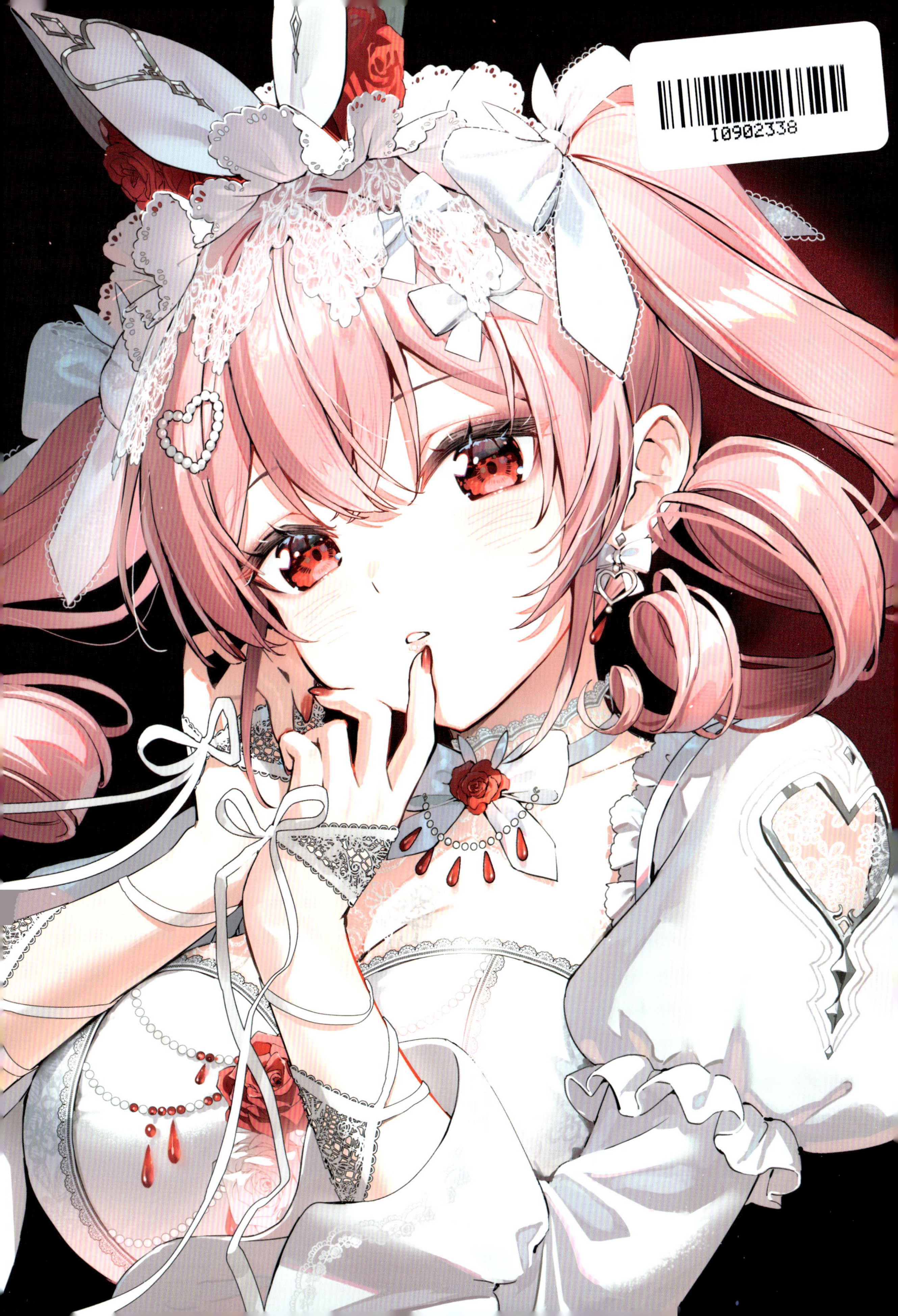

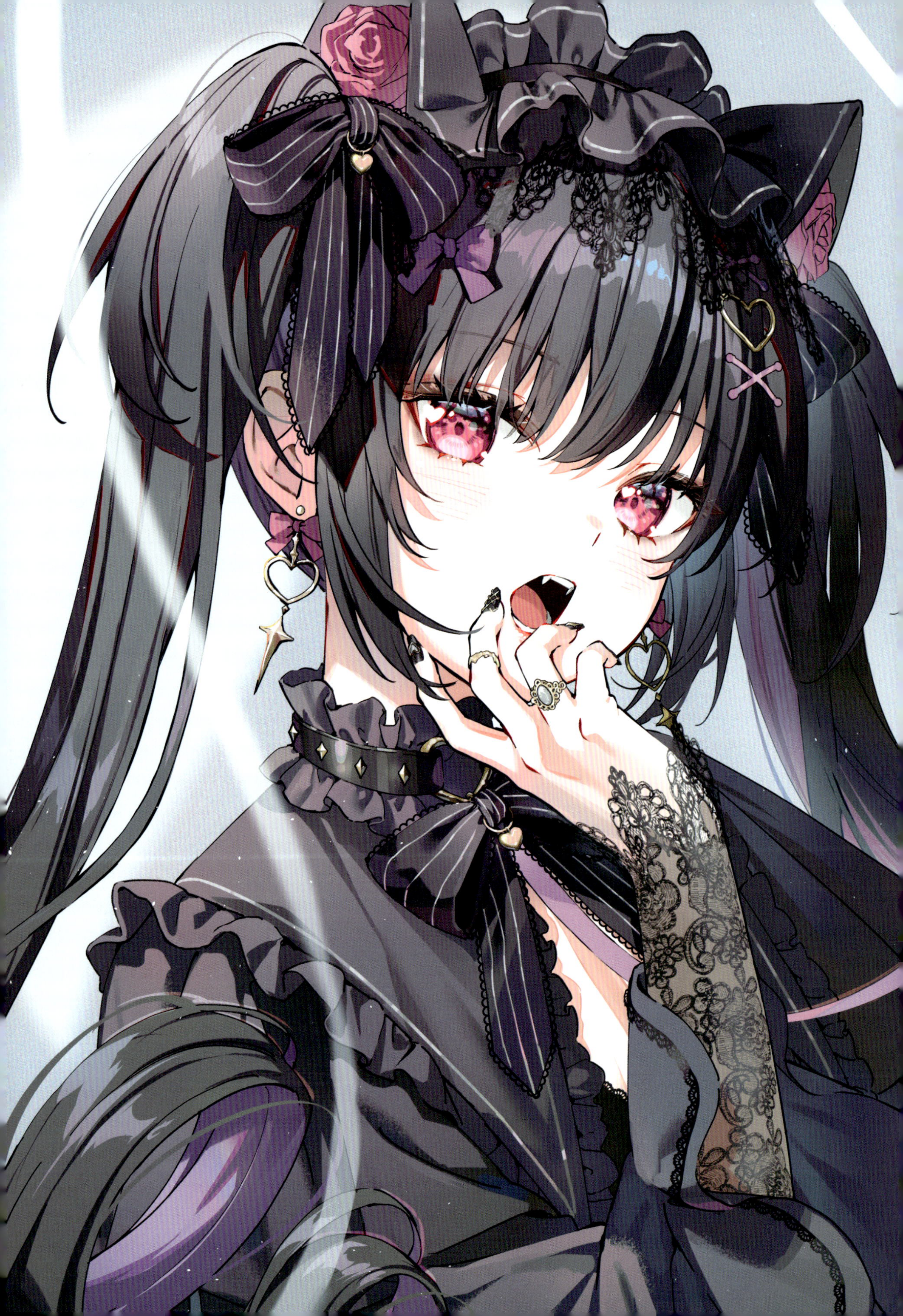

serenity

The Art of Rosuuri

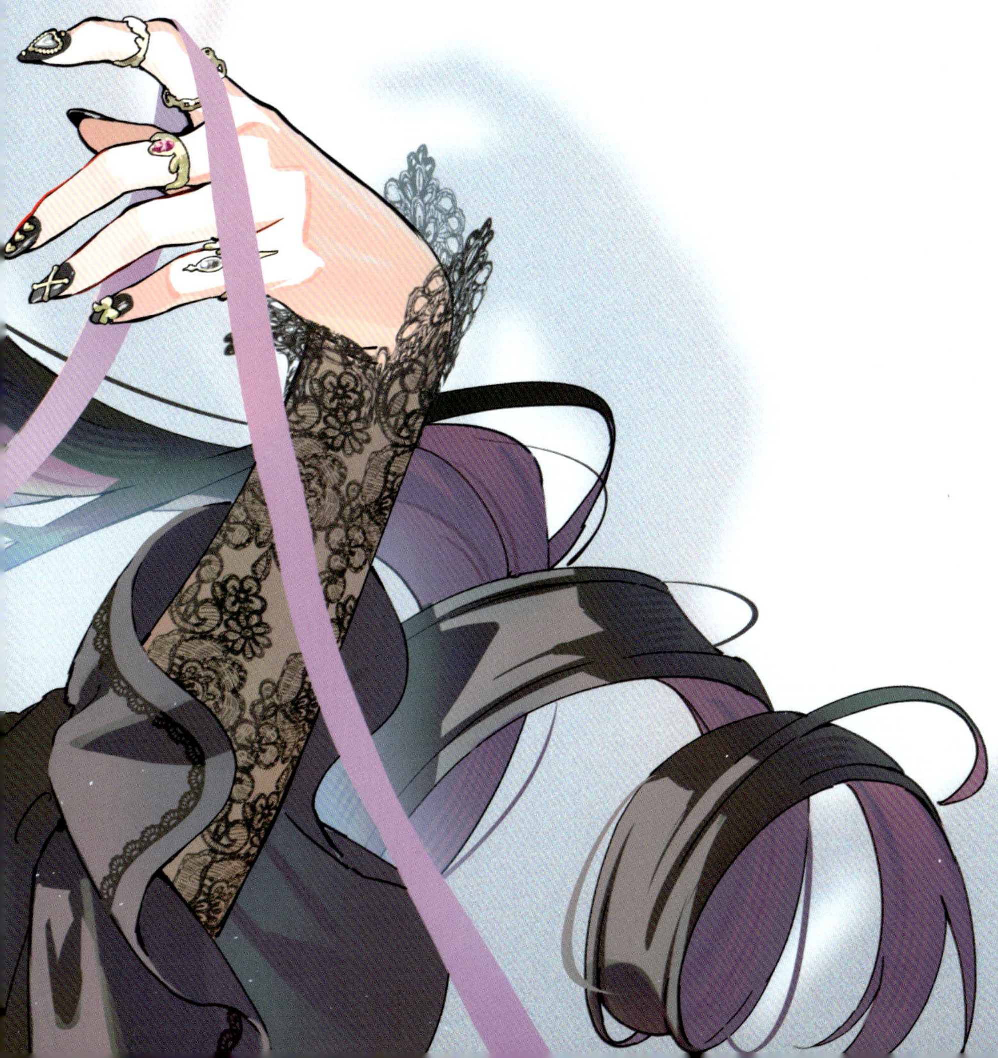

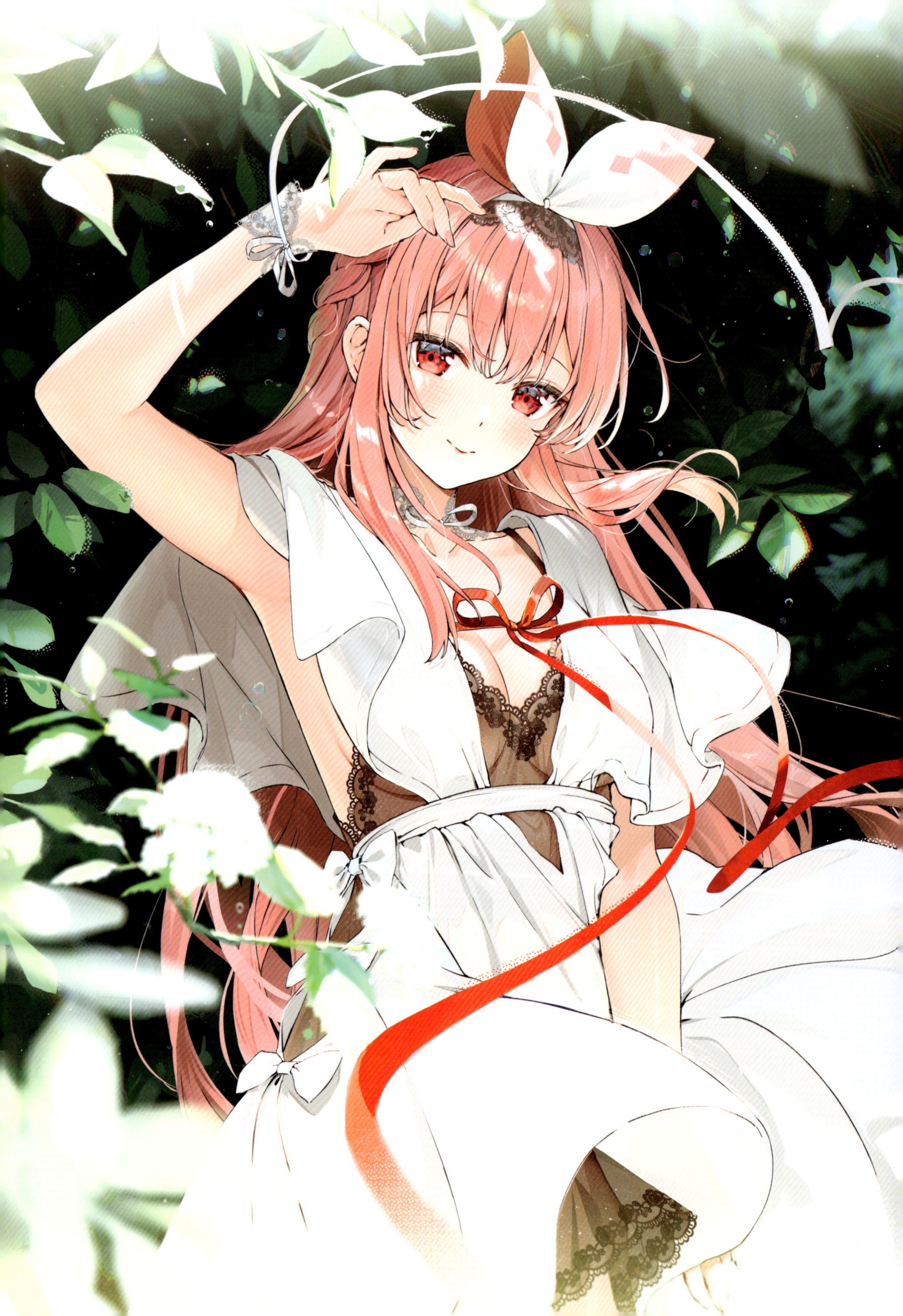

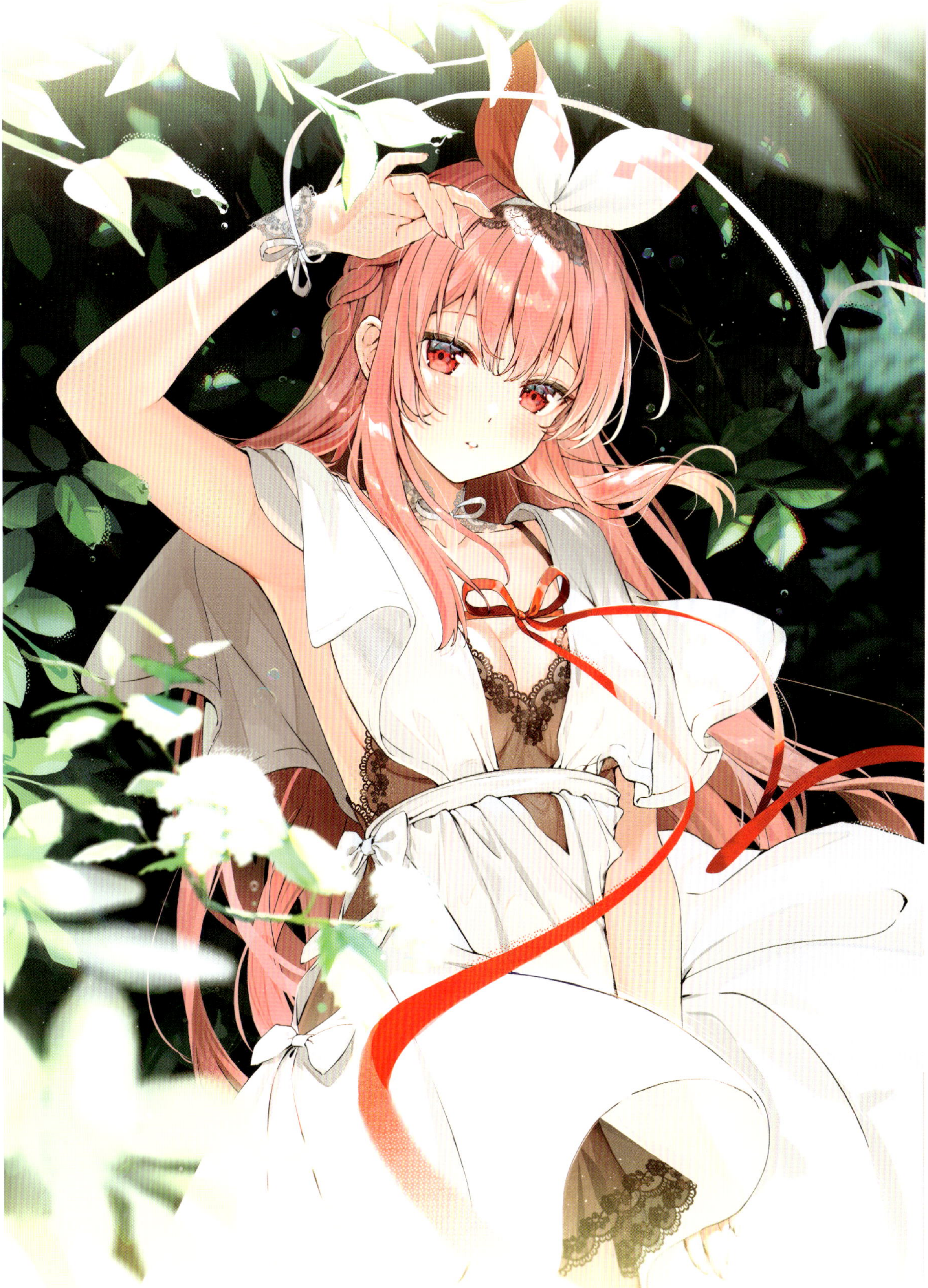

Original Works

The Art of Rosuuri

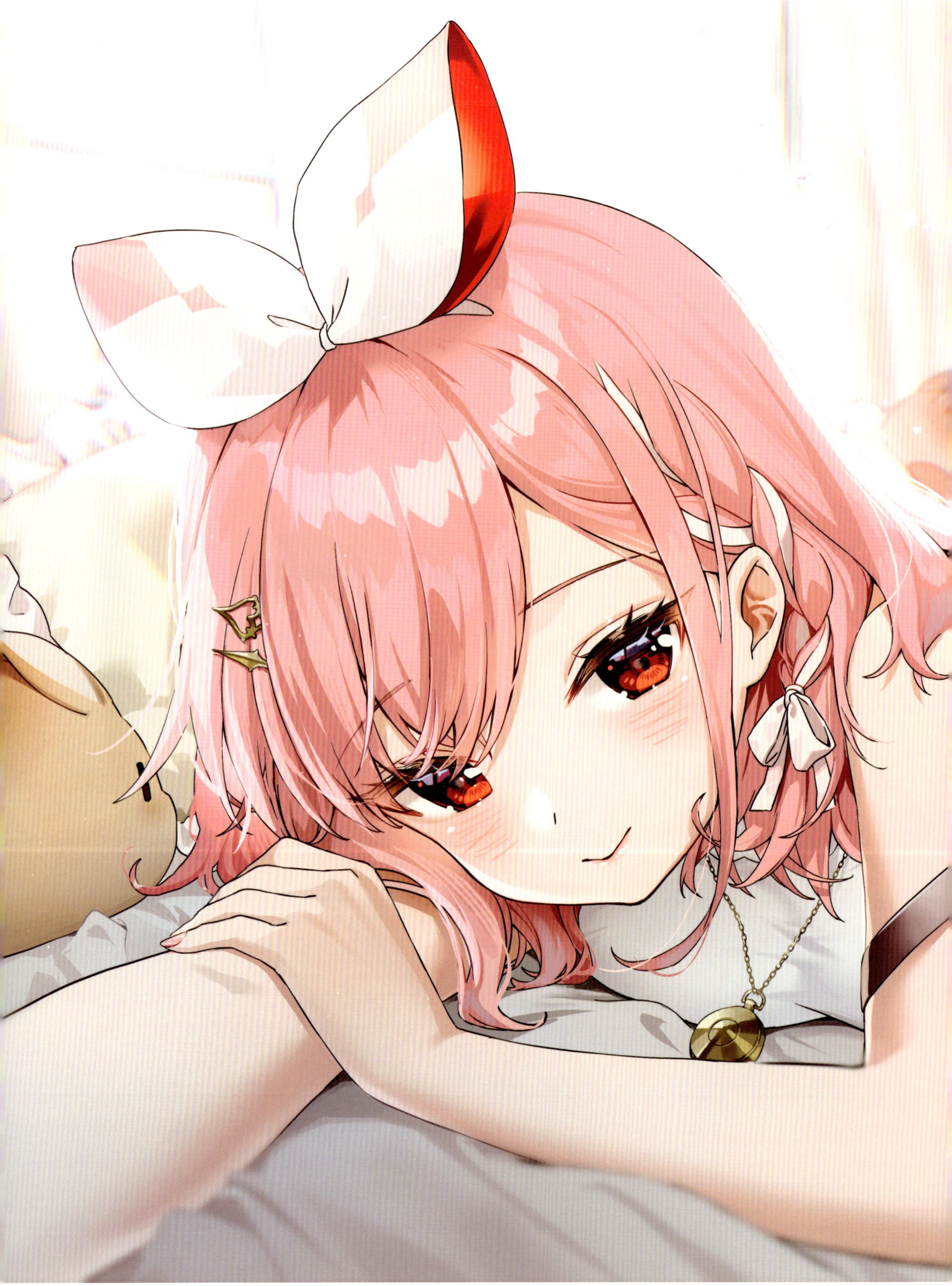

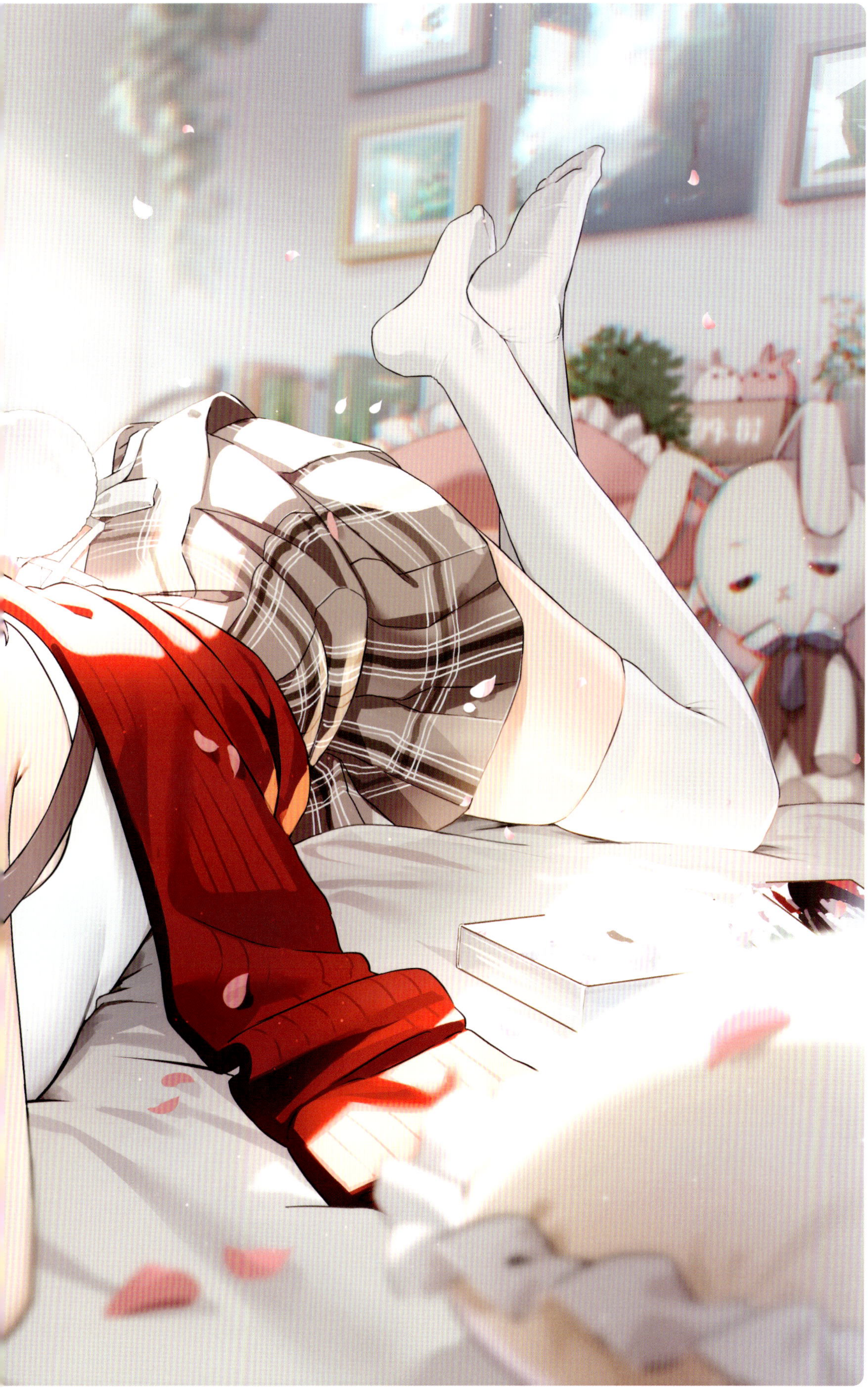

Rosu

White Rabbit

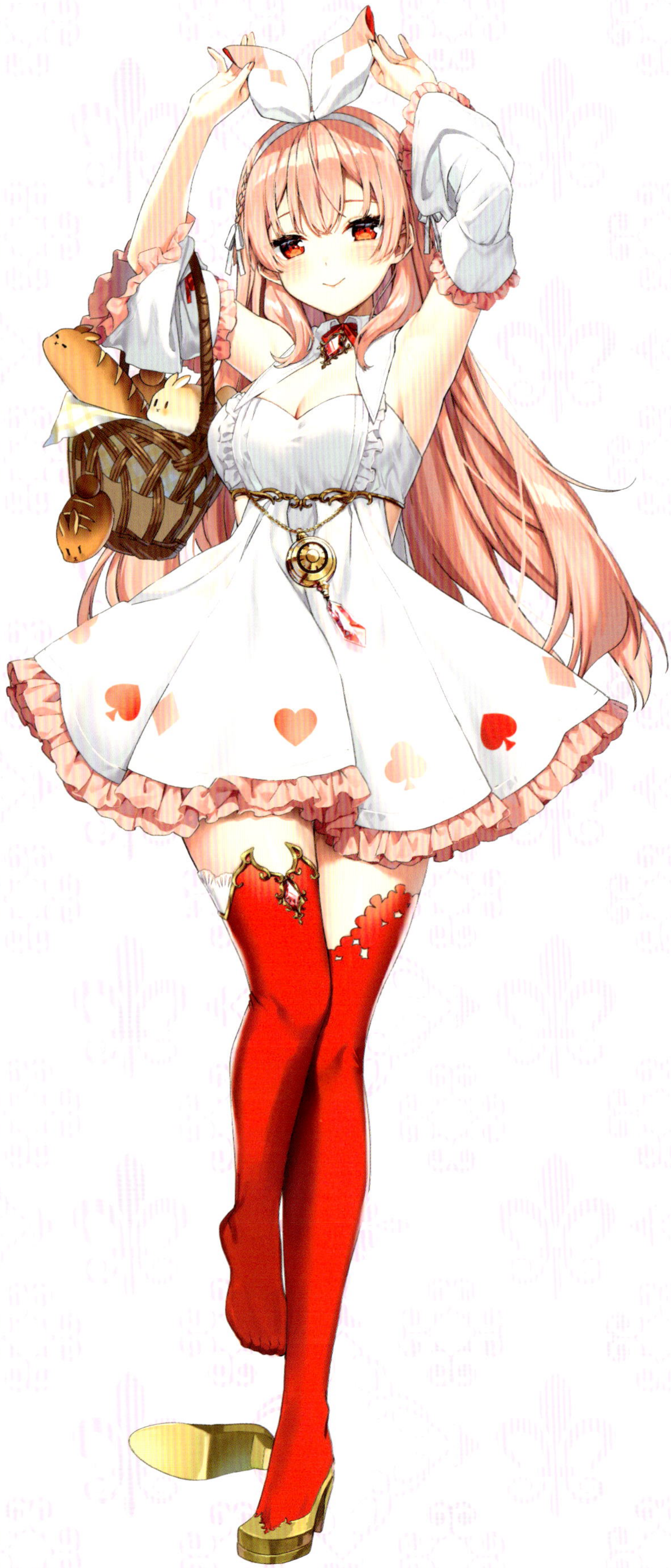

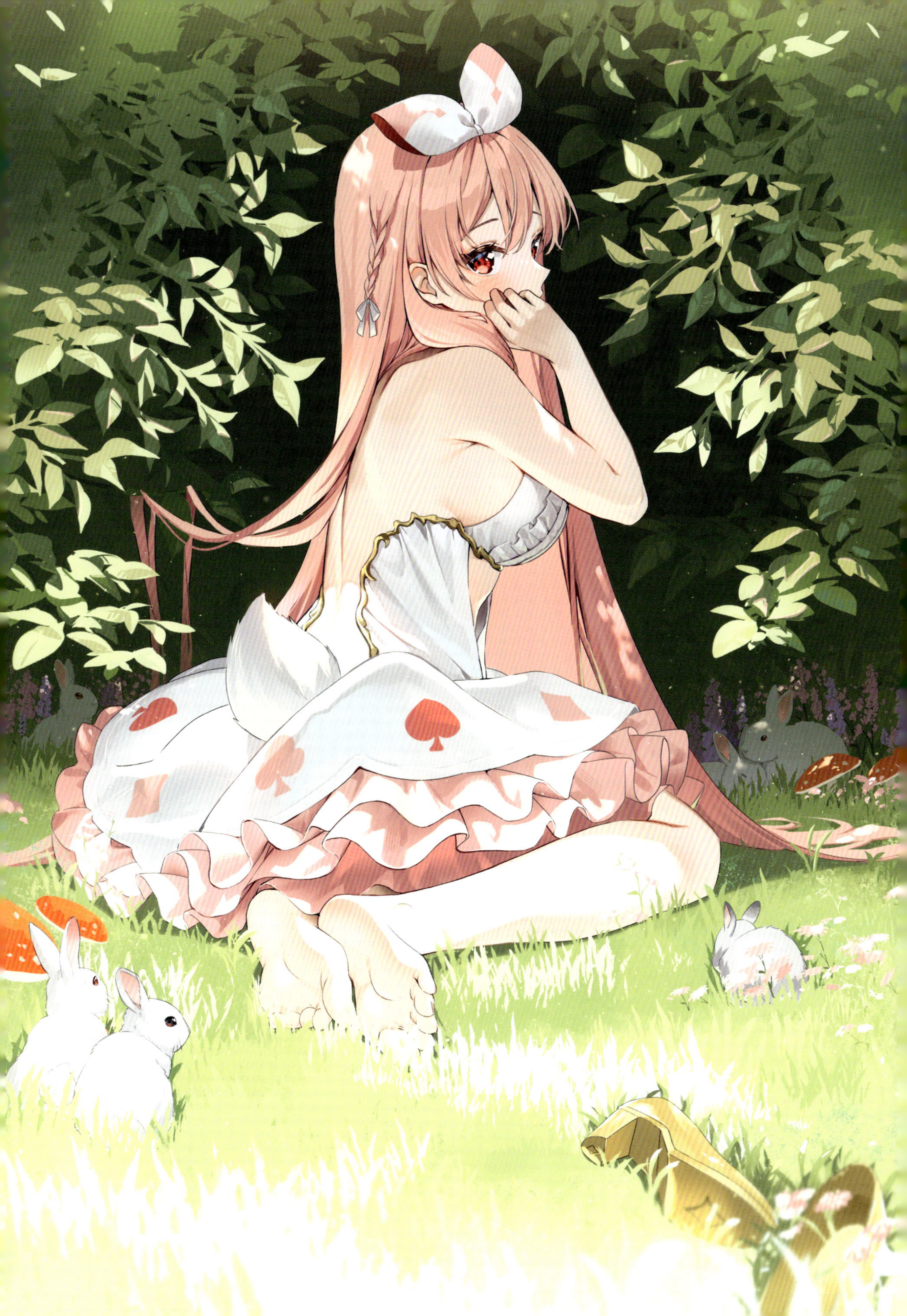

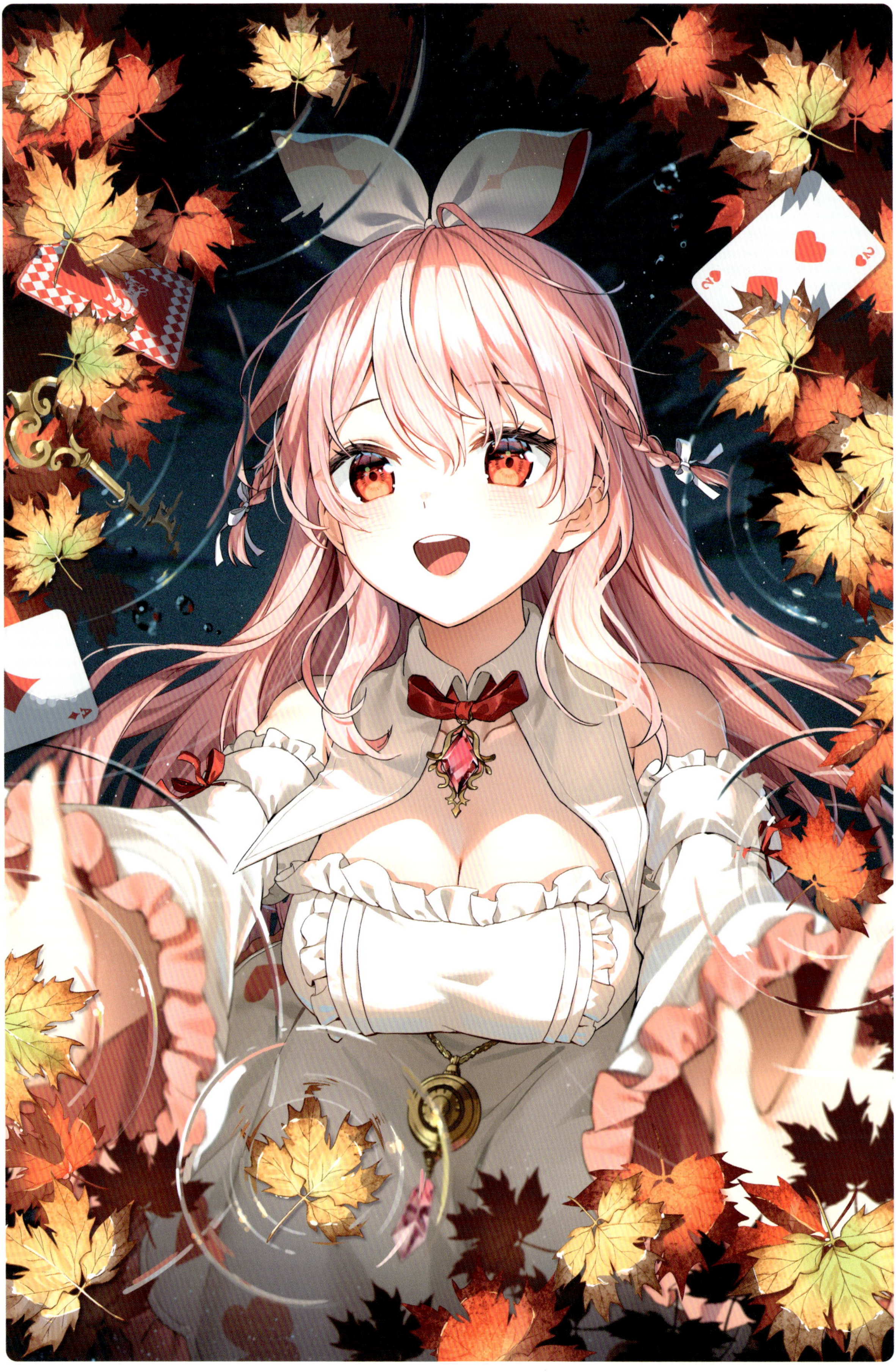

Serenity

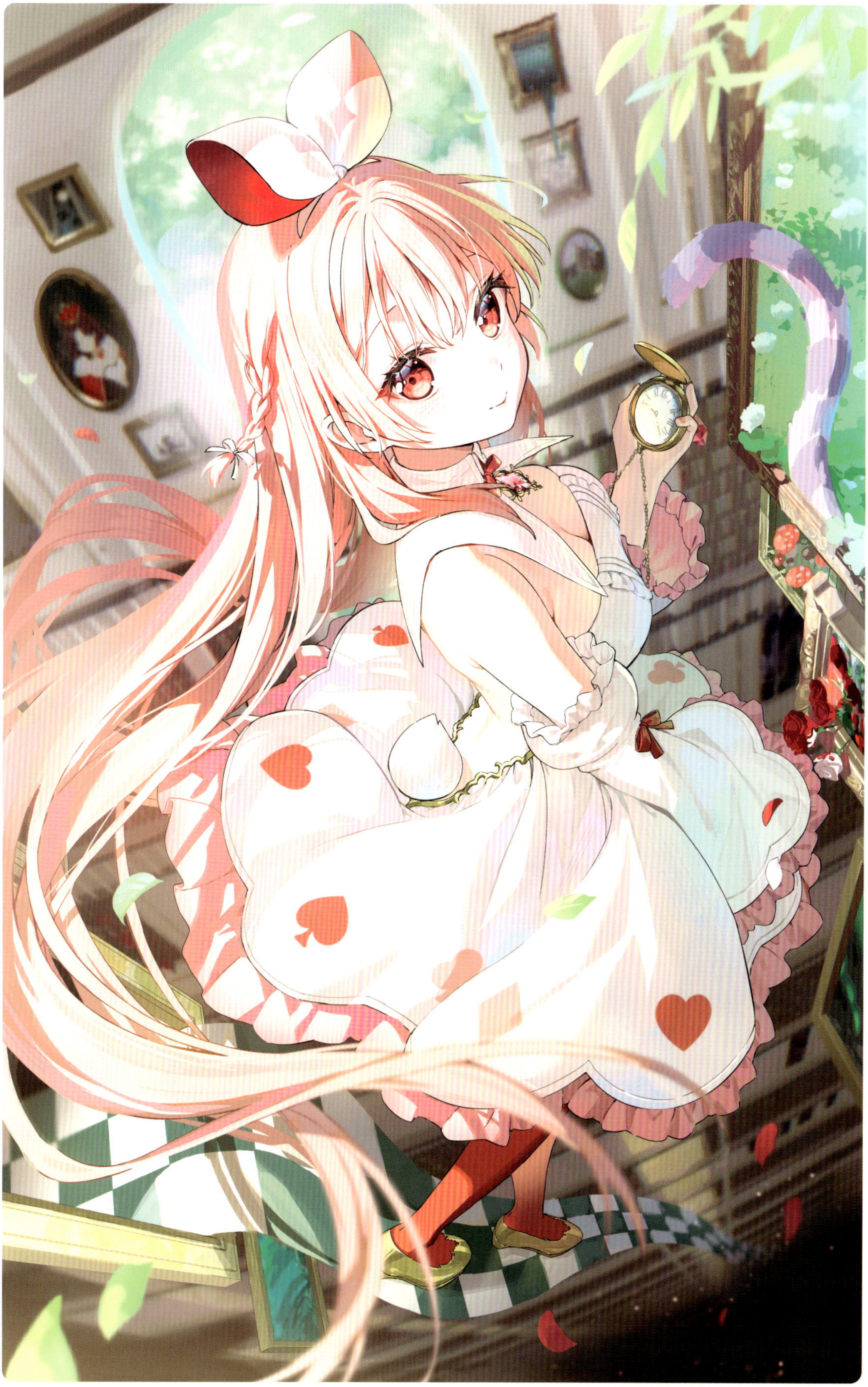

Serenity

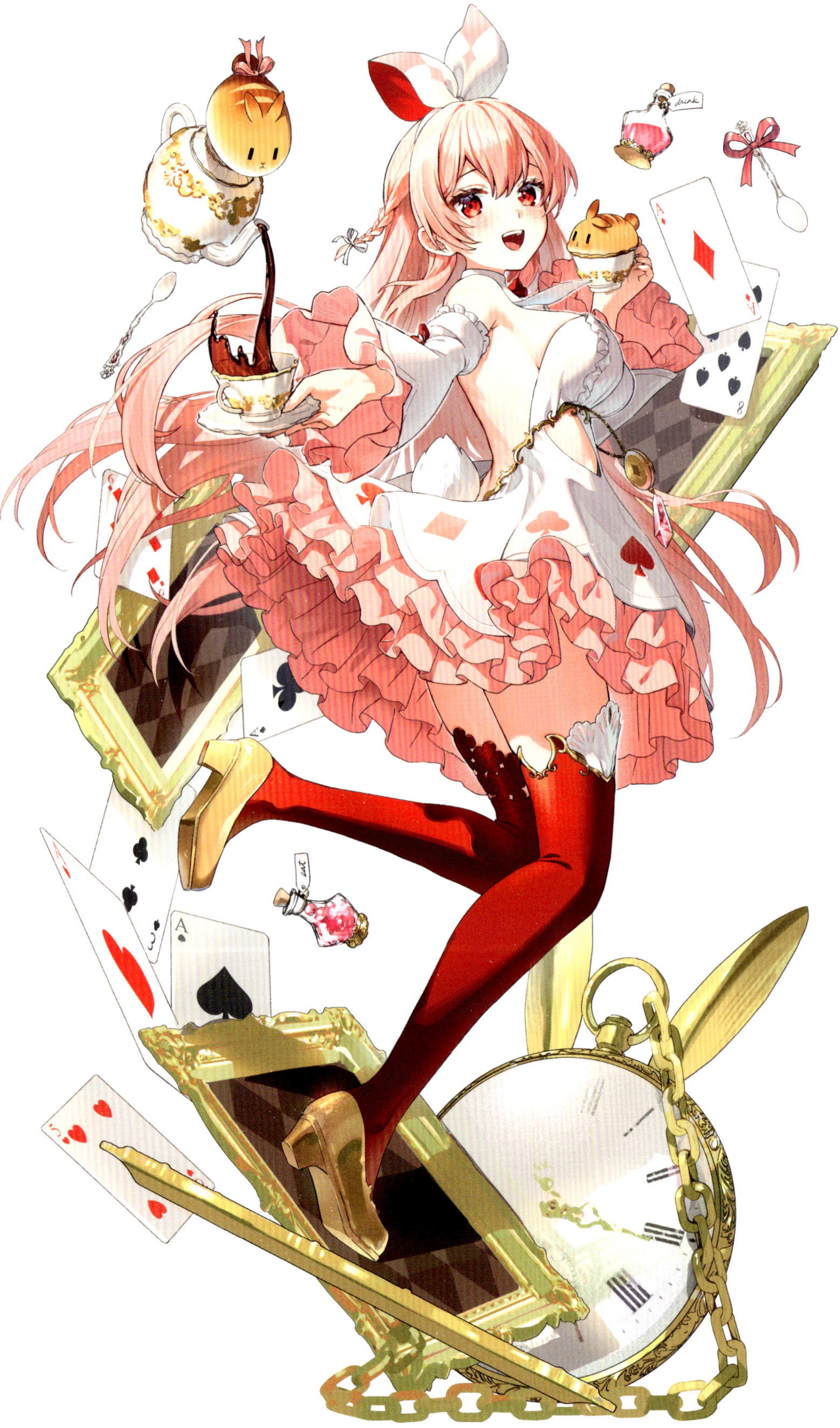

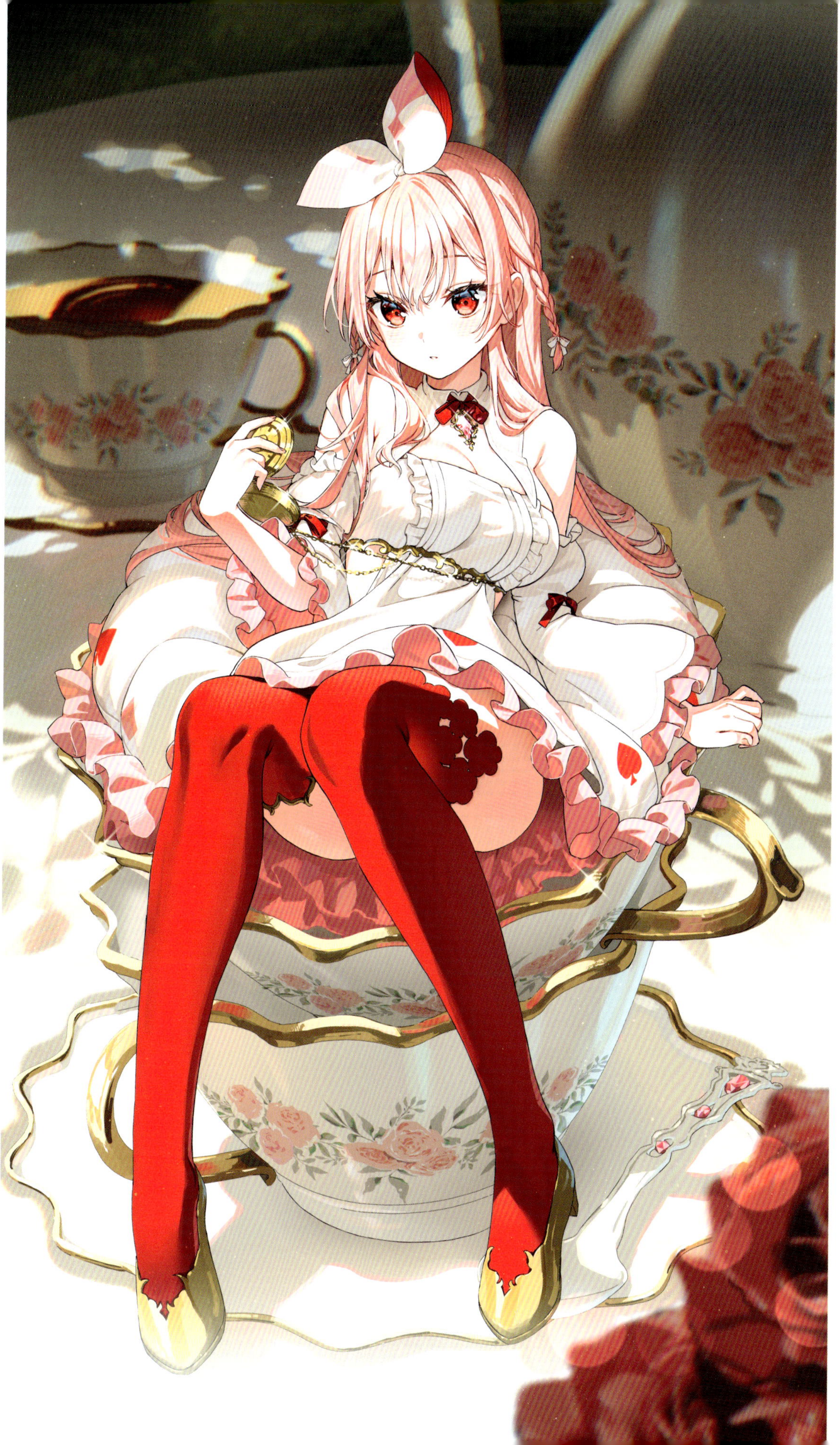

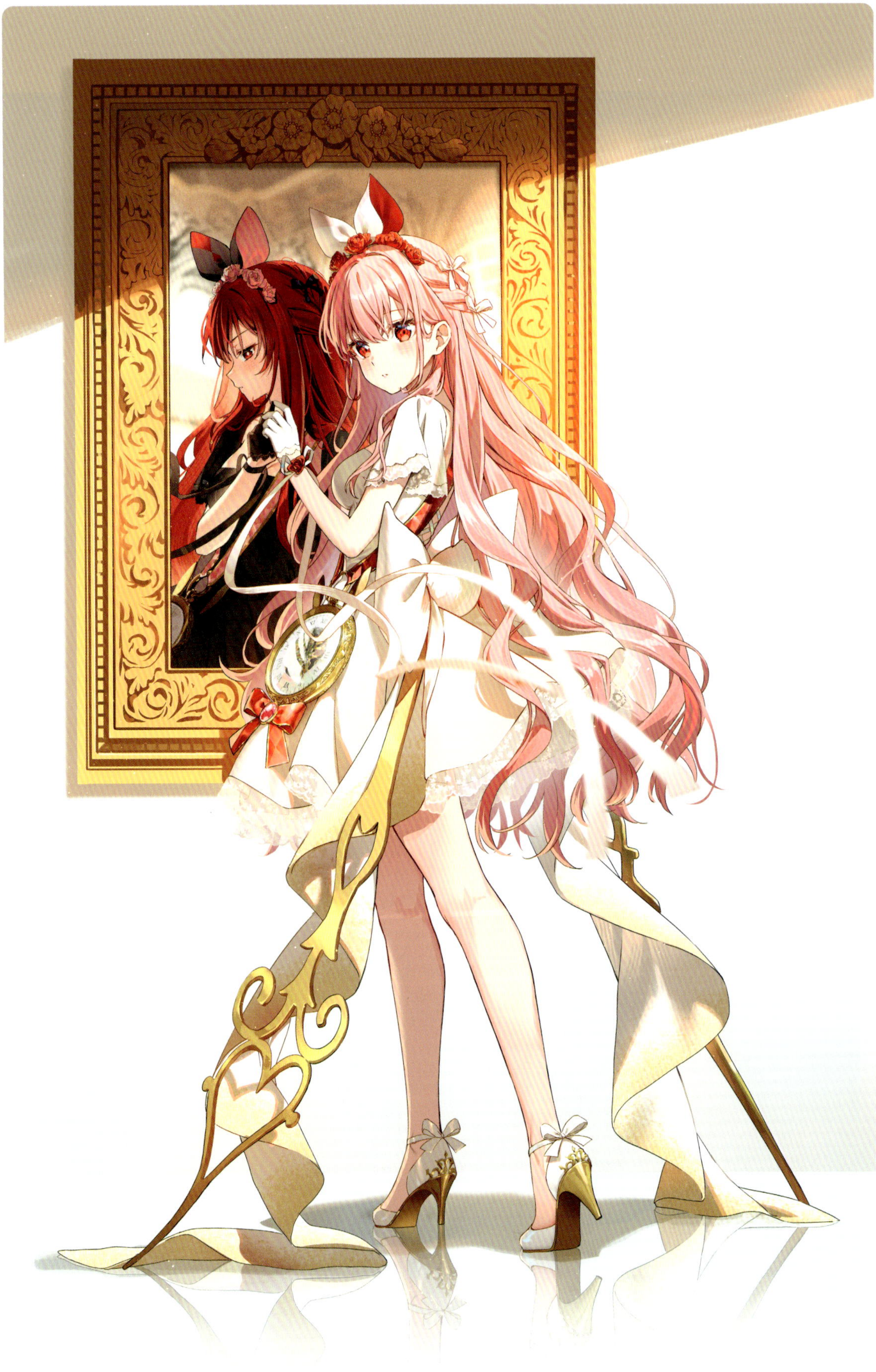

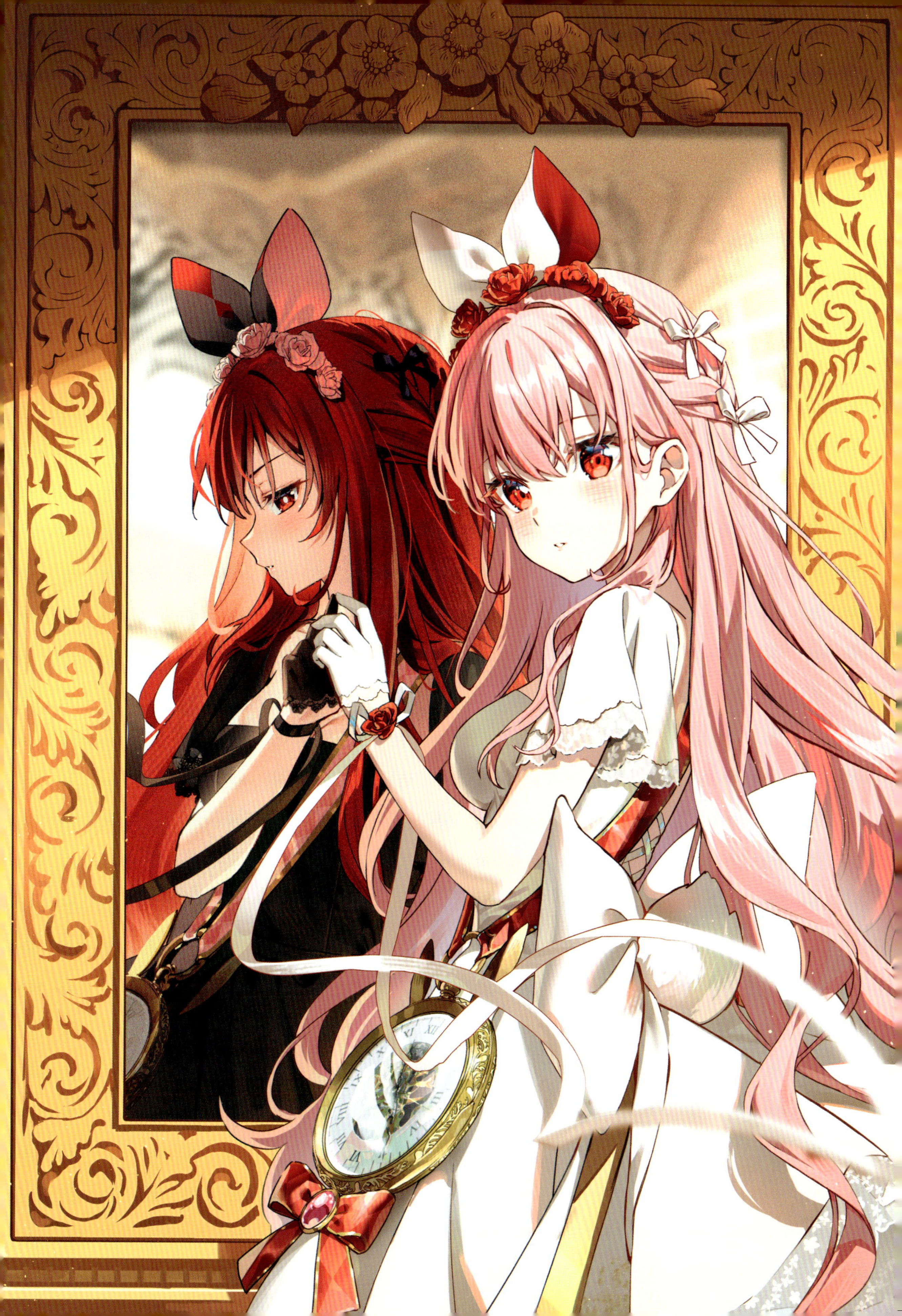

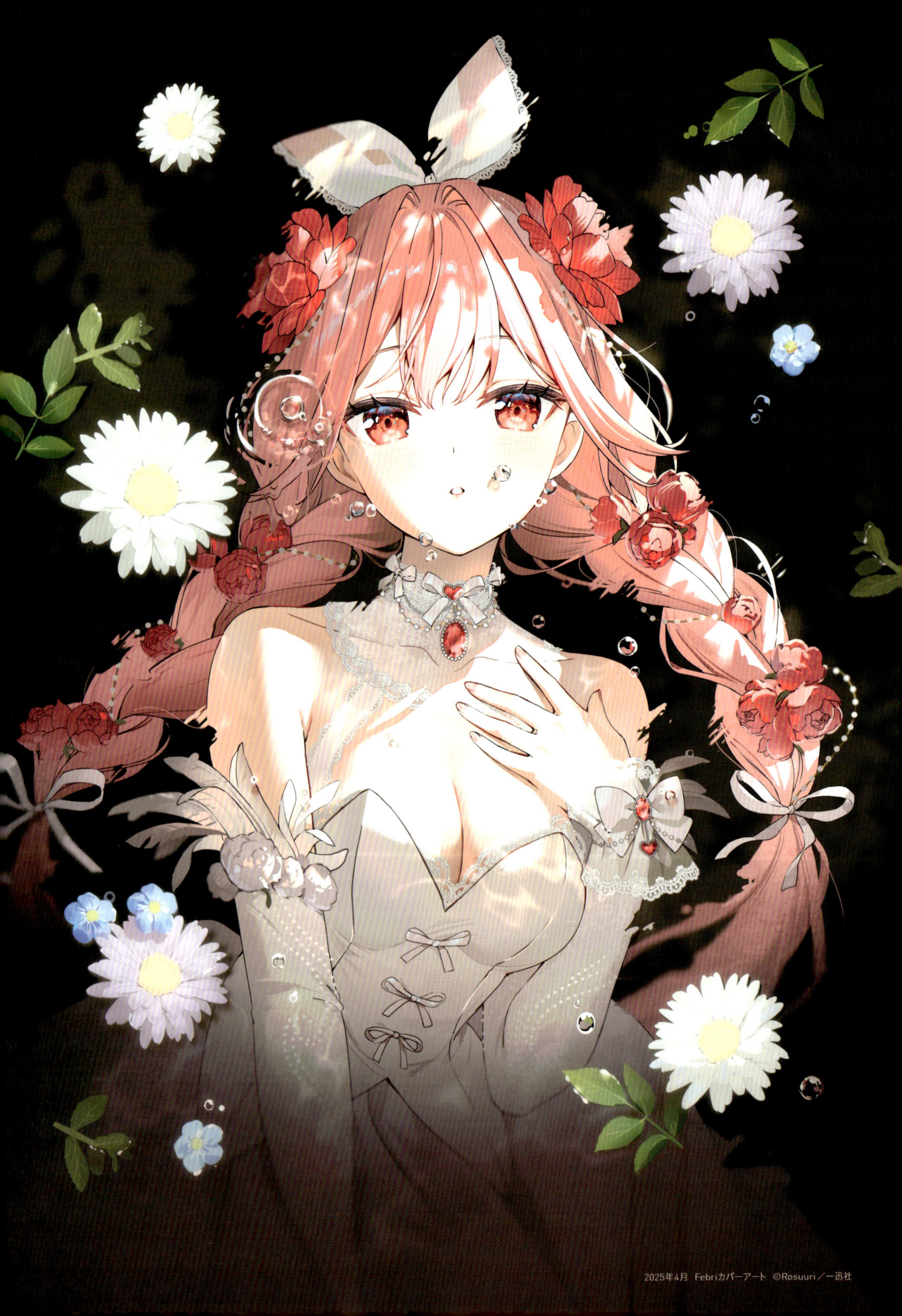

2025年4月　Febriカバーアート　

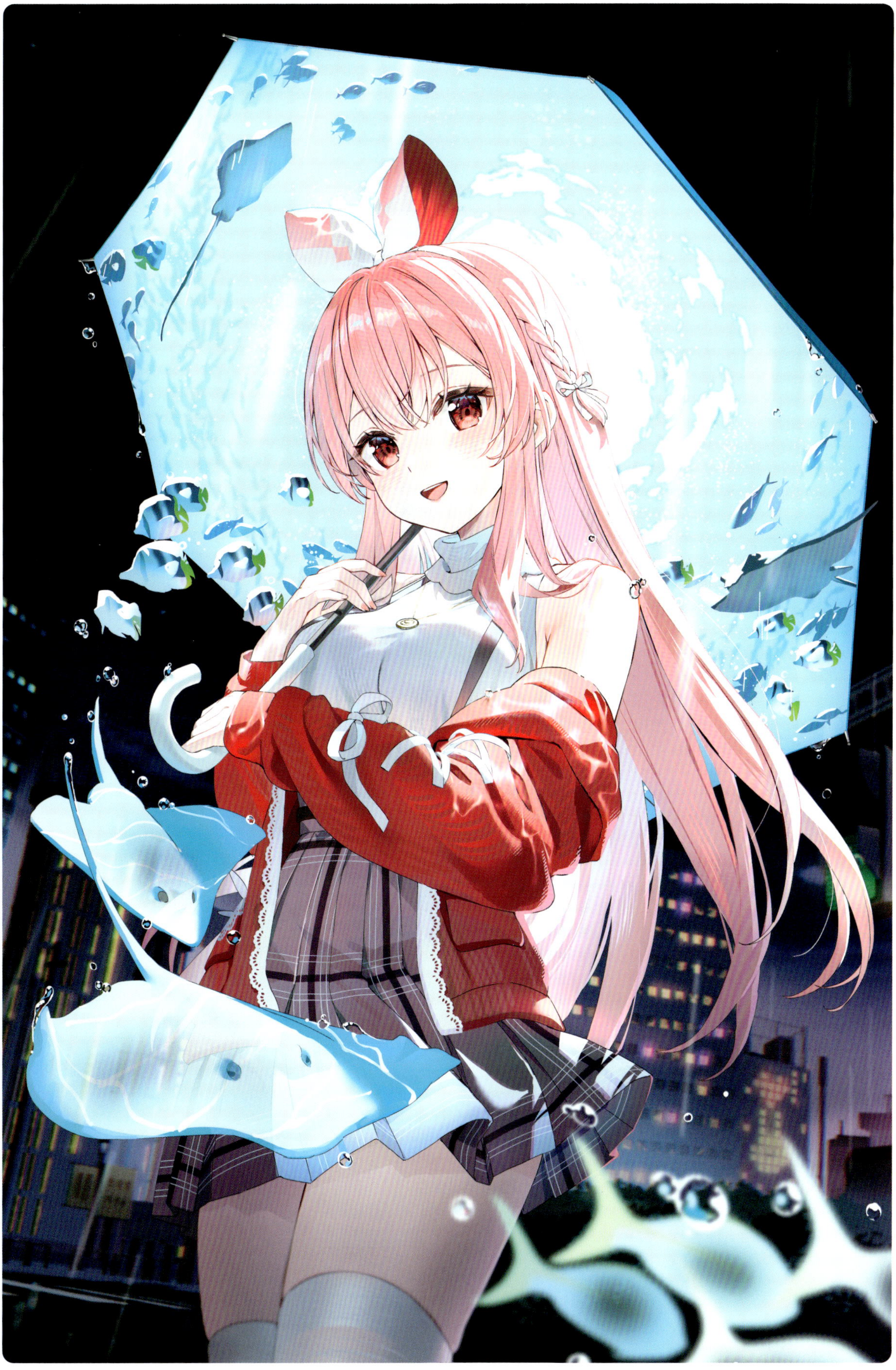

IGX2025 描き下ろしイラスト

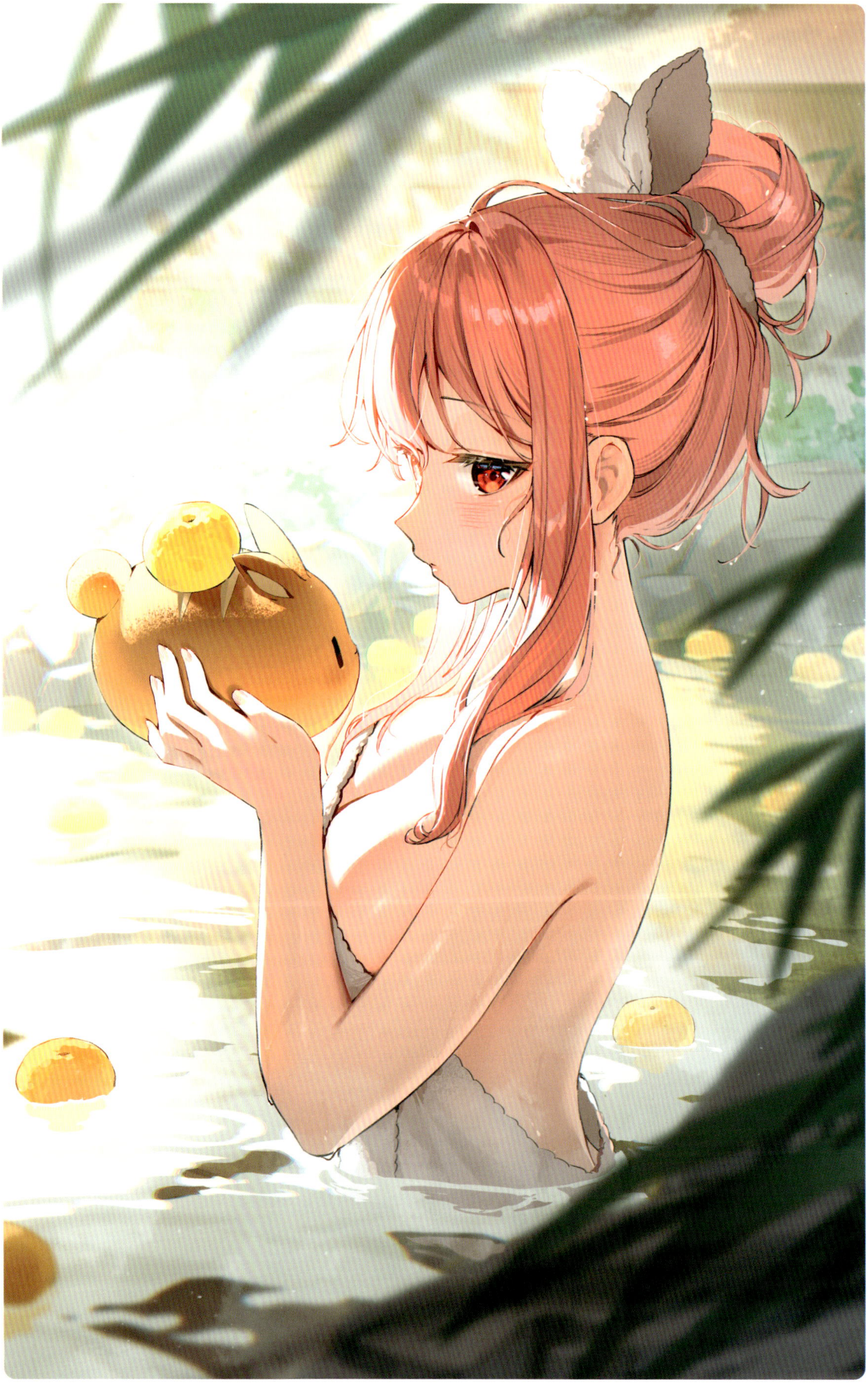

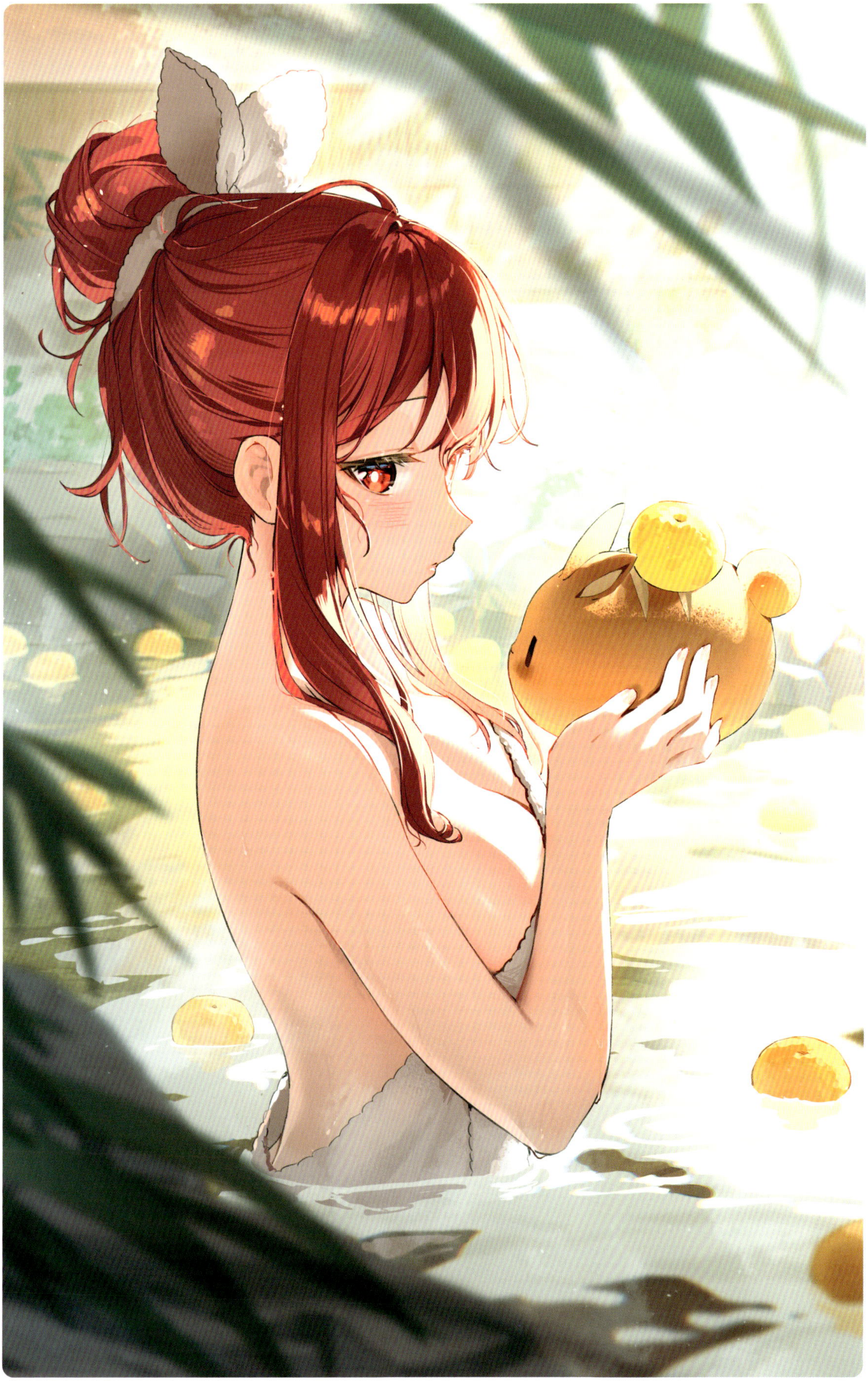

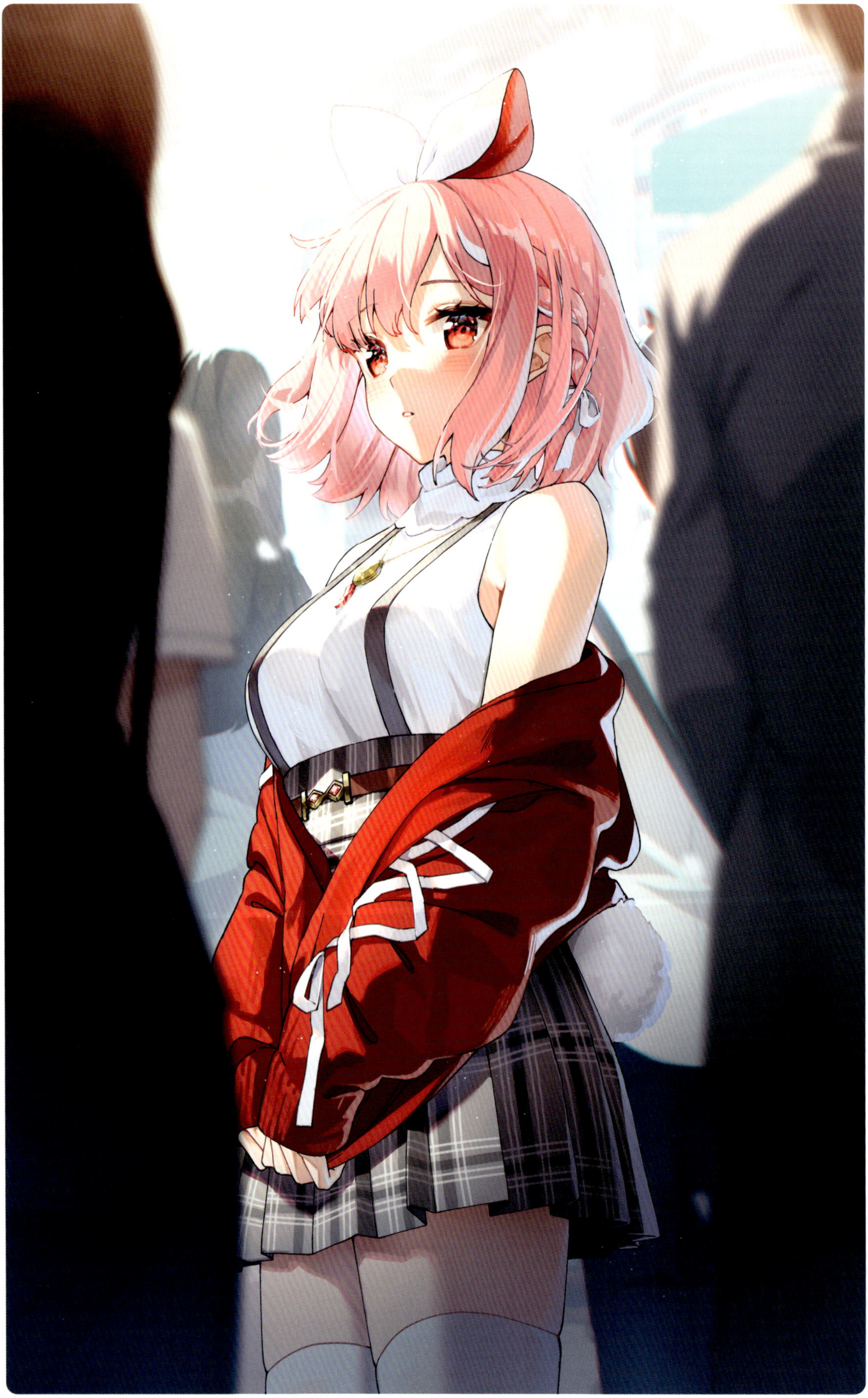

Comic **01**

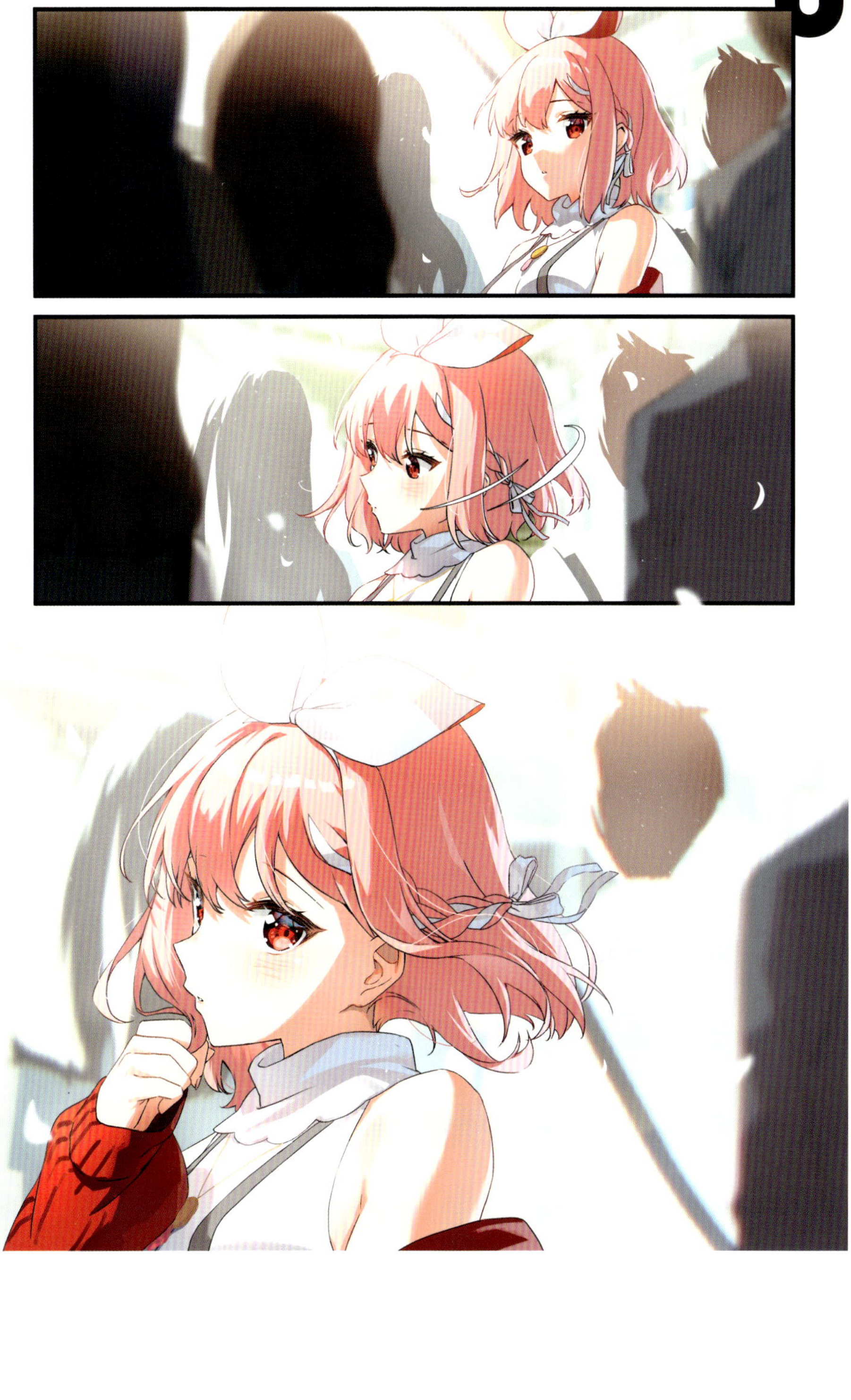

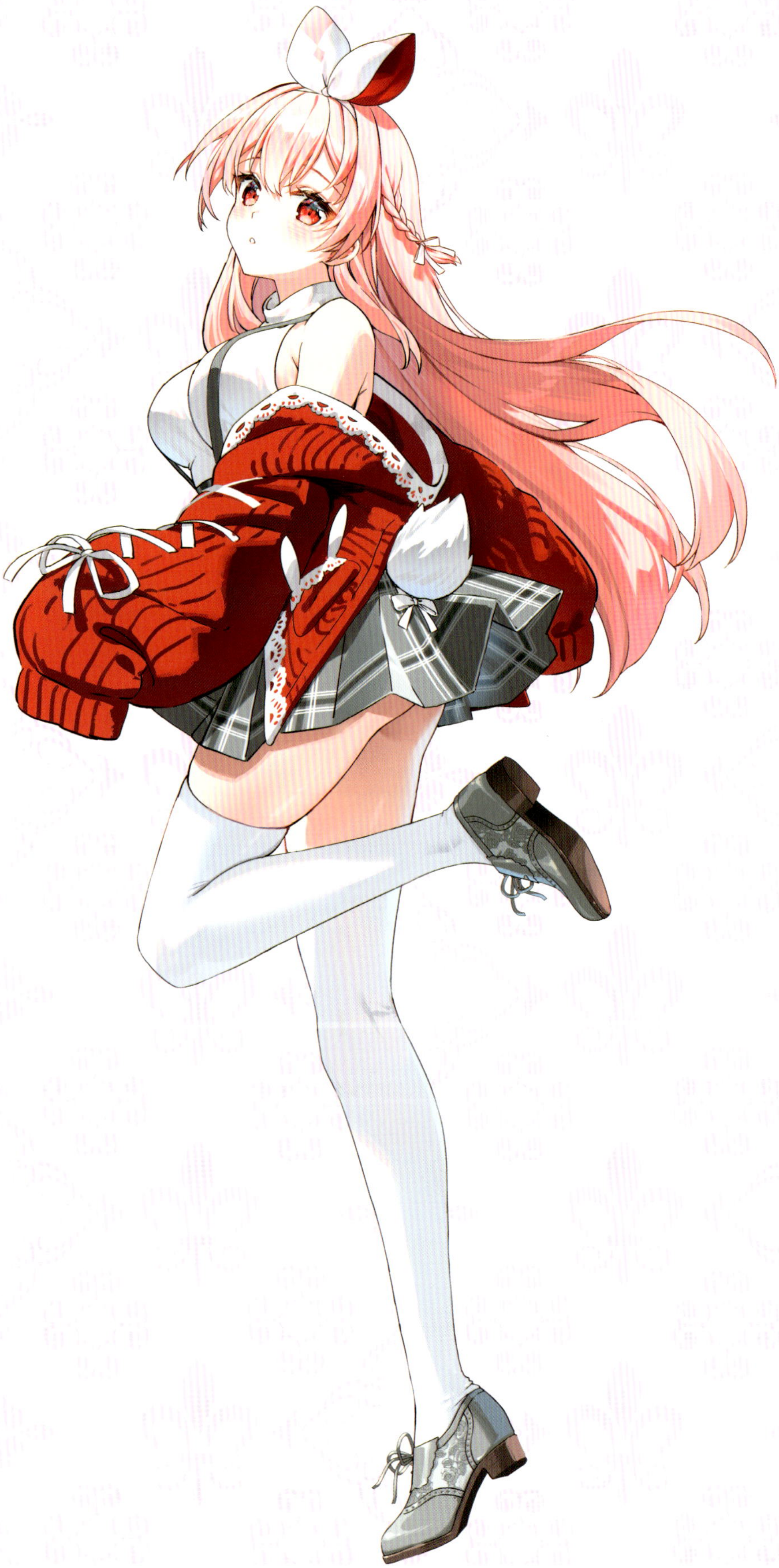

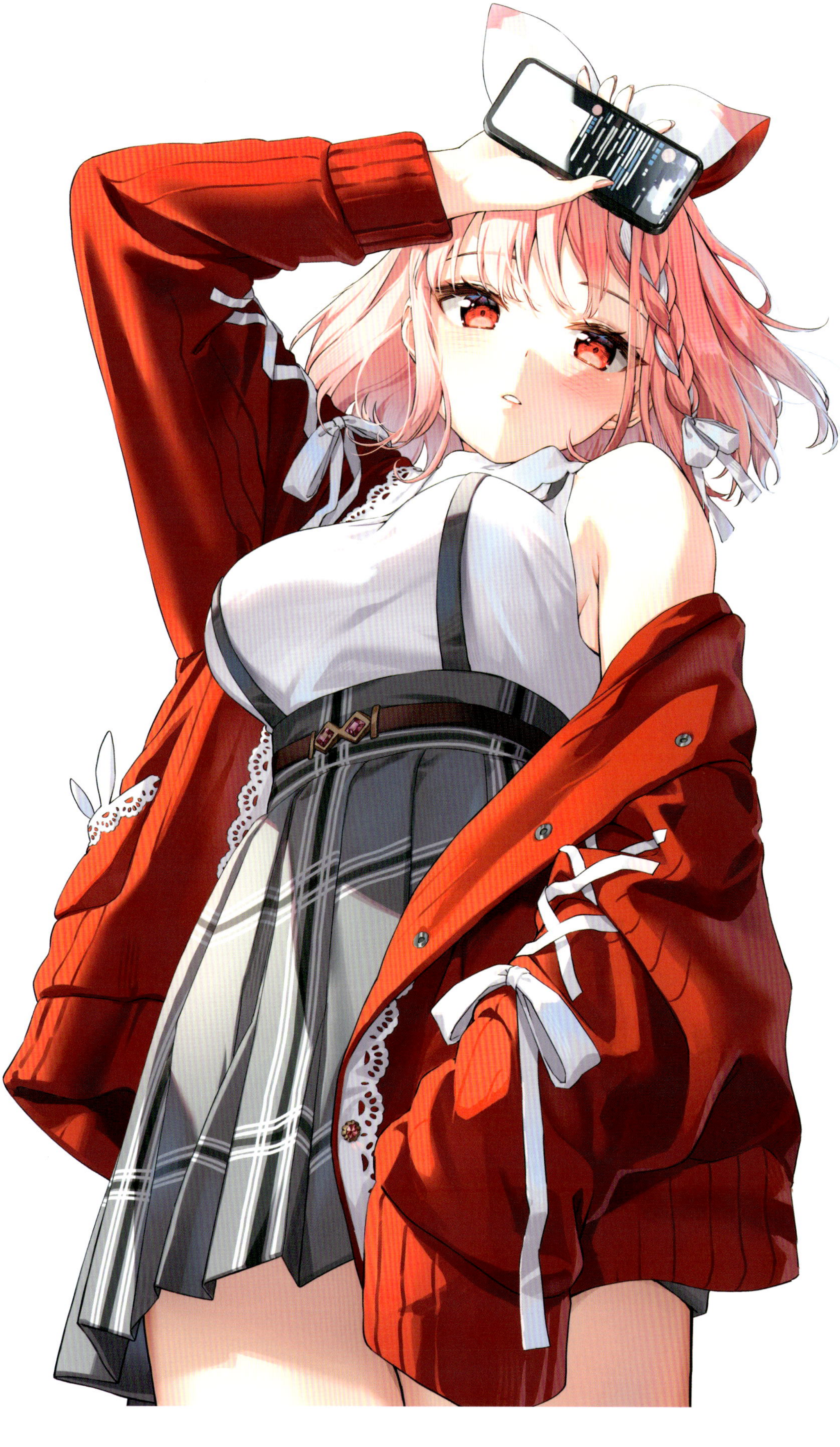

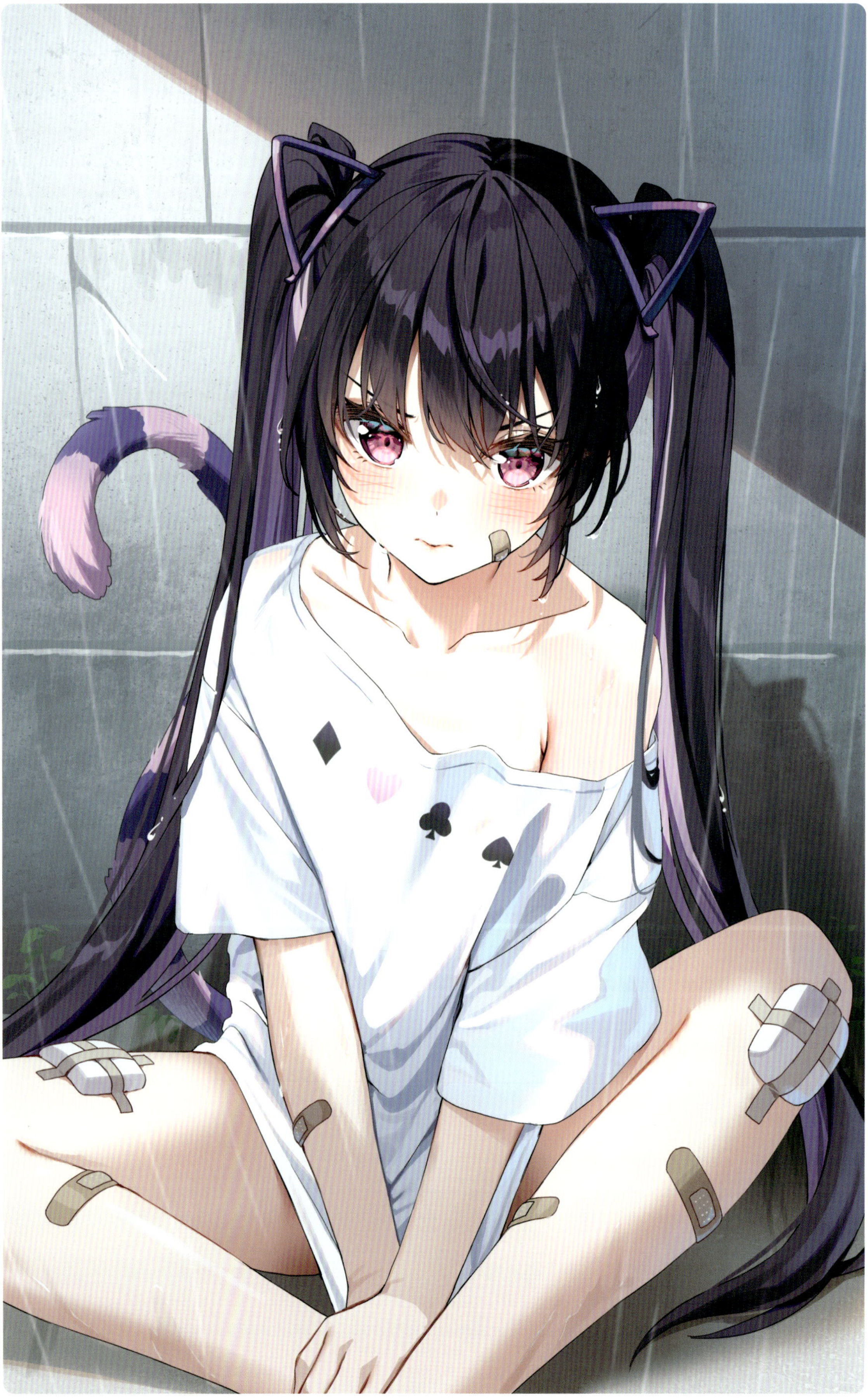

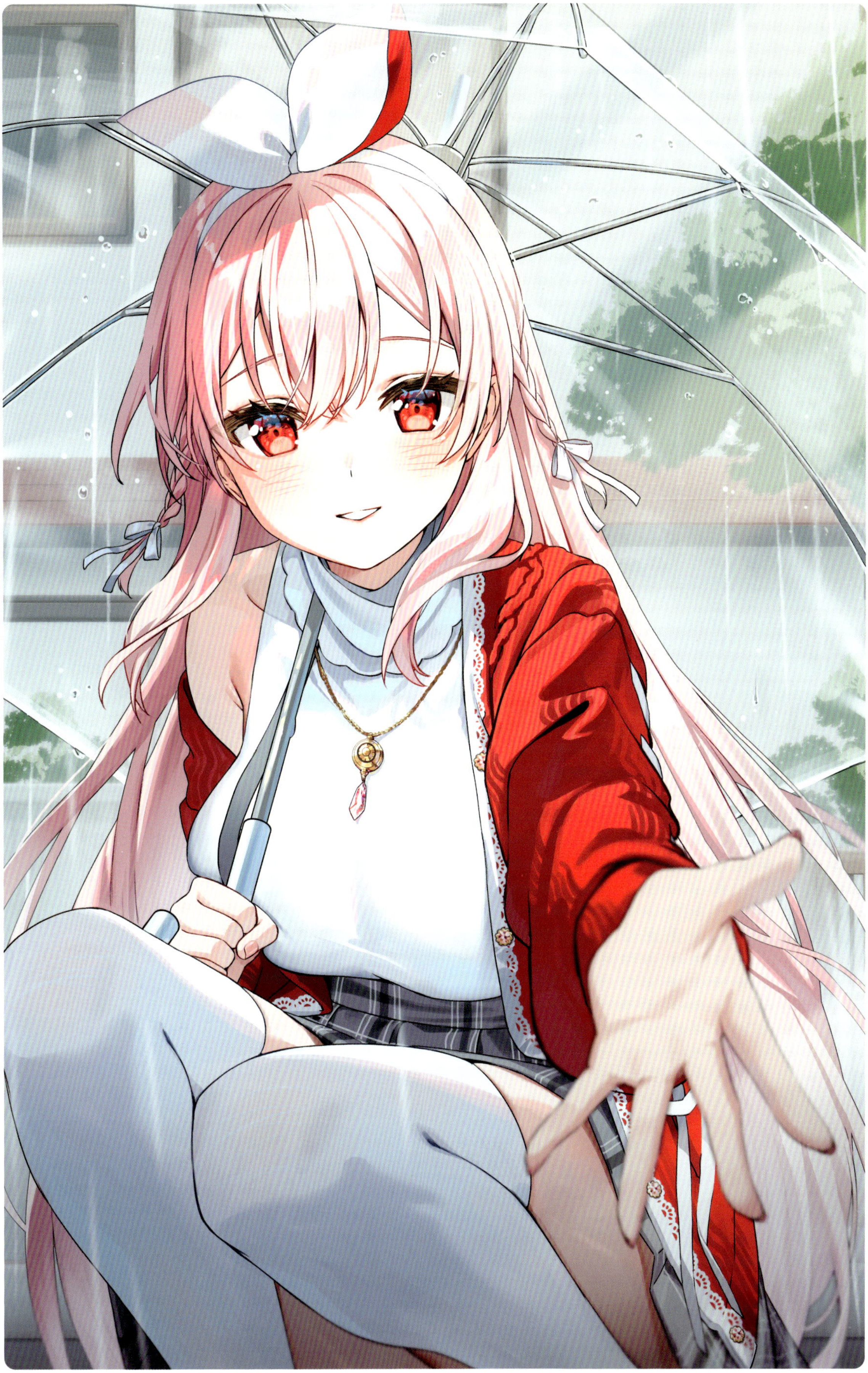

Comic 02

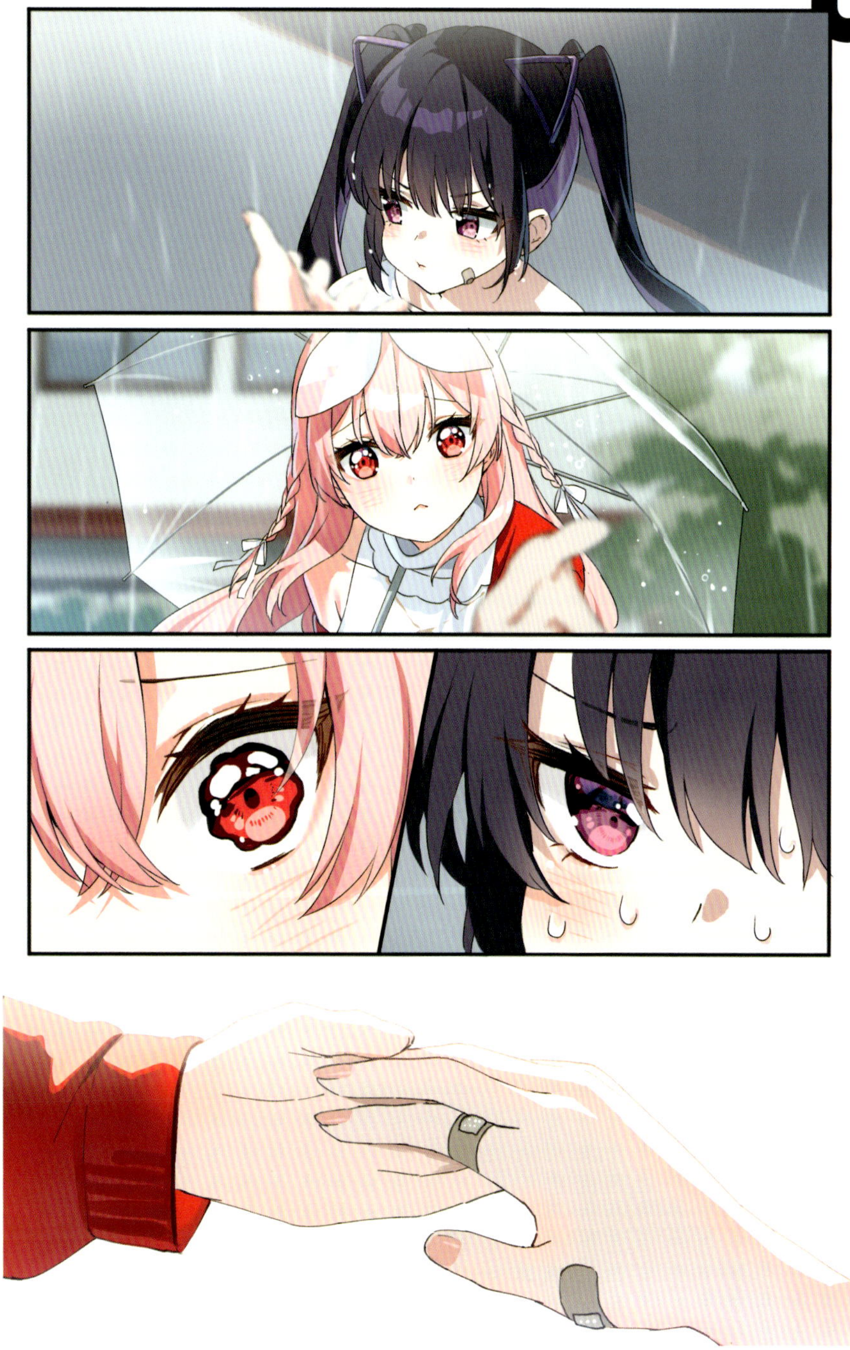

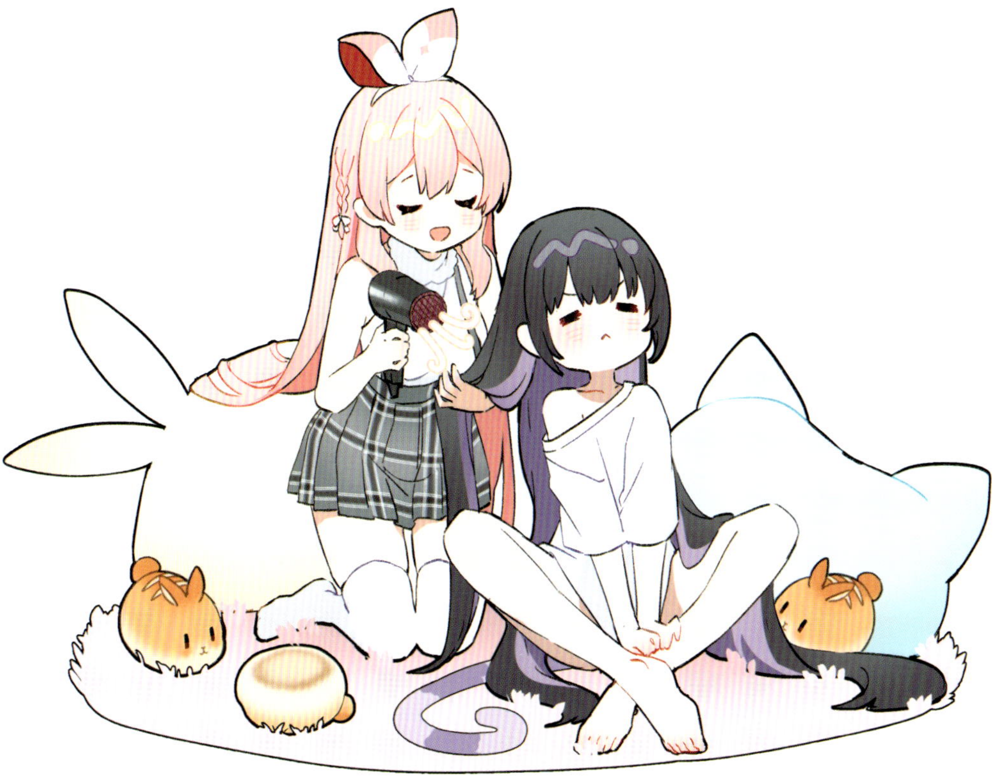

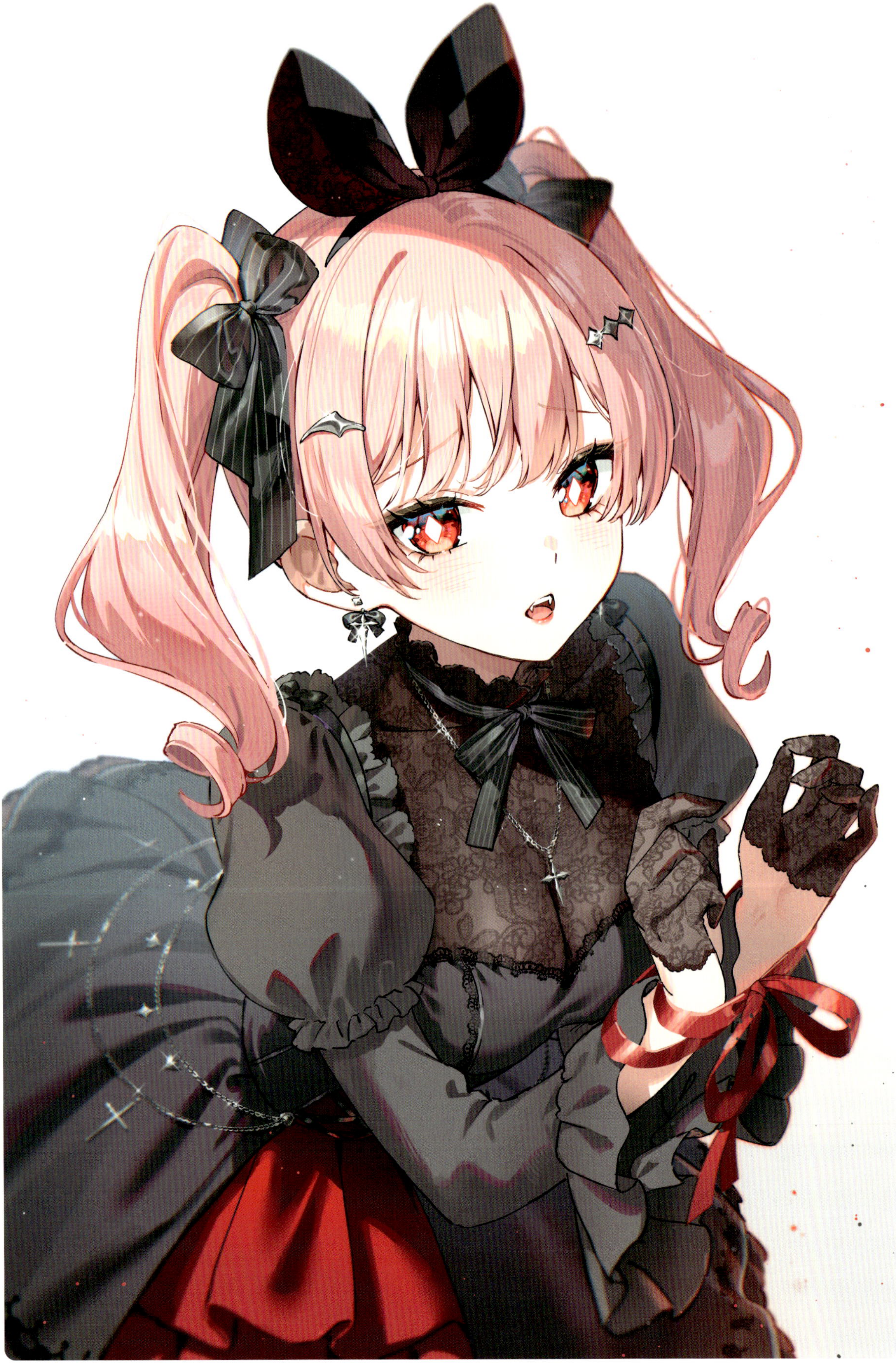

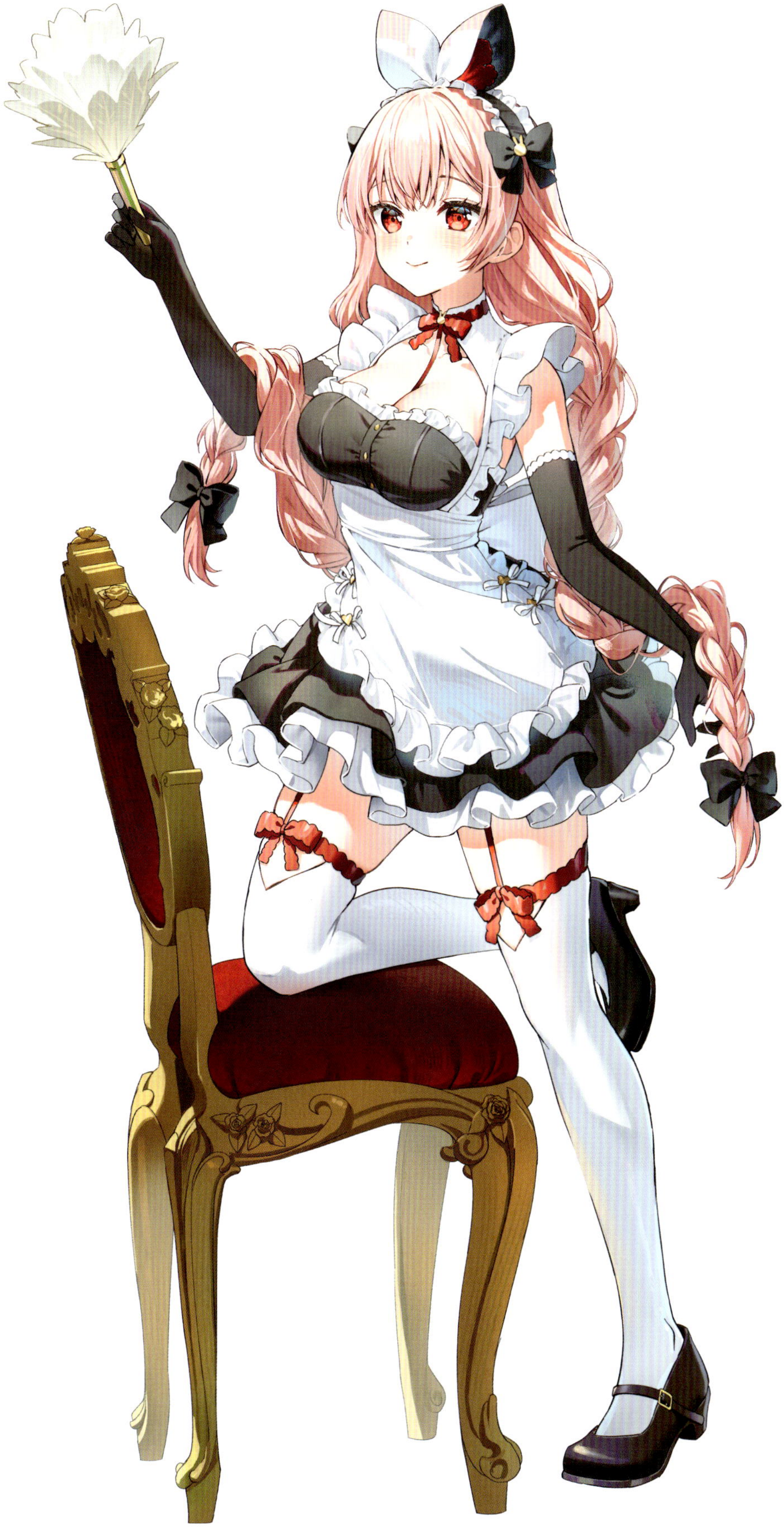

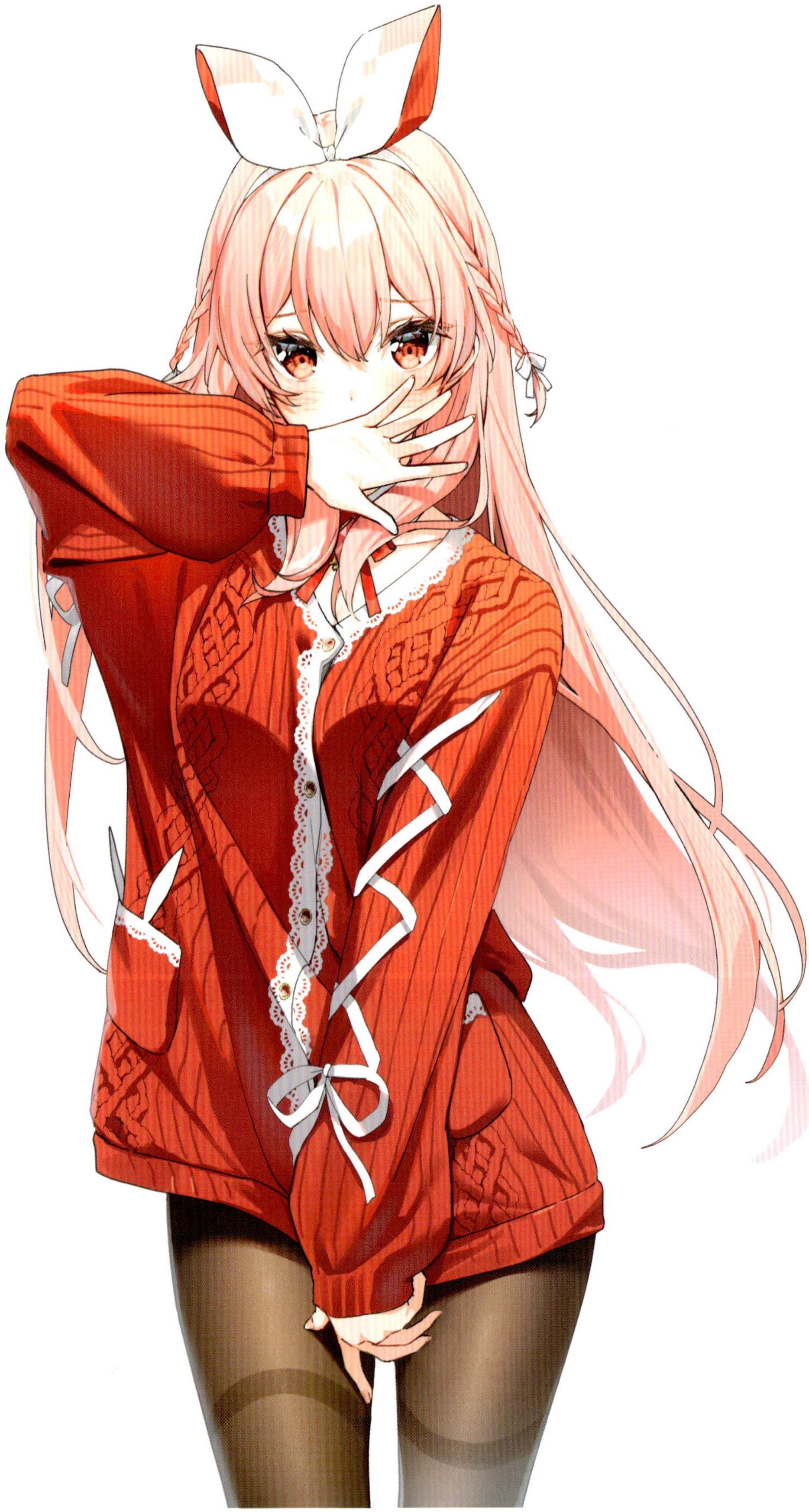

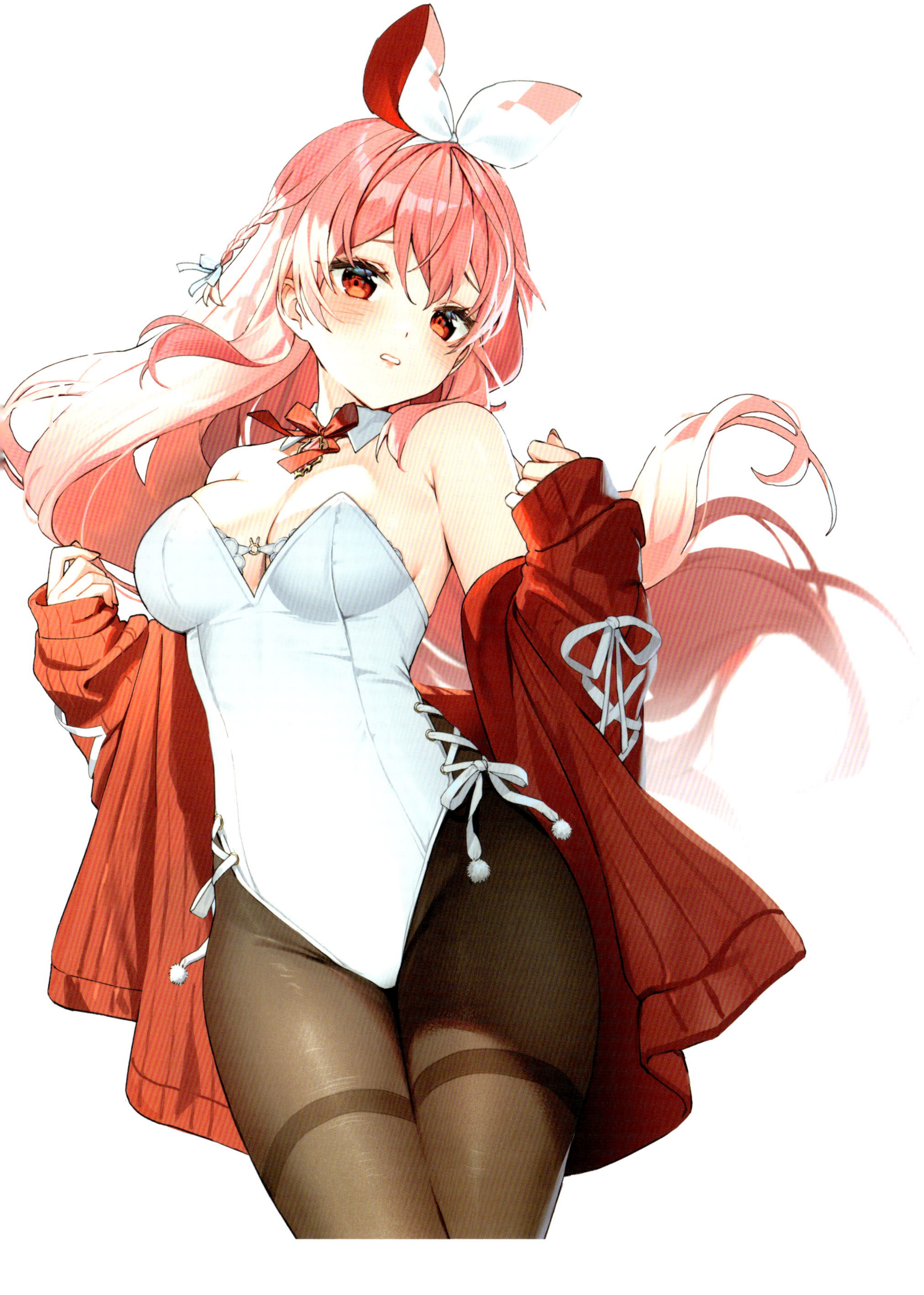

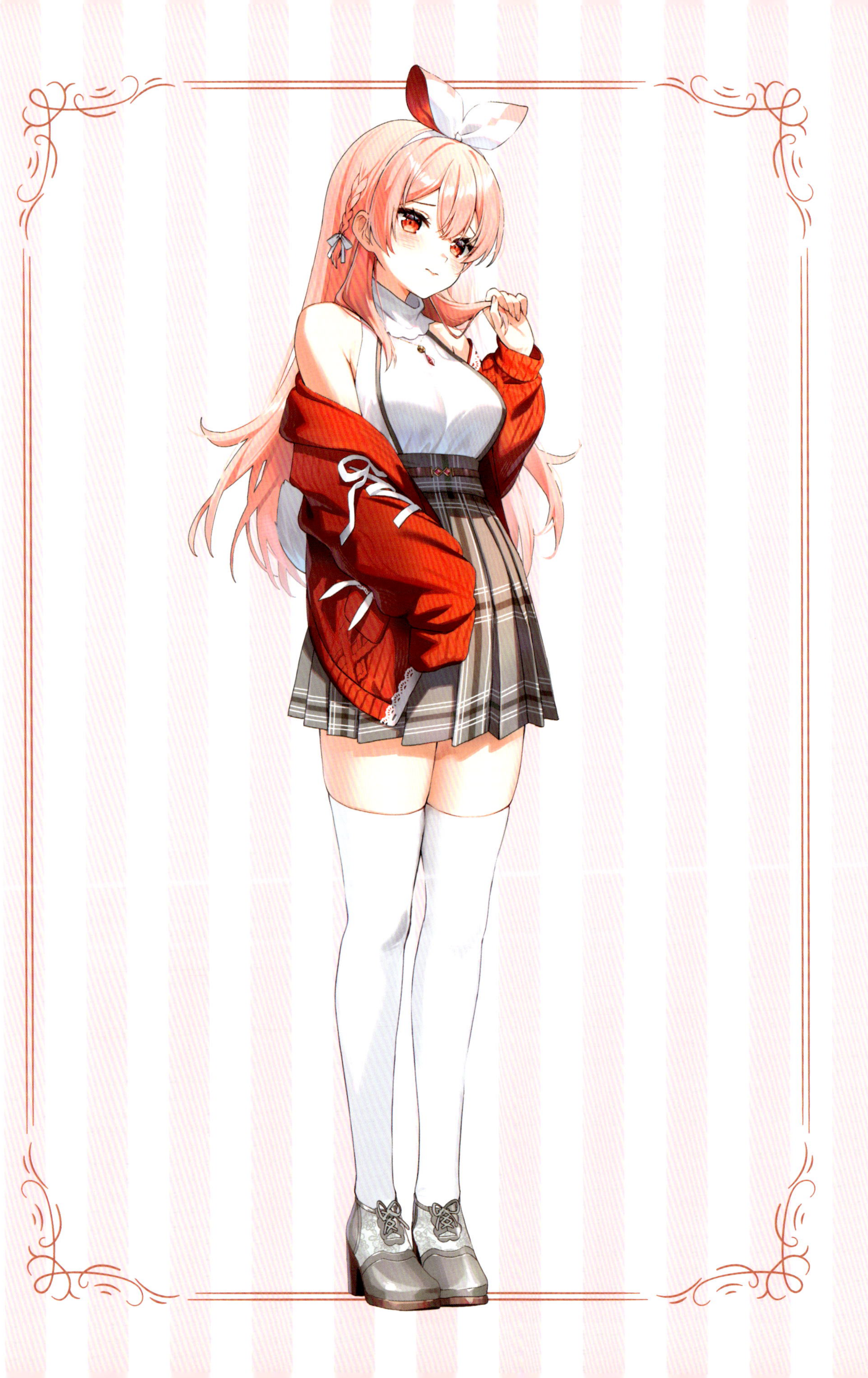

White Rabbit

Rosu

Rosu is a White Rabbit from Wonderland.
She was tasked with finding Alice,
but is procrastinating instead and having fun in the real world.

White Rabbit is a shy and easily flustered girl
who appears to be 20 years old,
though it is well known that time flows differently in Wonderland.

白ウサギのロスは、不思議の国出身。
アリスを捜すという任務を先延ばしにしており、
現在は不思議の国の外での生活を楽しんでいる。
白ウサギは恥ずかしがり屋で、見た目は20歳前後、
すぐに動揺してしまう女の子です。
また、不思議の国では時間の流れ方が
変わっていることはよく知られています。

Mika

Cheshire Cat

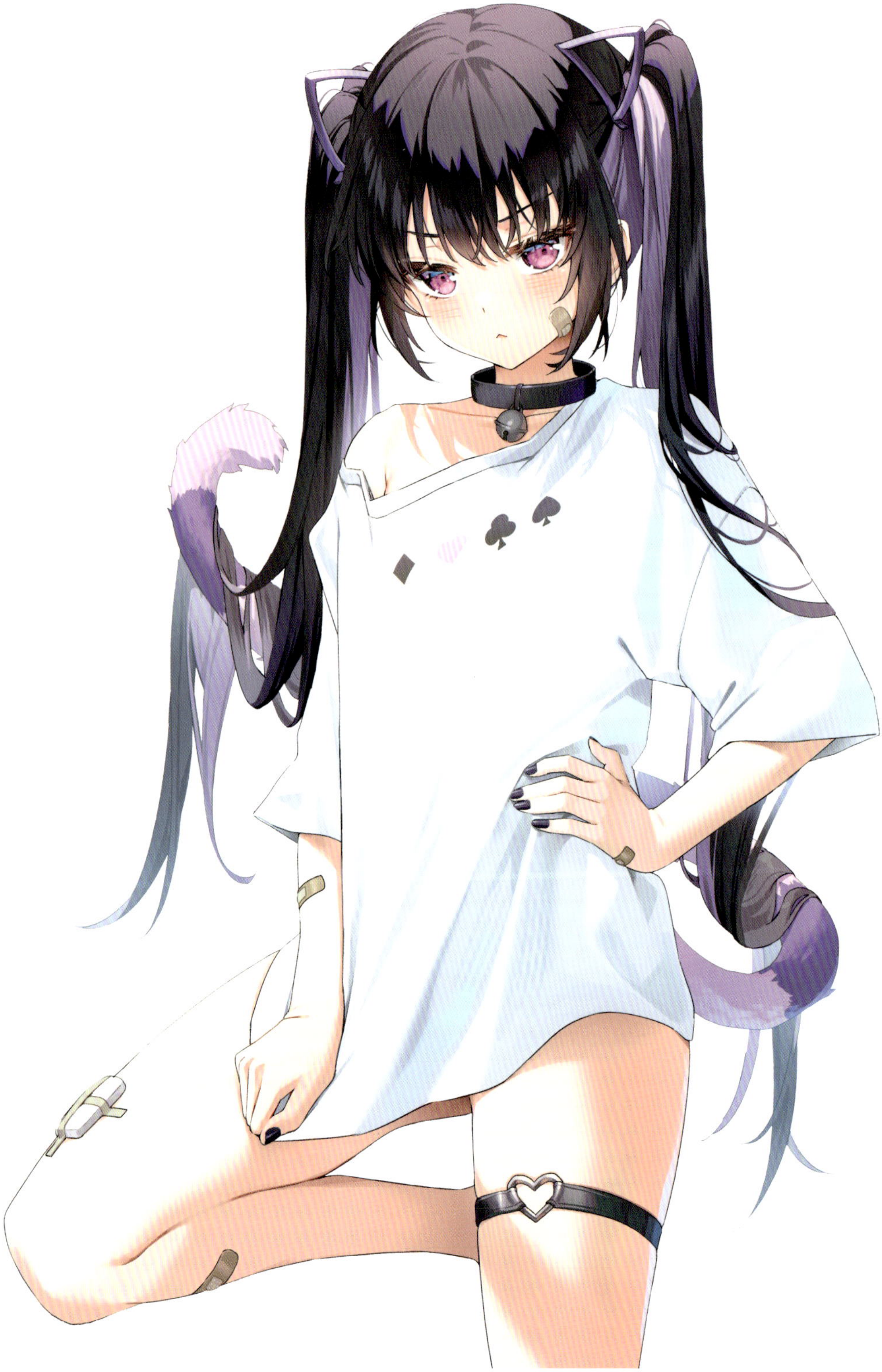

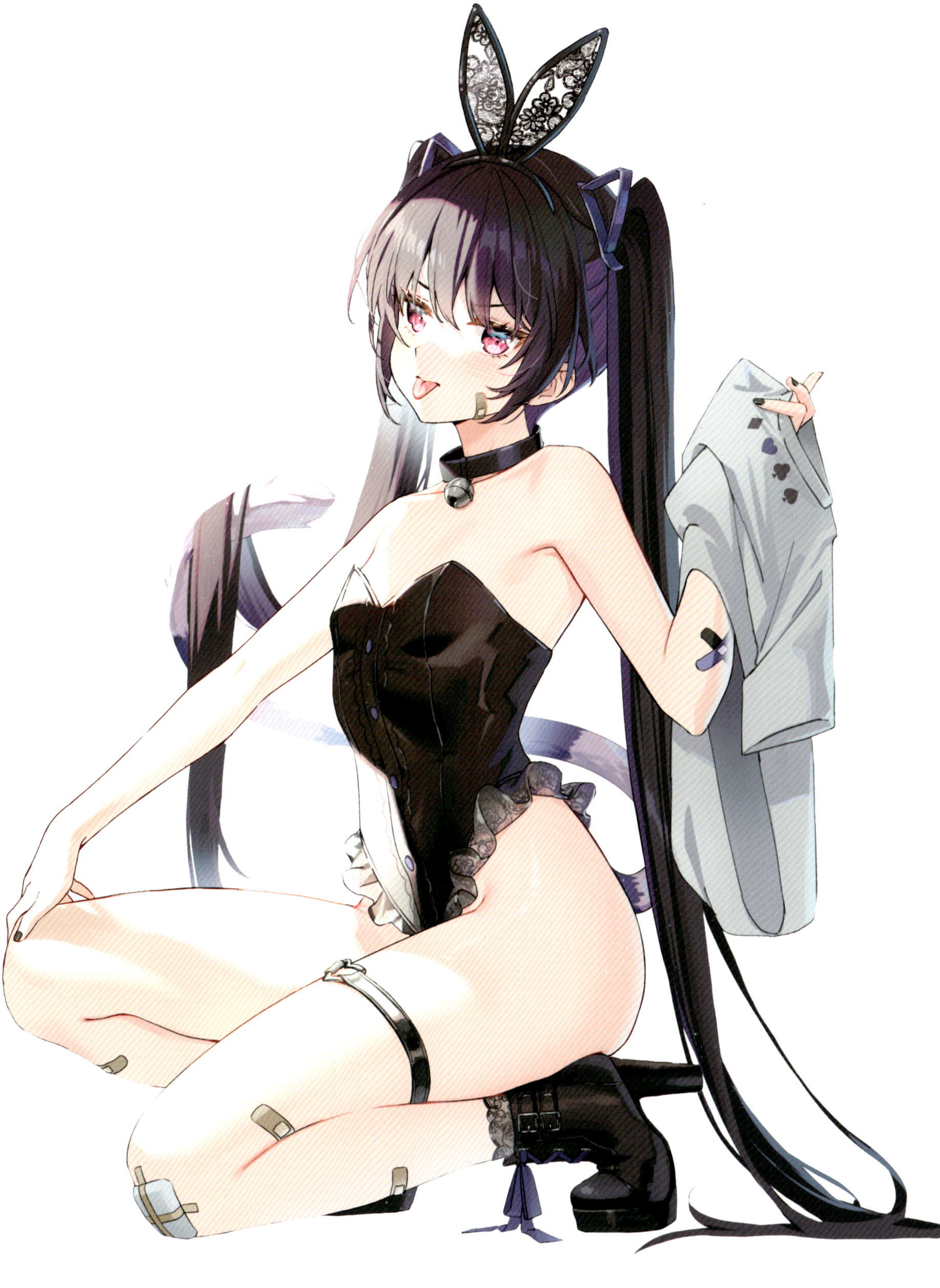

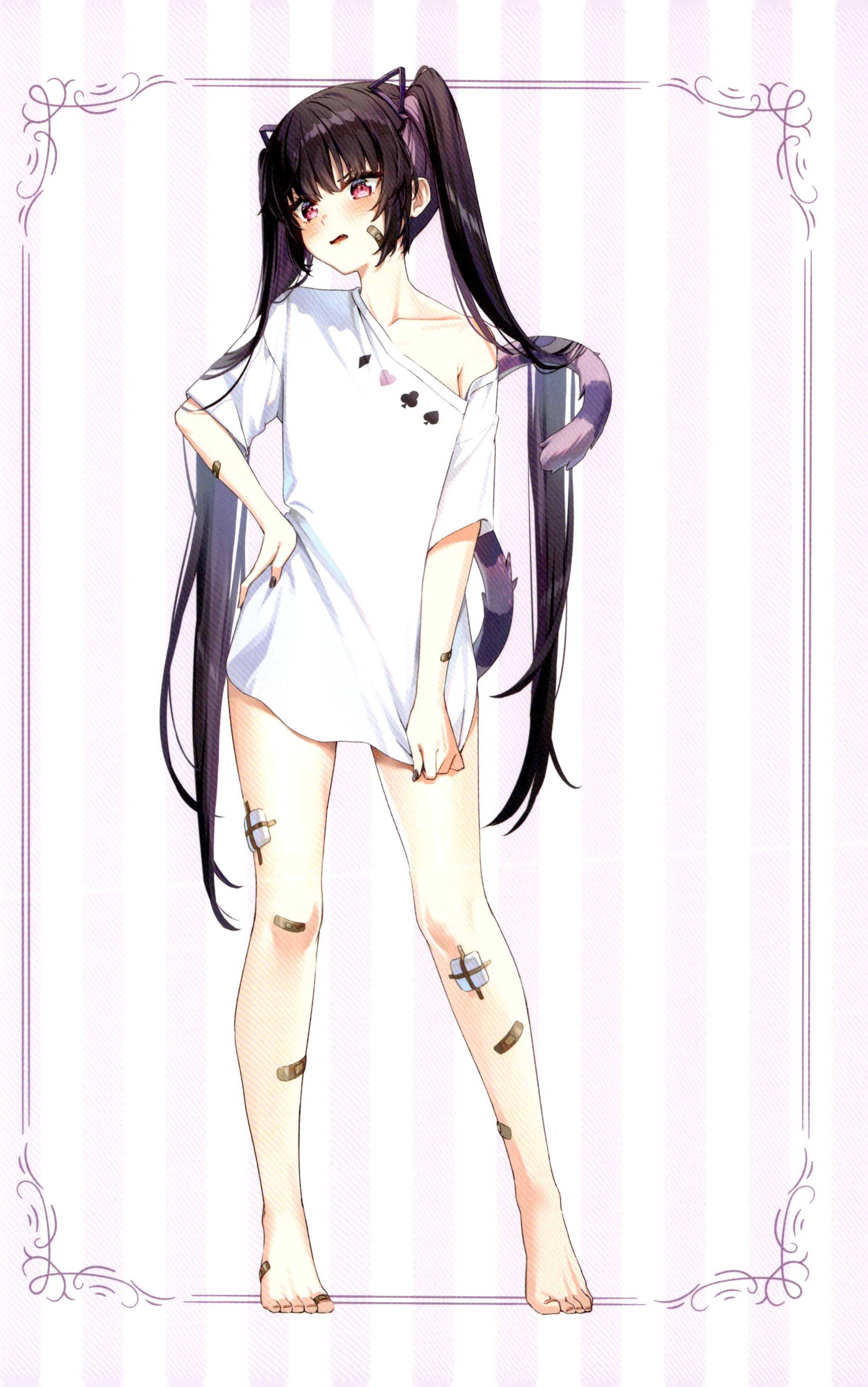

Cheshire Cat

Mika

Mika is a mysterious runaway Cheshire Cat.
White Rabbit recently adopted this stray Cheshire,
which has made her daily life more colorful
in all the most fun and troublesome of ways.
She is not very sociable and tends to glare at people.
She likes wearing cute outfits, but is embarrassed to be seen in them.

白ウサギは最近、迷子のチェシャ猫を保護しました。
この謎めいたチェシャ猫は、白ウサギの手を常にわずらわせ、
同時に日常を最高に楽しく彩る存在になりました。
チェシャ猫ミカは、人見知りで知らない人を睨みつける癖があります。
また、かわいい服を着ることは好きですが、
それを人に見られるのは恥ずかしいようです。

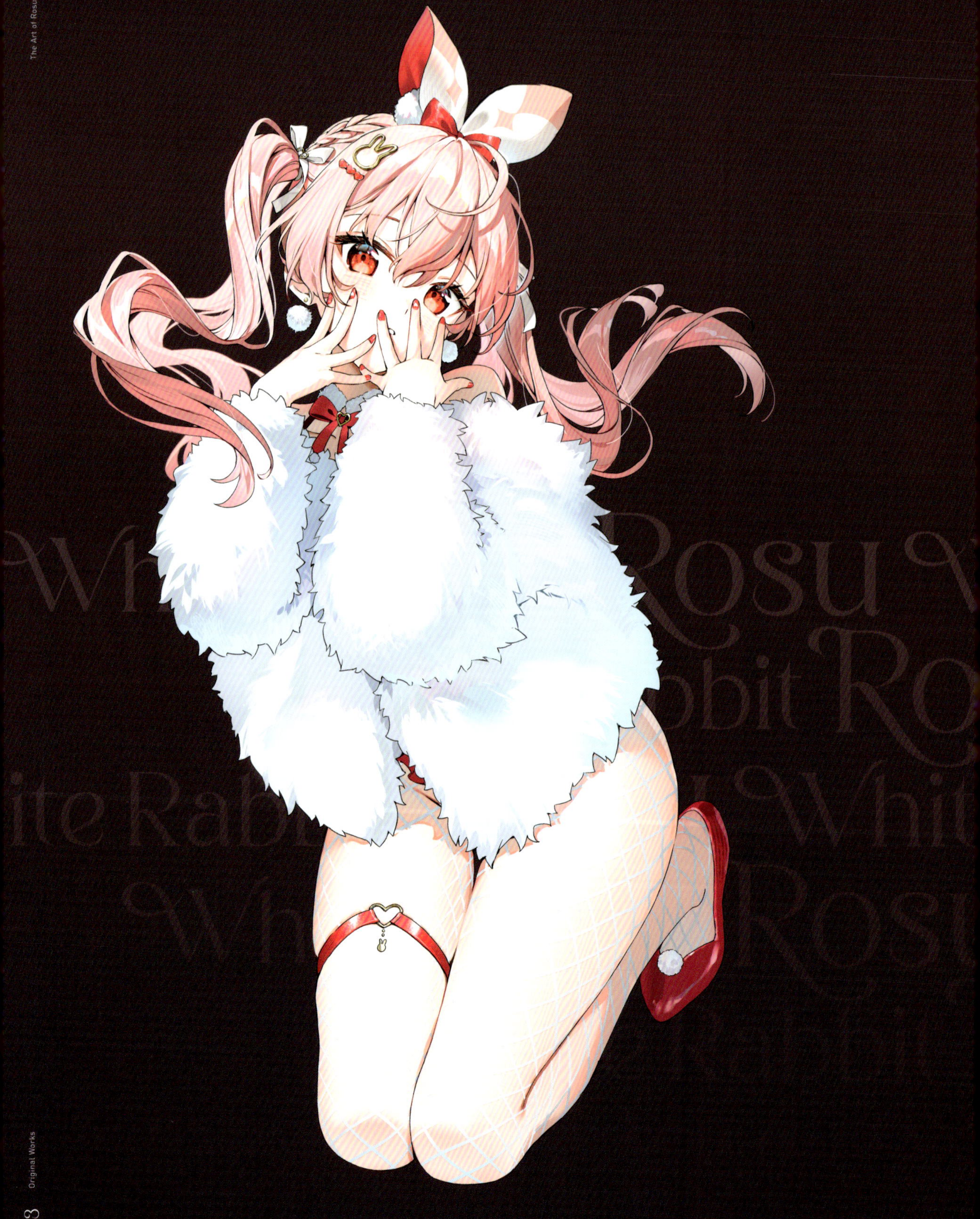
Rosu

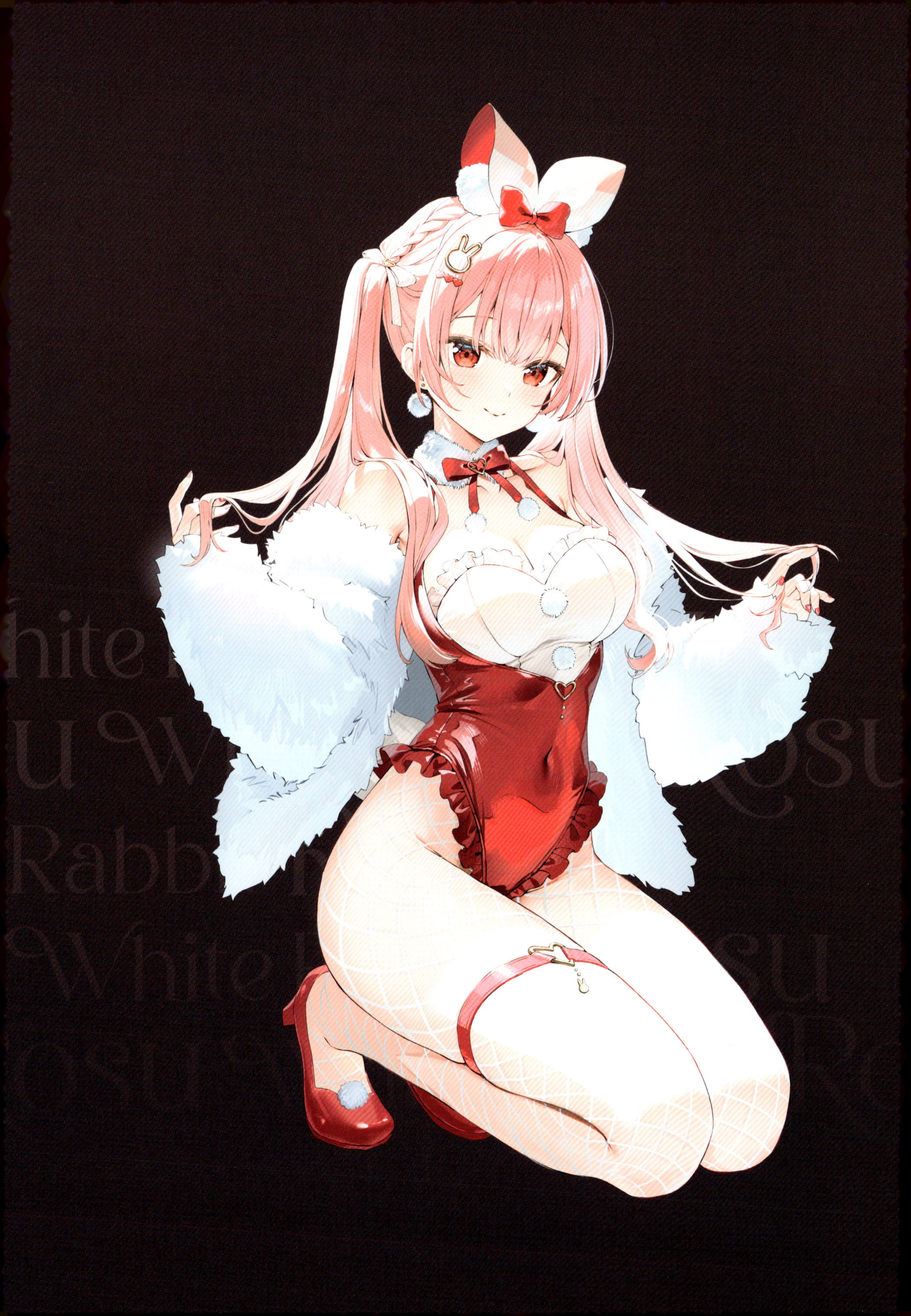

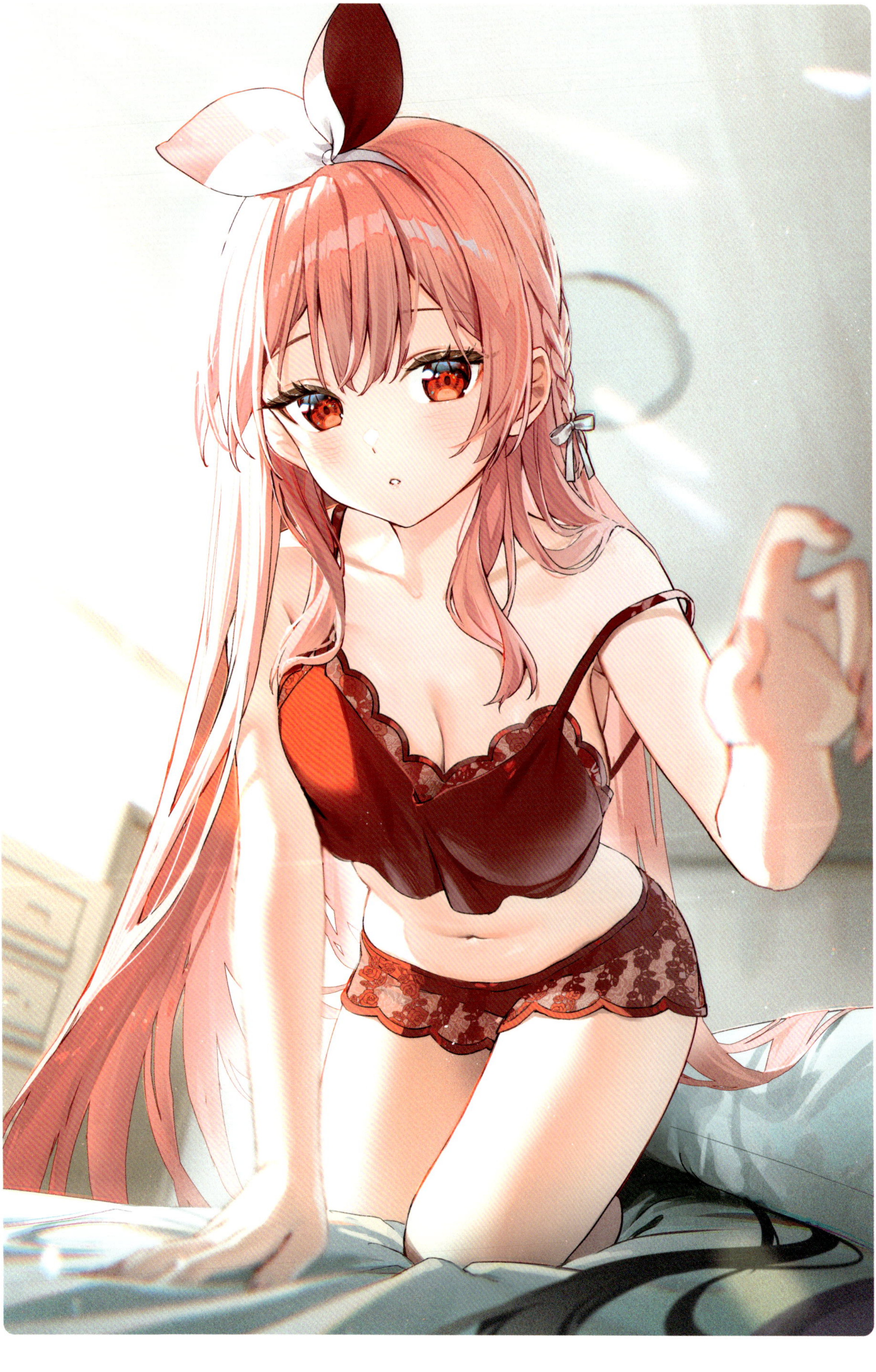

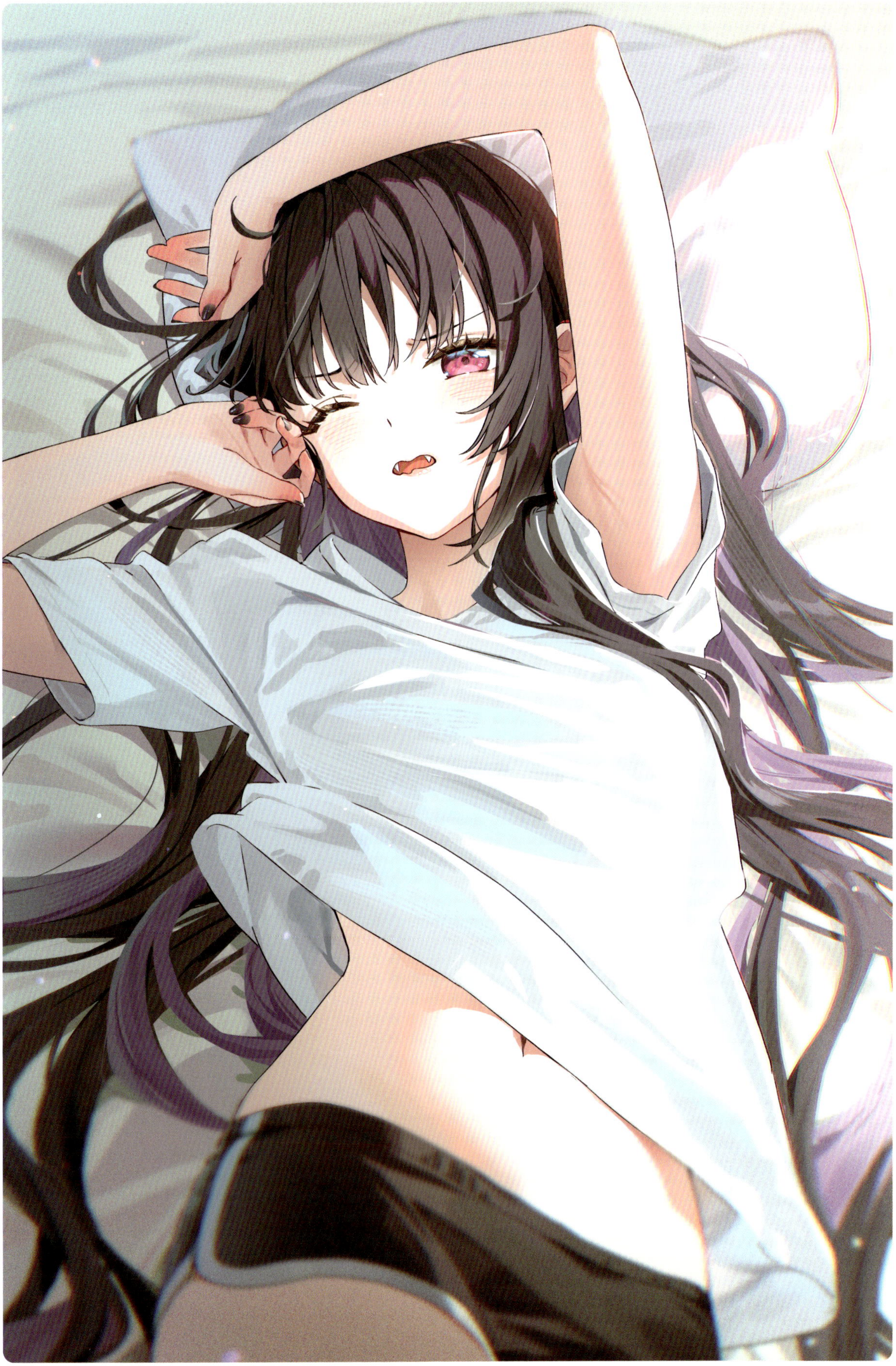

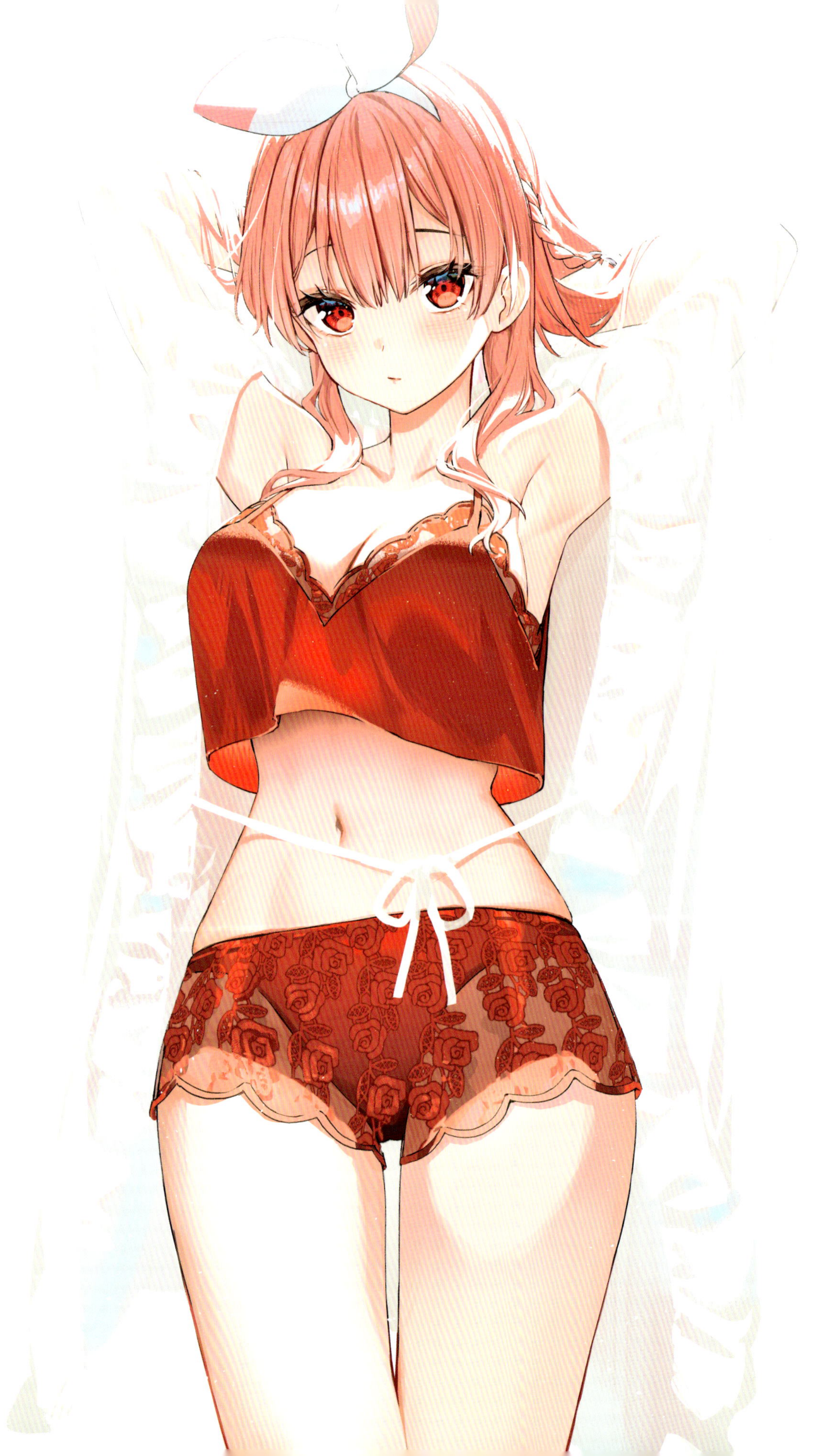

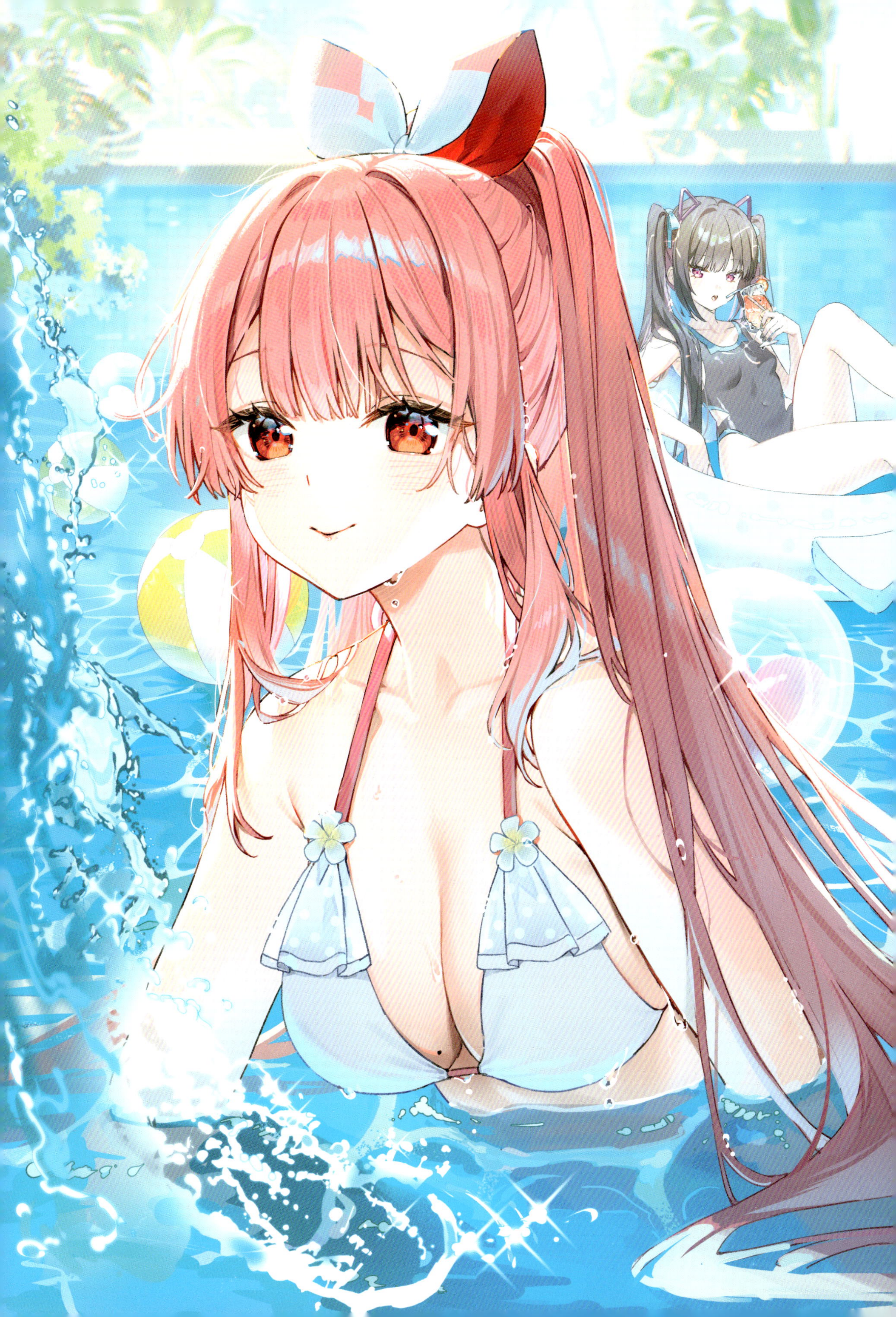

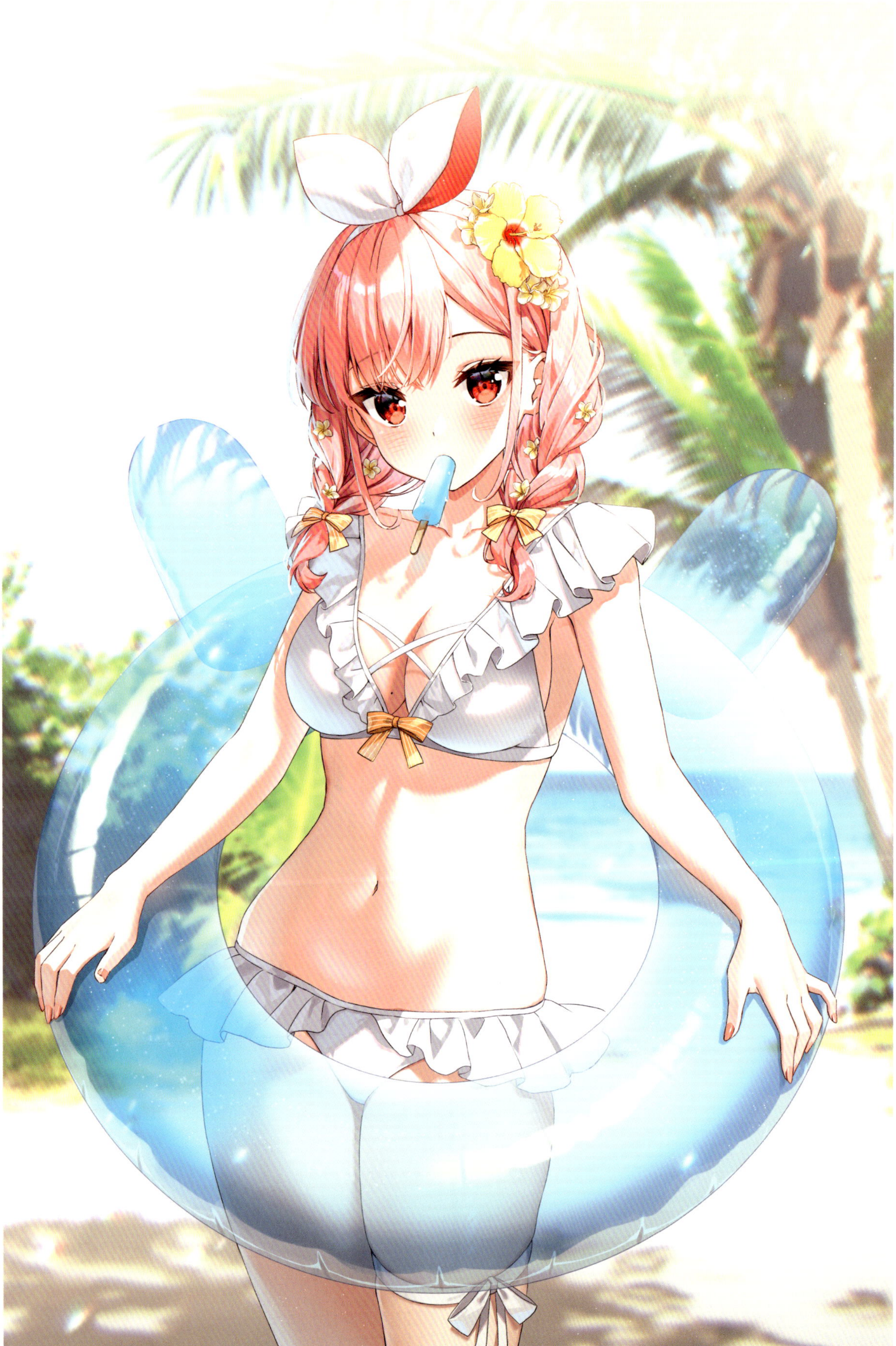

Comic 03

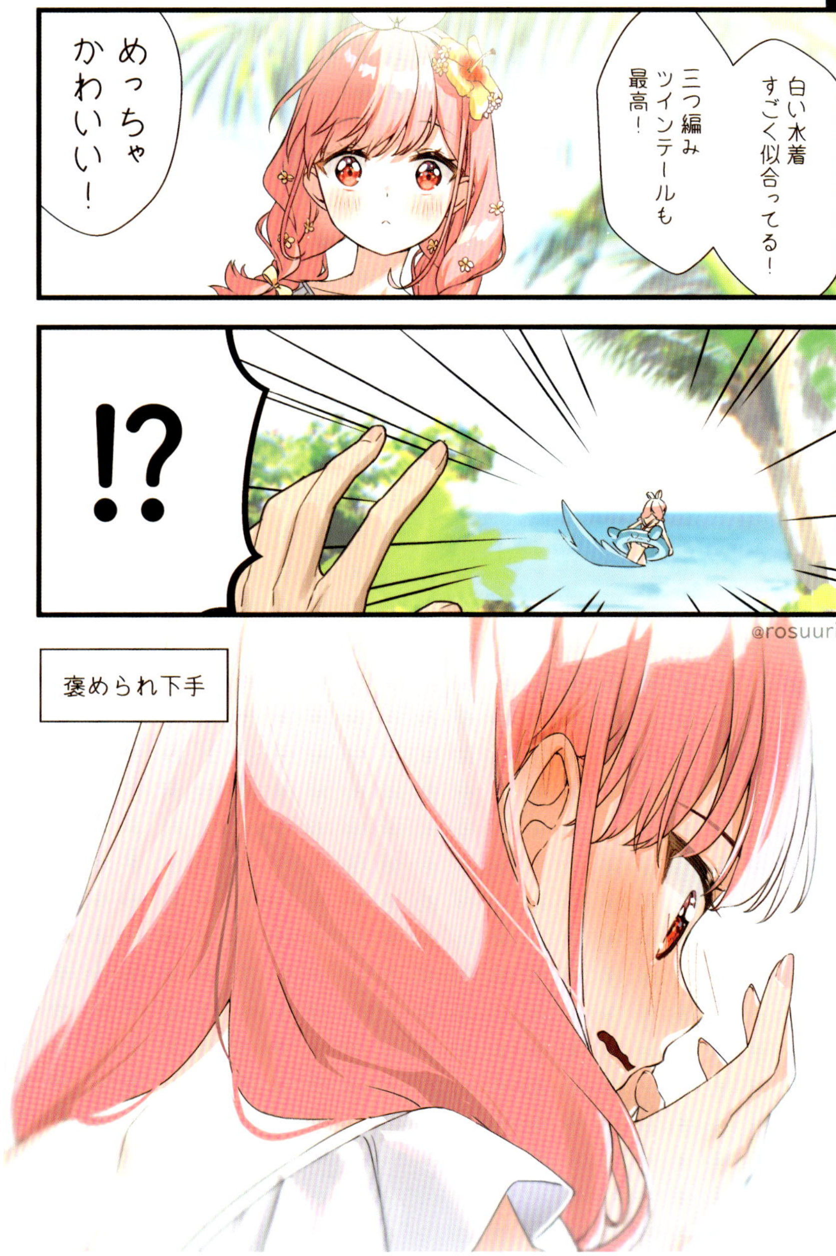

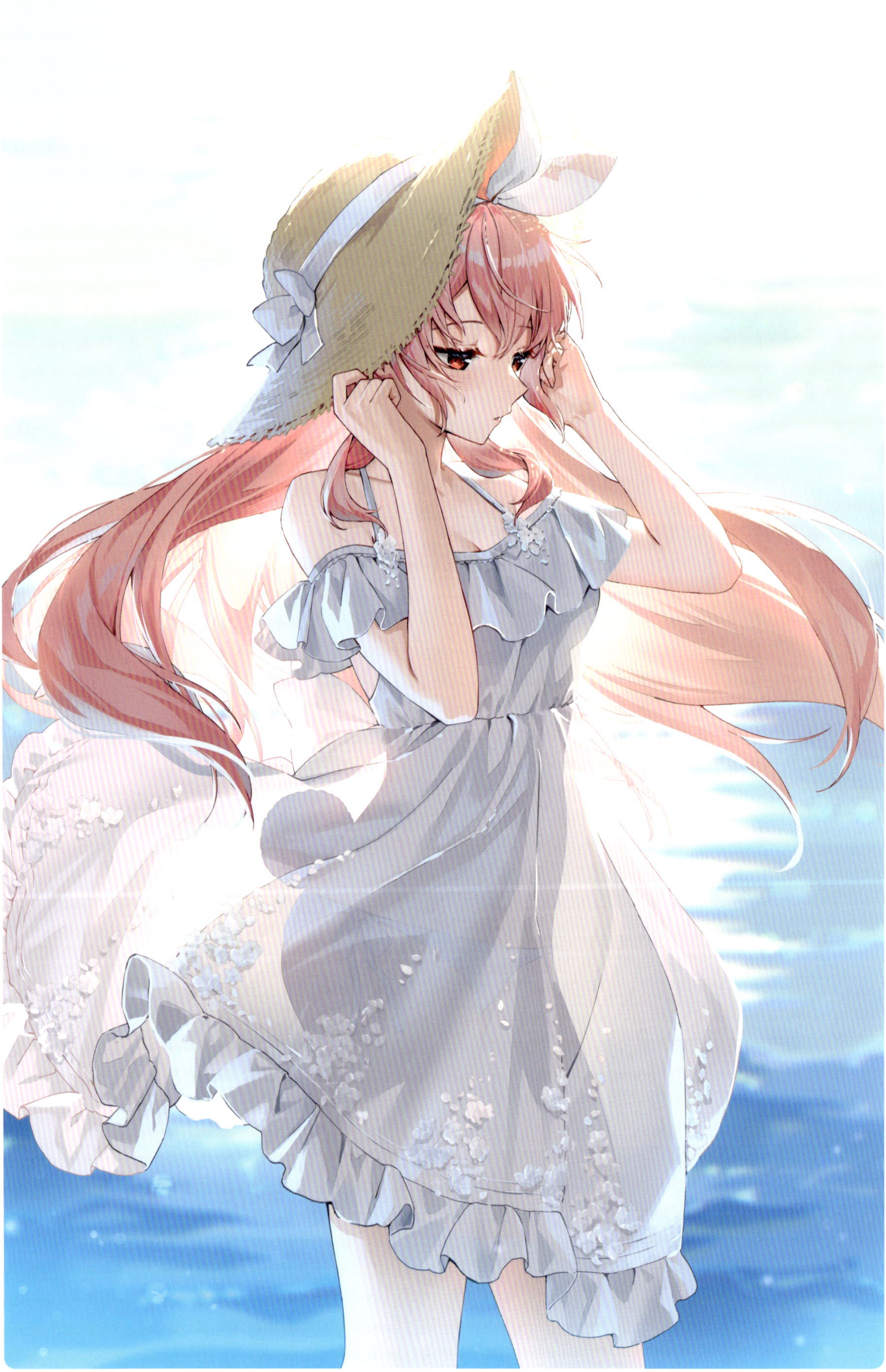

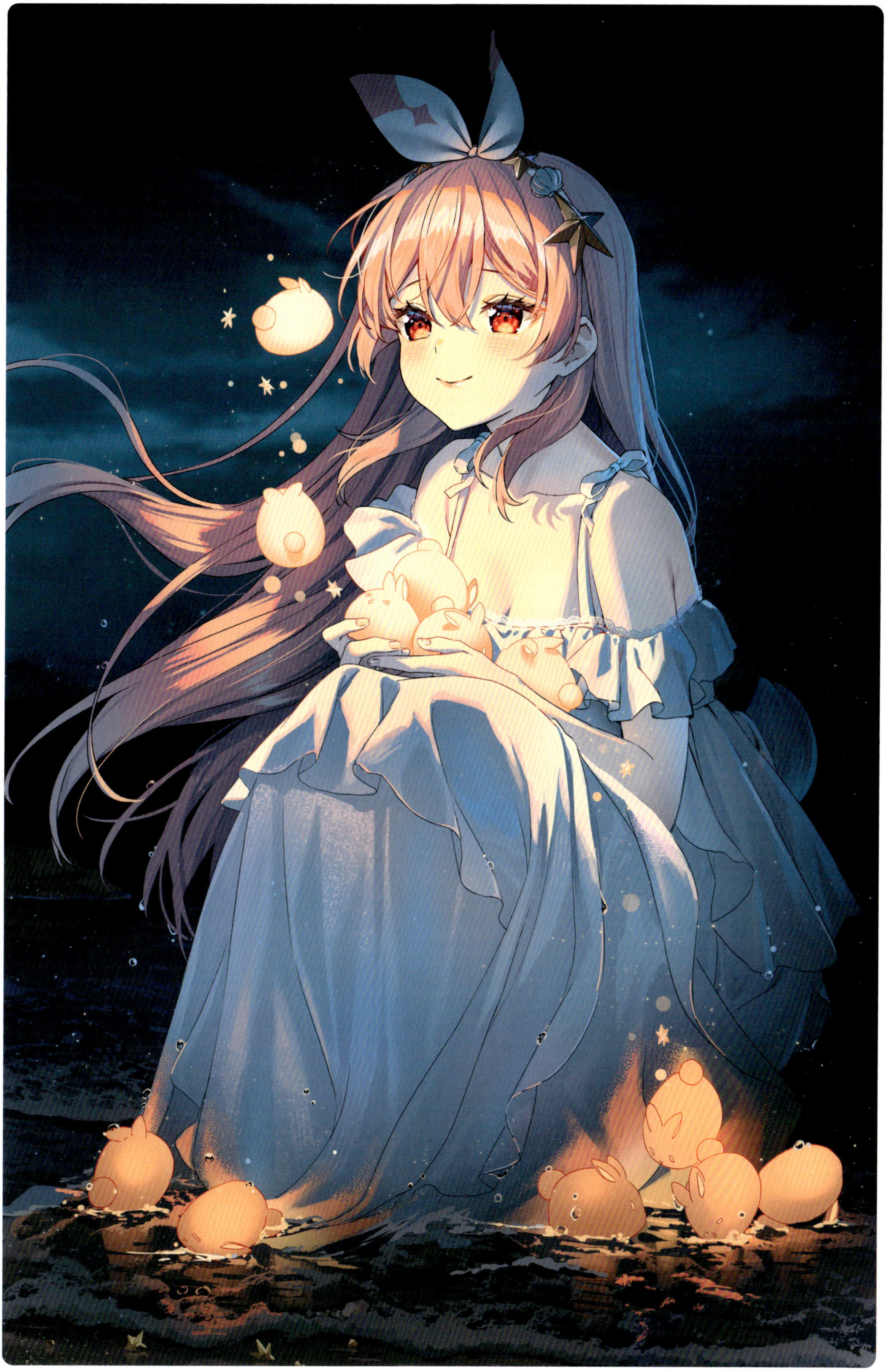

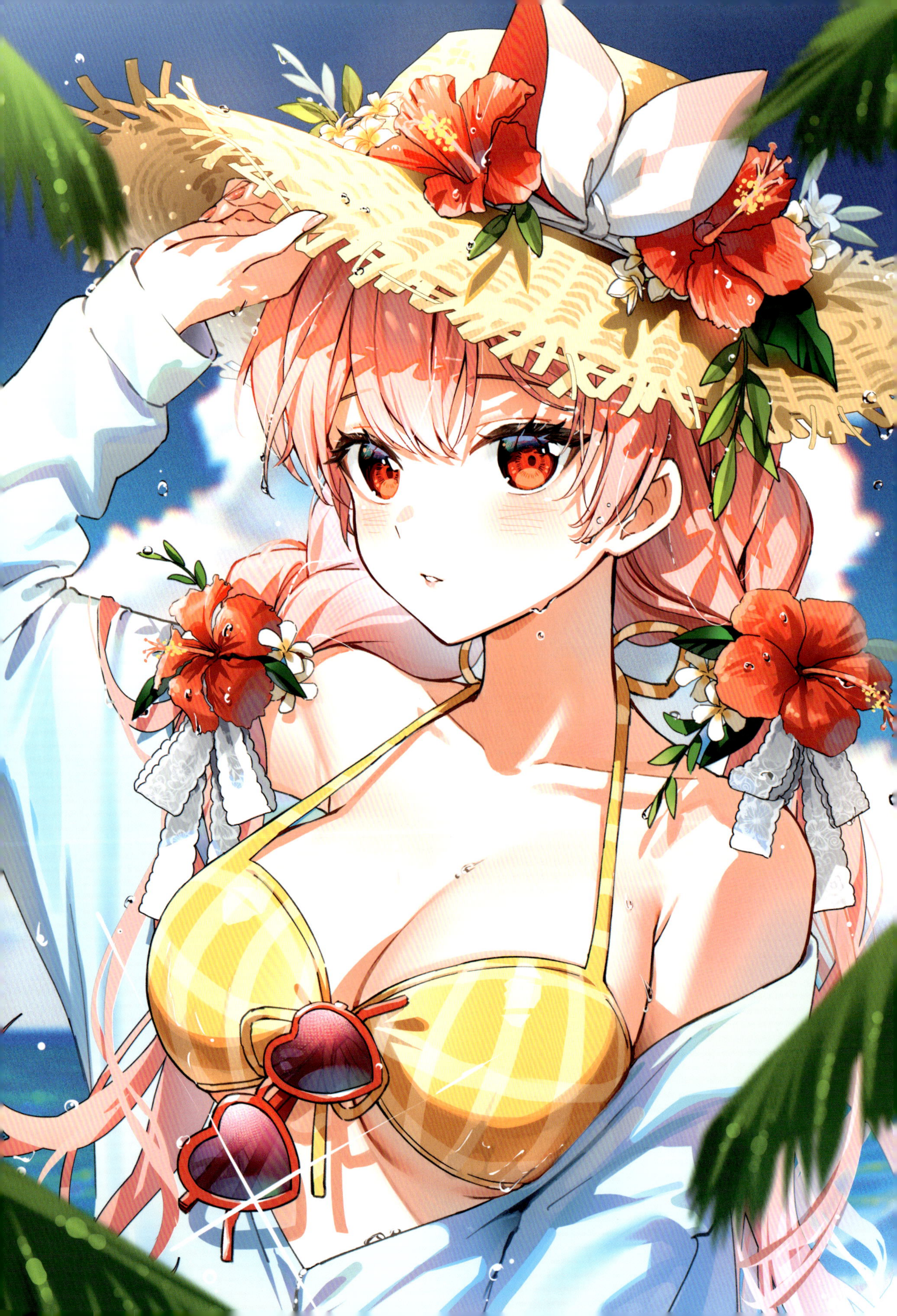

Comic **04**

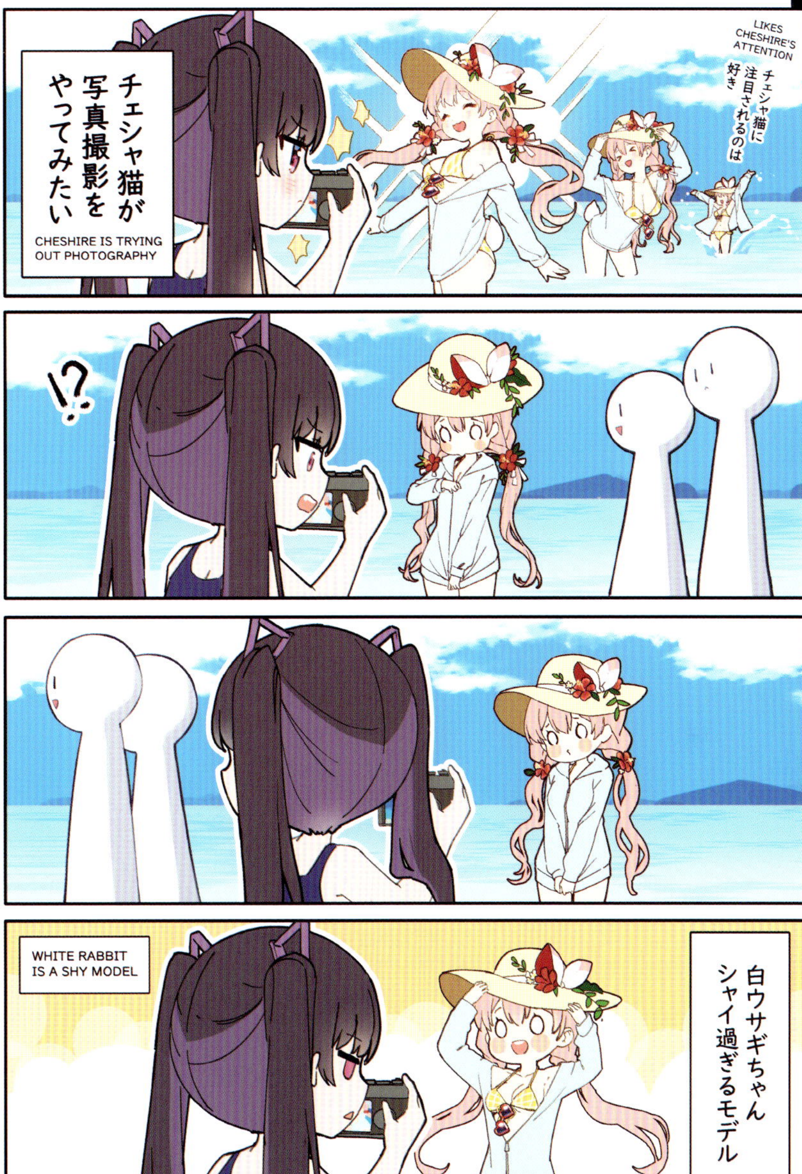
チェシャ猫が写真撮影をやってみたい
CHESHIRE IS TRYING OUT PHOTOGRAPHY
LIKES CHESHIRE'S ATTENTION
チェシャ猫に注目されるのは好き
!?
WHITE RABBIT IS A SHY MODEL
白ウサギちゃんシャイ過ぎるモデル

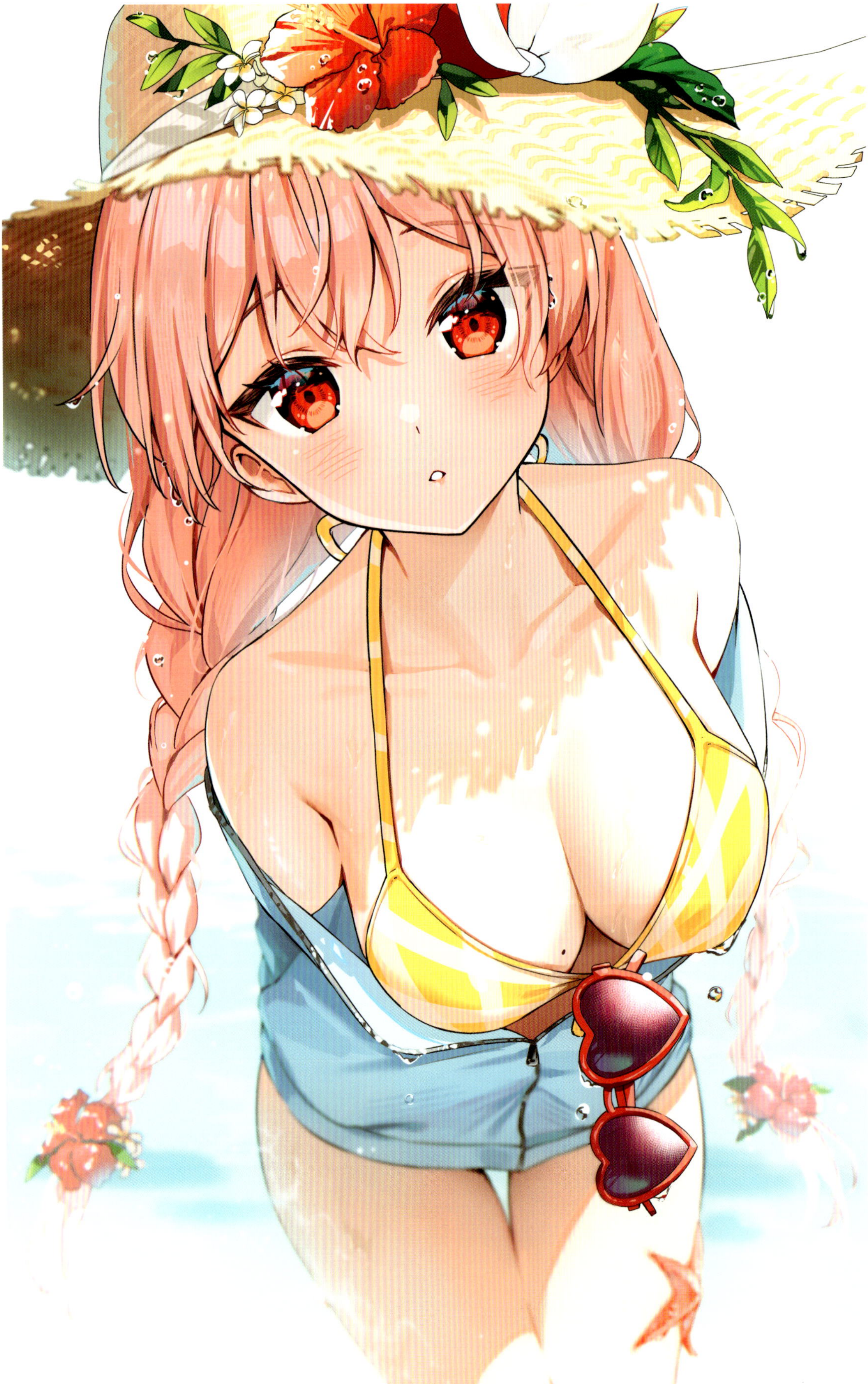

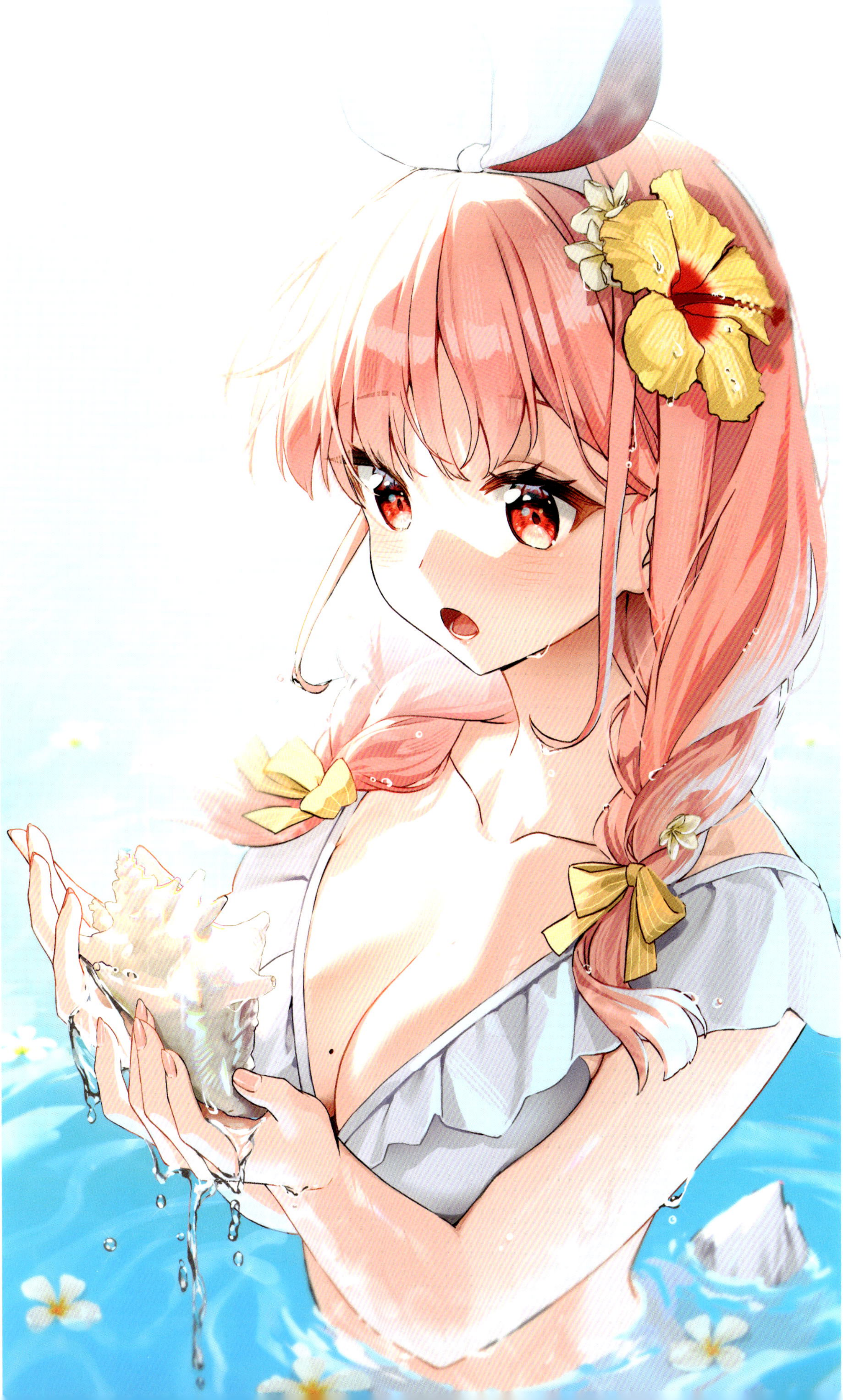

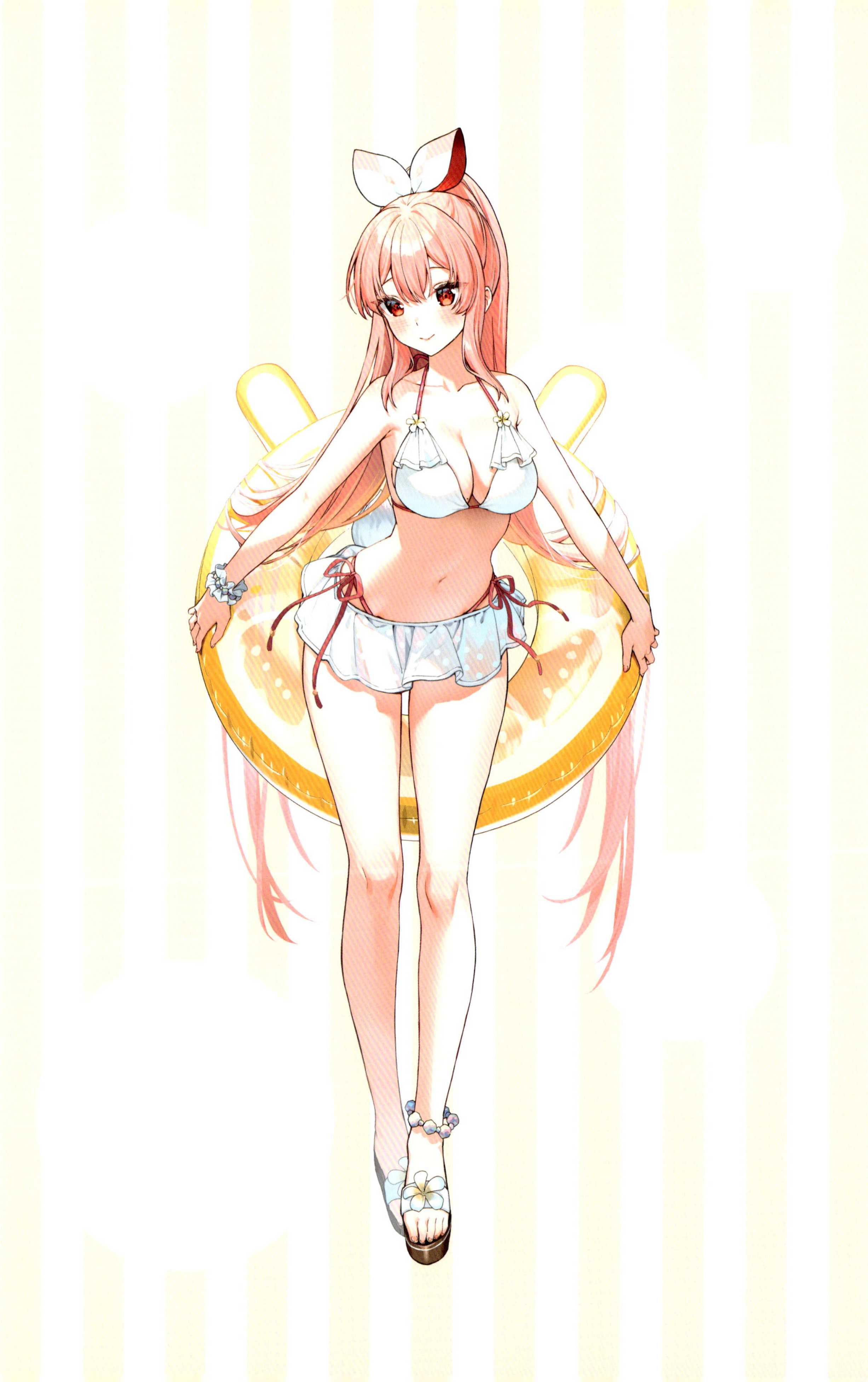

Serenity

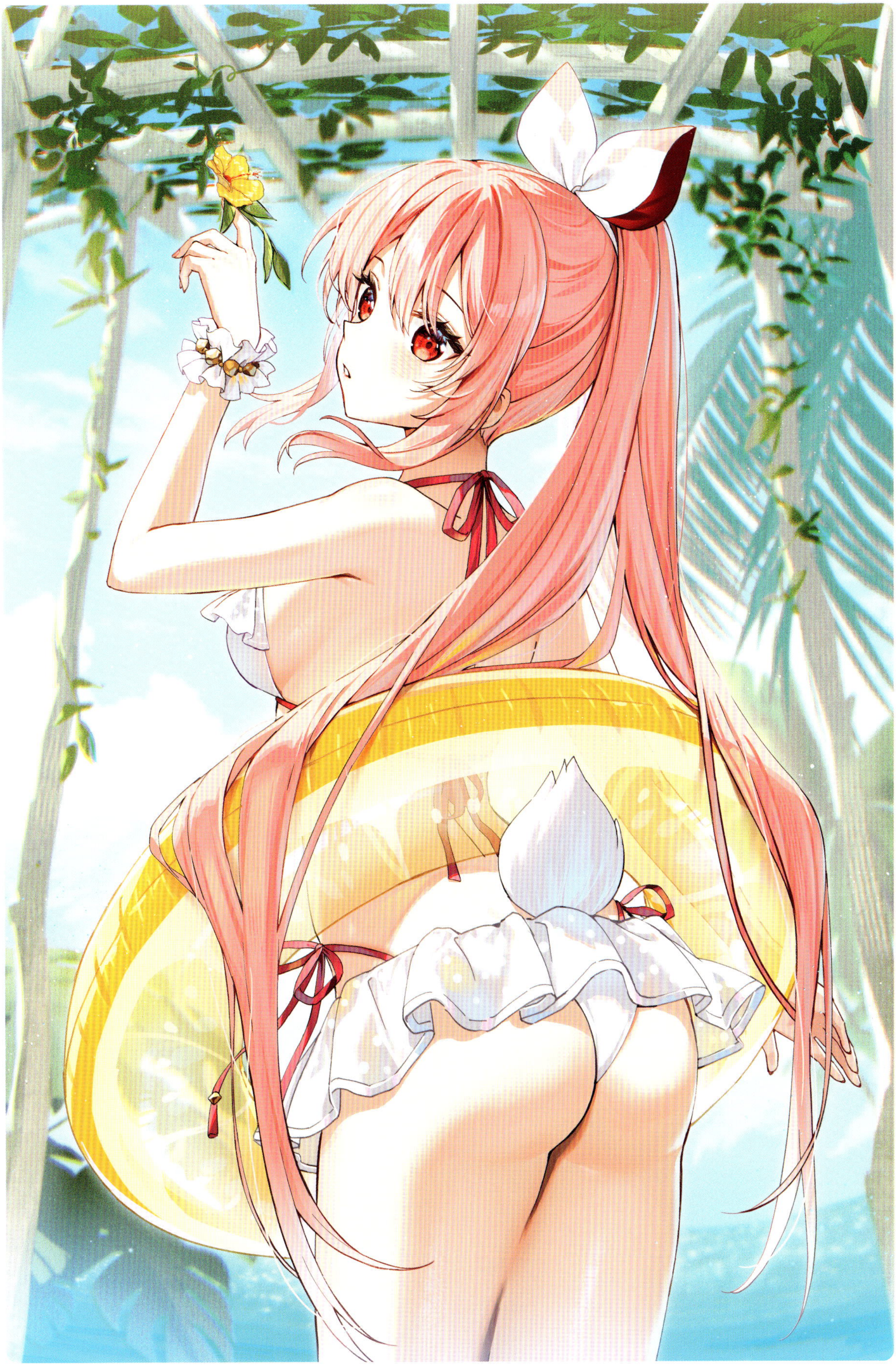

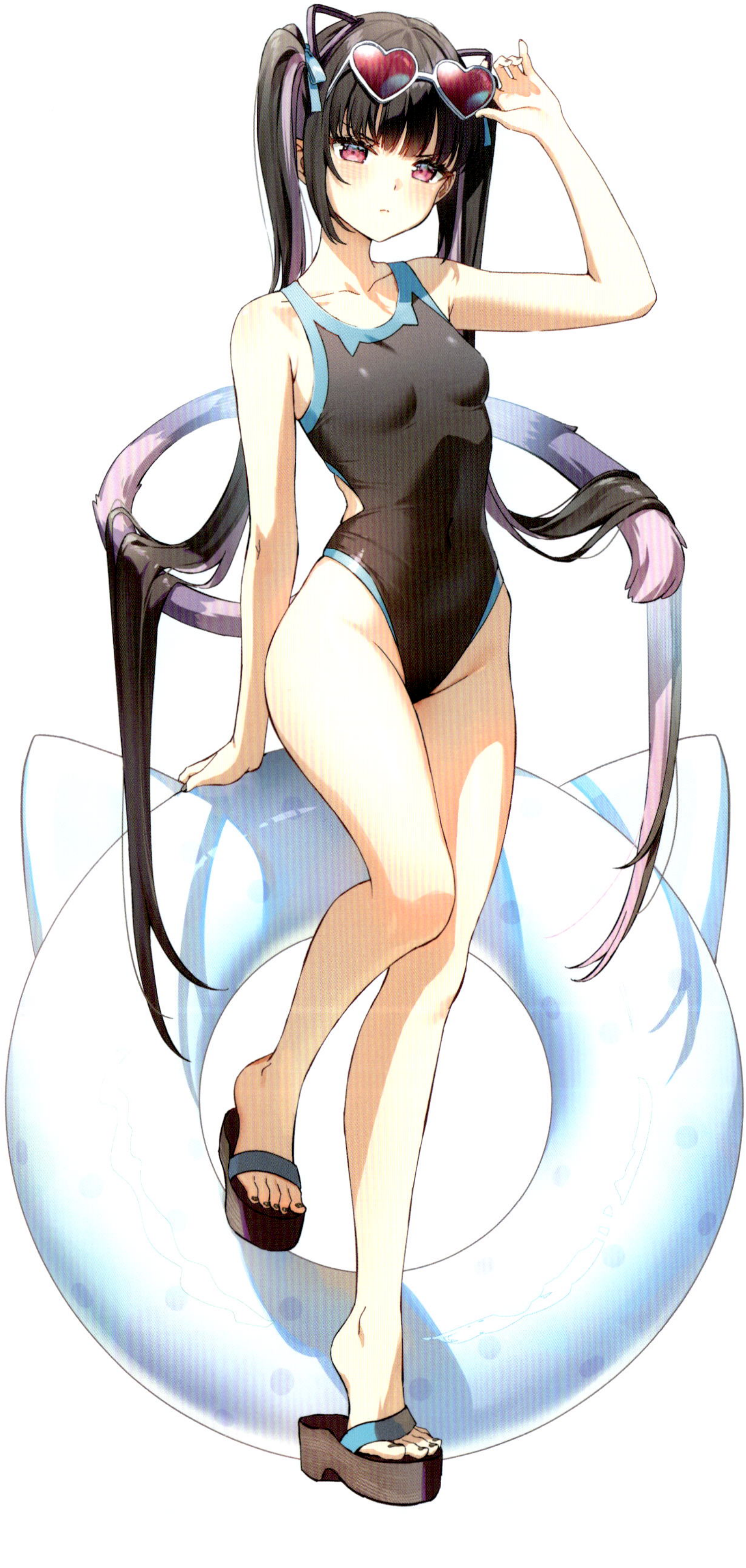

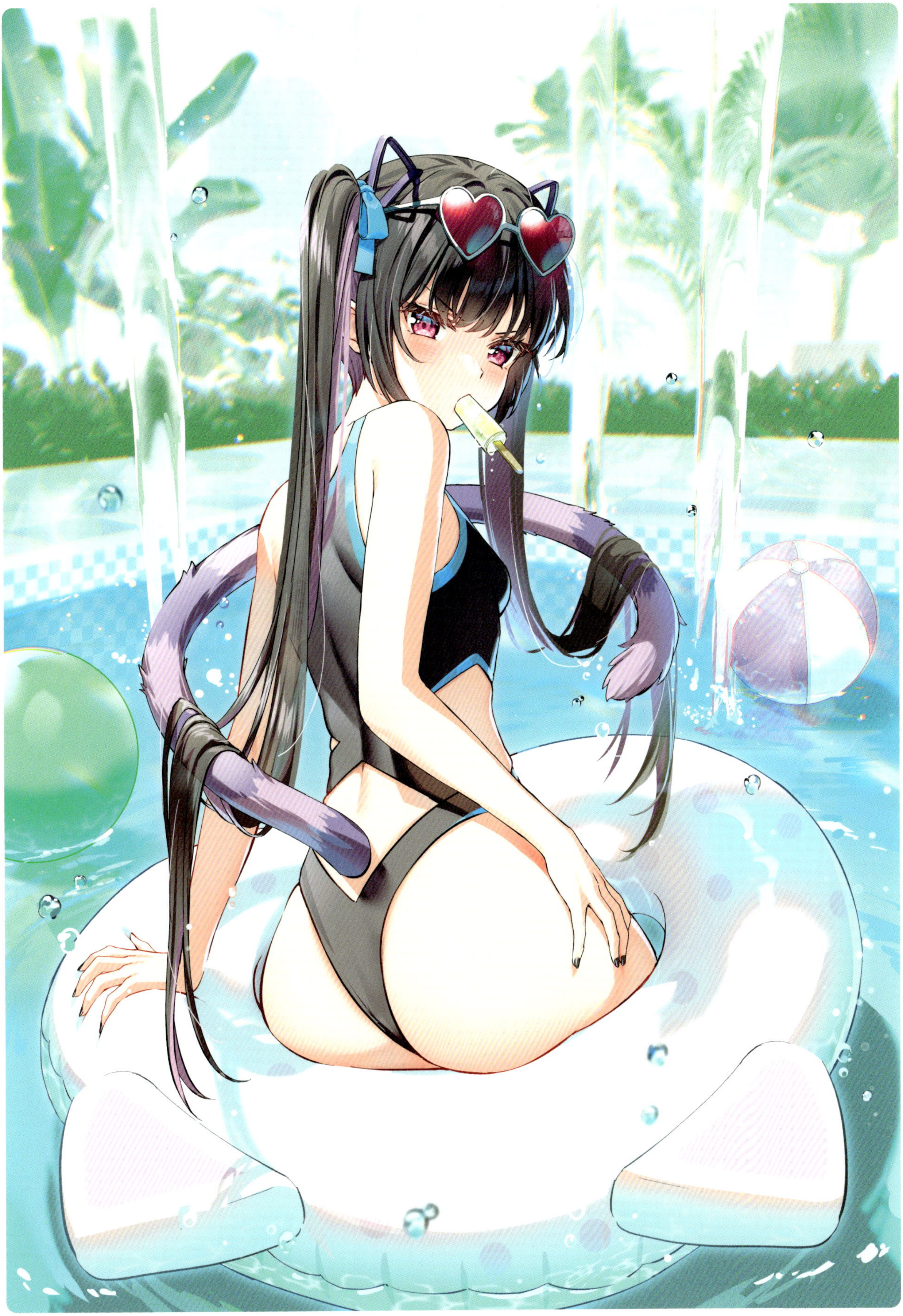

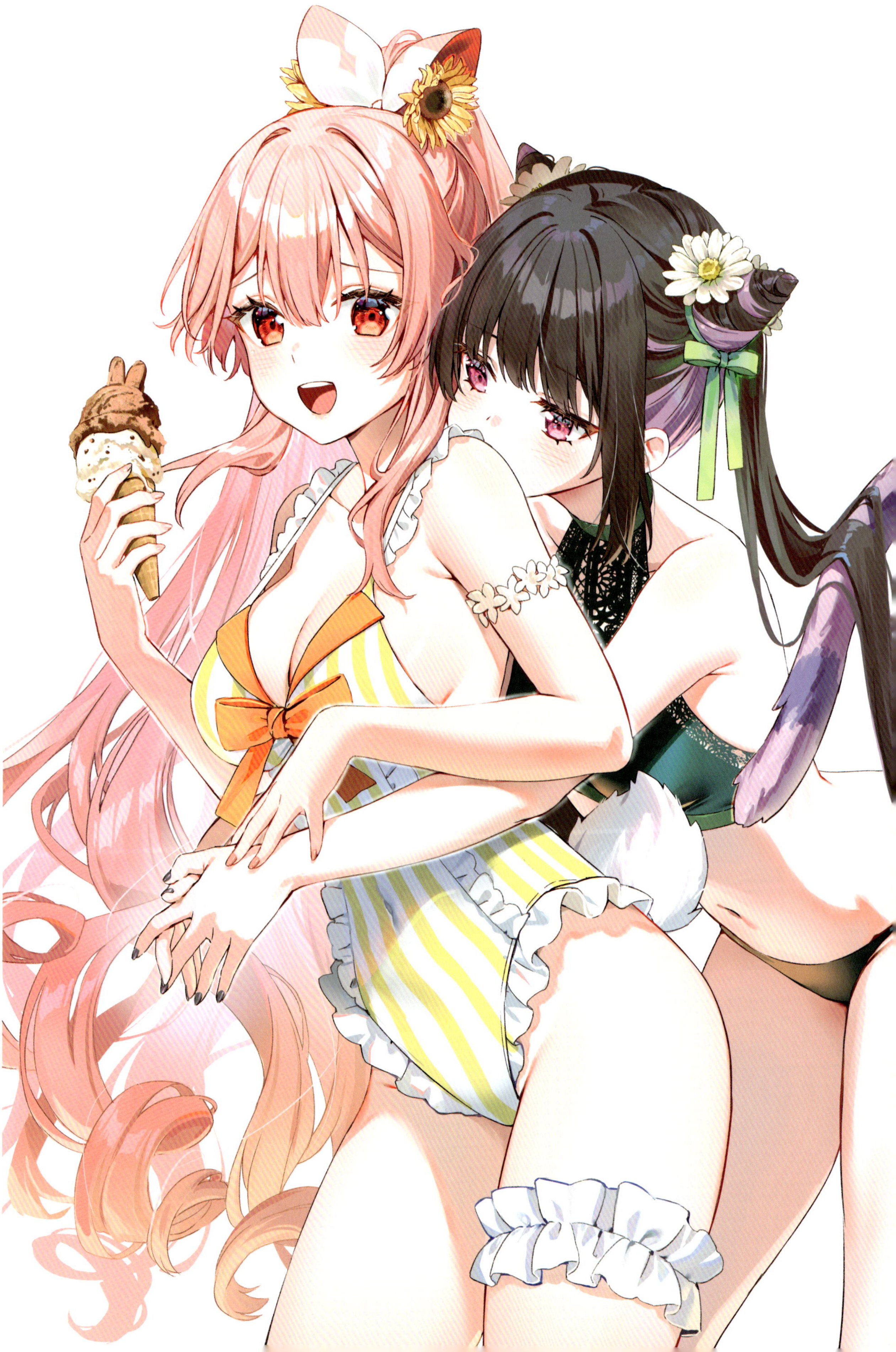

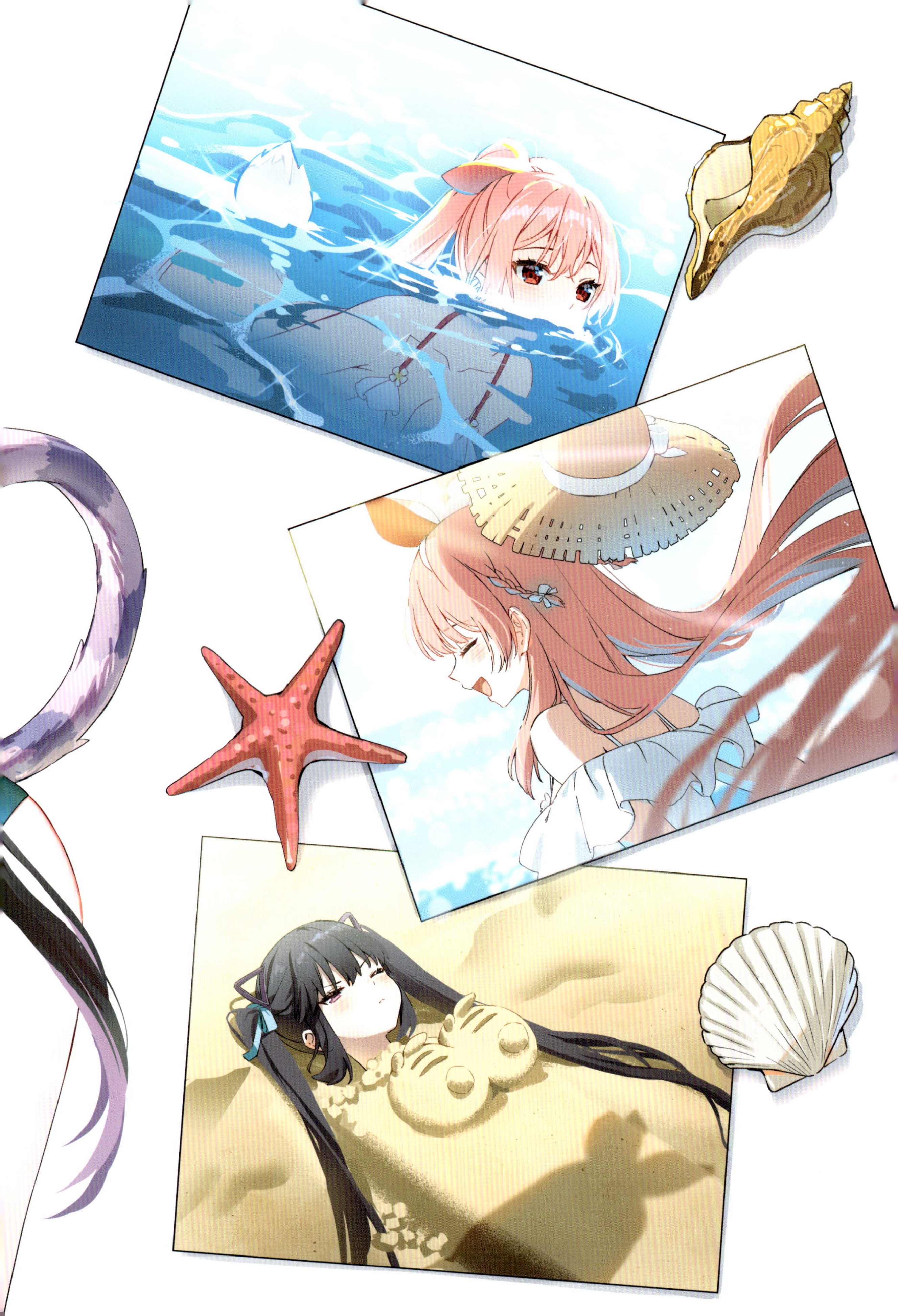

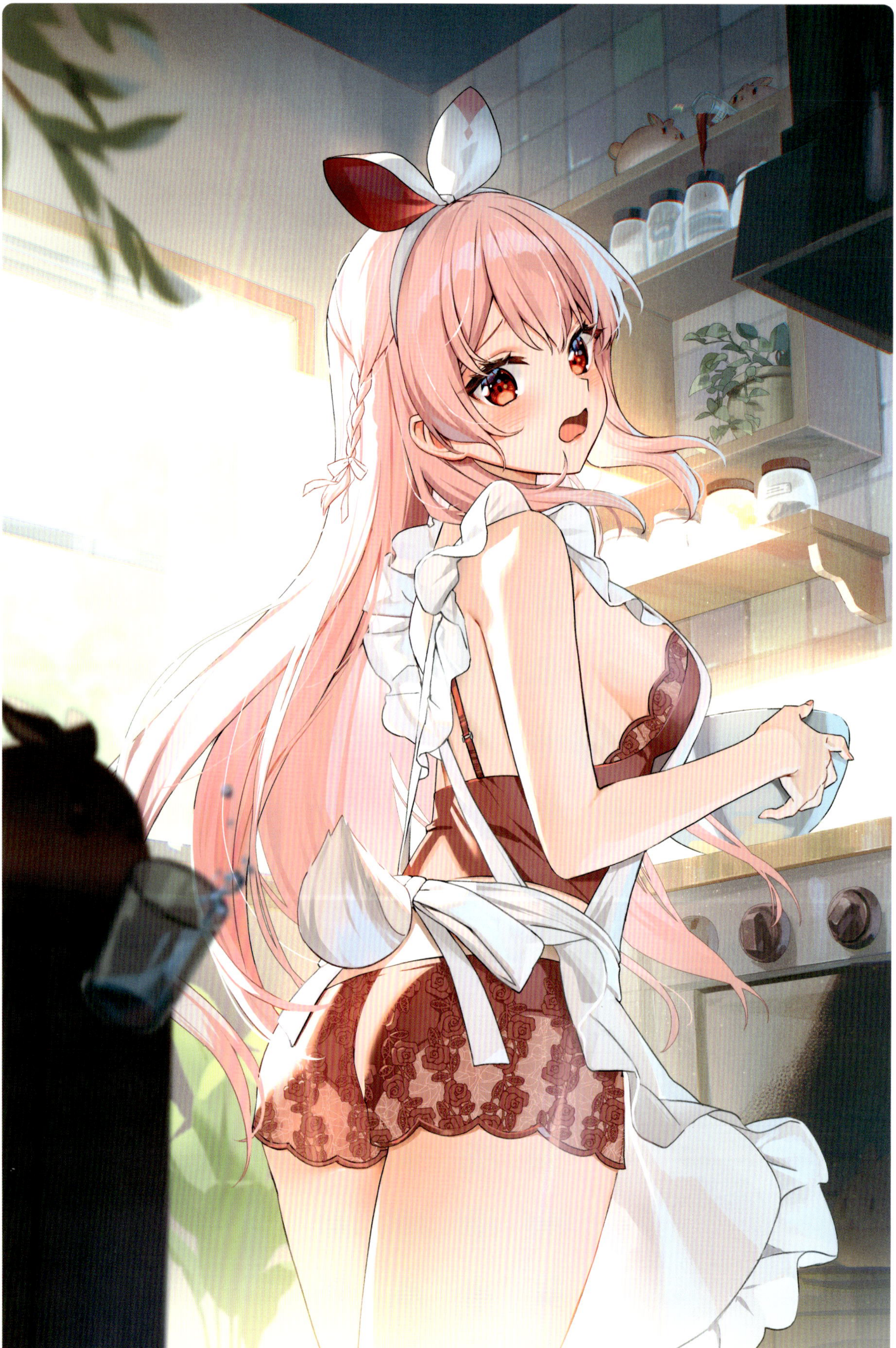

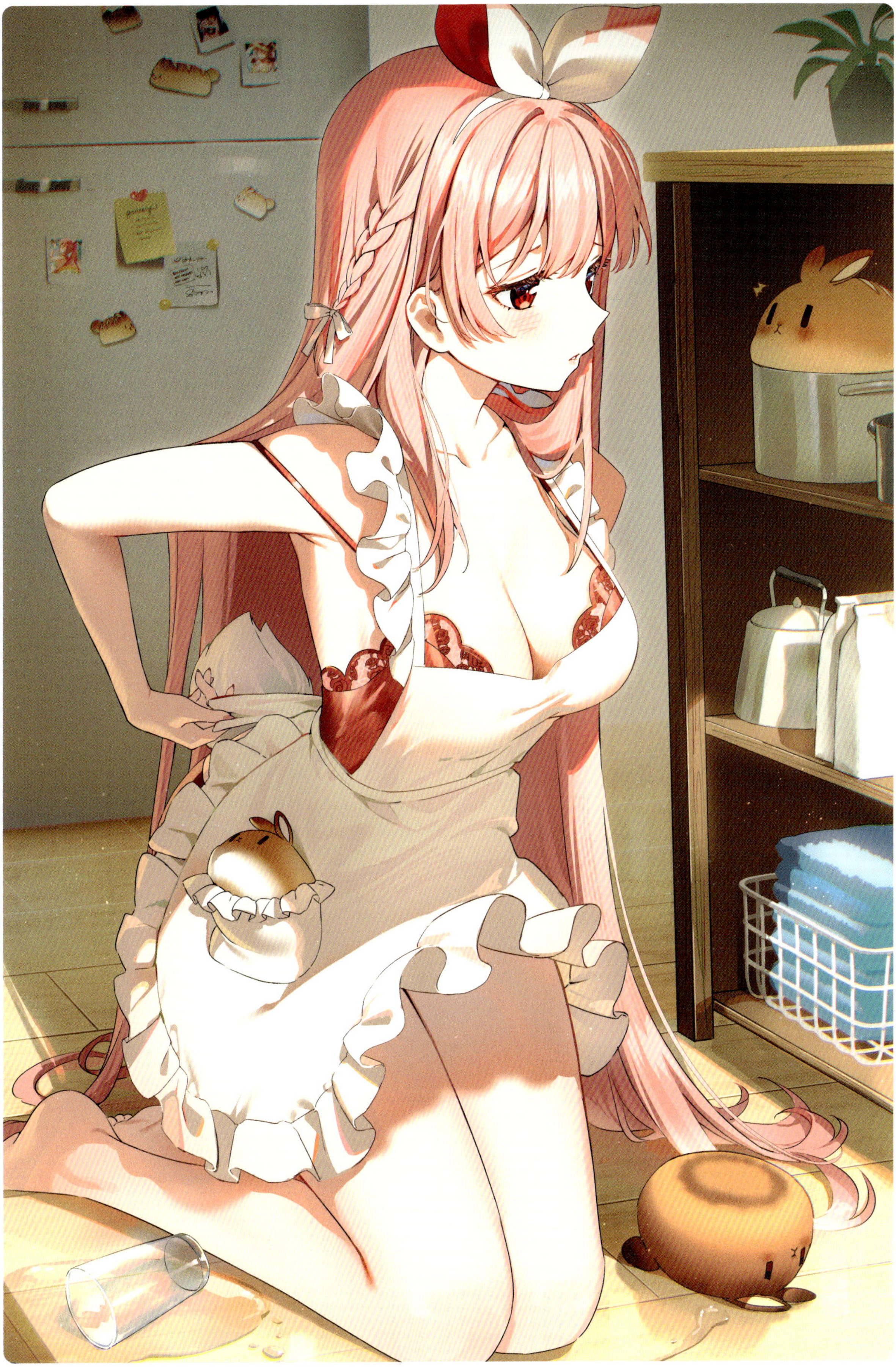

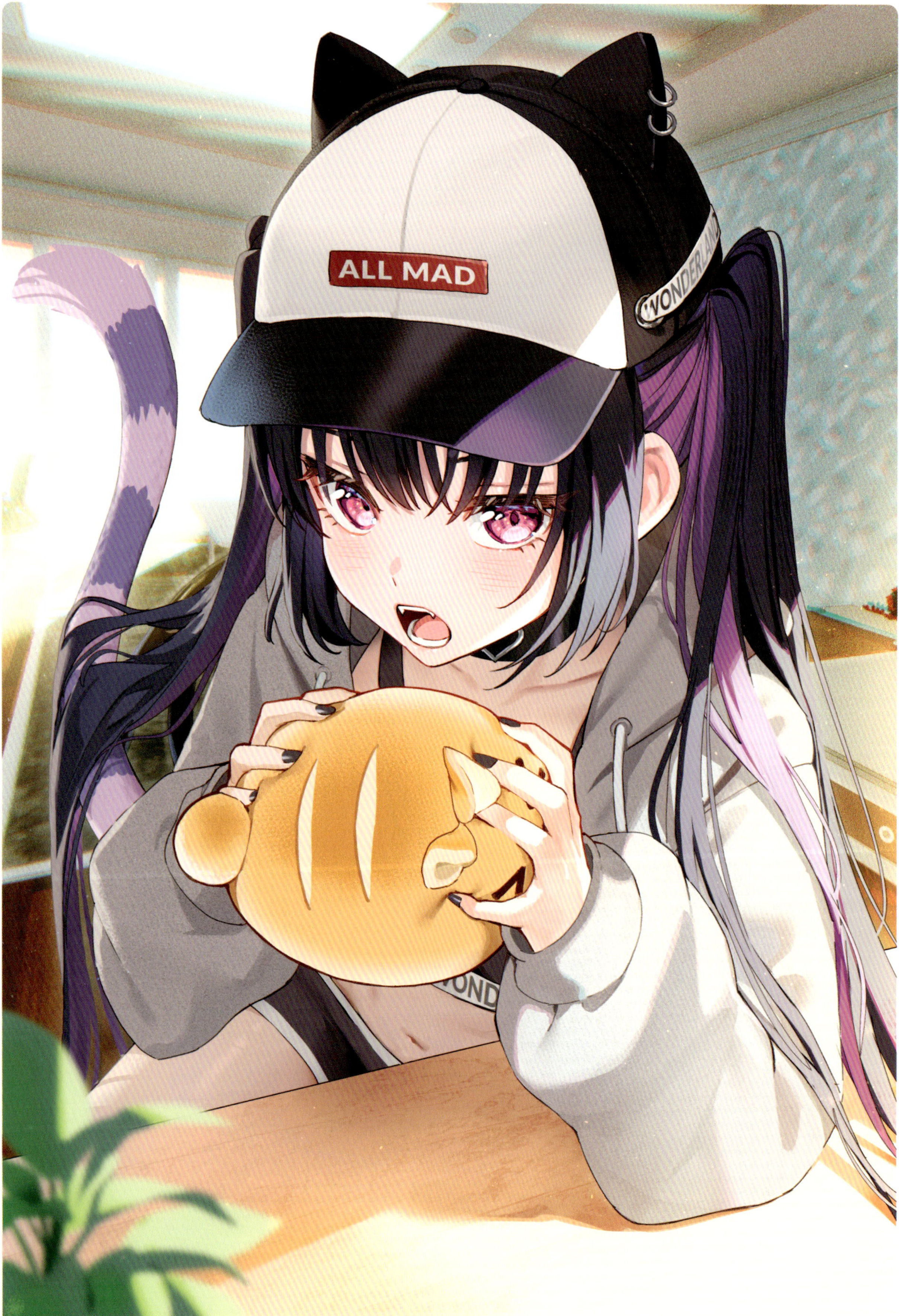
ALL MAD

Comic 05

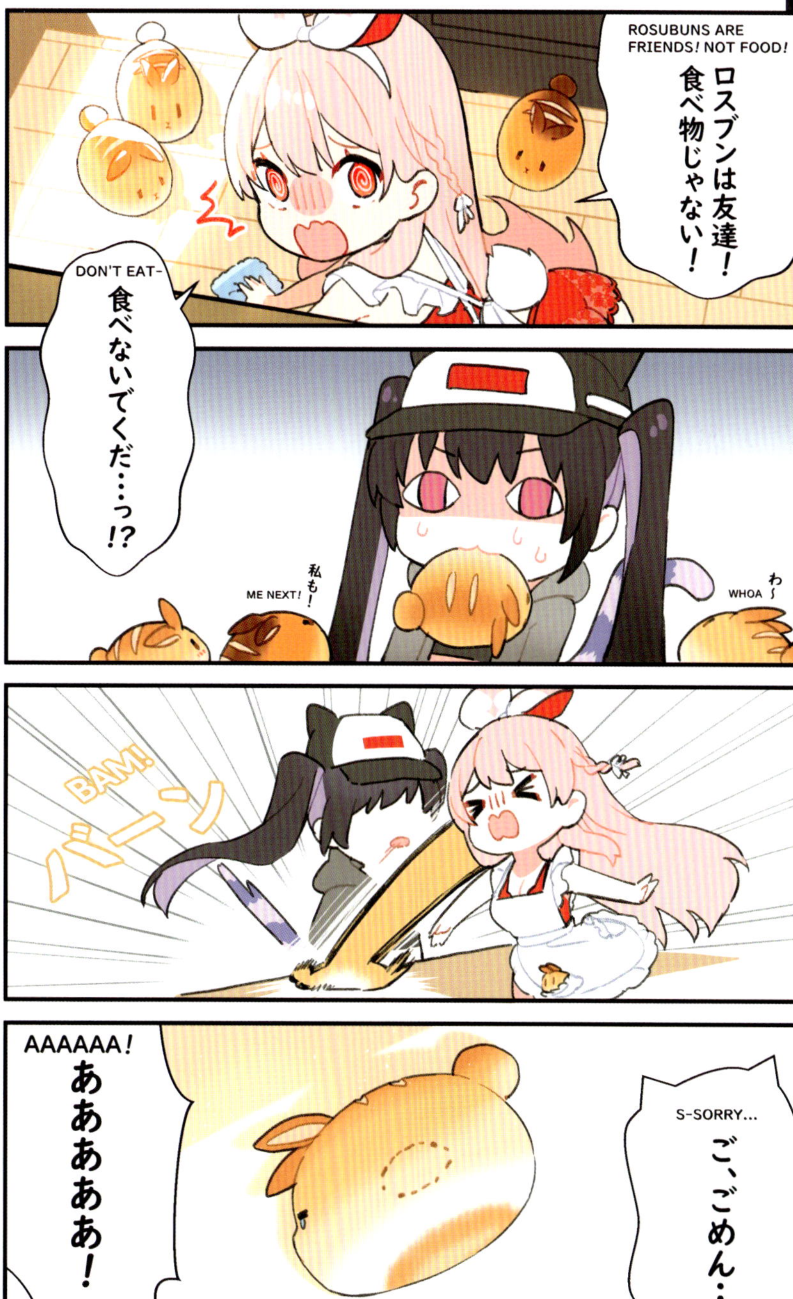

ROSUBUNS ARE FRIENDS! NOT FOOD!
ロスブンは友達！食べ物じゃない！
DON'T EAT-
食べないでくだ…っ!?
WHOA
わ～
ME NEXT!
私も！
BAM!
バーン
AAAAAA!
ああああ！
S-SORRY...
ご、ごめん…

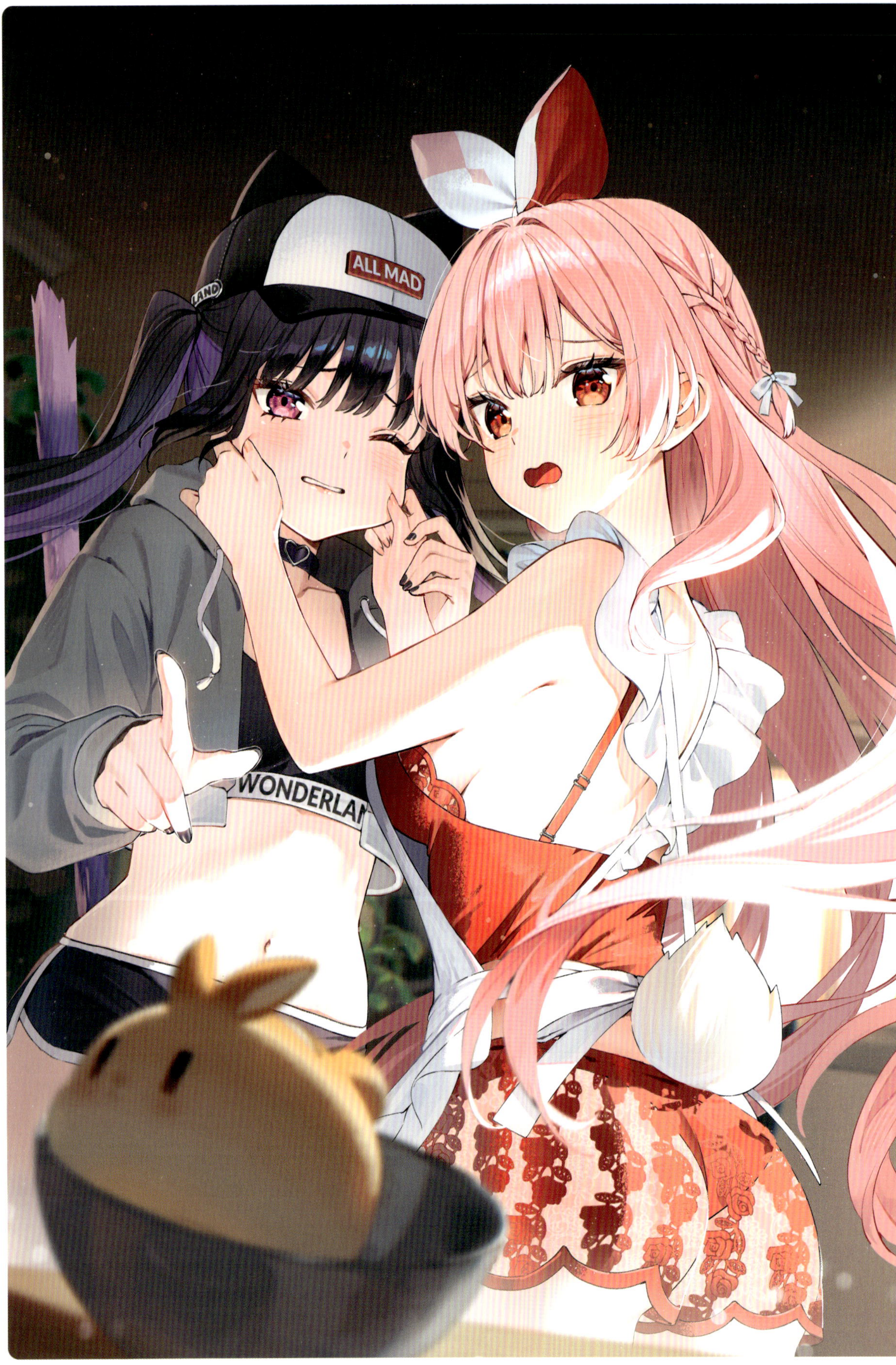
ALL MAD
LAND
WONDERLAN

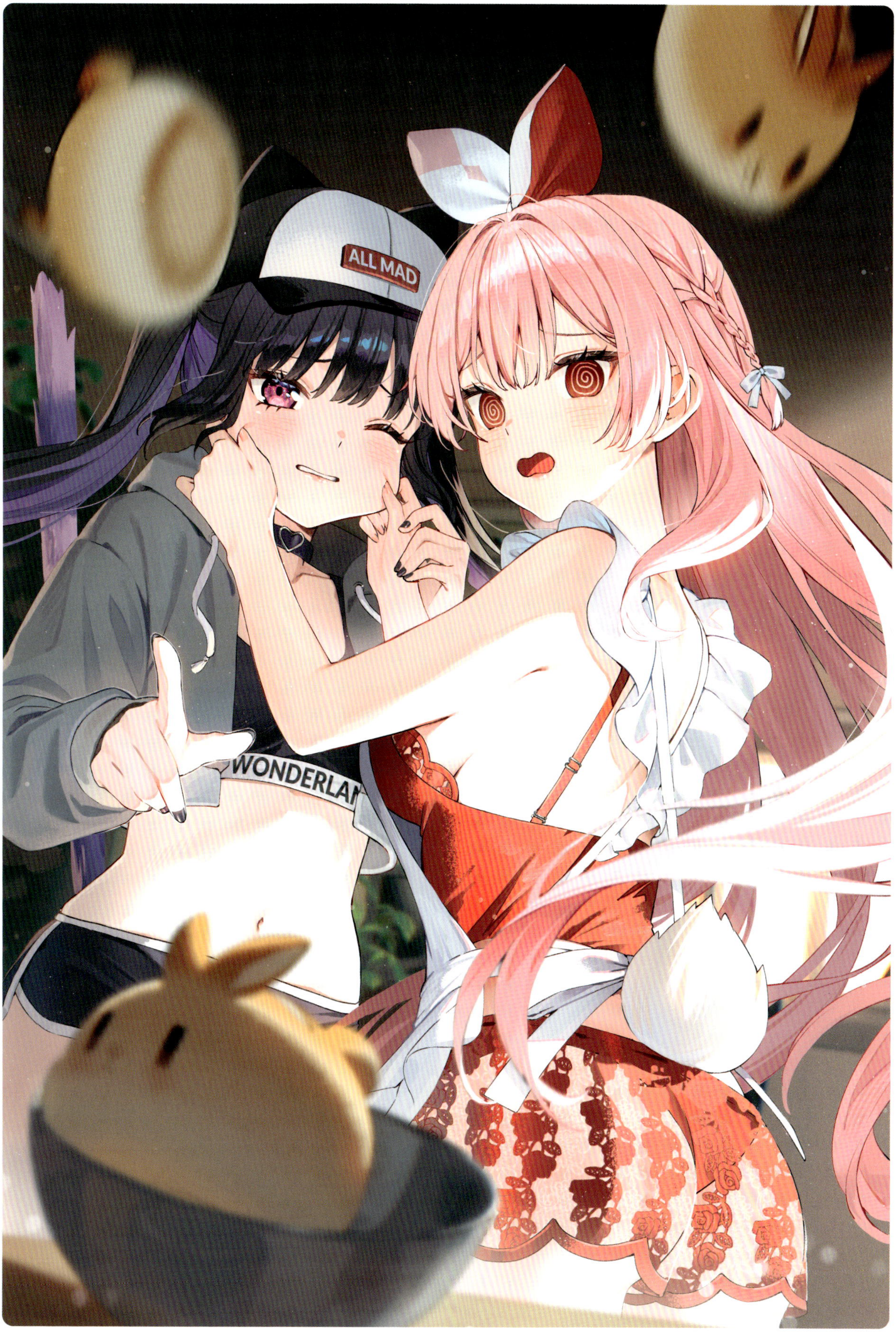
ALL MAD
WONDERLAN

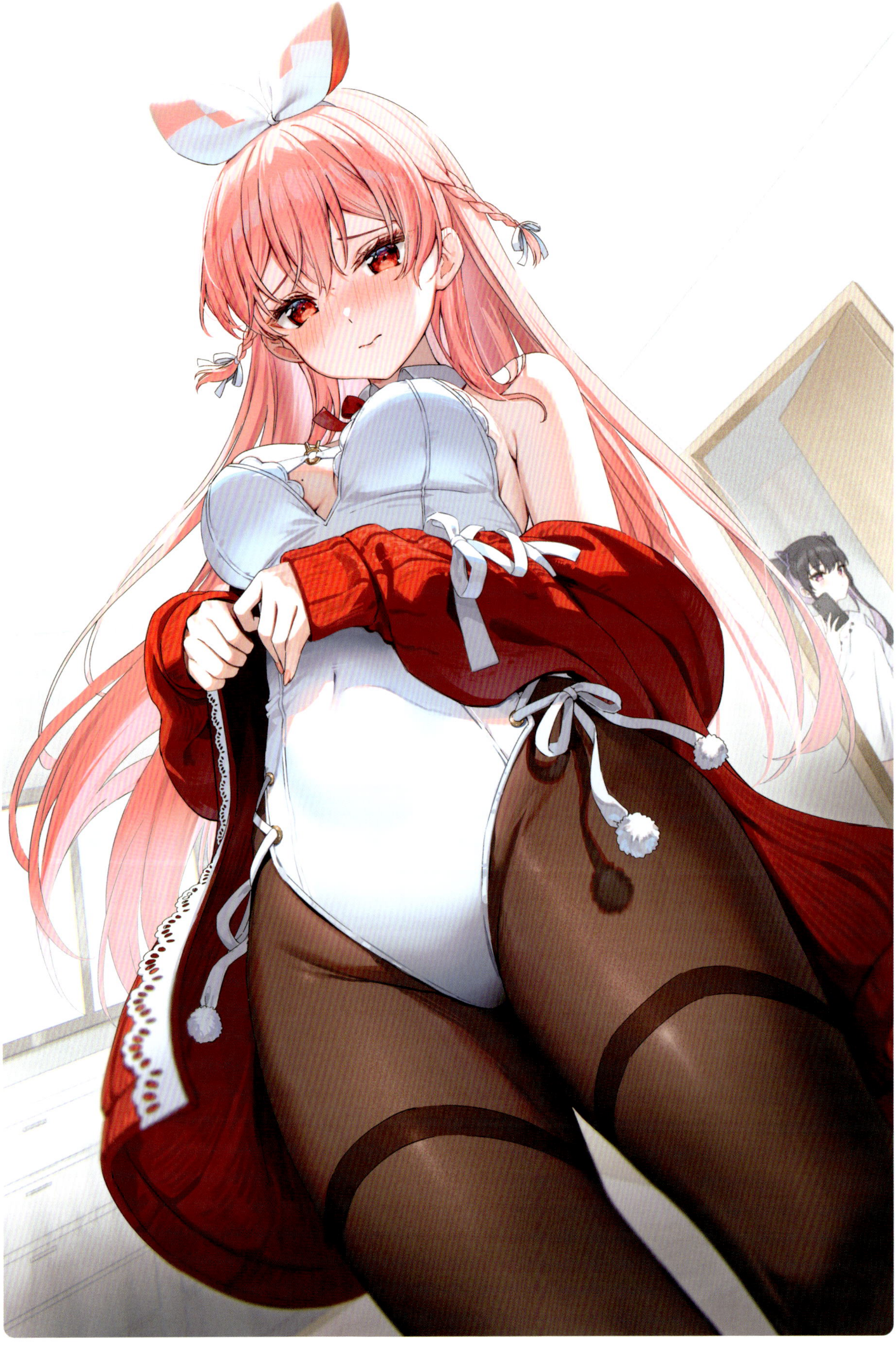

Comic 06

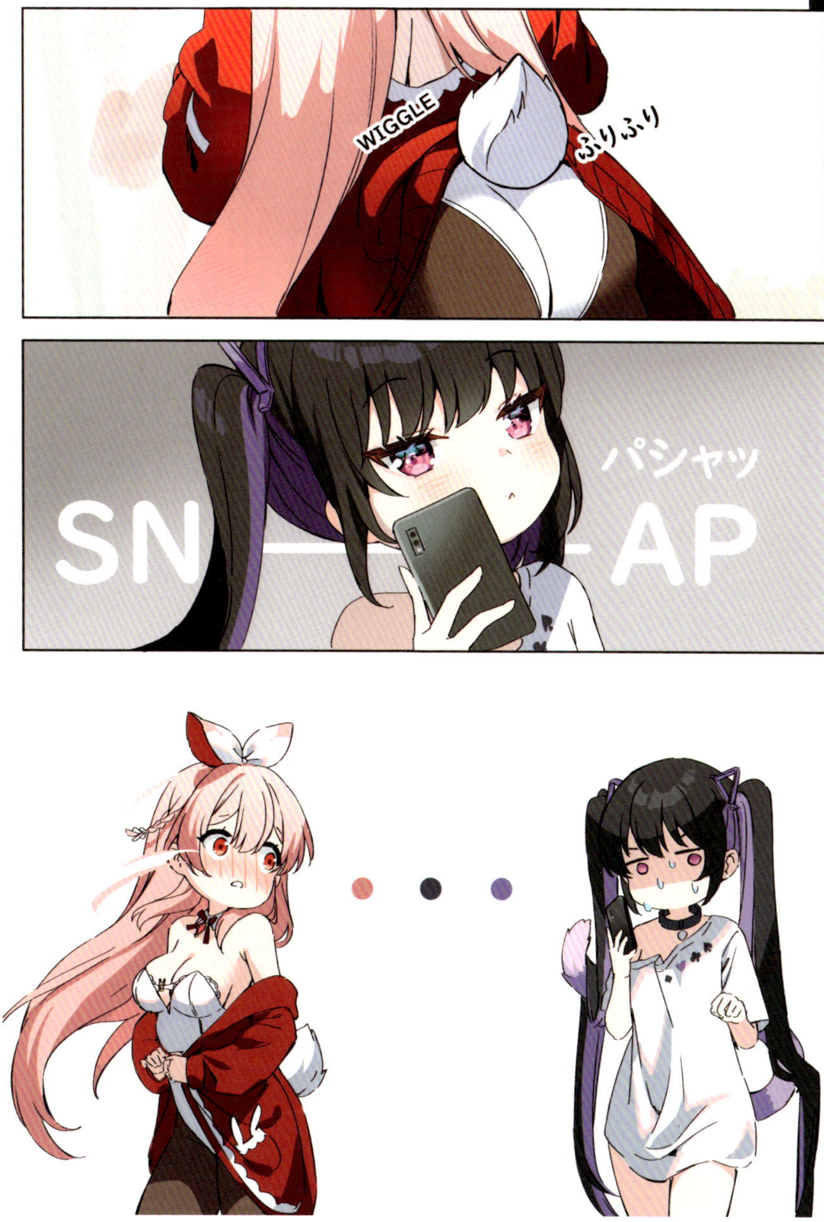

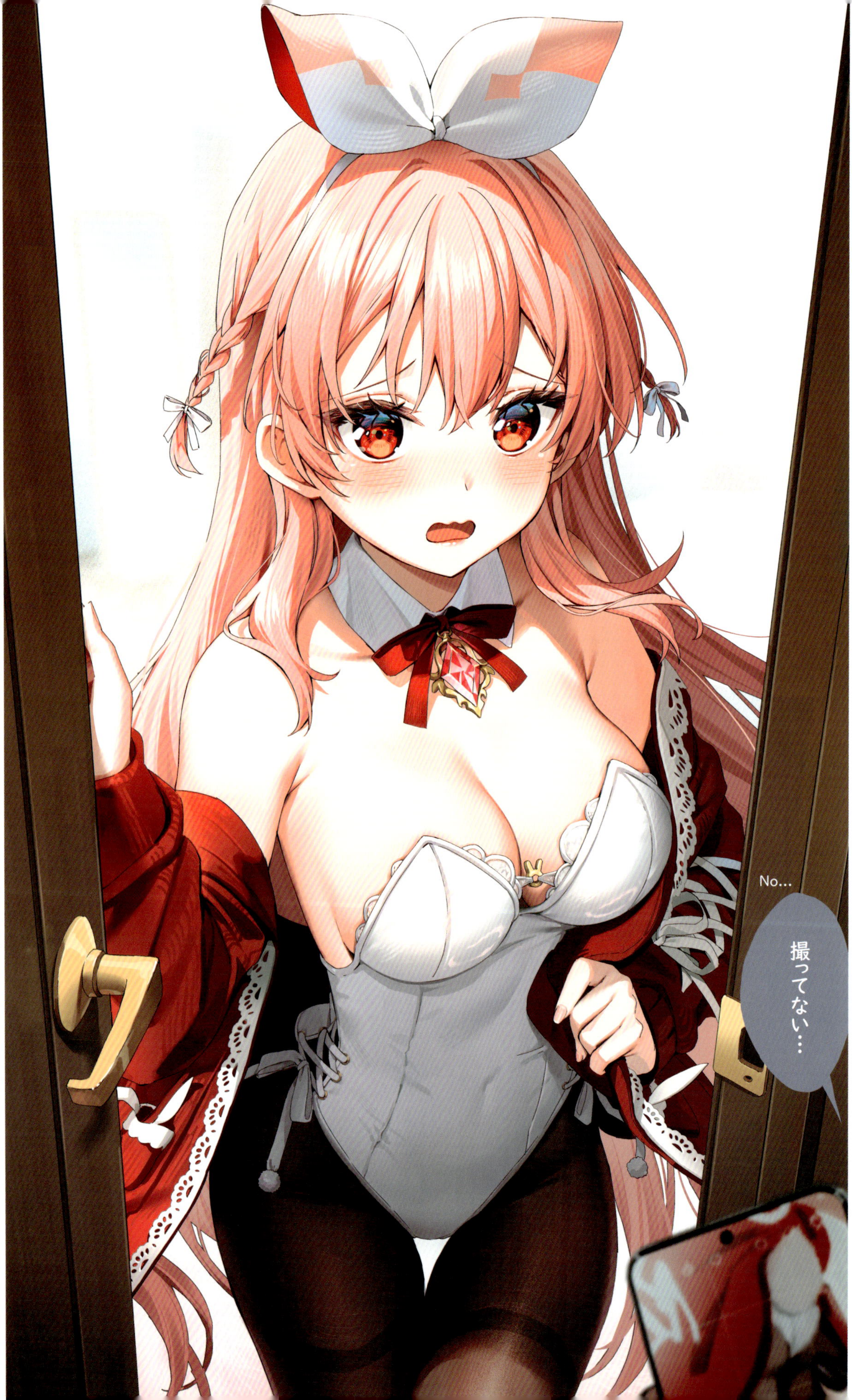
No…
撮ってない…

Comic **07**

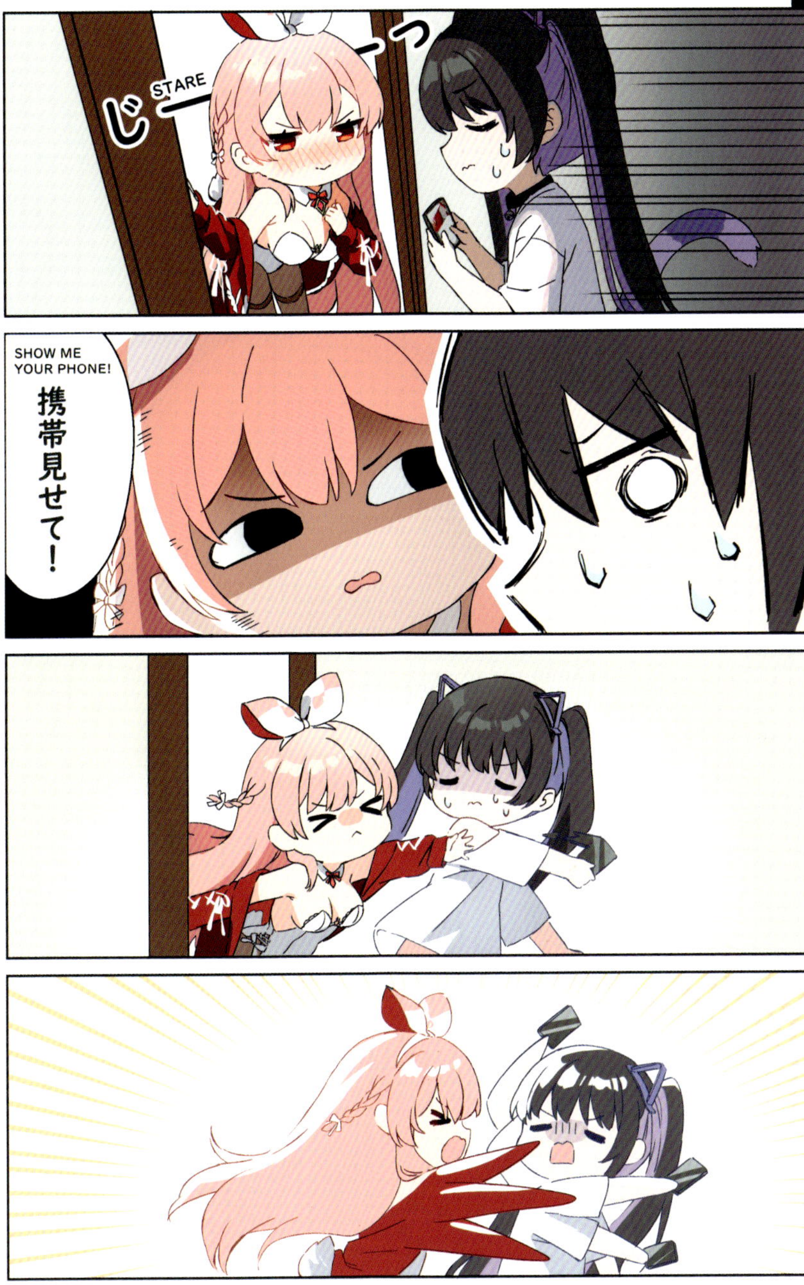

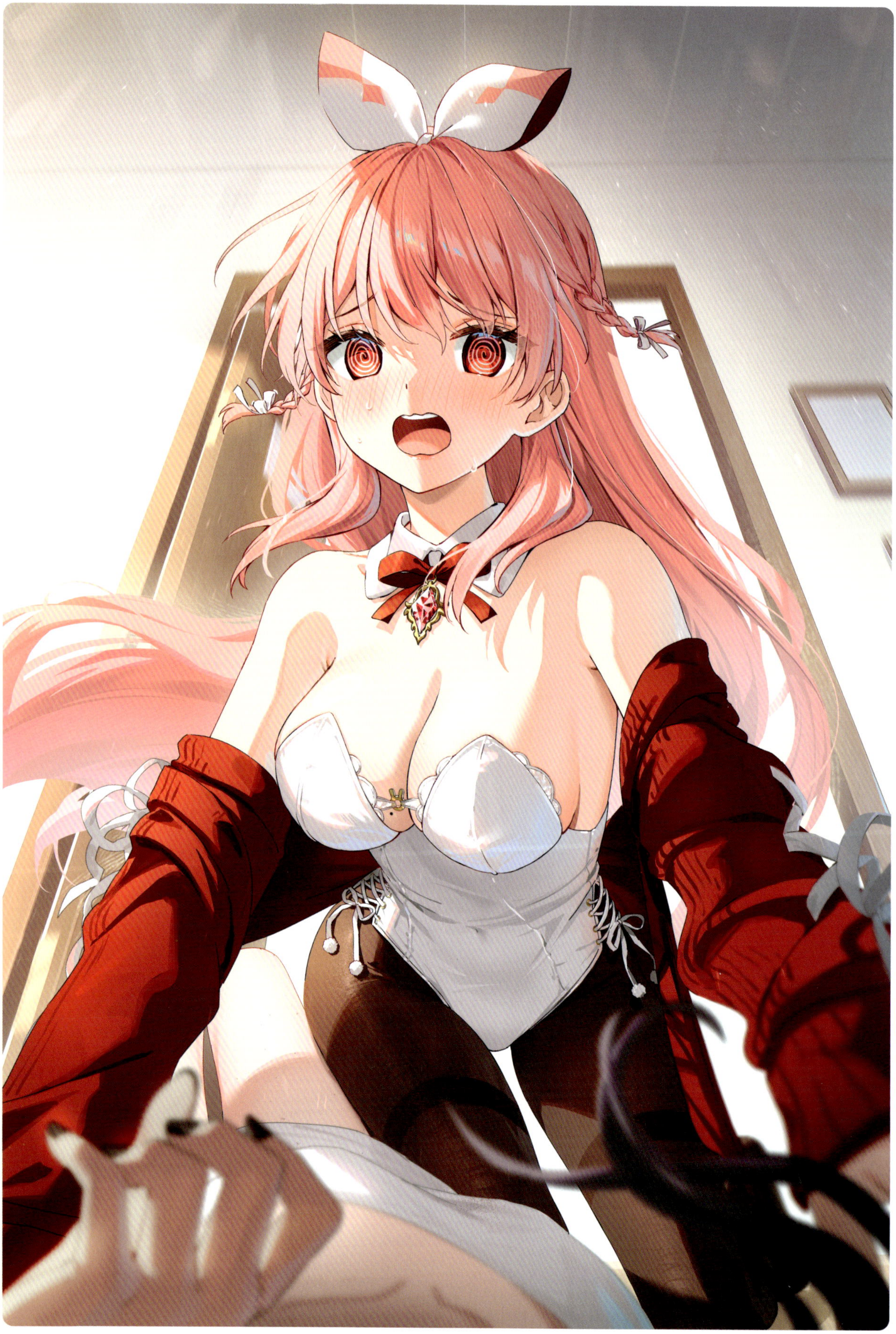

Comic 08

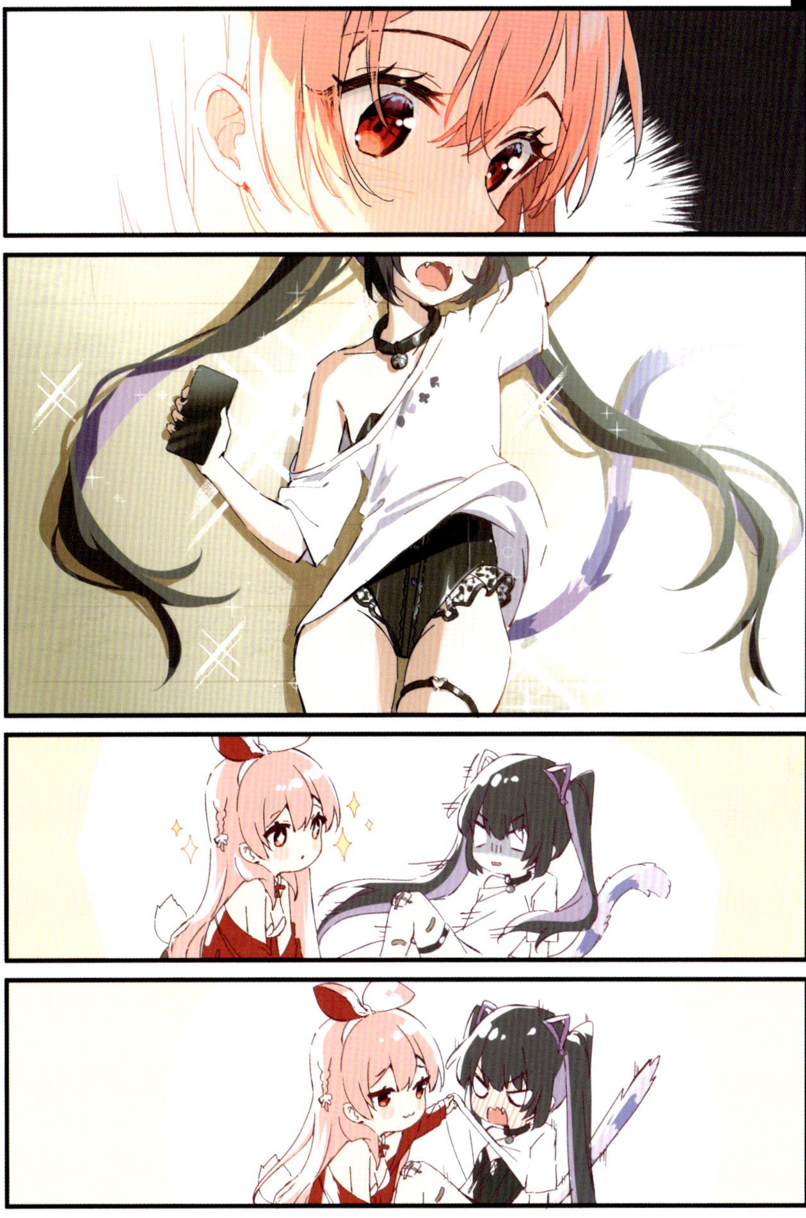

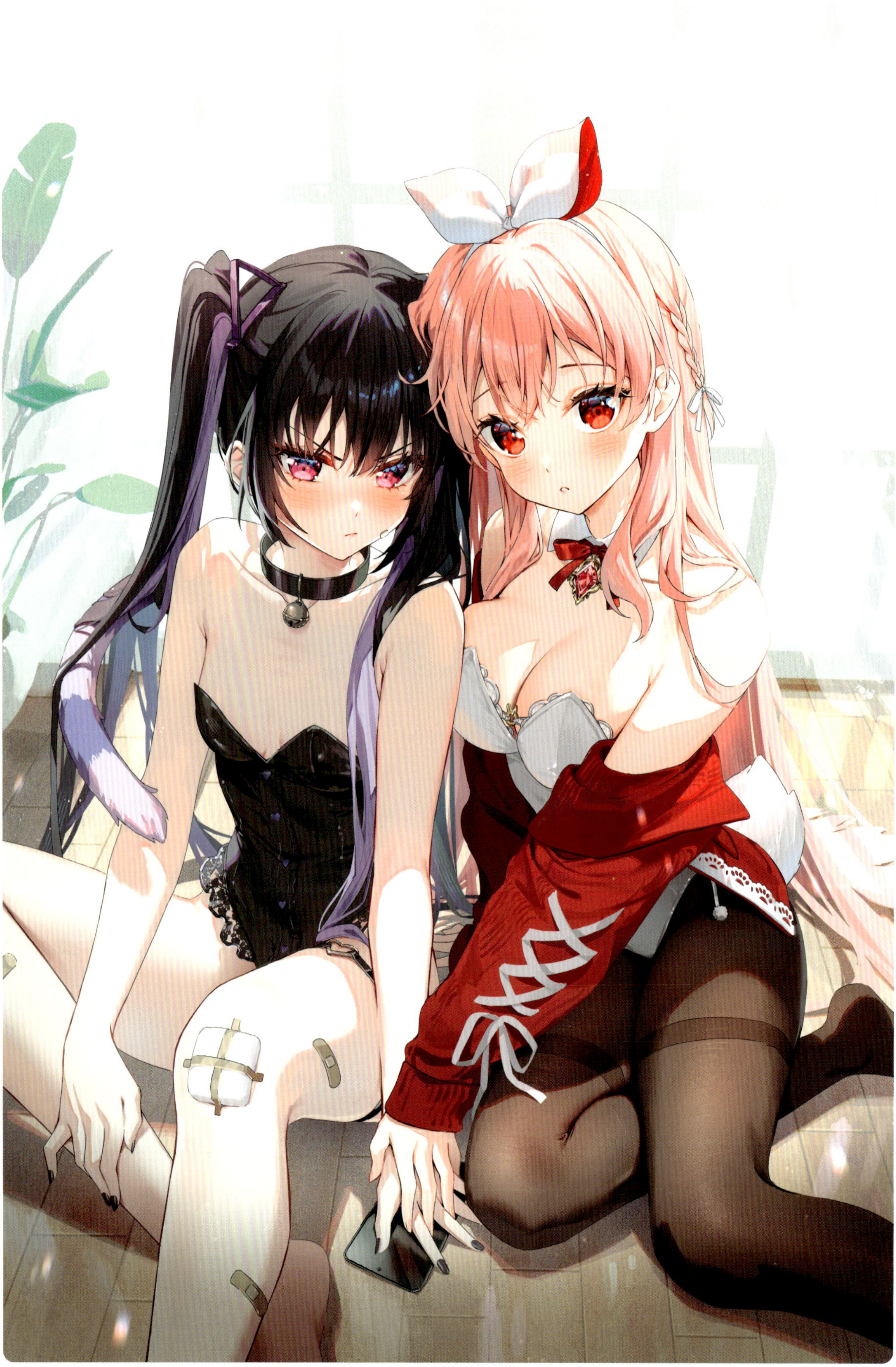

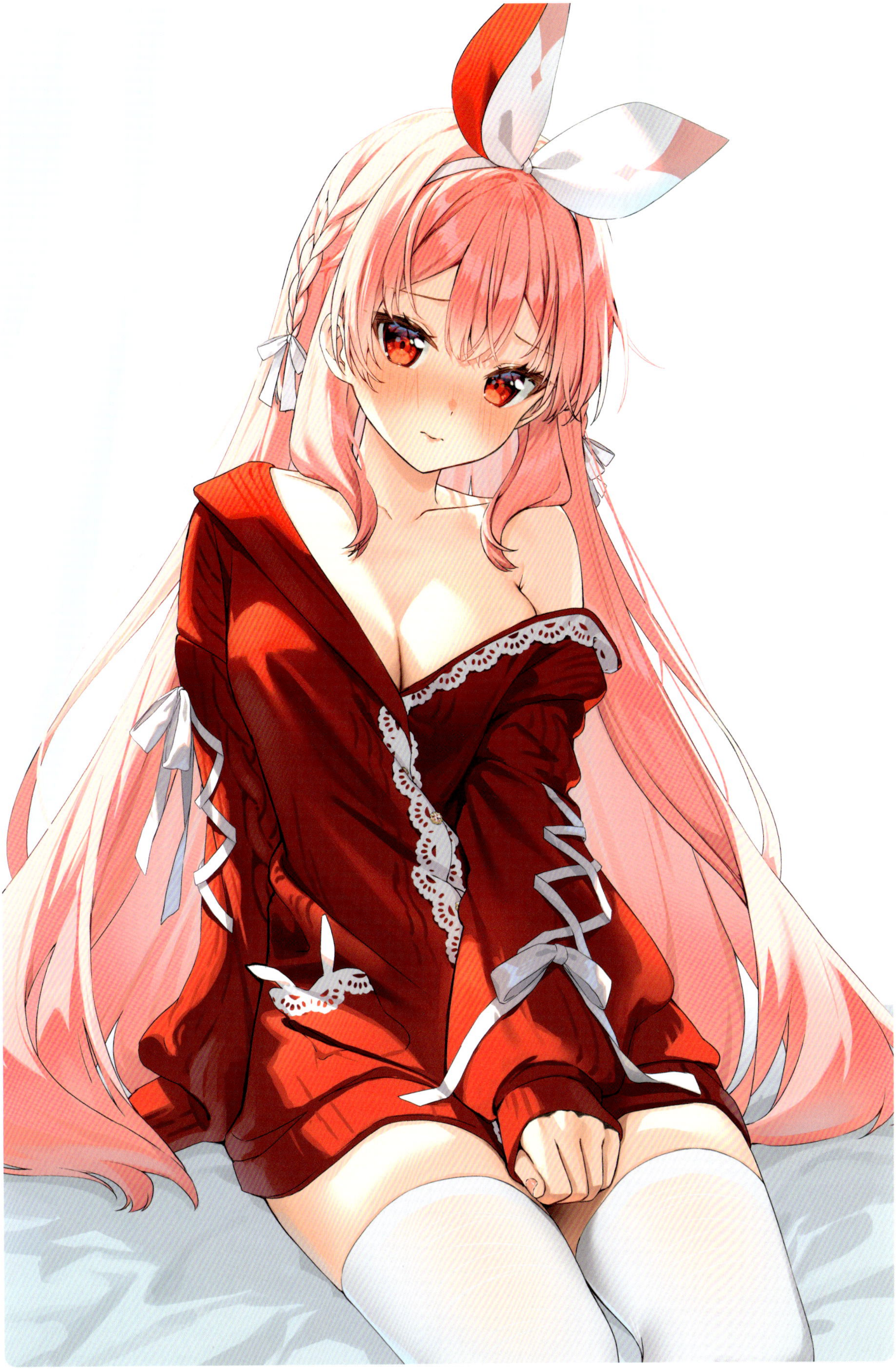

Serenity

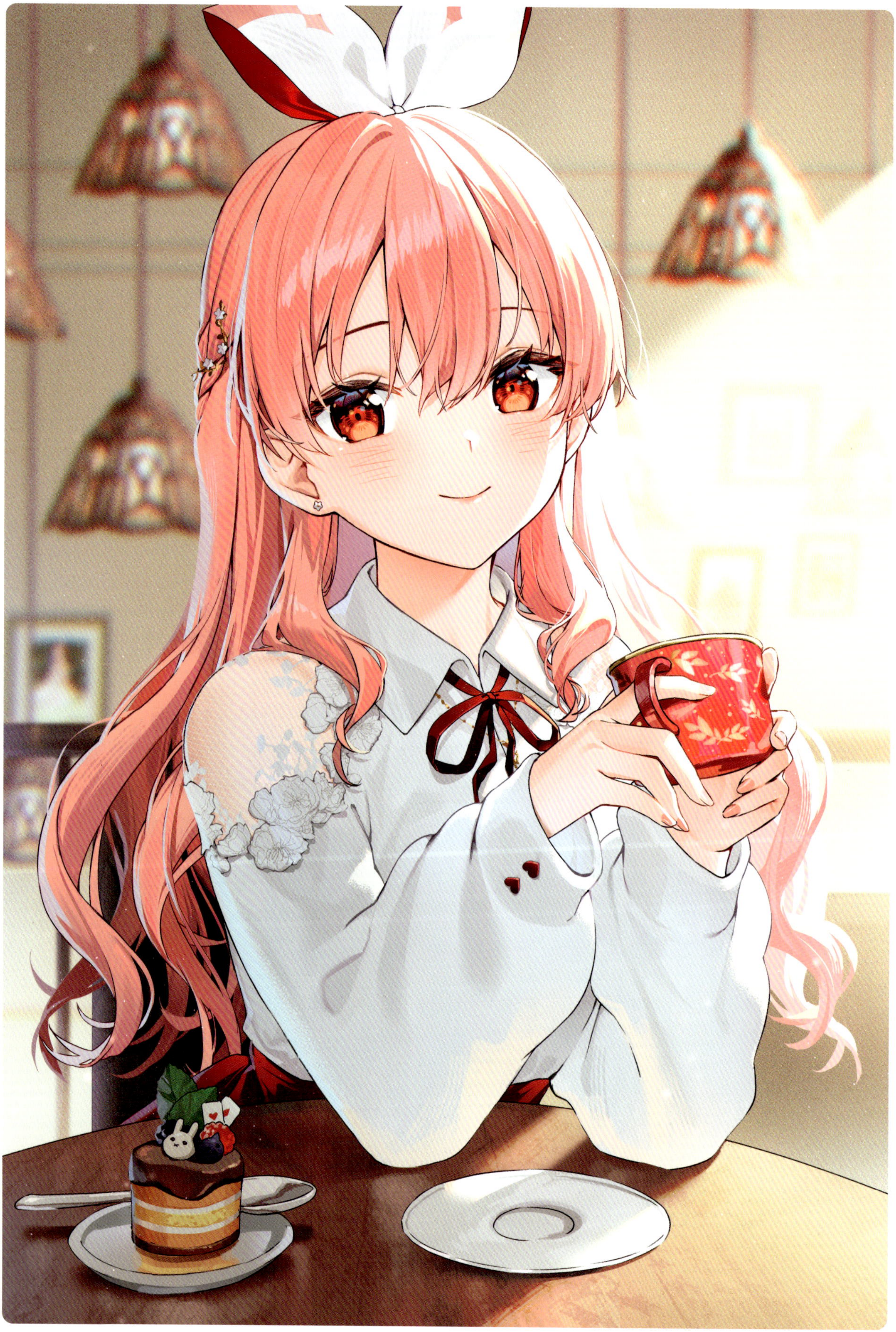

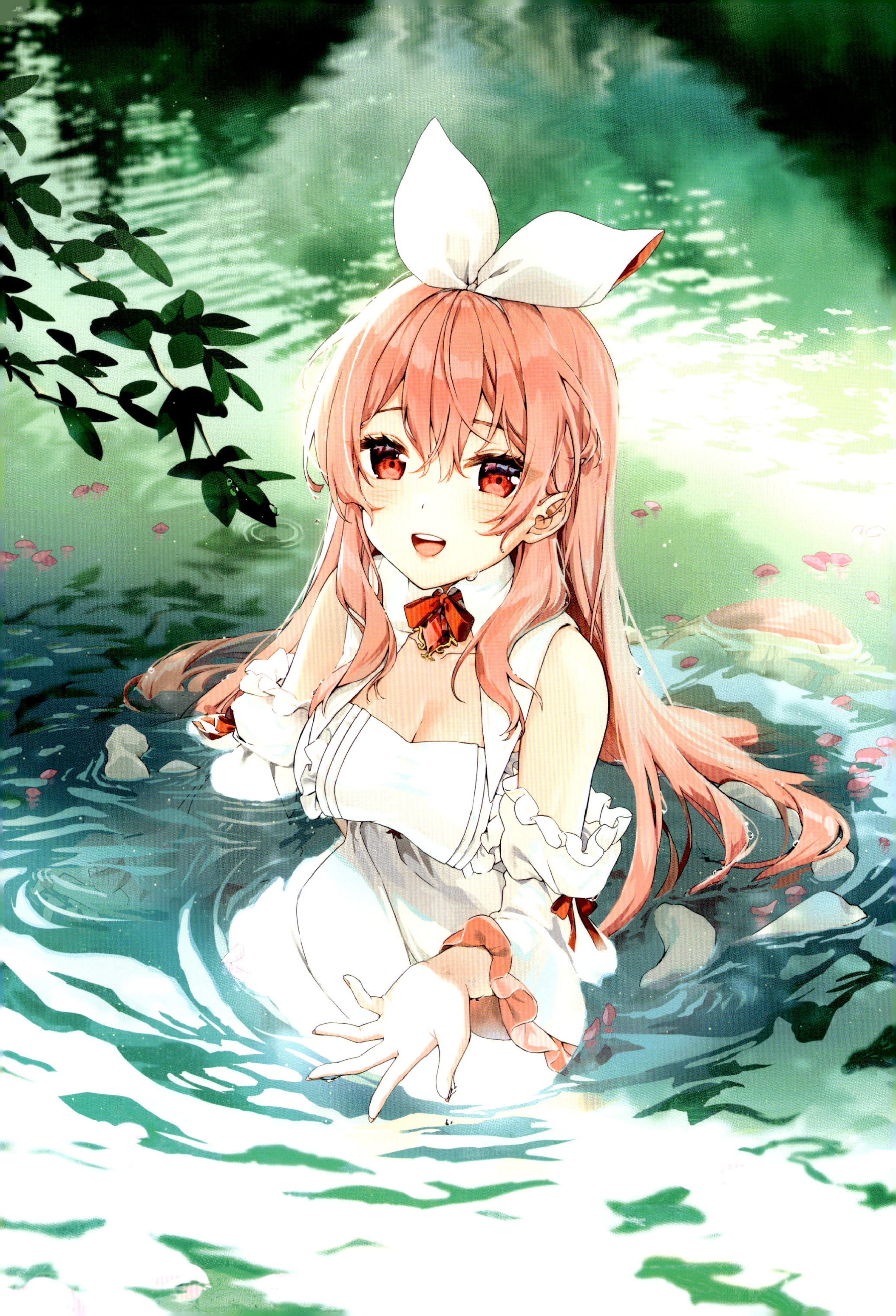

Serenity

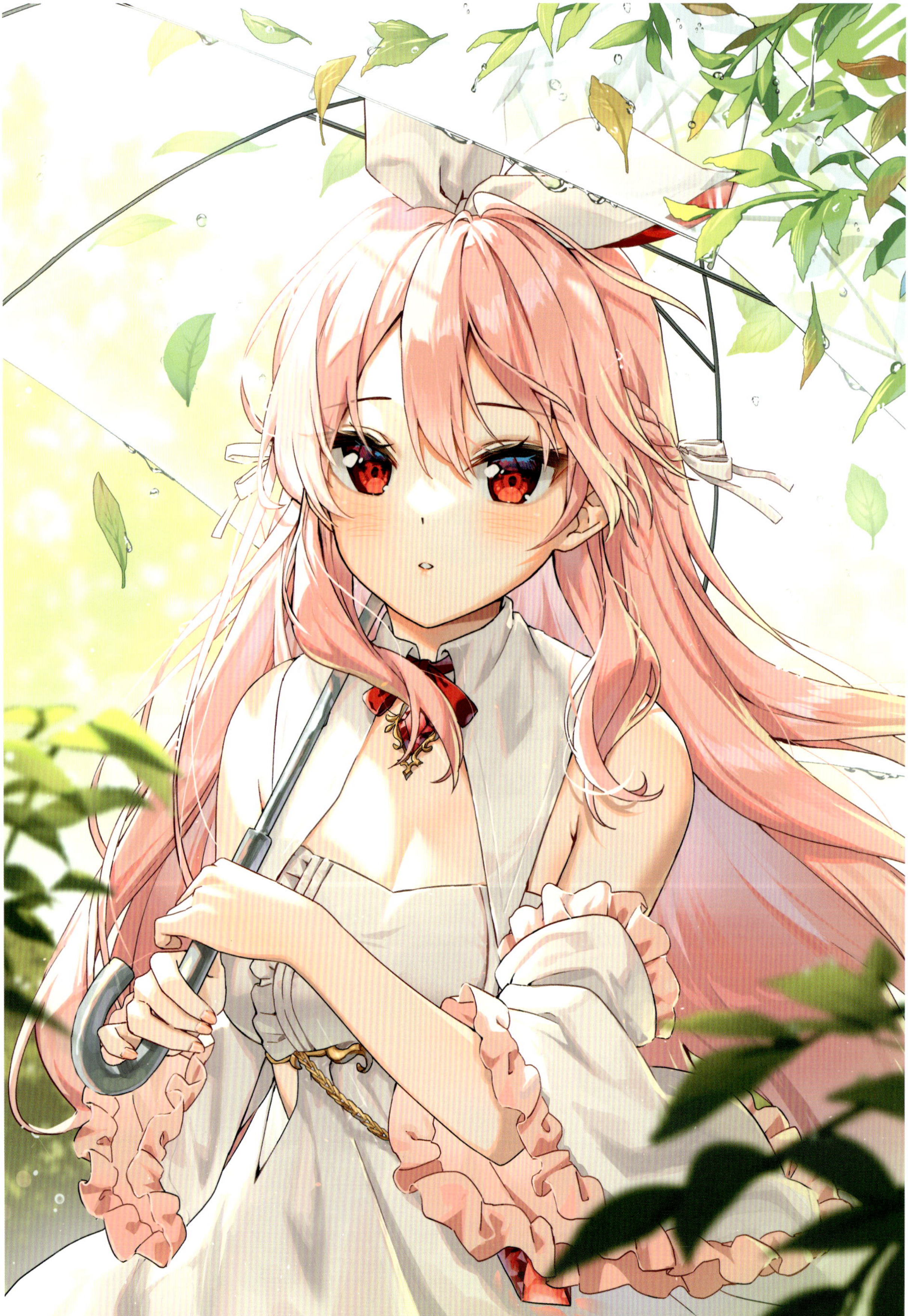

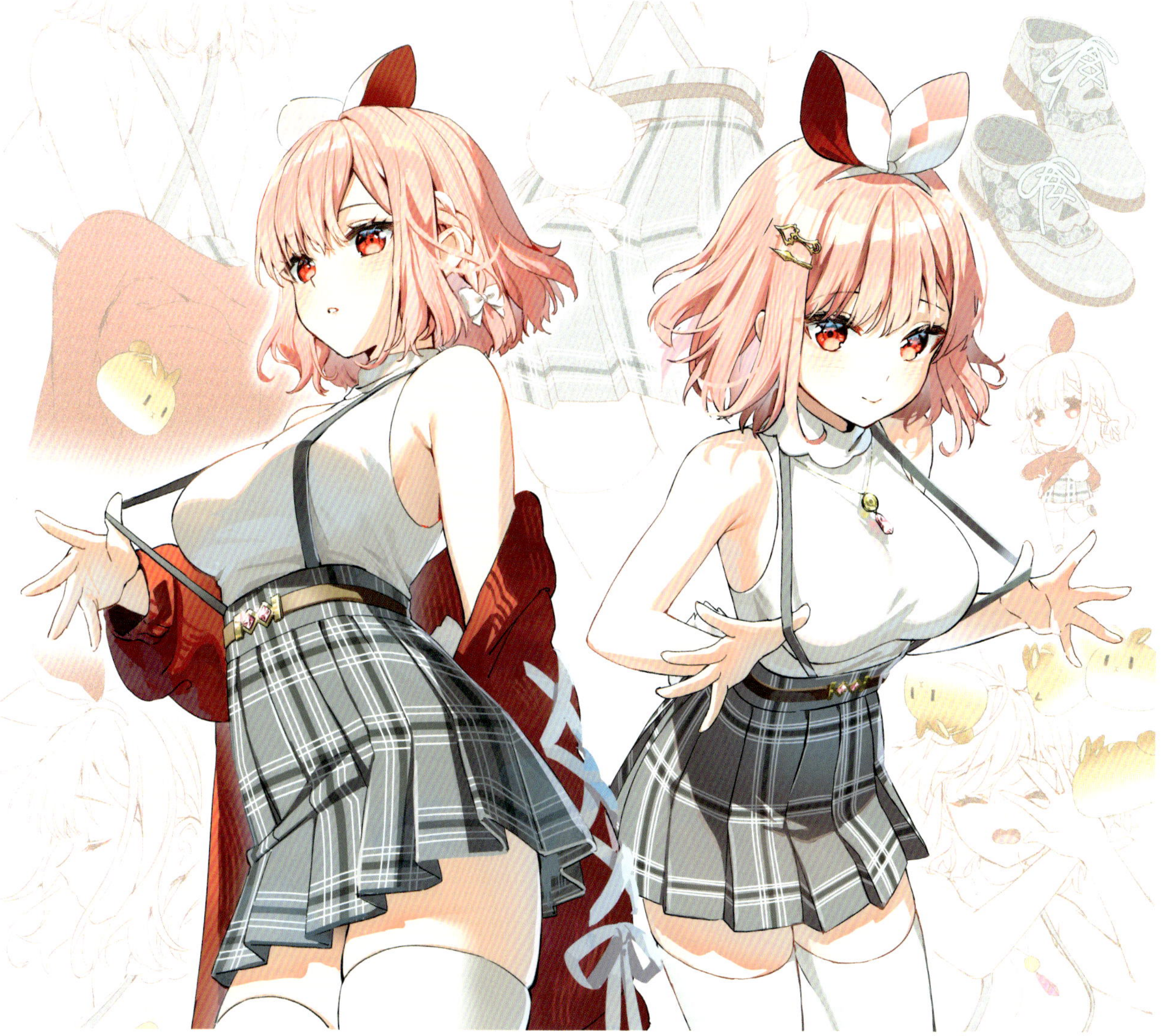

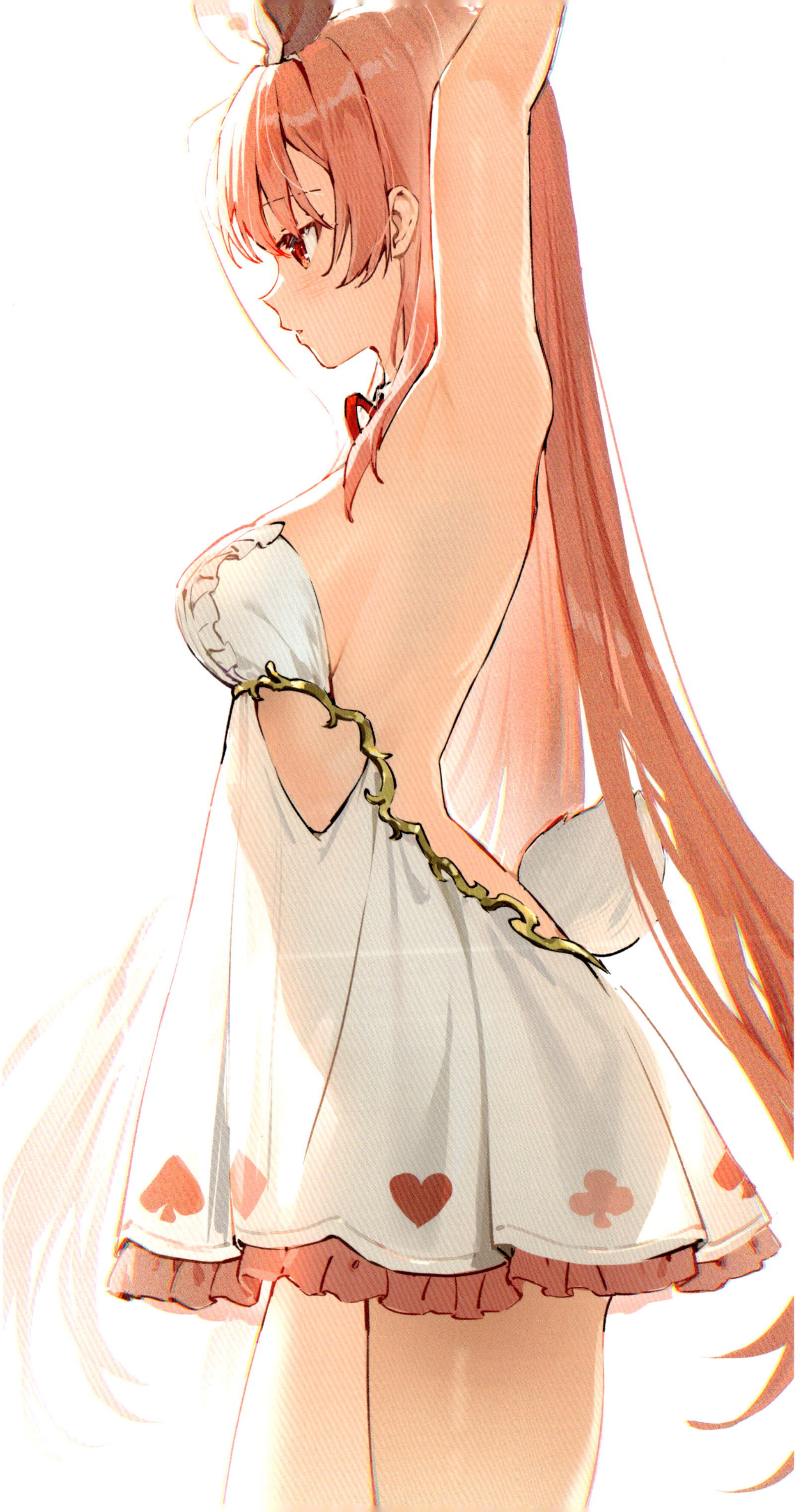

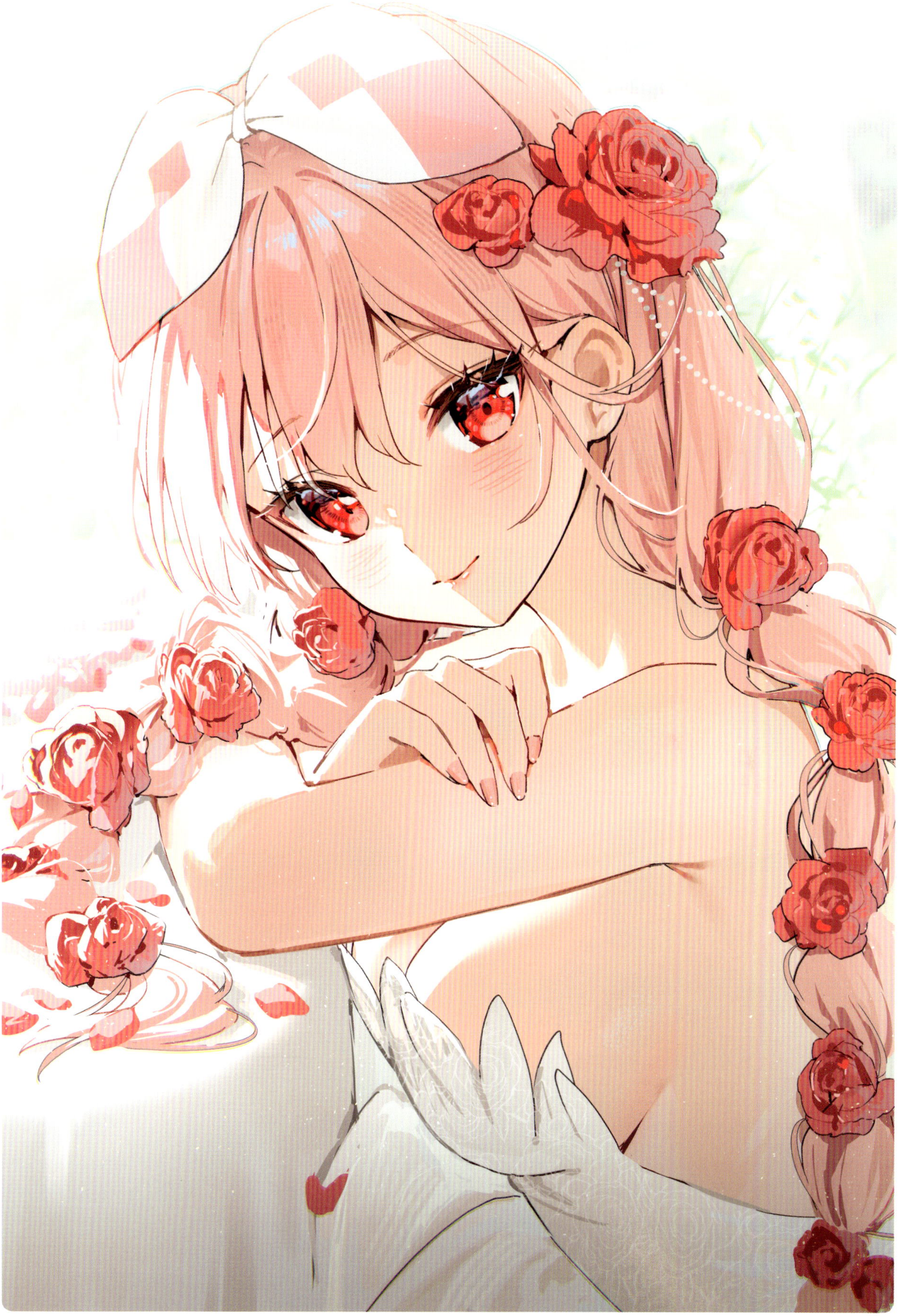

Serenity

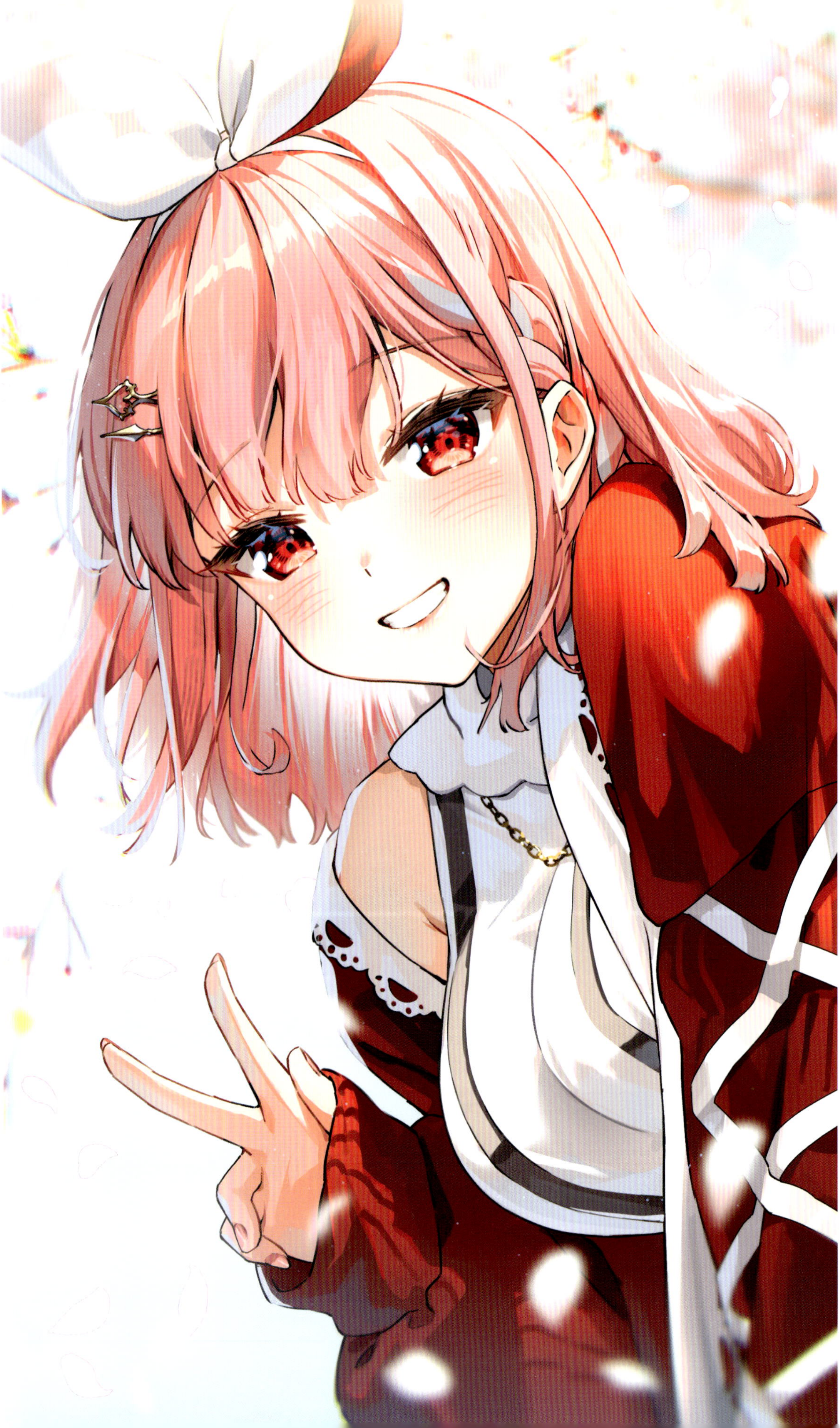

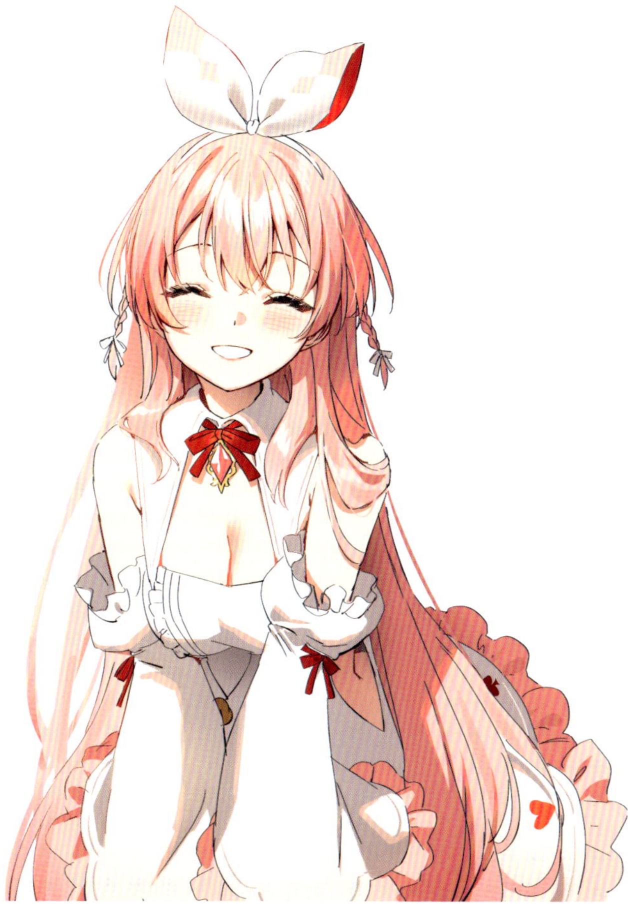

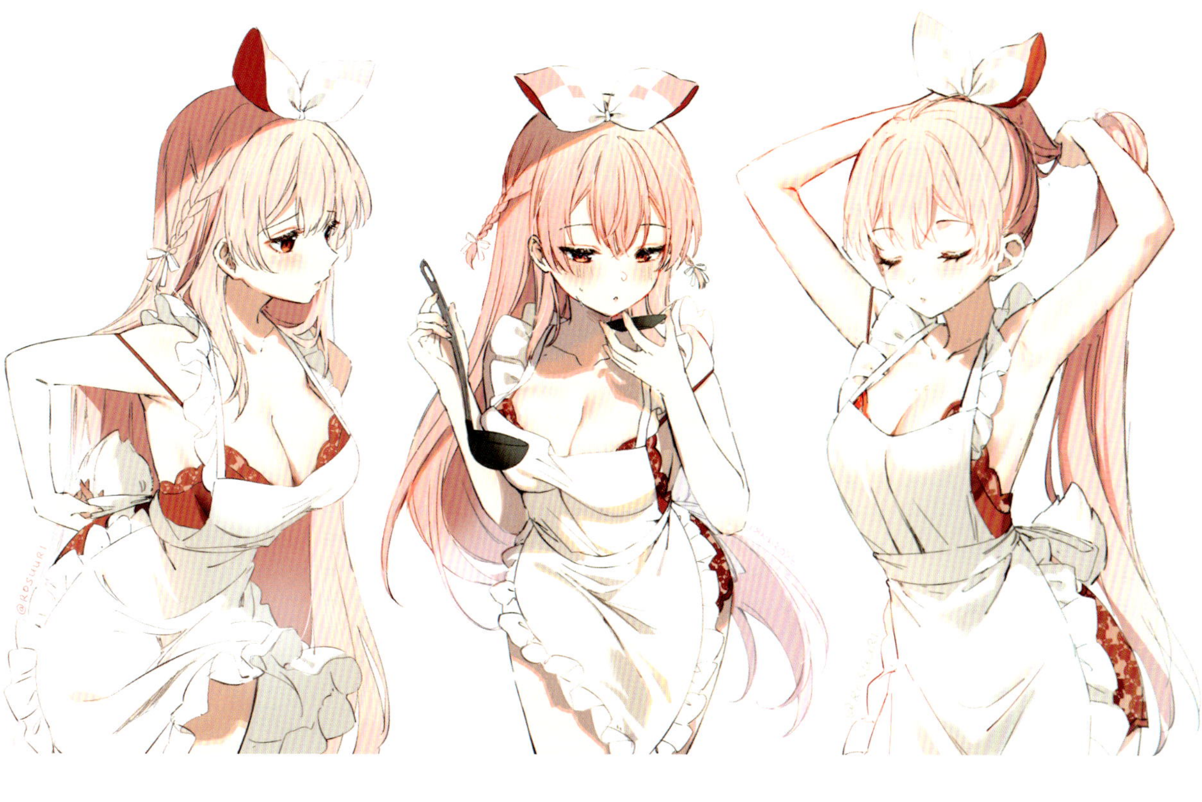

Alter

White Rabbit

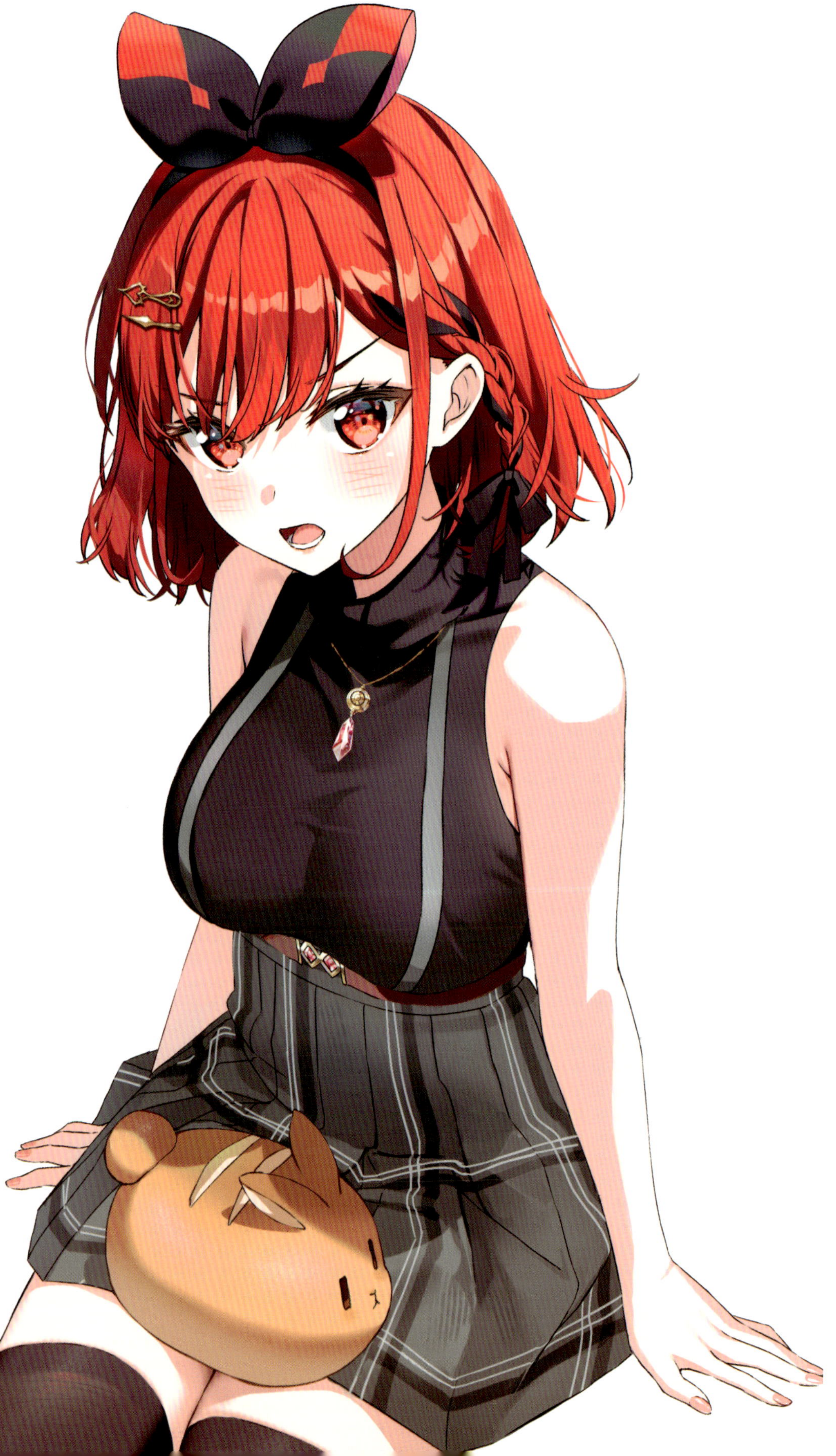

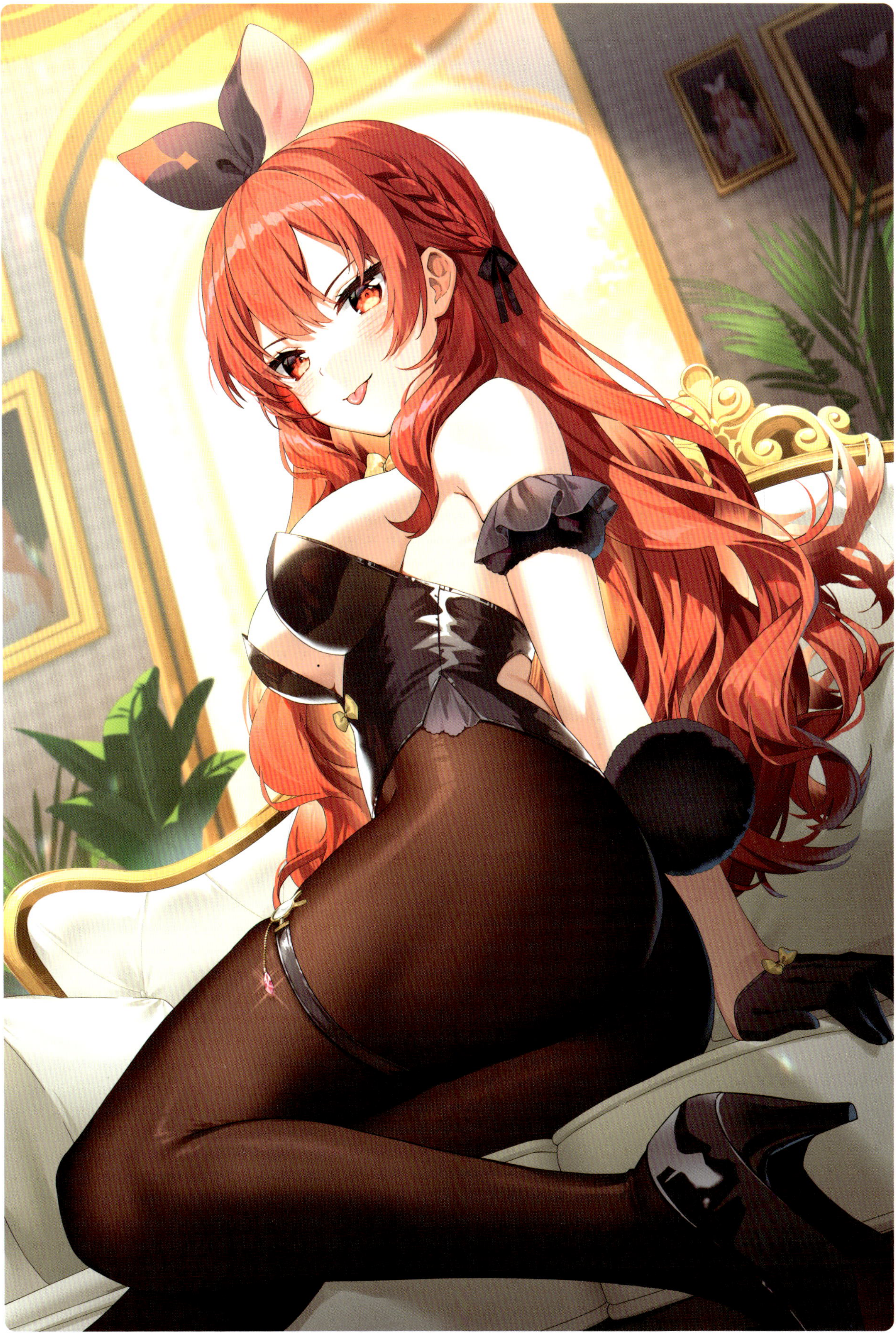

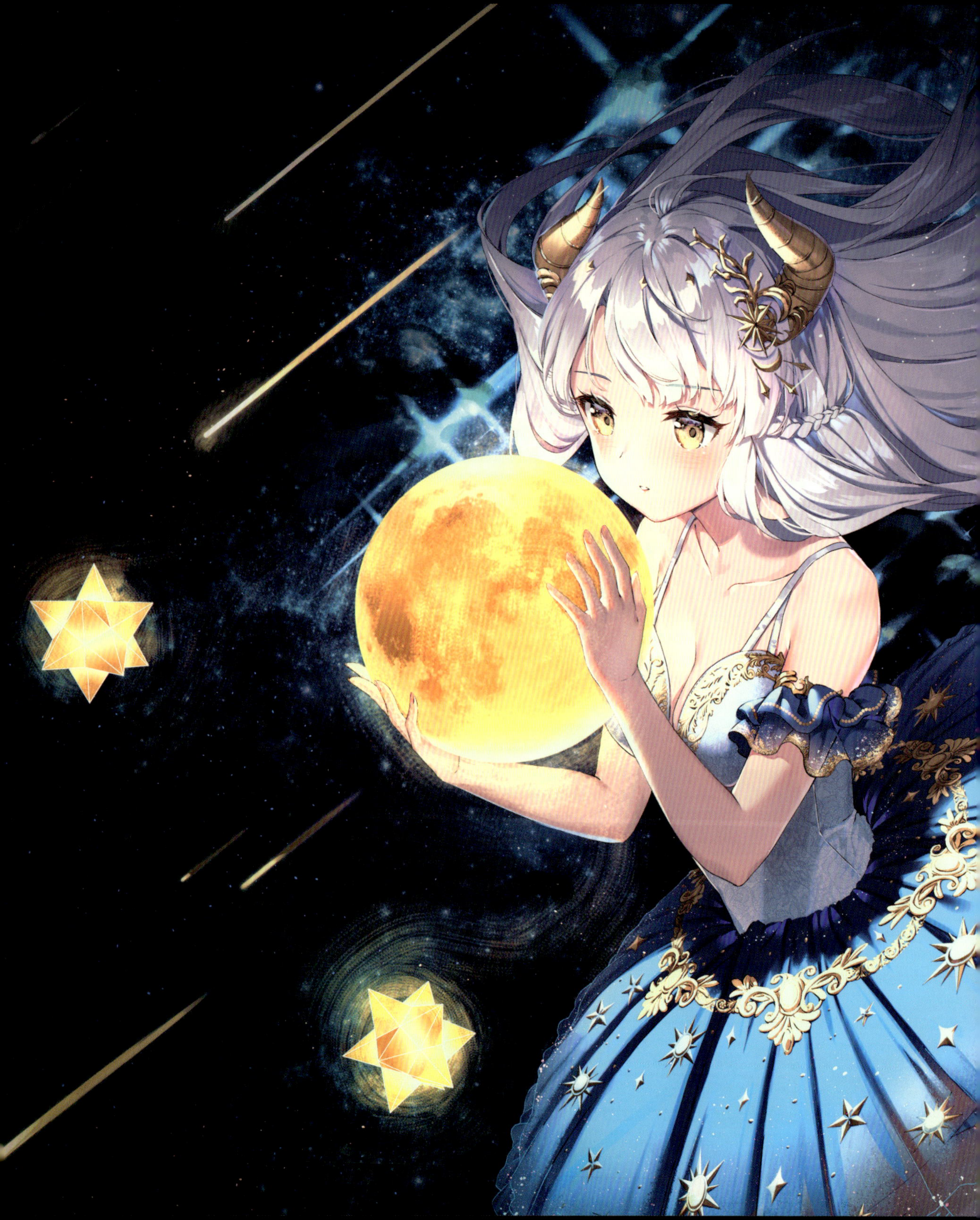

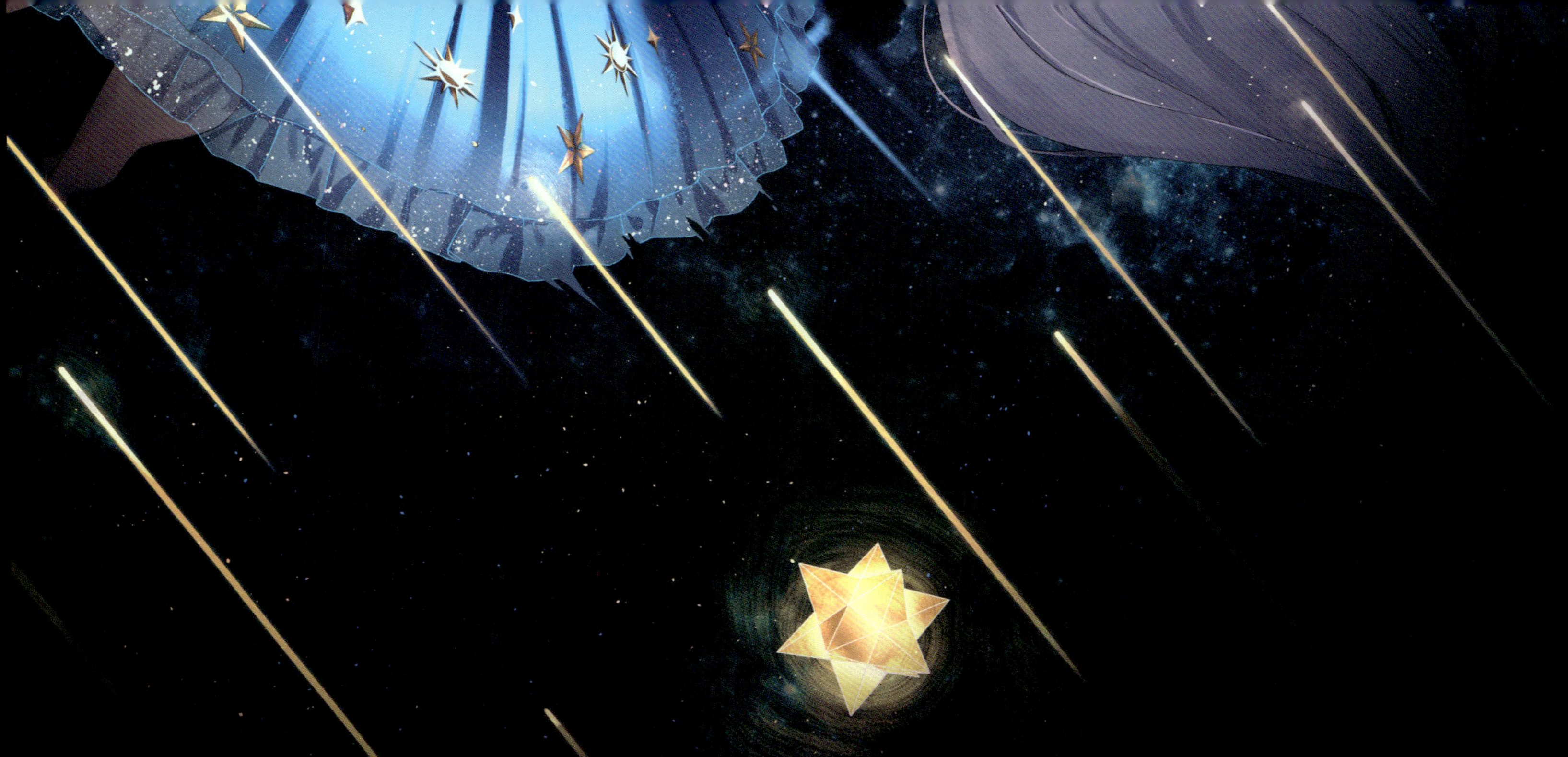

Astrea

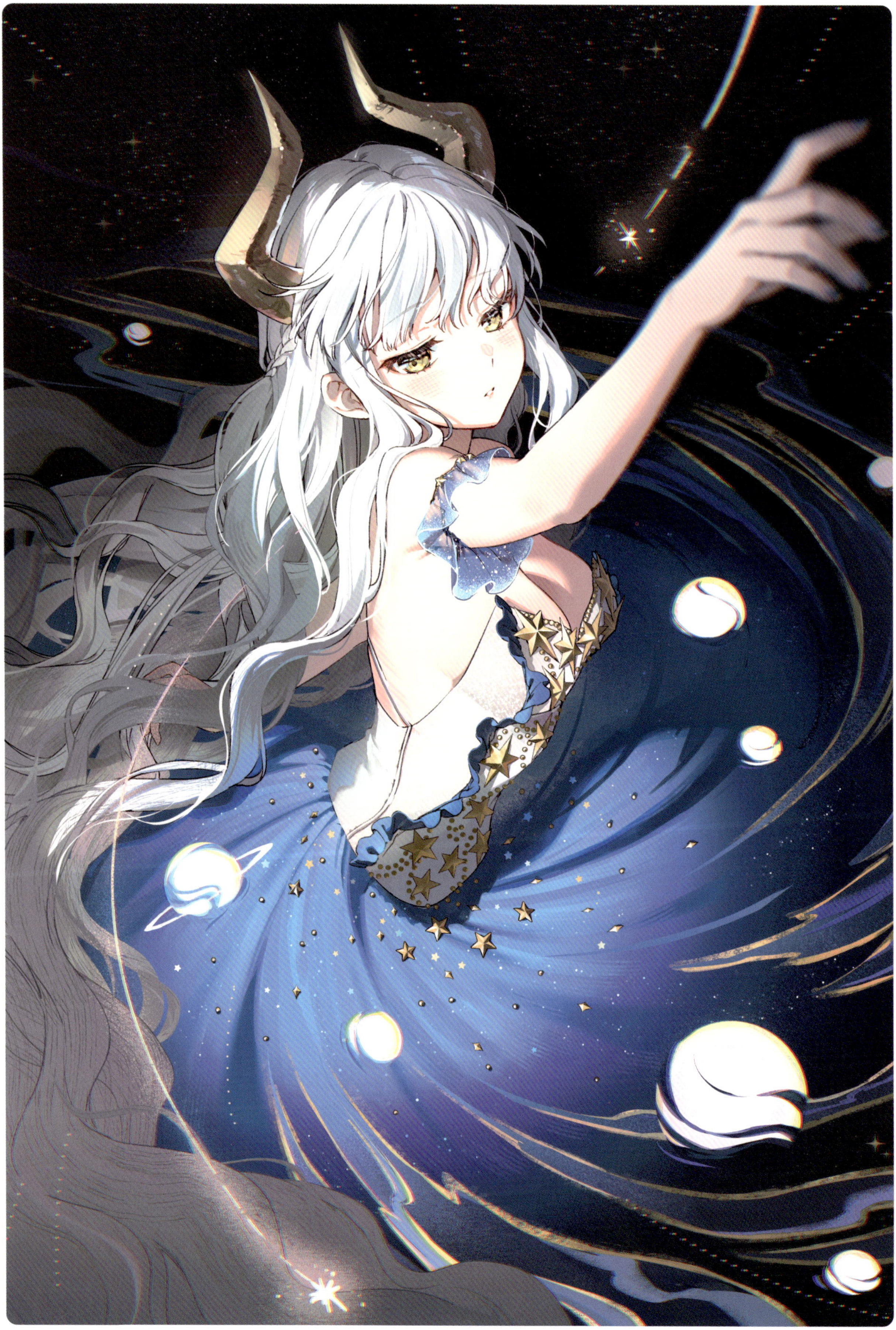

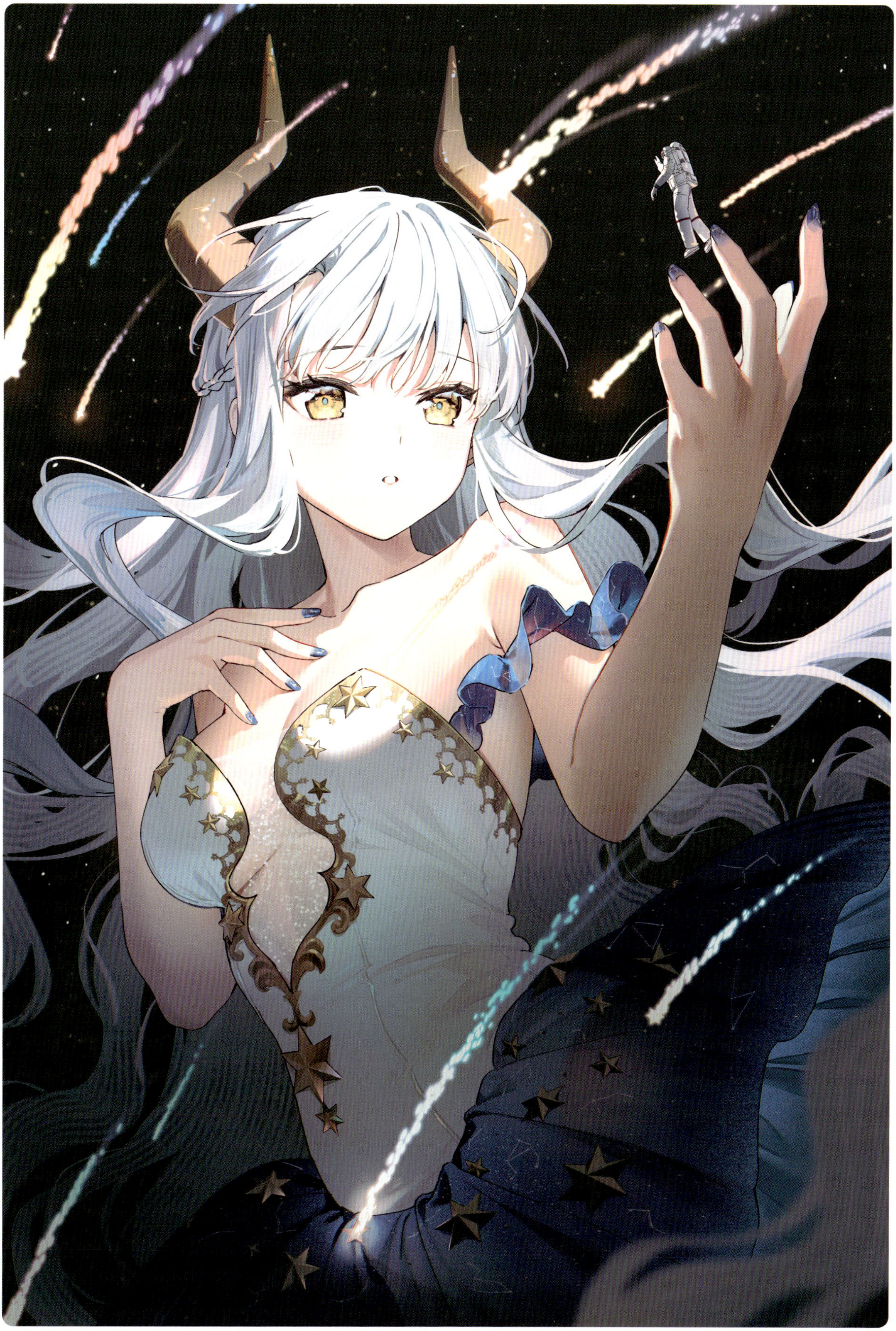

Artist of the Month 描き下ろしイラスト © XART Inc. / Rosuuri

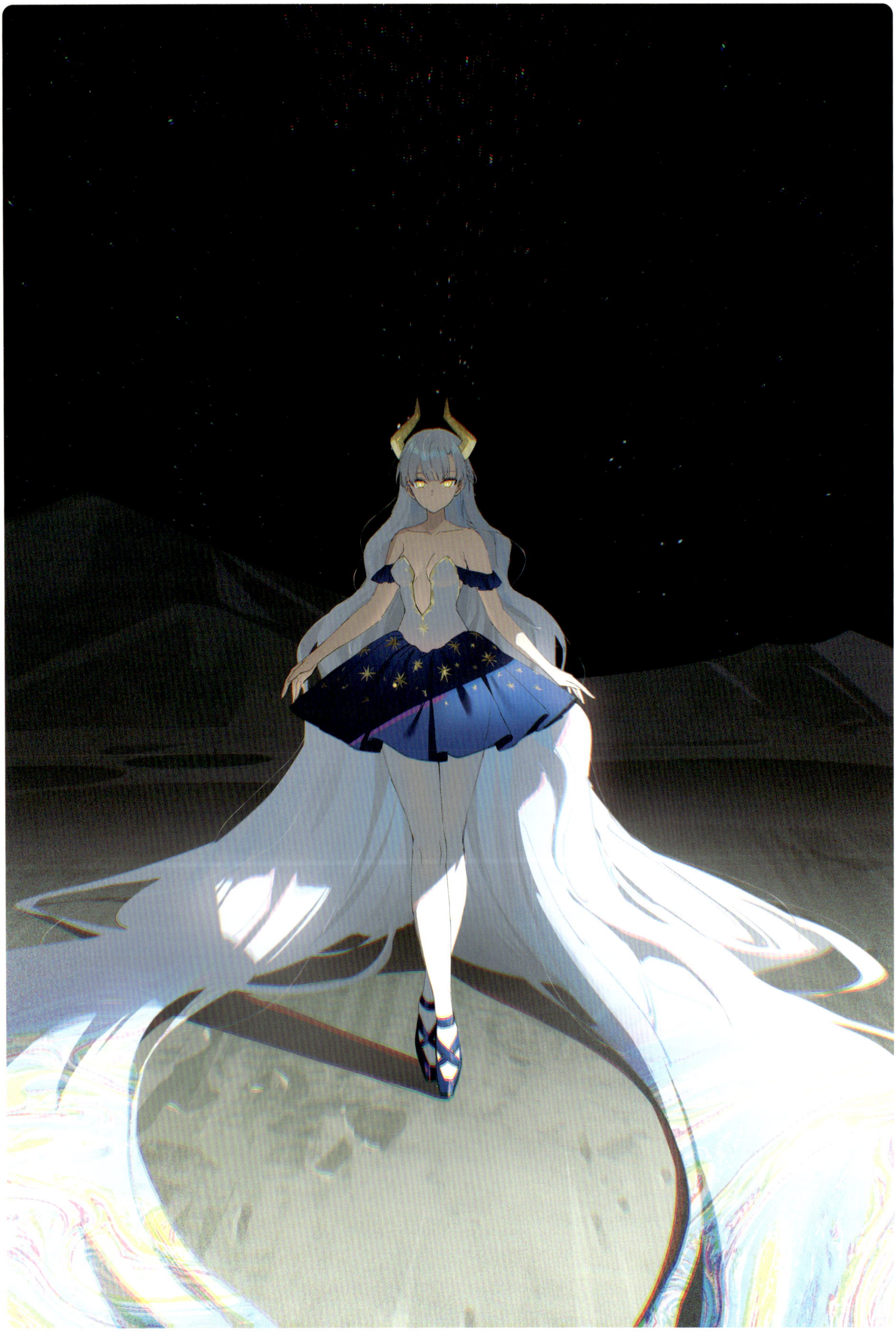

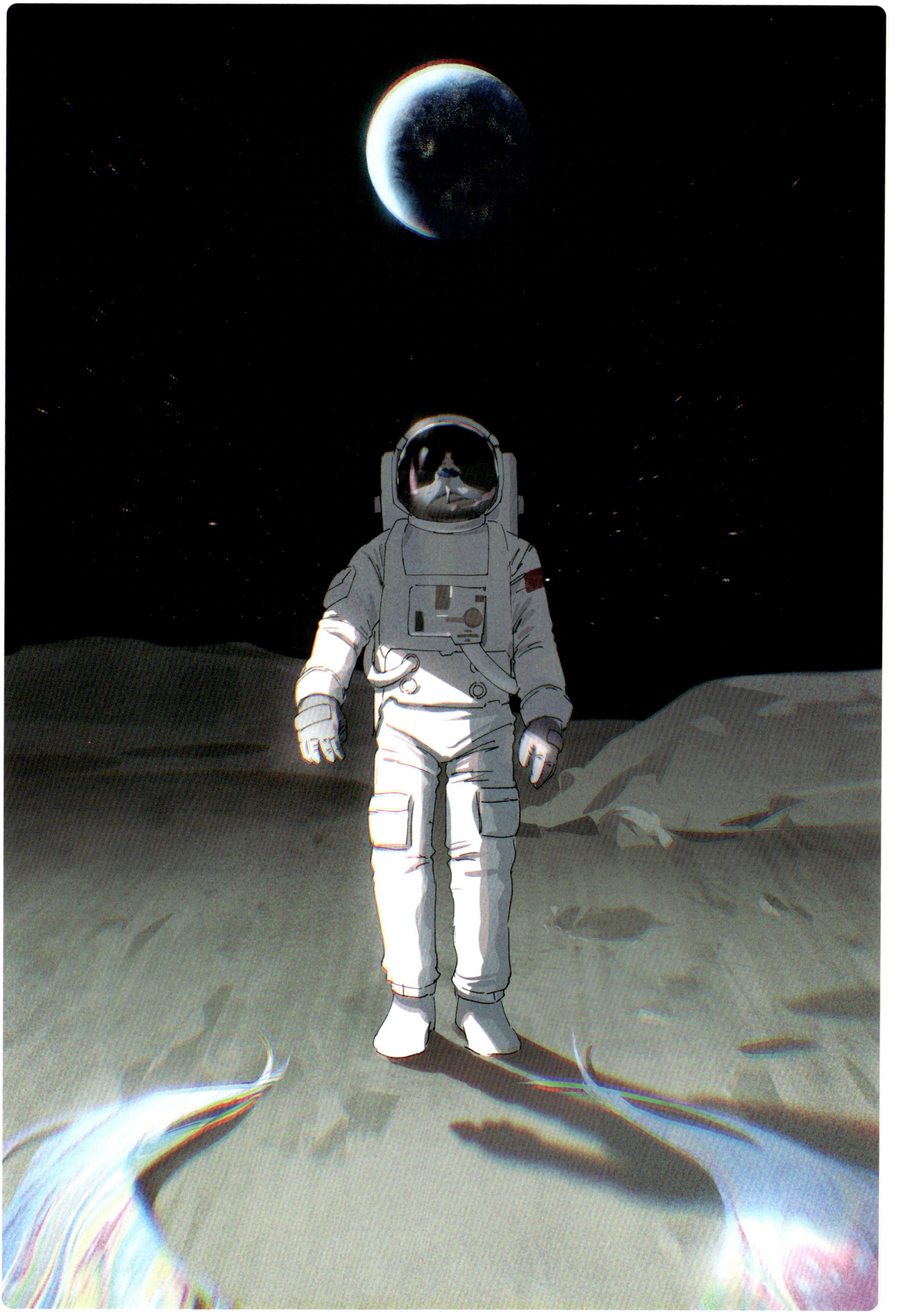

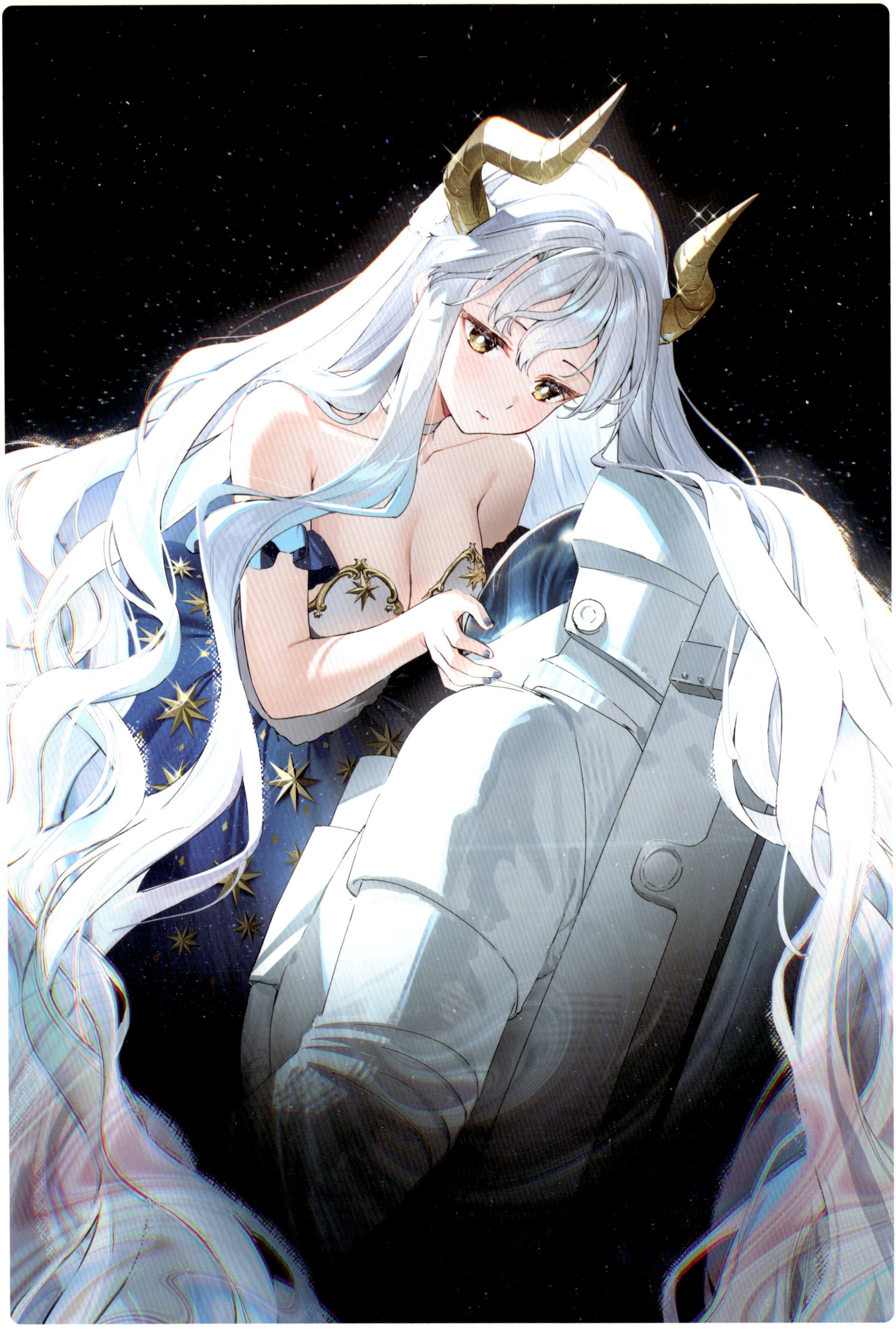

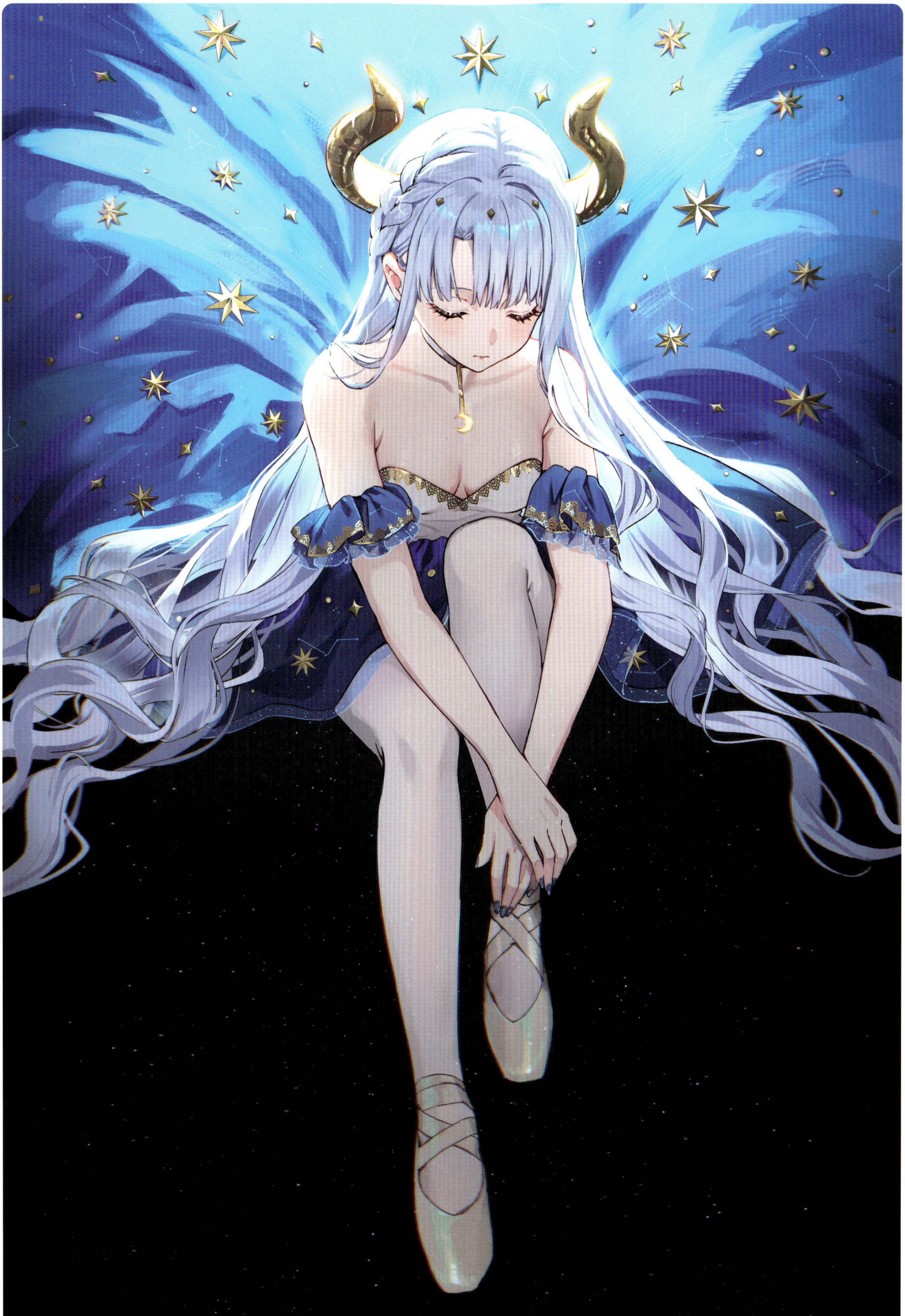

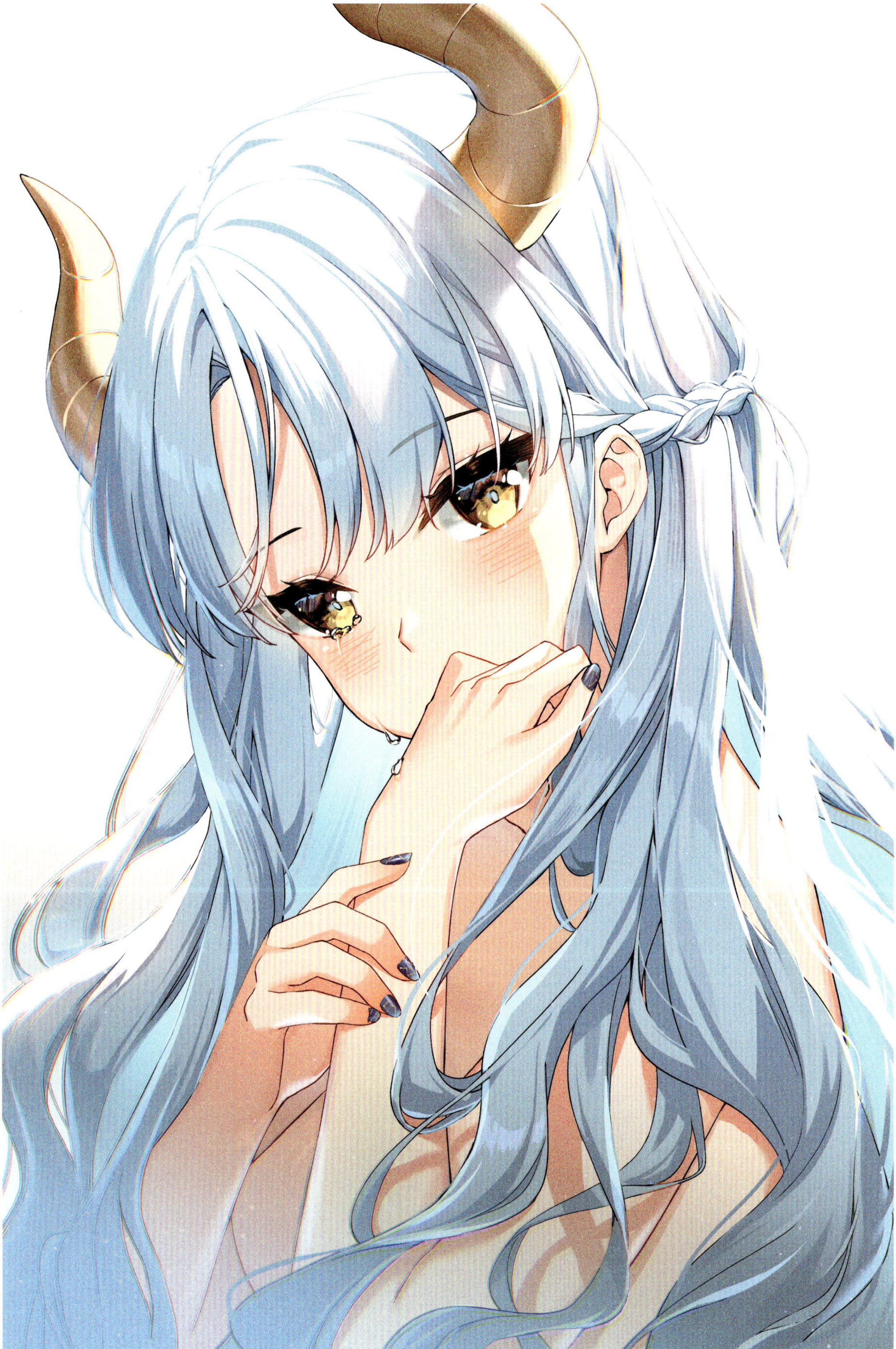

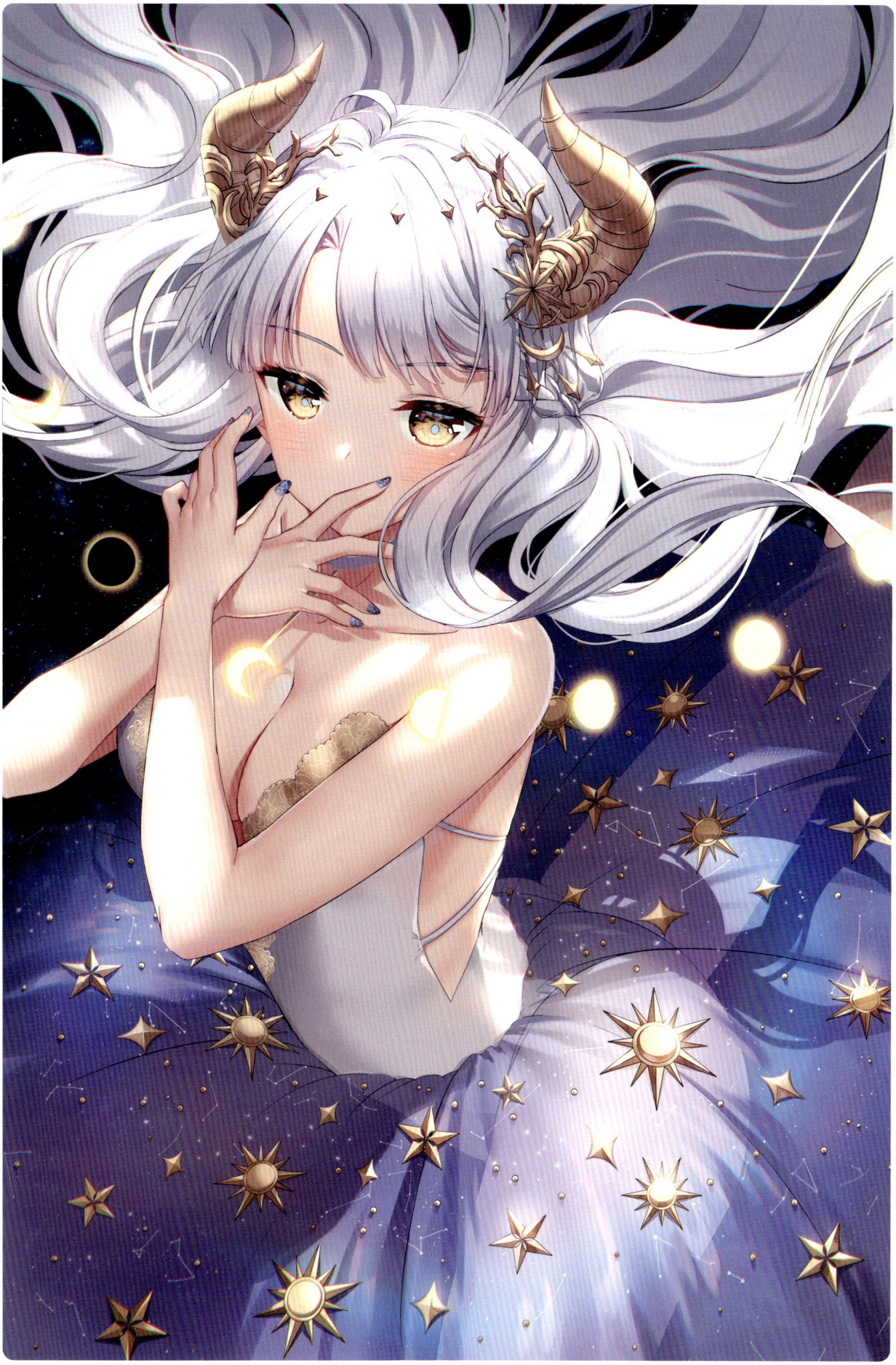

Astrea

Long ago a lone celestial being came into existence.
She had words and thoughts, but nobody to share them with –
and so began her ballet across the astral sphere.
She has some control over matter, which she uses to change her size and
appearance at will, and to manifest rooms
in a celestial palace she inhabits alone.
Mostly she spends her limitless time in the guise of a ballerina,
dancing gracefully from star to star in search of a friend.

遥か昔、天界にひとりの存在が誕生しました。
彼女は思考と言葉を持っていましたが、それらを共有する相手はいませんでした。
それから、彼女の天界での孤独な舞踊が始まりました。
彼女は物質を操る能力を持ち、それを用いて自由に姿形や大小を変化させ、
ひとりで住む天界の宮殿を出現させました。
彼女は無限の時間を主にバレリーナの姿で過ごし、
星から星へと優雅に舞いながら、友を探し求めています。

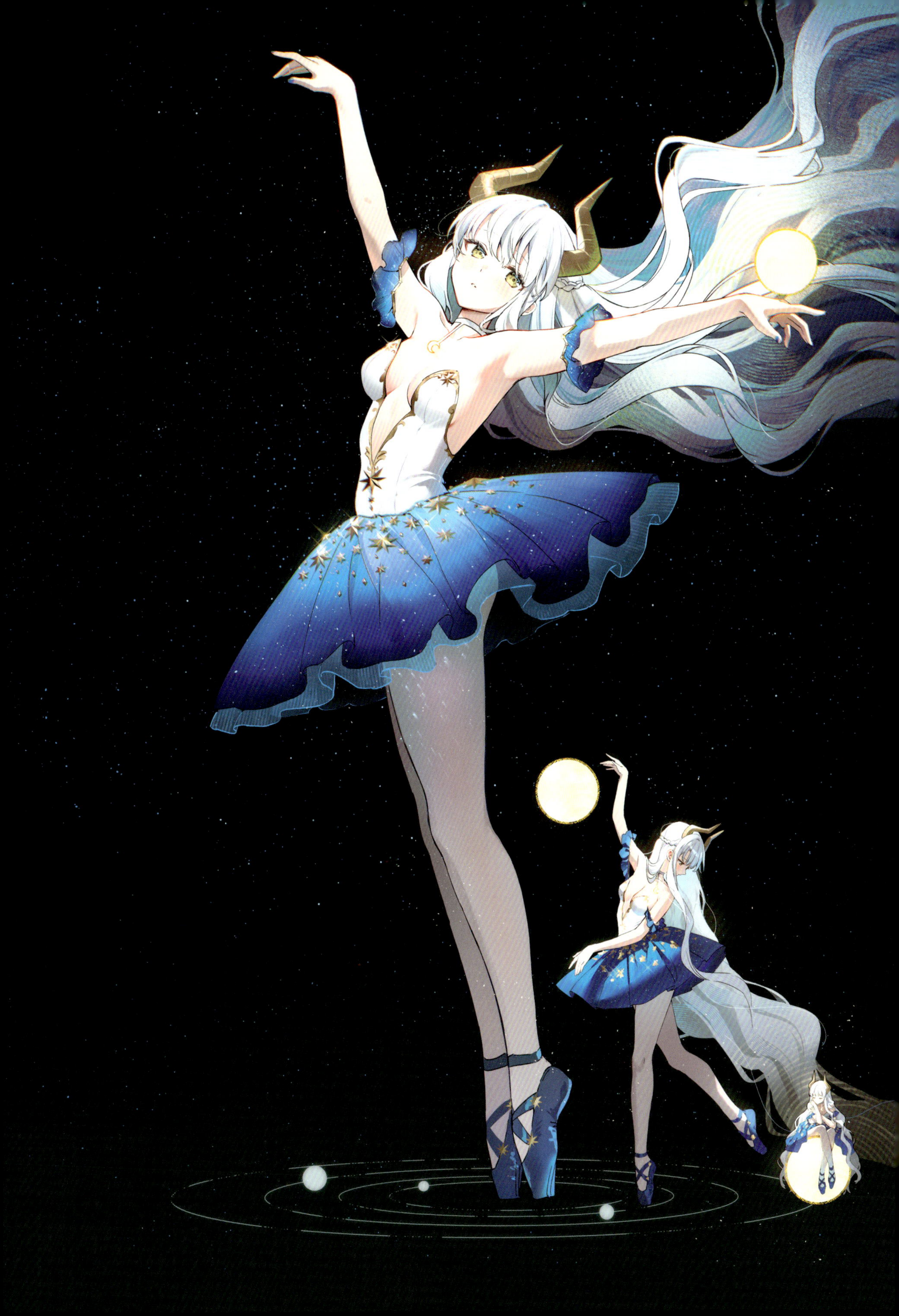

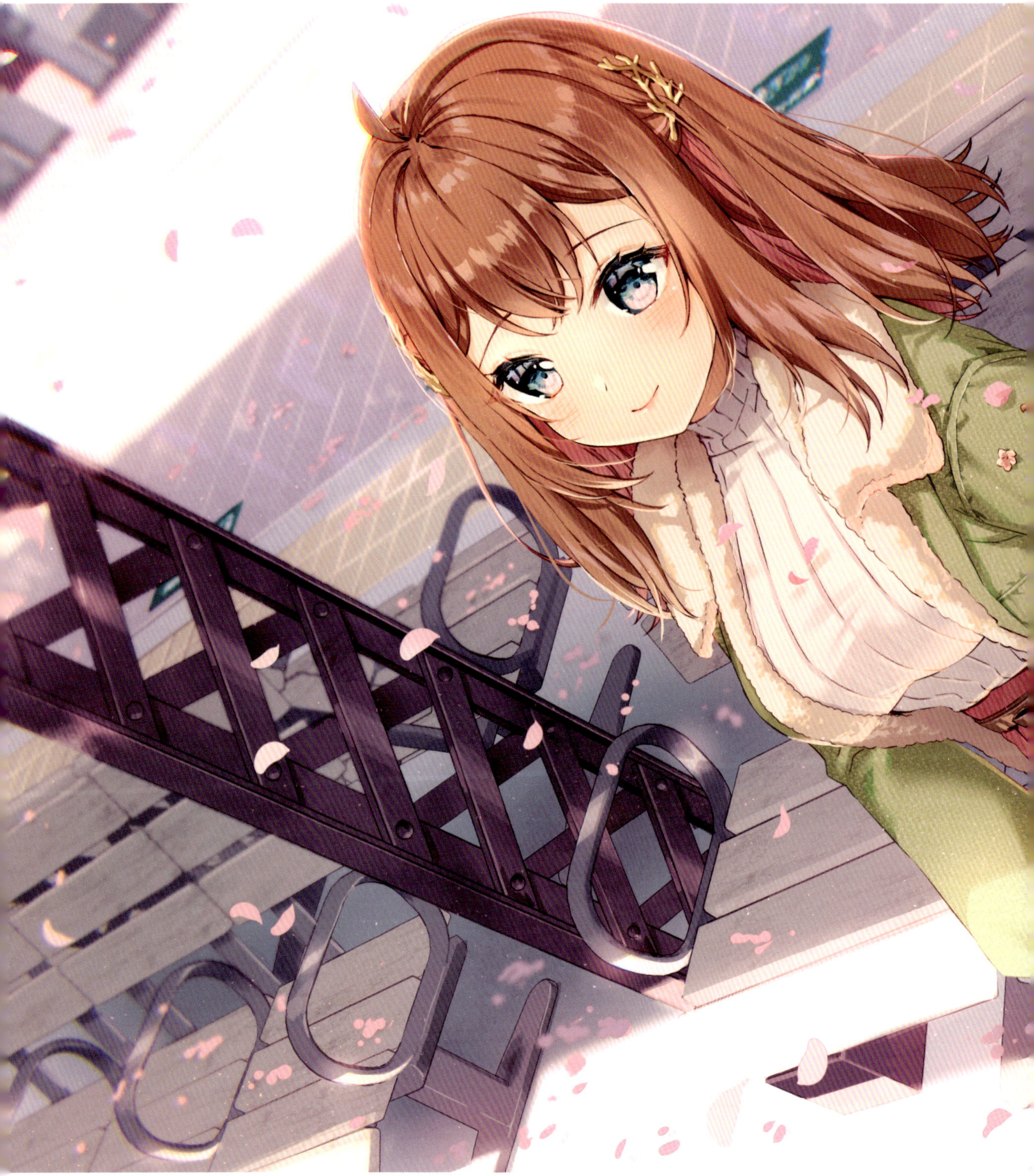

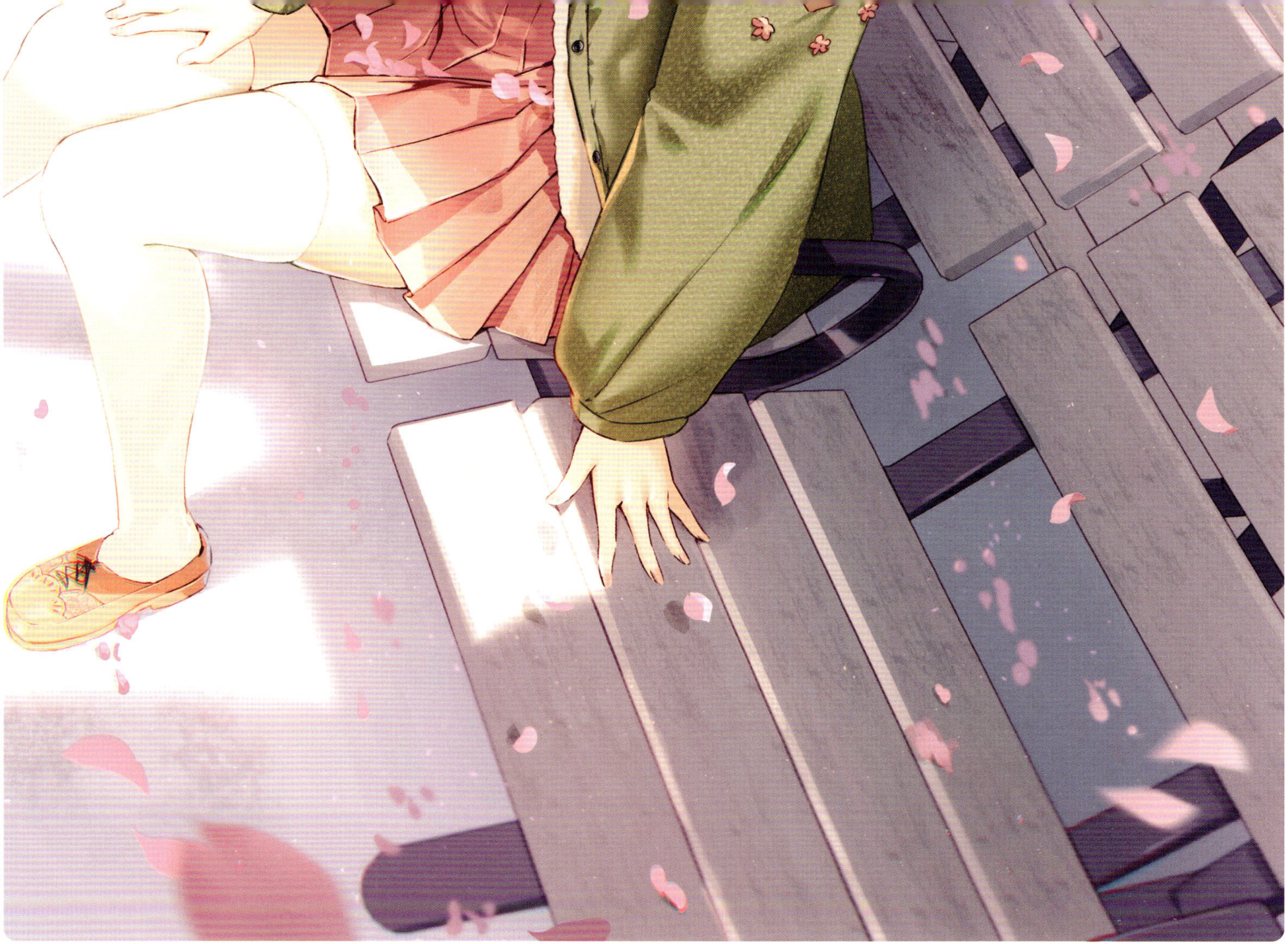

Deer **Chiharu**

Serenity

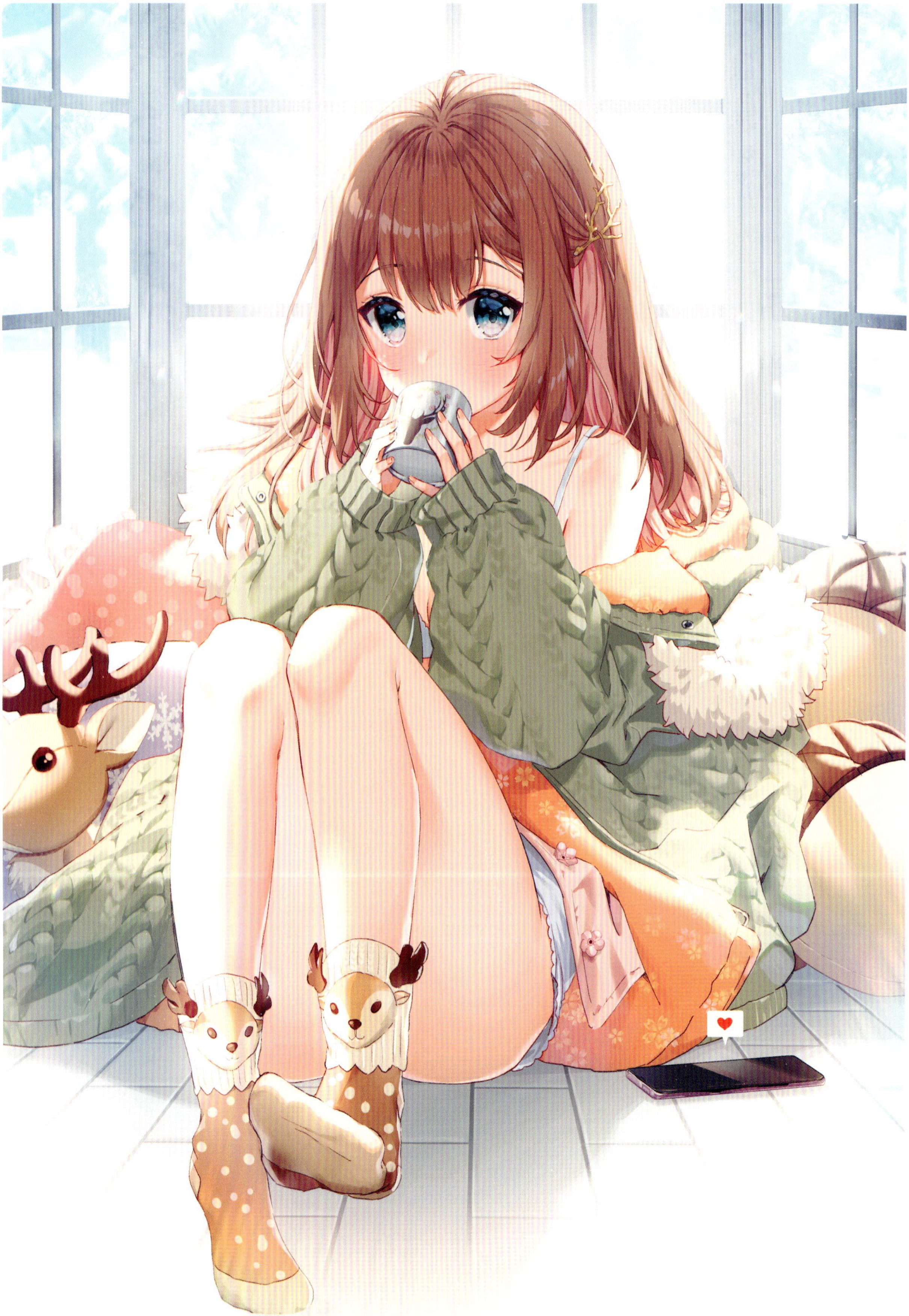

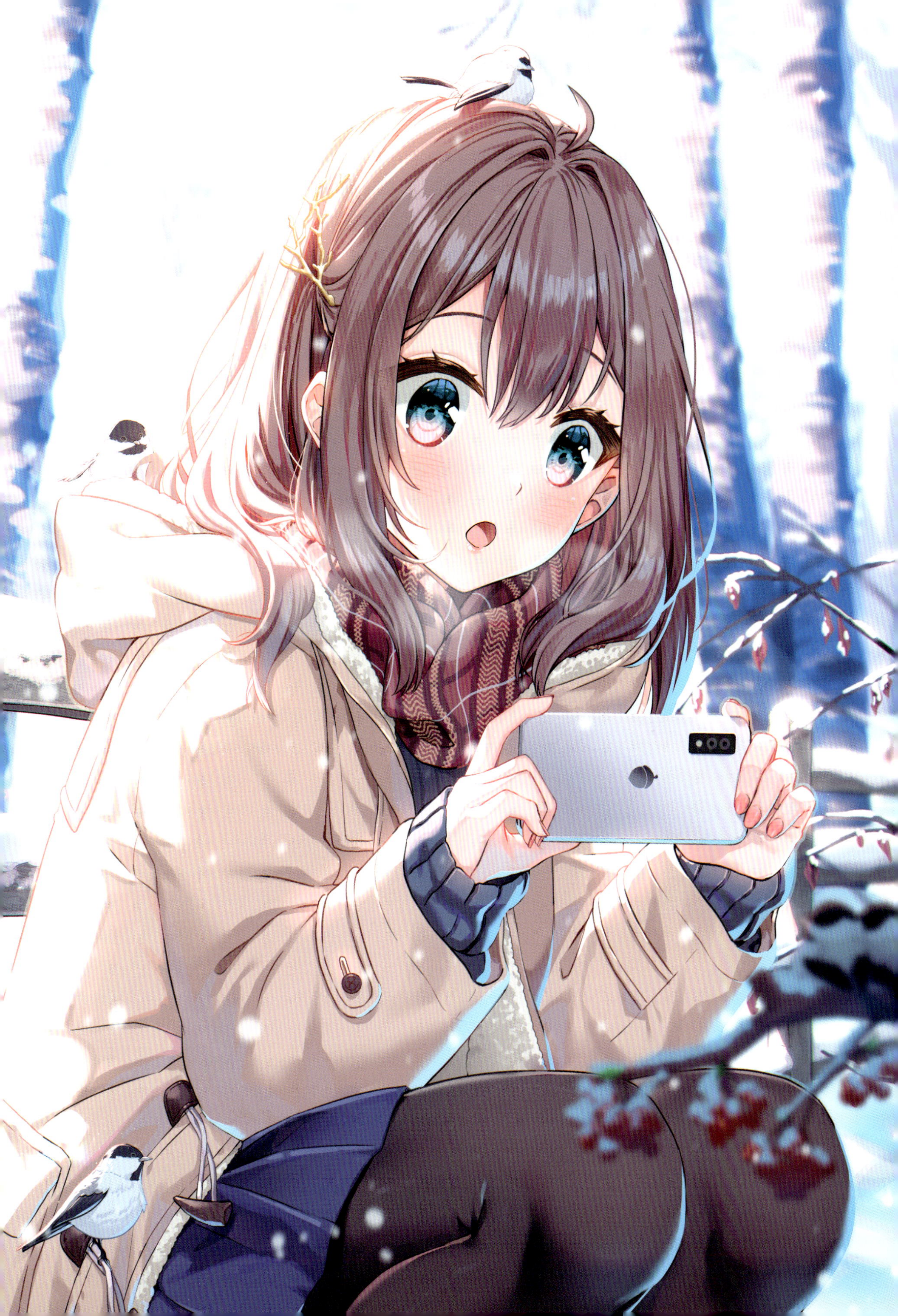

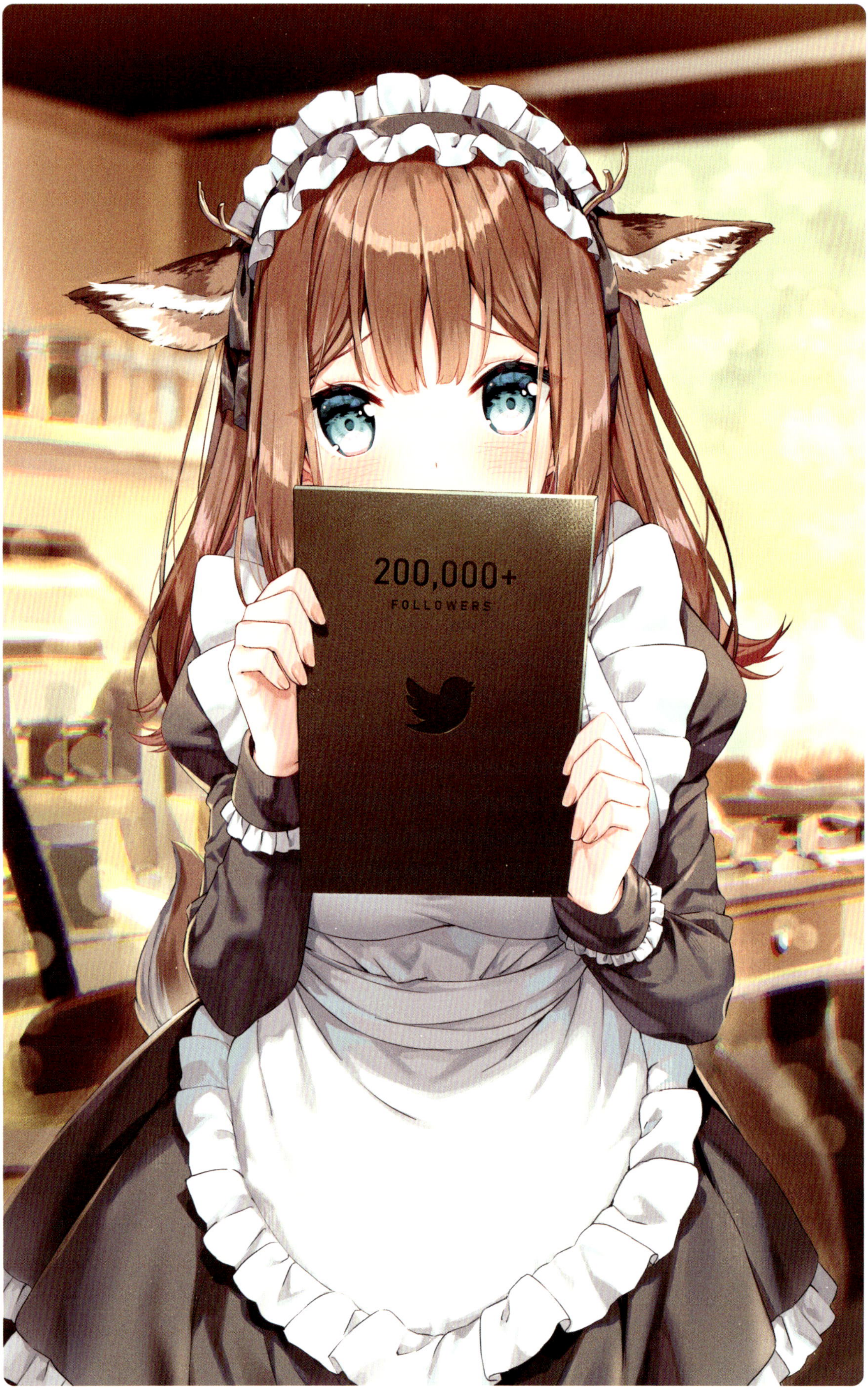
200,000+
FOLLOWERS

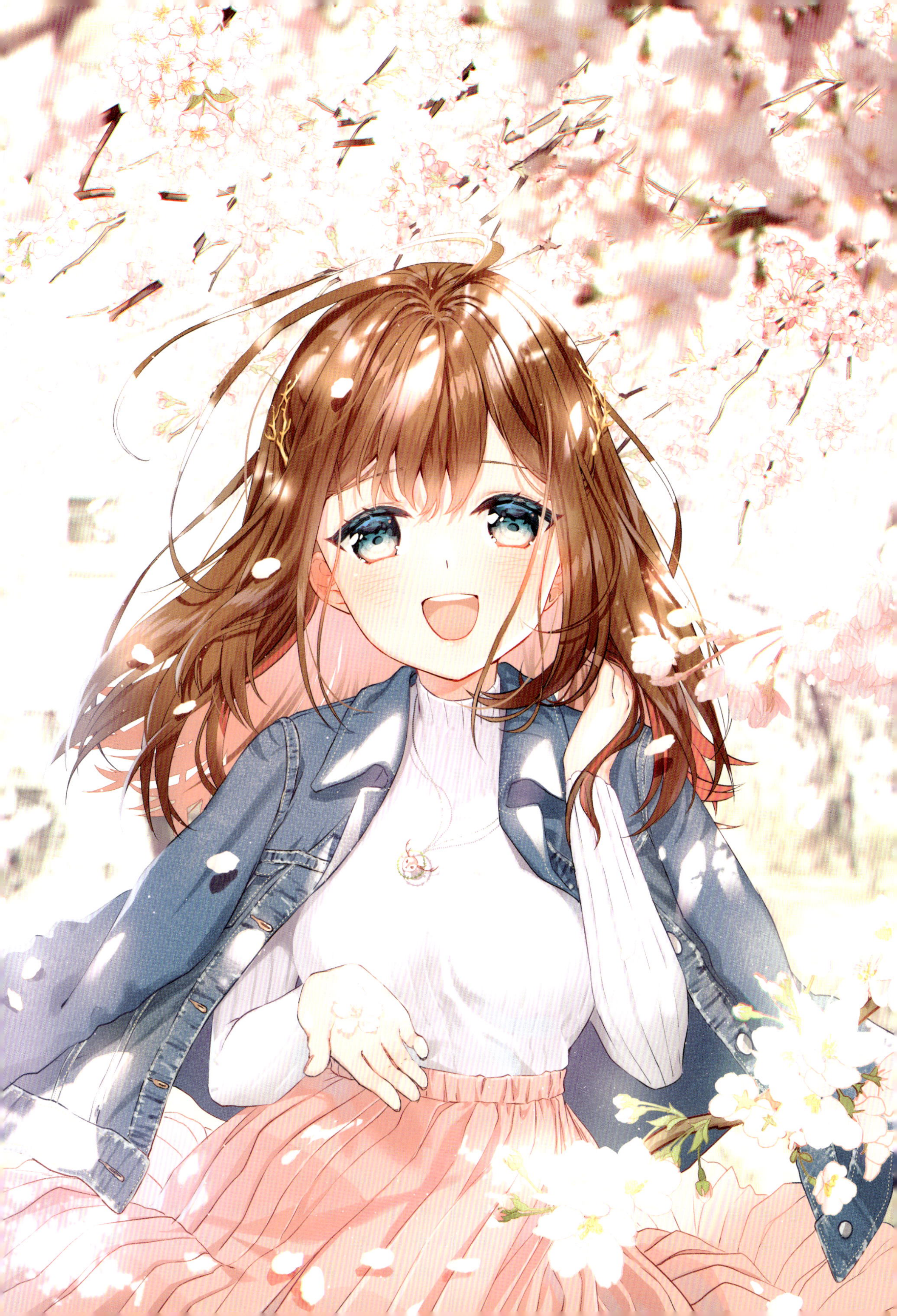

Snake Eve

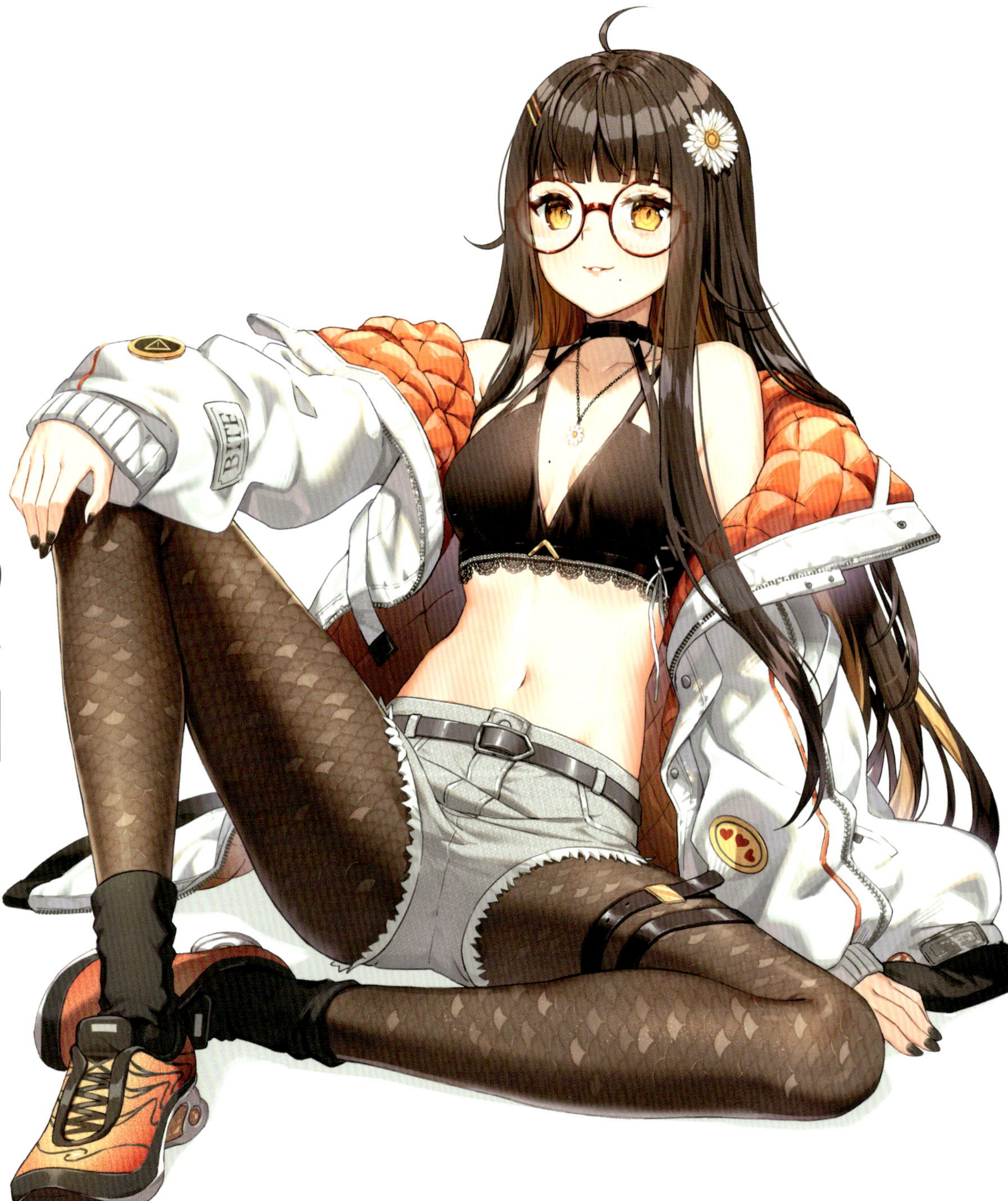

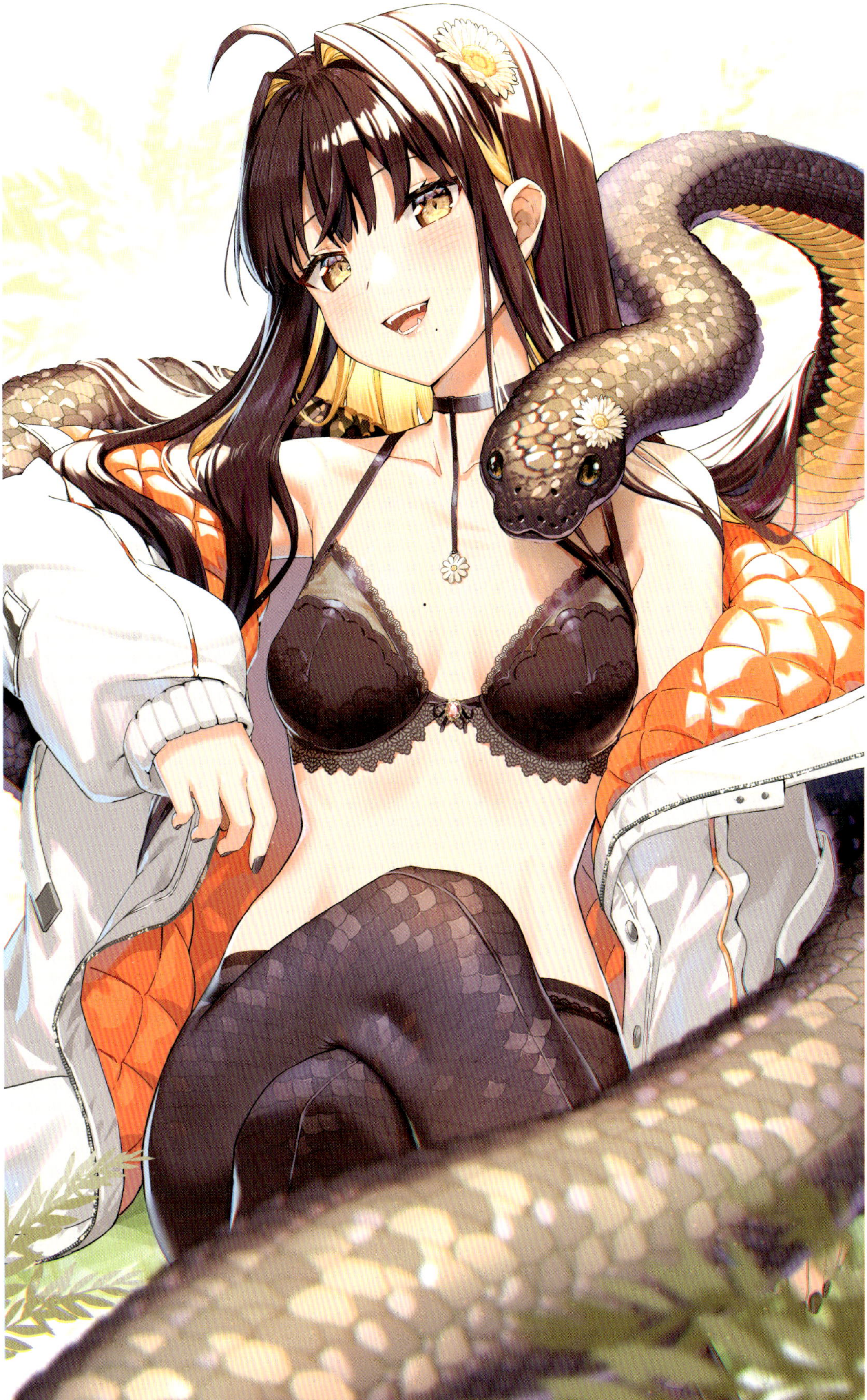

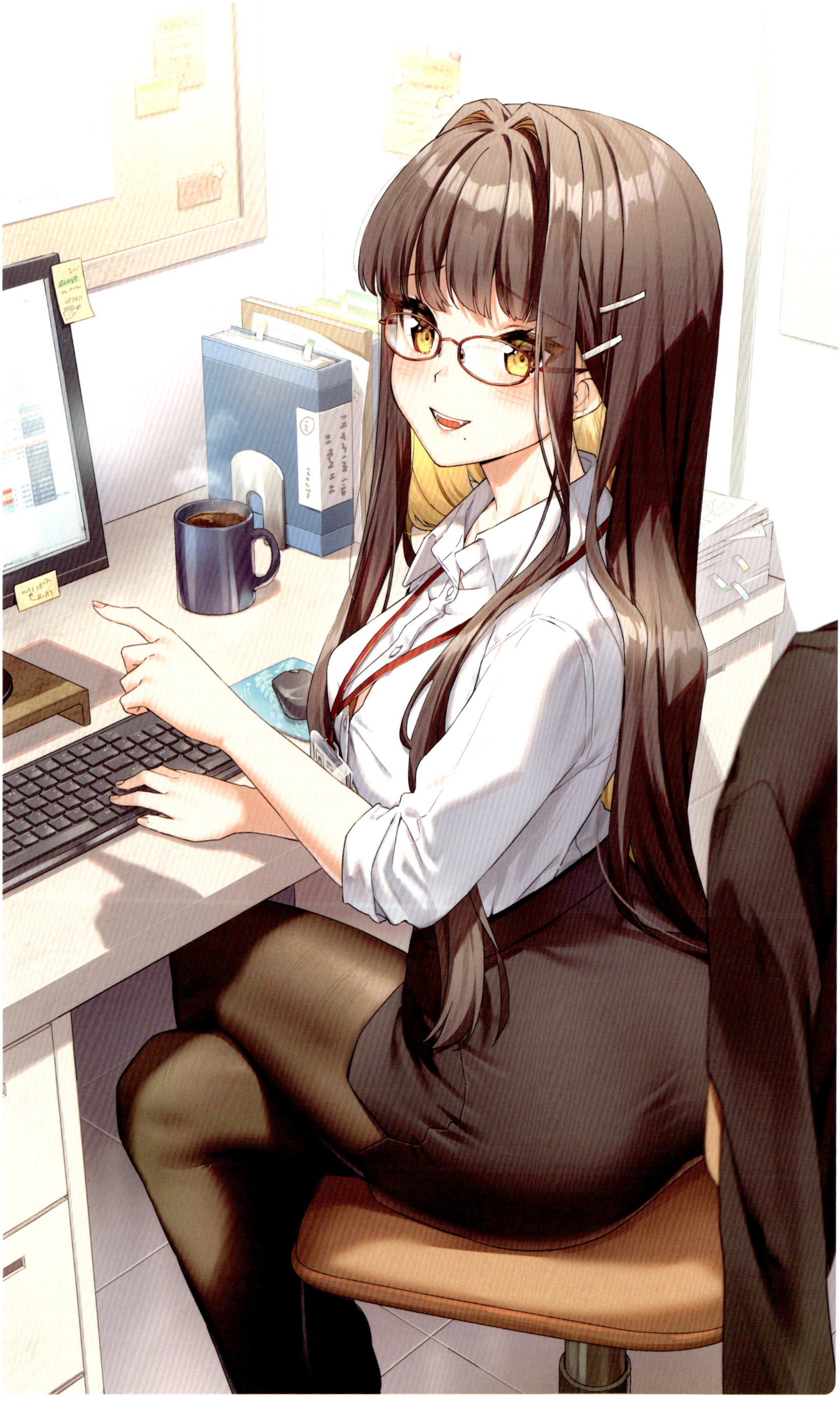

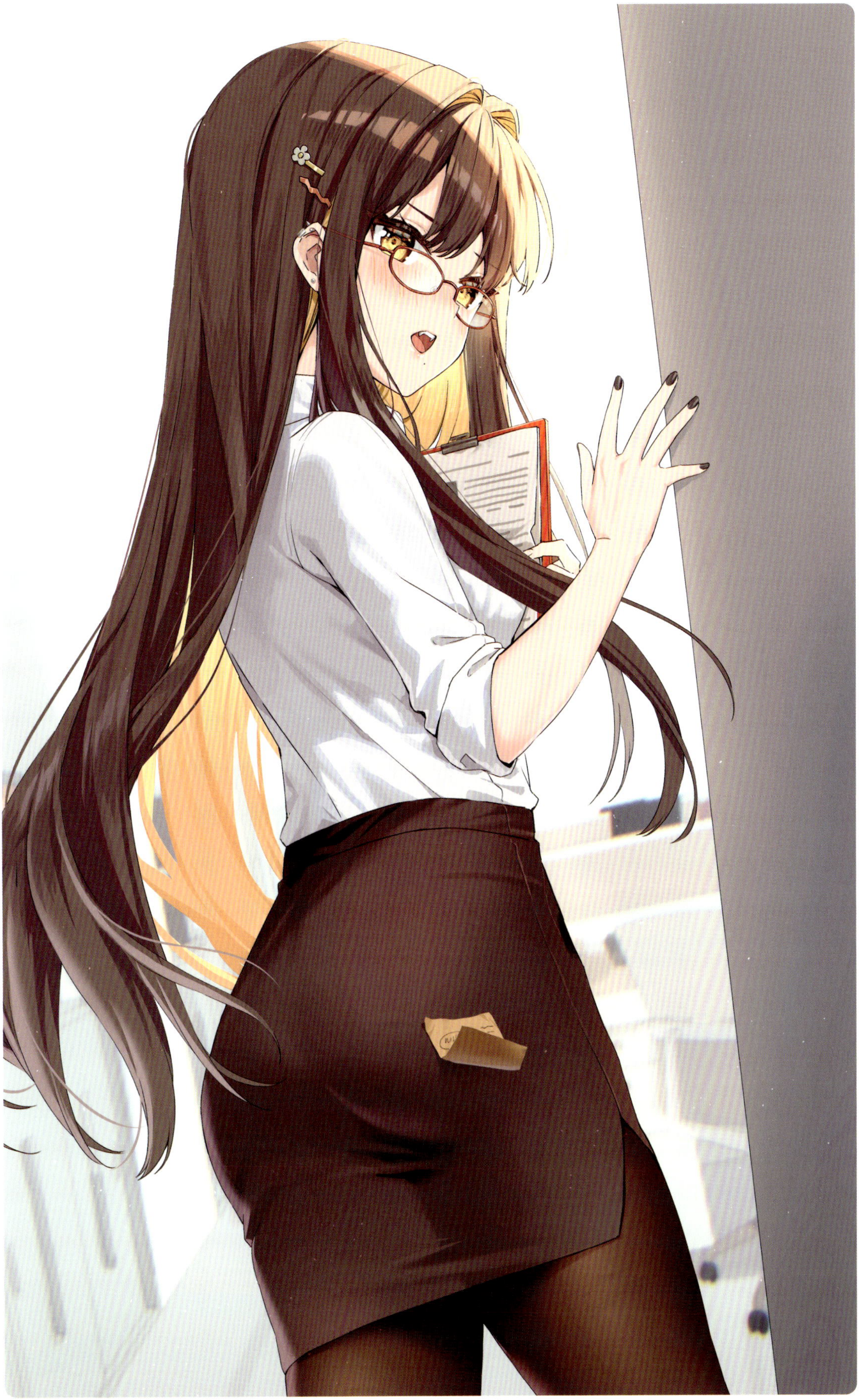

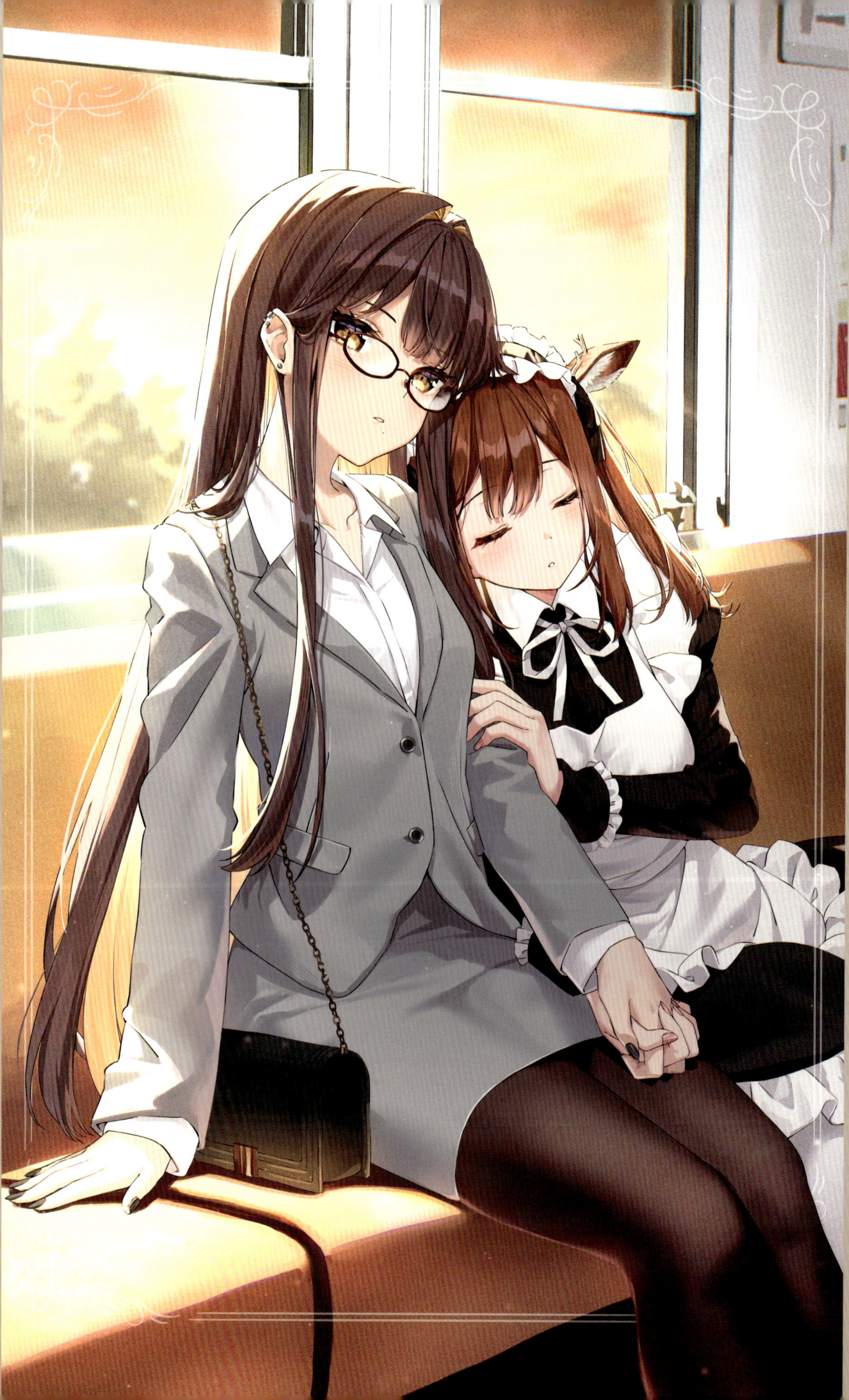

Chiharu & Eve

Chiharu is a gentle and warm-hearted girl with a deep affinity for deer!
She enjoys traveling, taking photos, and trying out local delicacies
in the prefectures she visits throughout Japan.
She works part-time at a maid cafe to save money
for her dream of traveling outside of Japan to see the world!

Eve is a cunning and mischievous girl who is known for her bold personality and long, slender frame.
She works as a regular office lady in the daytime.
She's a bit clumsy, but she gets the job done!
She especially enjoys playfully teasing people who react in cute and interesting ways,
which at least partly explains her unlikely and dear friendship with Chiharu.

千春は、鹿に深い愛情を注ぐ心優しい女の子です。
彼女は旅をして、写真撮影や日本各地を訪れた際のご当地グルメを楽しんでいます。
いつかは日本を飛び出し、世界中を旅するという夢を叶えるため、
普段はメイドカフェでアルバイトをしています！

イヴは、スレンダーな体格で性格は大胆、そして狡猾でいたずら好きな女の子です。
昼間はオフィスワーカーとして働いています。少し不器用ですが、仕事はしっかりこなします！
かわいい・面白いリアクションの人をからかうことが大好きで、
これが千春と親しい友情を結んでいる理由のひとつでもあります。

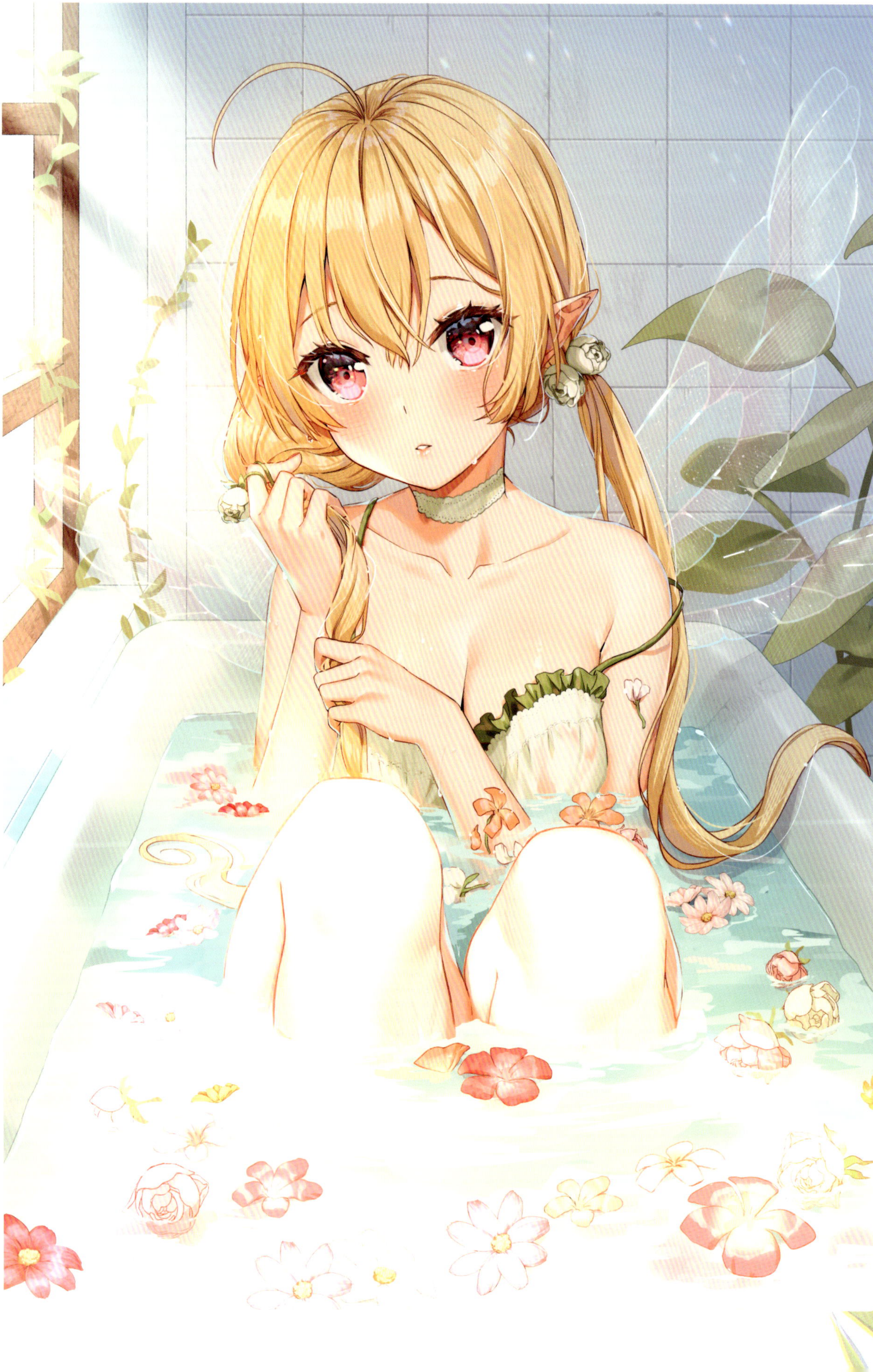

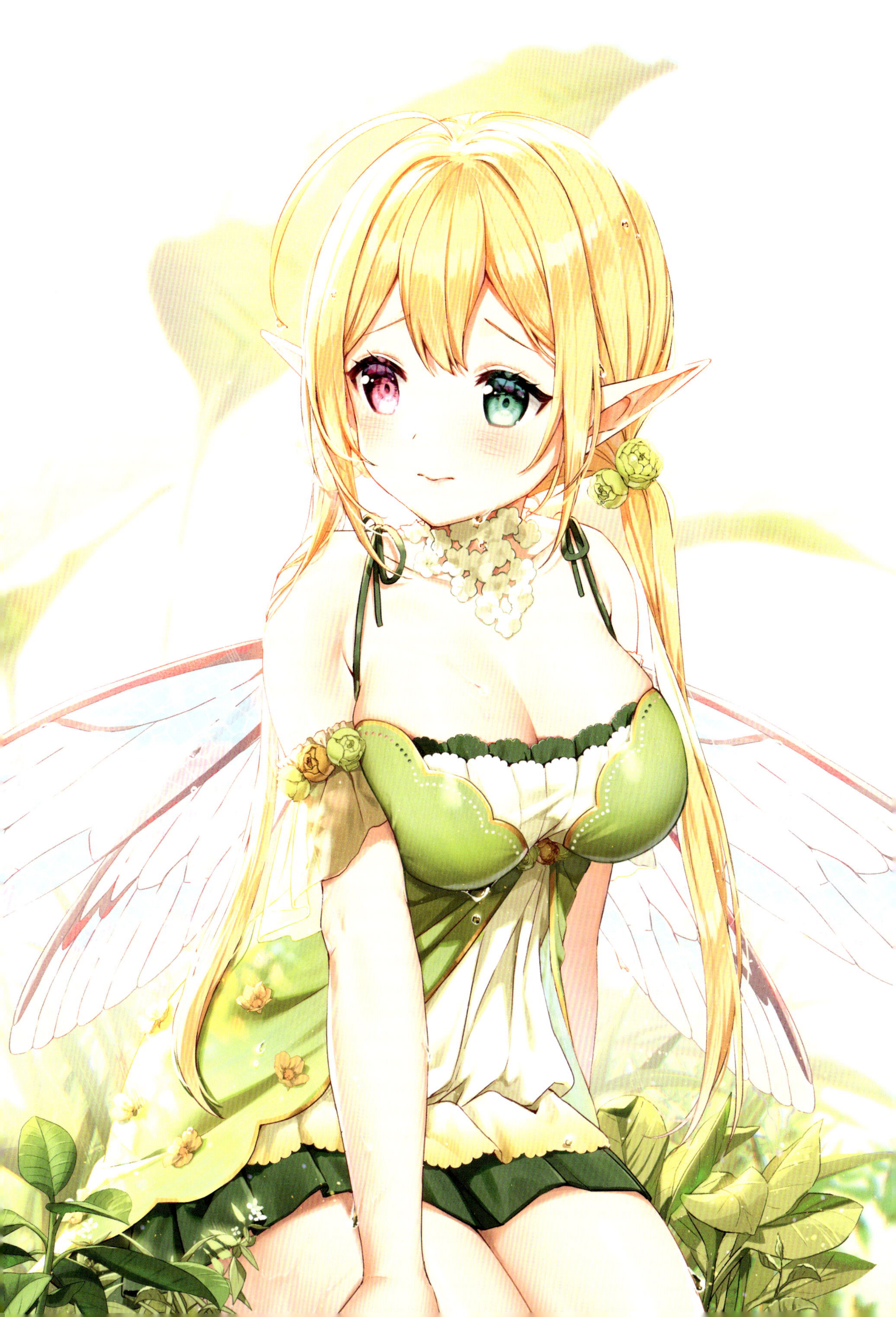

Client Works

The Art of Rosuuri

Hatsune Miku

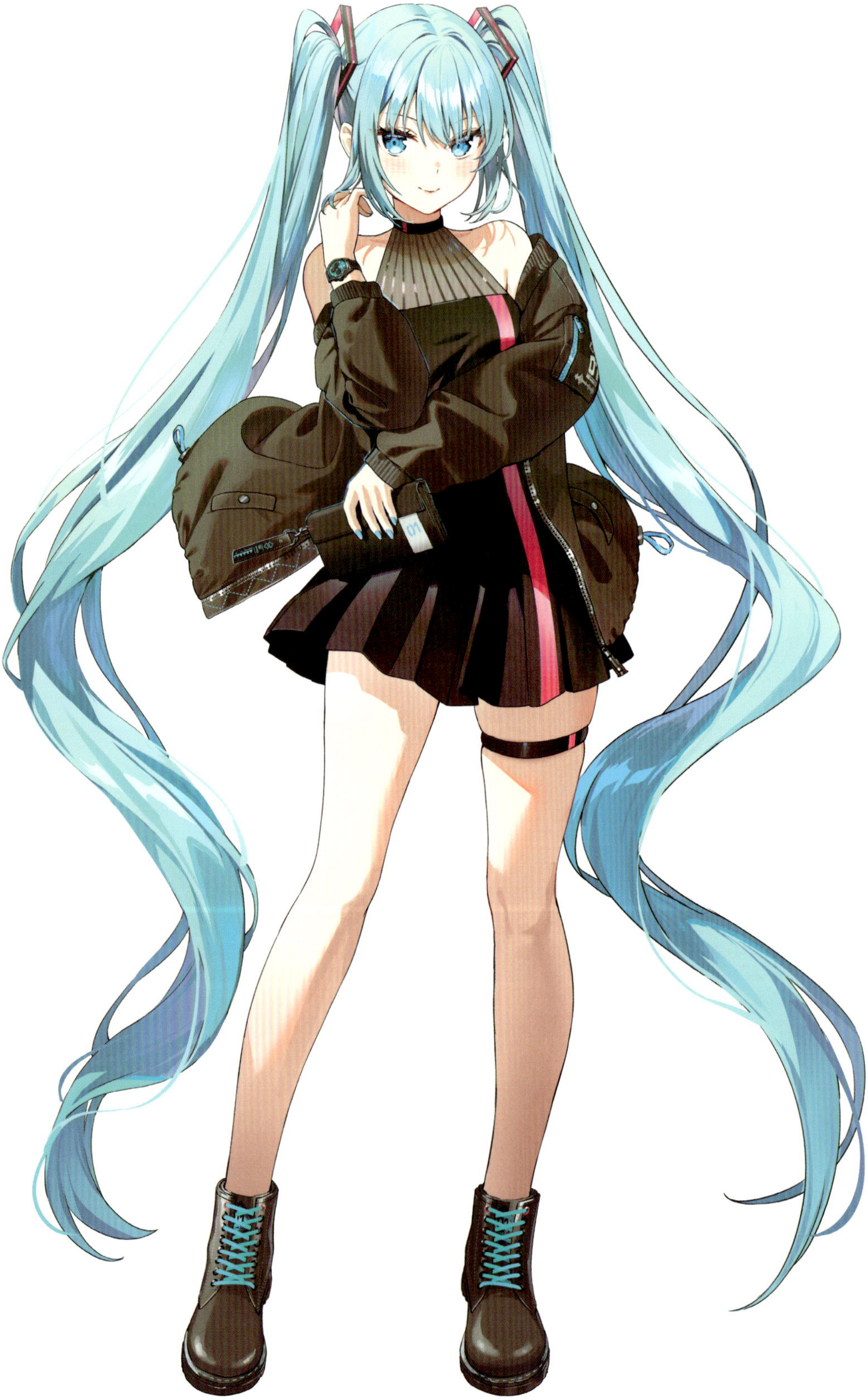

Key visual and card case art for Hatsune Miku x Super Groupies Collection

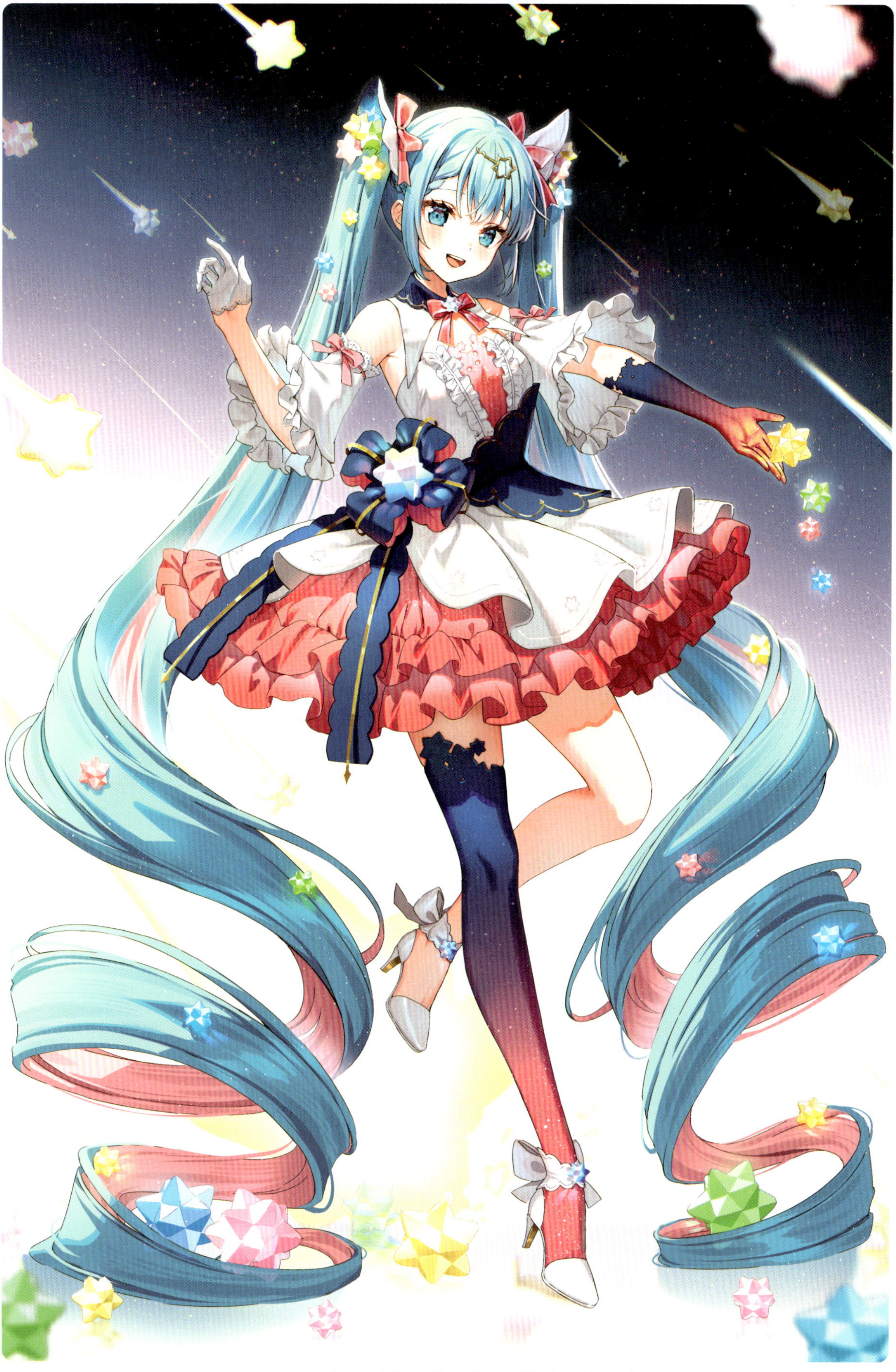

「Creators Collection Figure」 Hatsune Miku Rosuuri Ver.

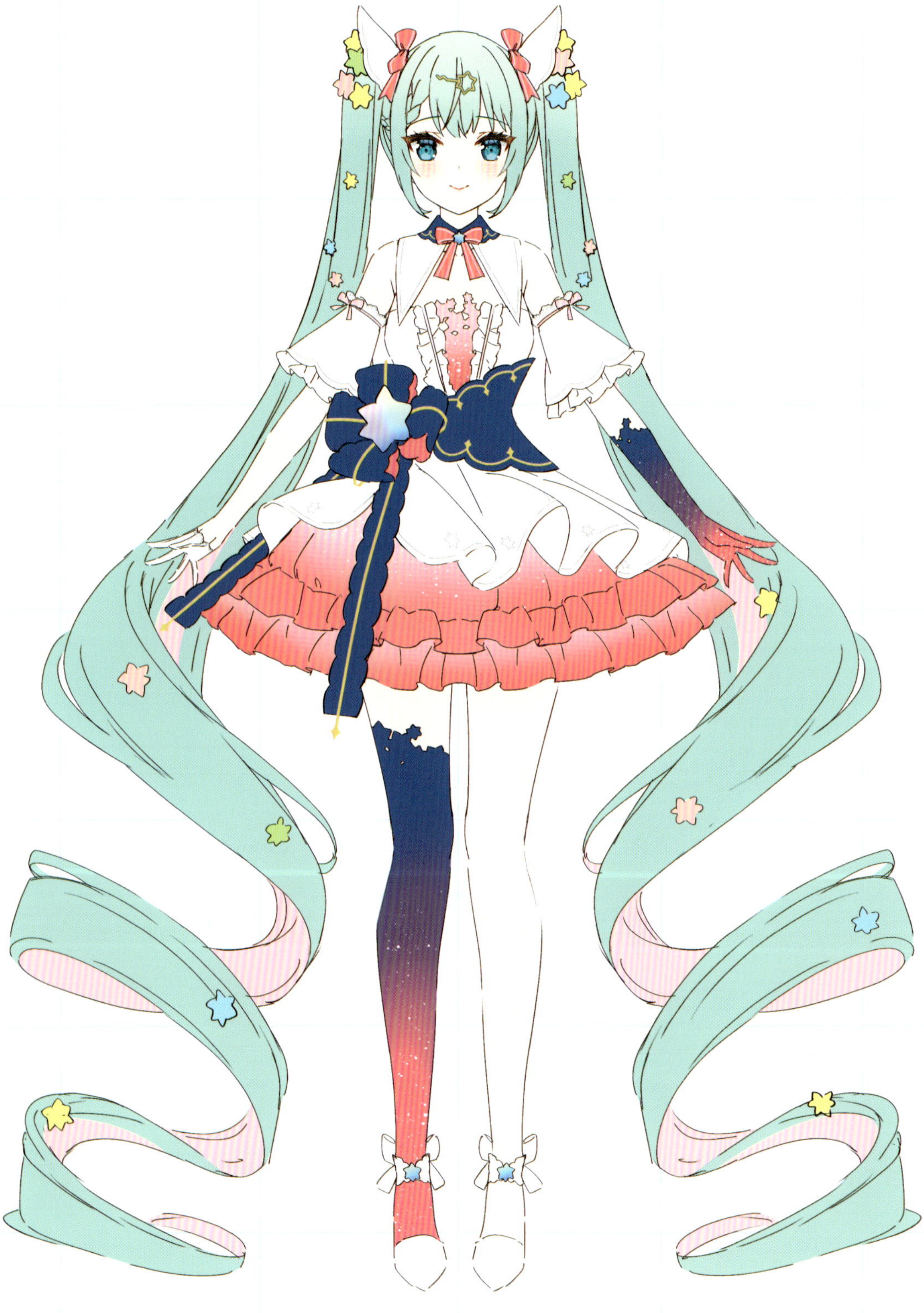

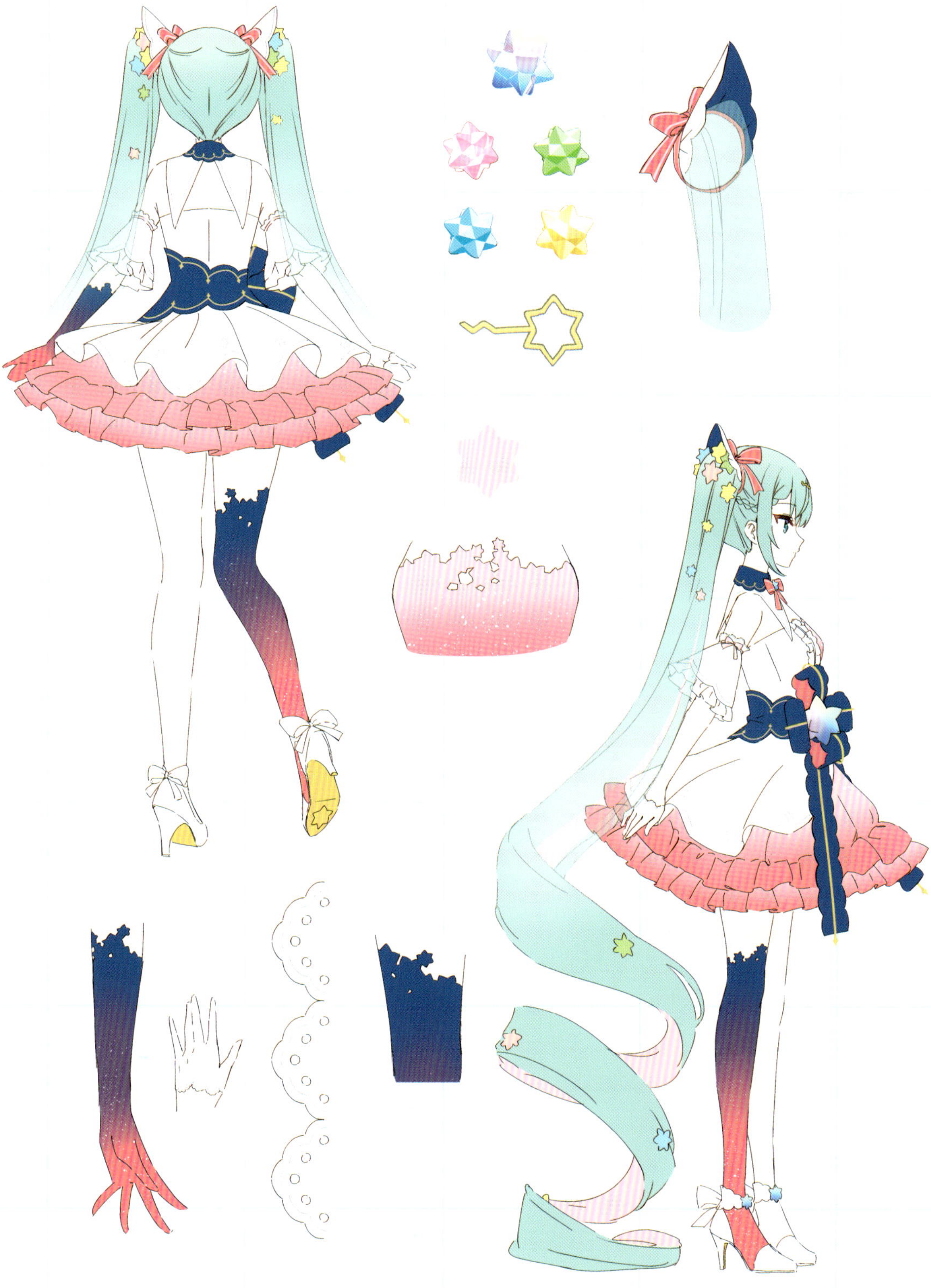

HATSUNE MIKU: COLORFUL STAGE!

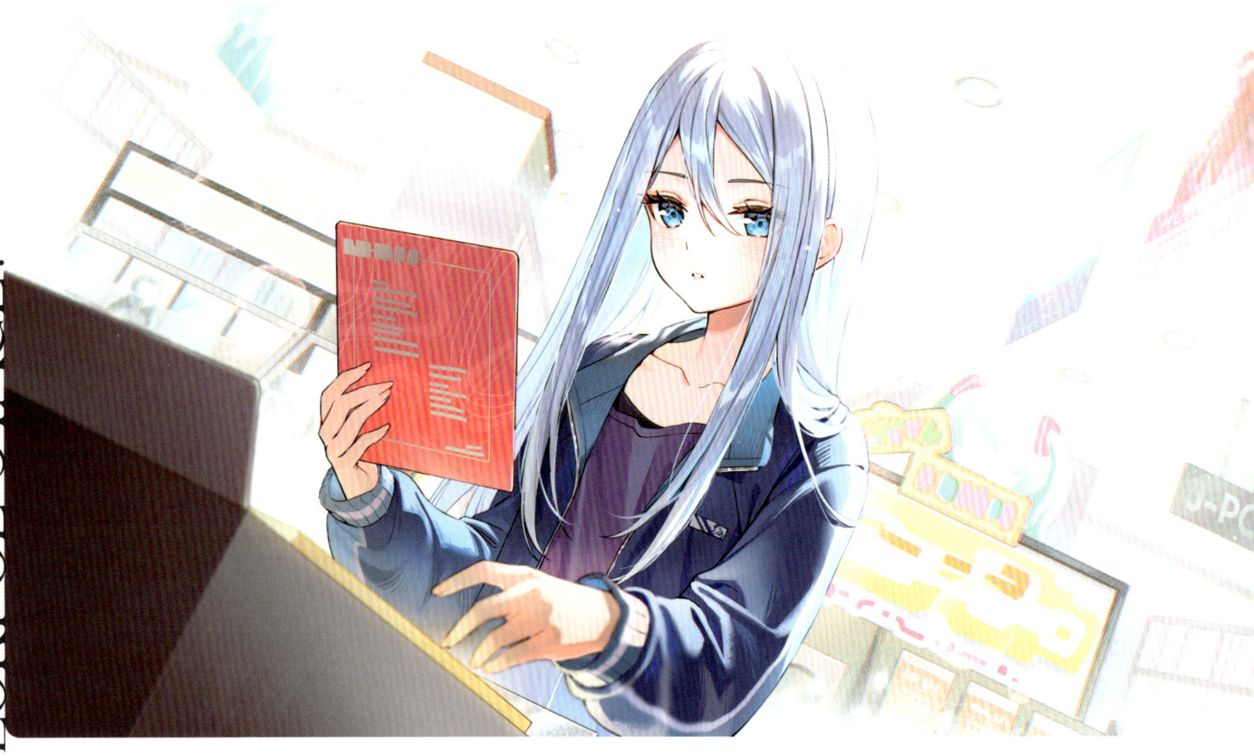

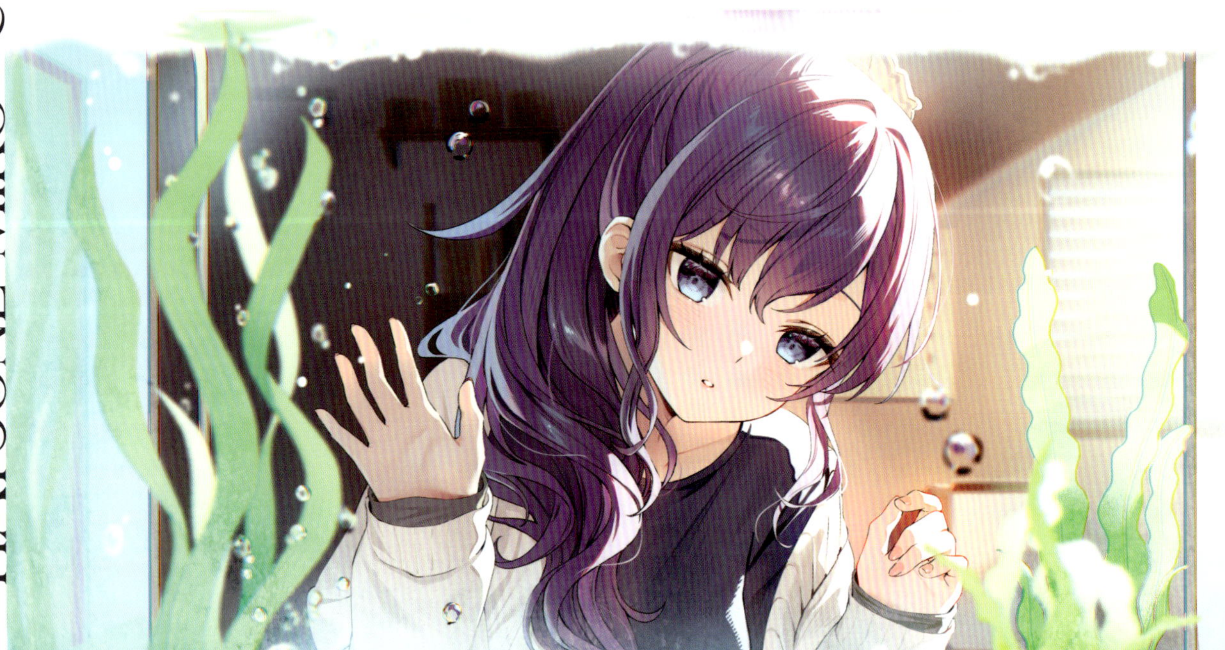

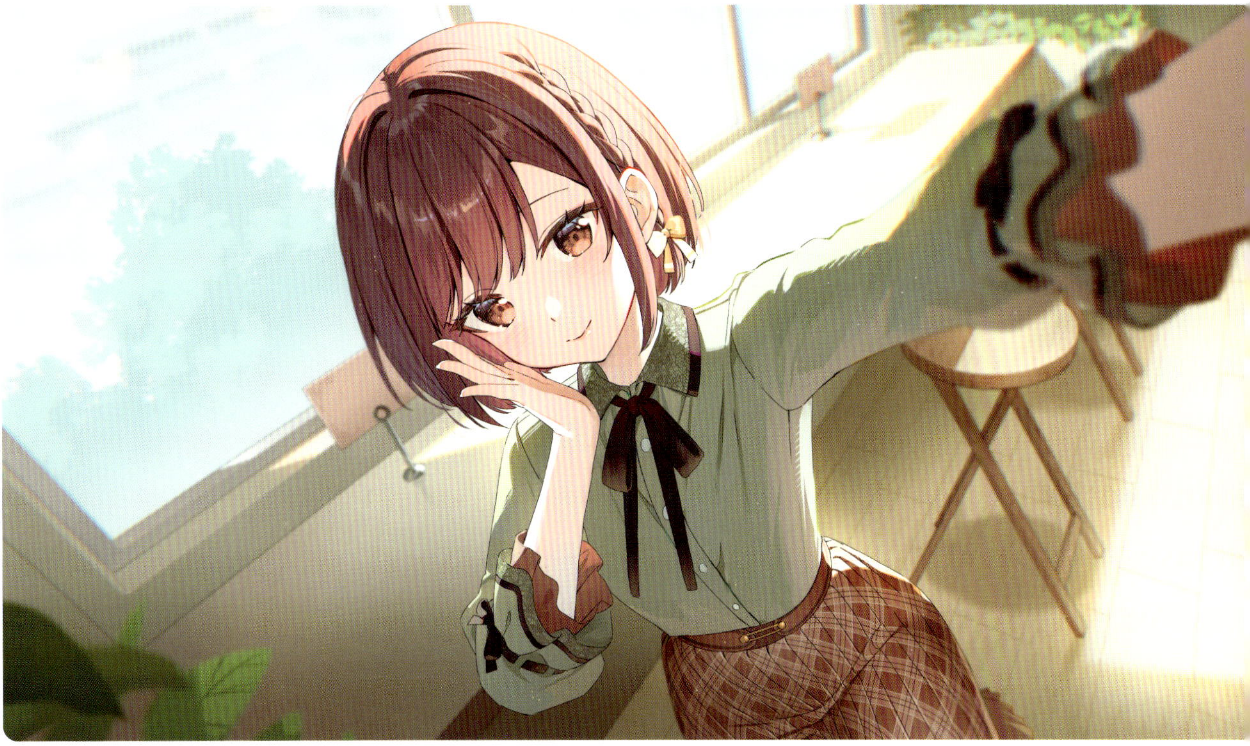

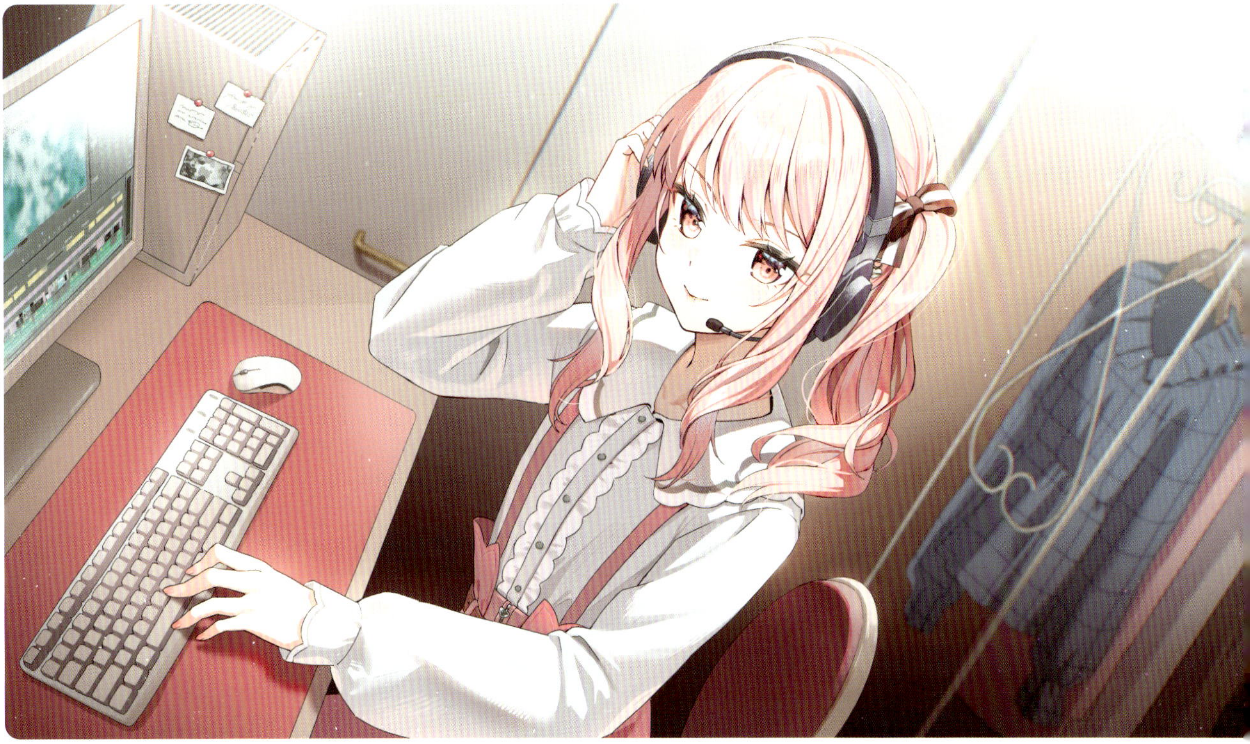

原神

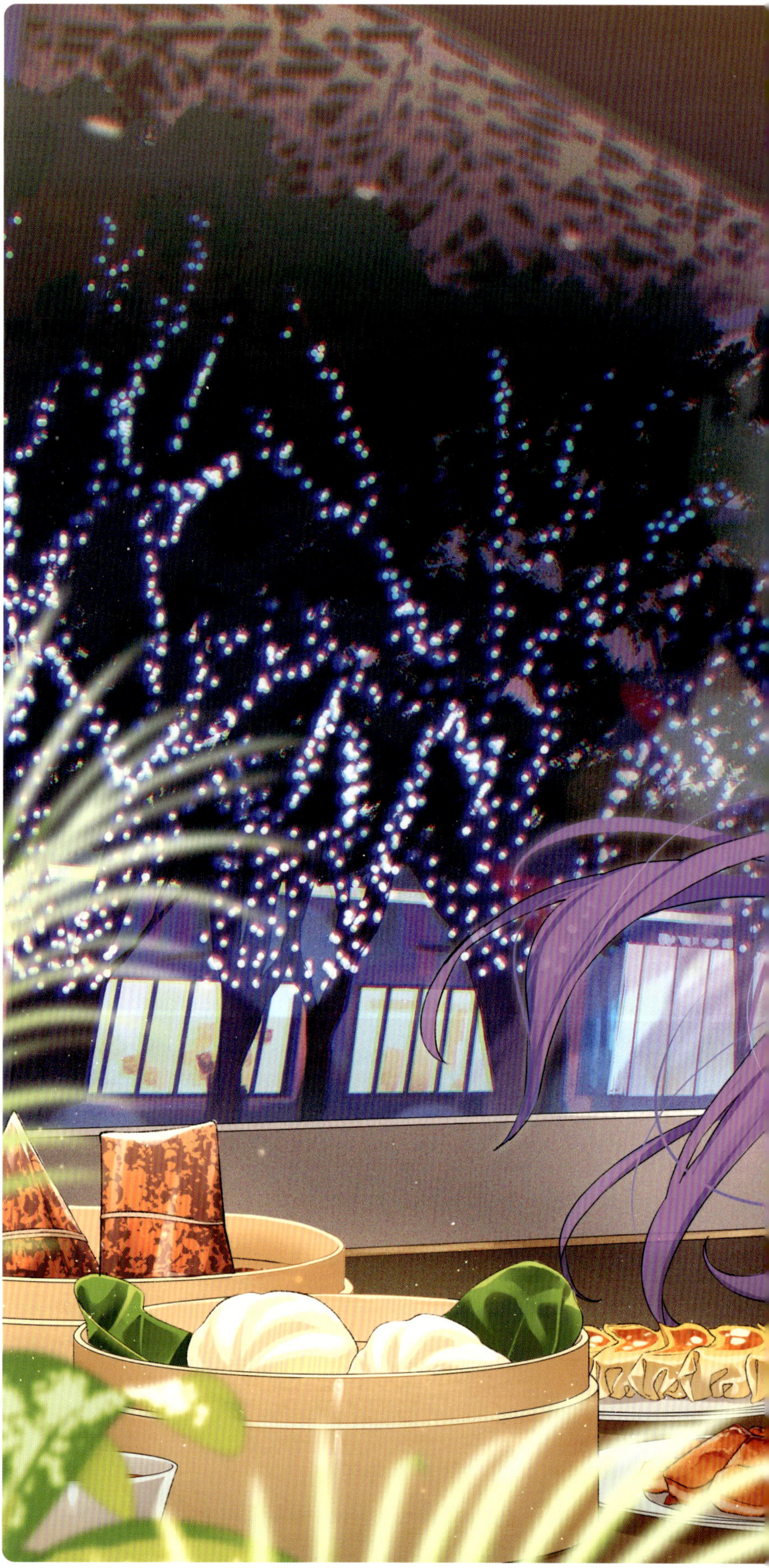

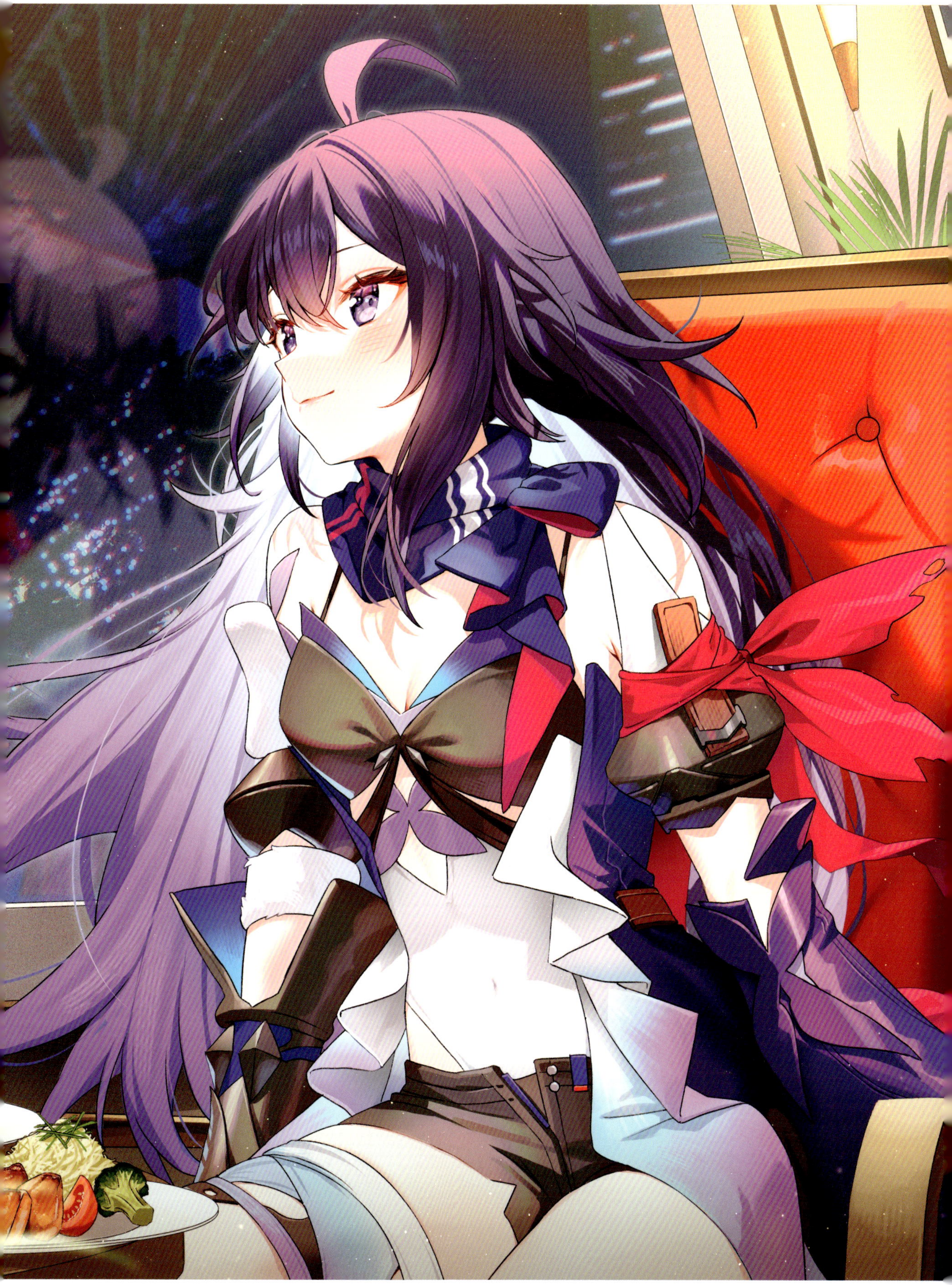

原神 ©miHoYo

崩壊：スターレイル

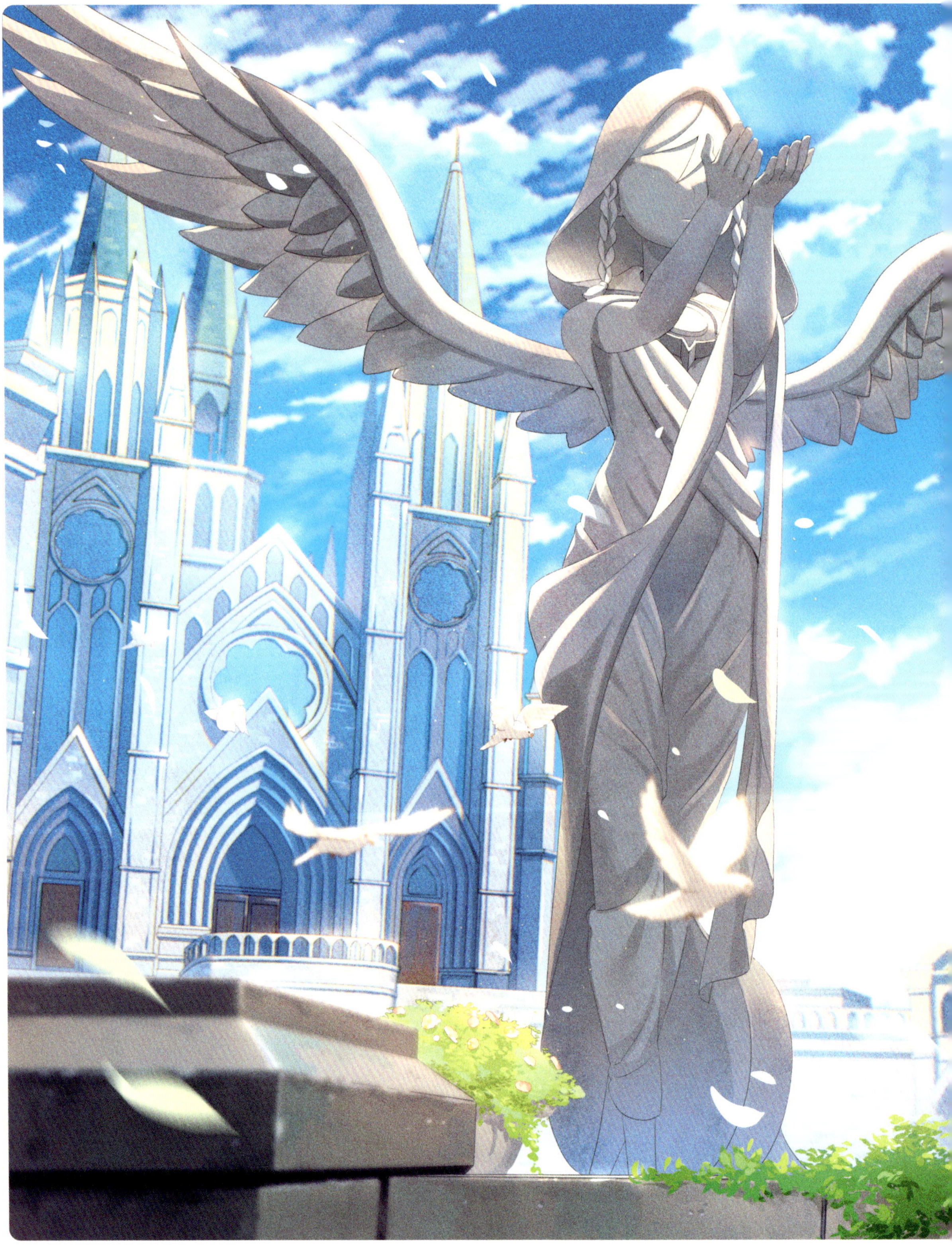

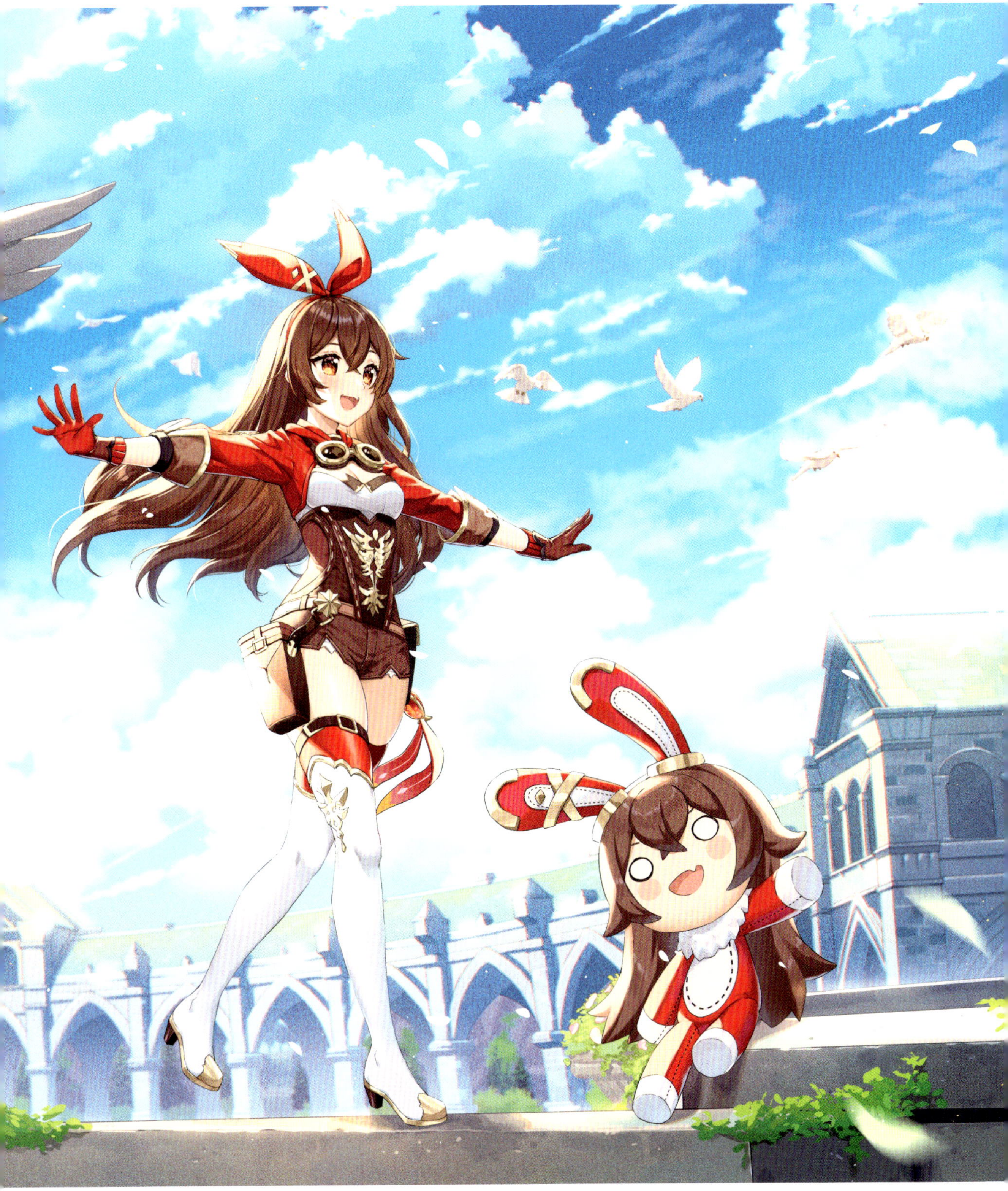

崩壊：スターレイル ©miHoYo

hololive

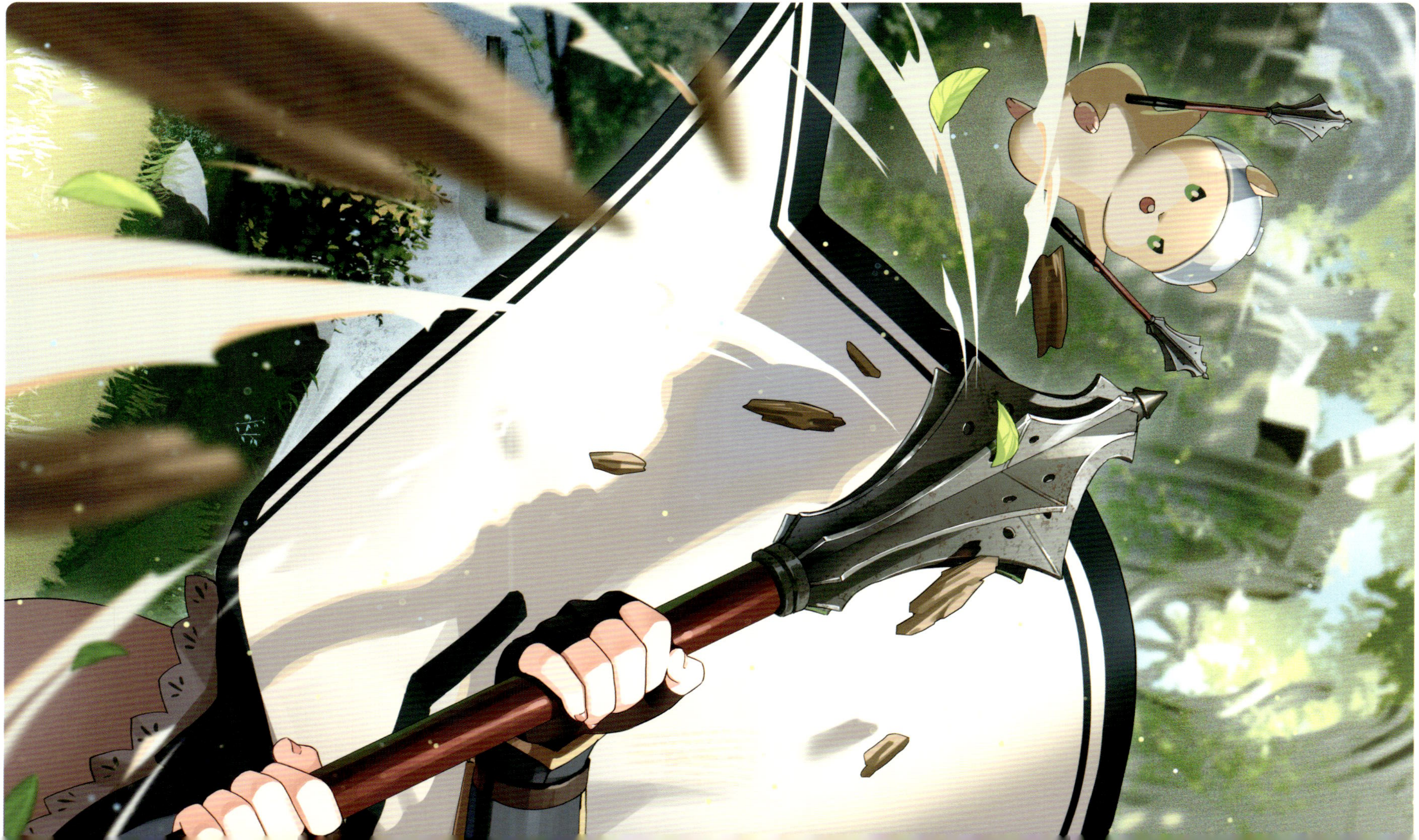

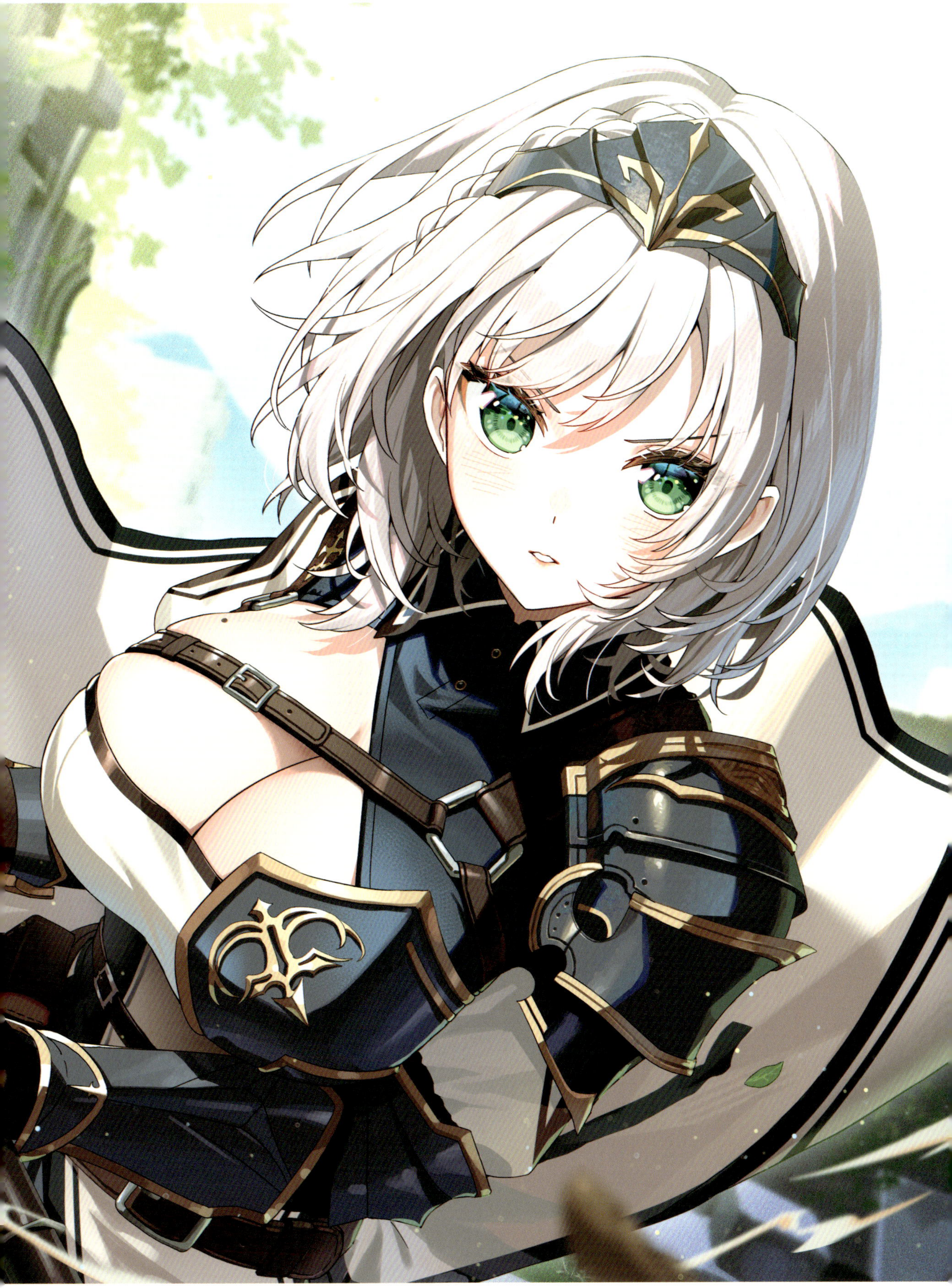

白銀ノエル4th記念グッズイラスト　© COVER

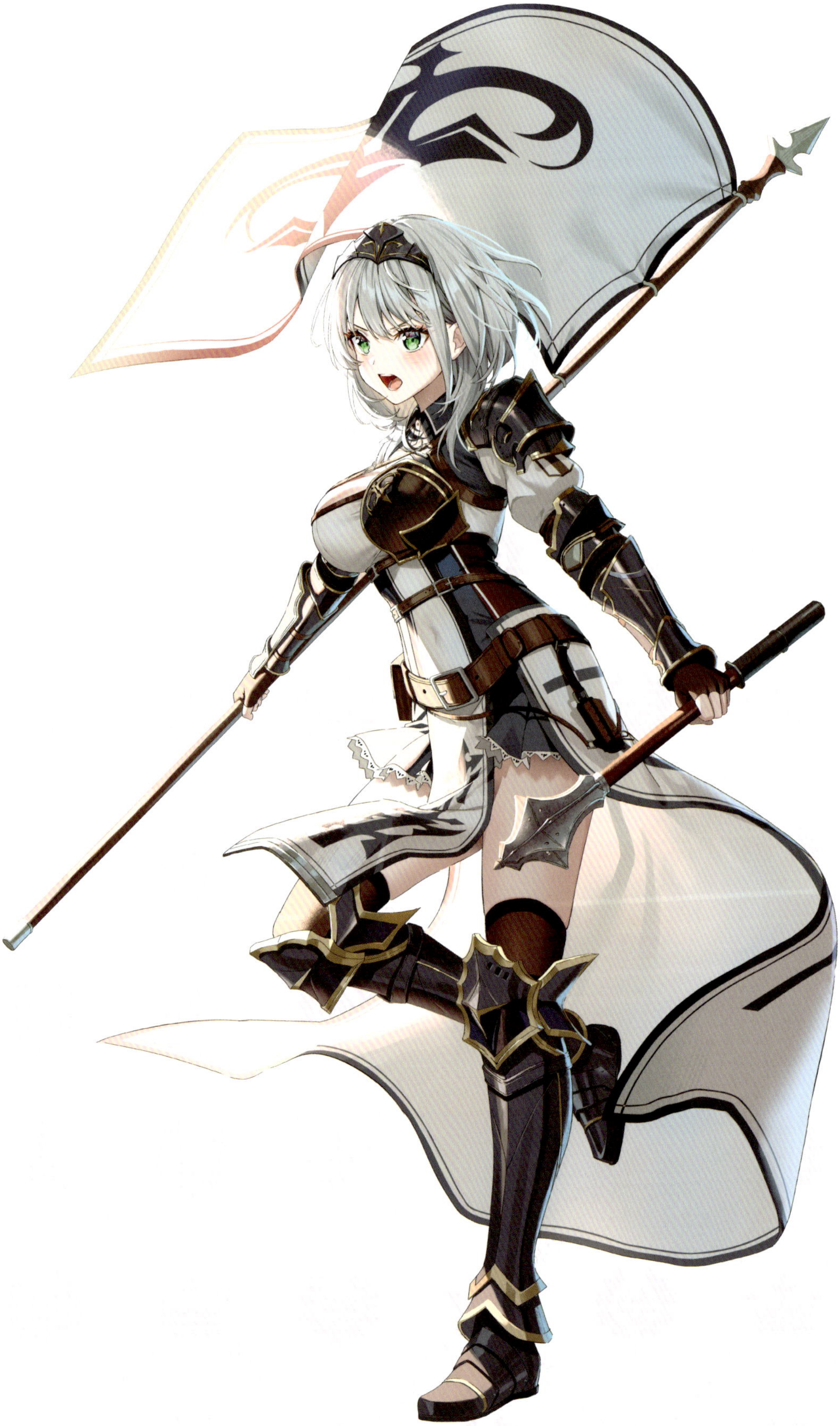

白銀ノエル 『NOEL'S GIN TONIC』明利酒類 コラボ © COVER

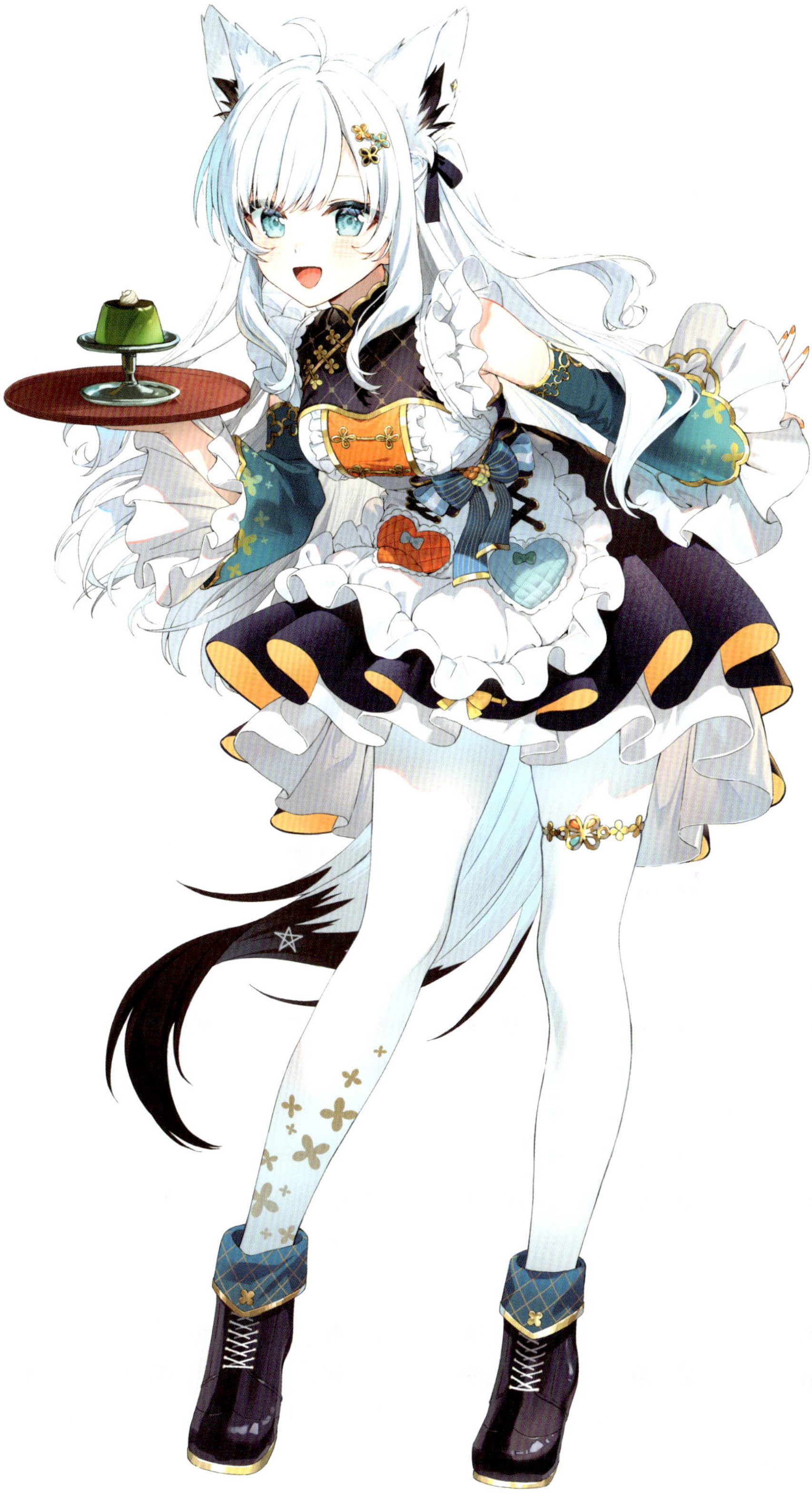

白上フブキ　フブキングダム御用達リキュール『酔う抹茶プディング』明利酒類コラボ　© COVER

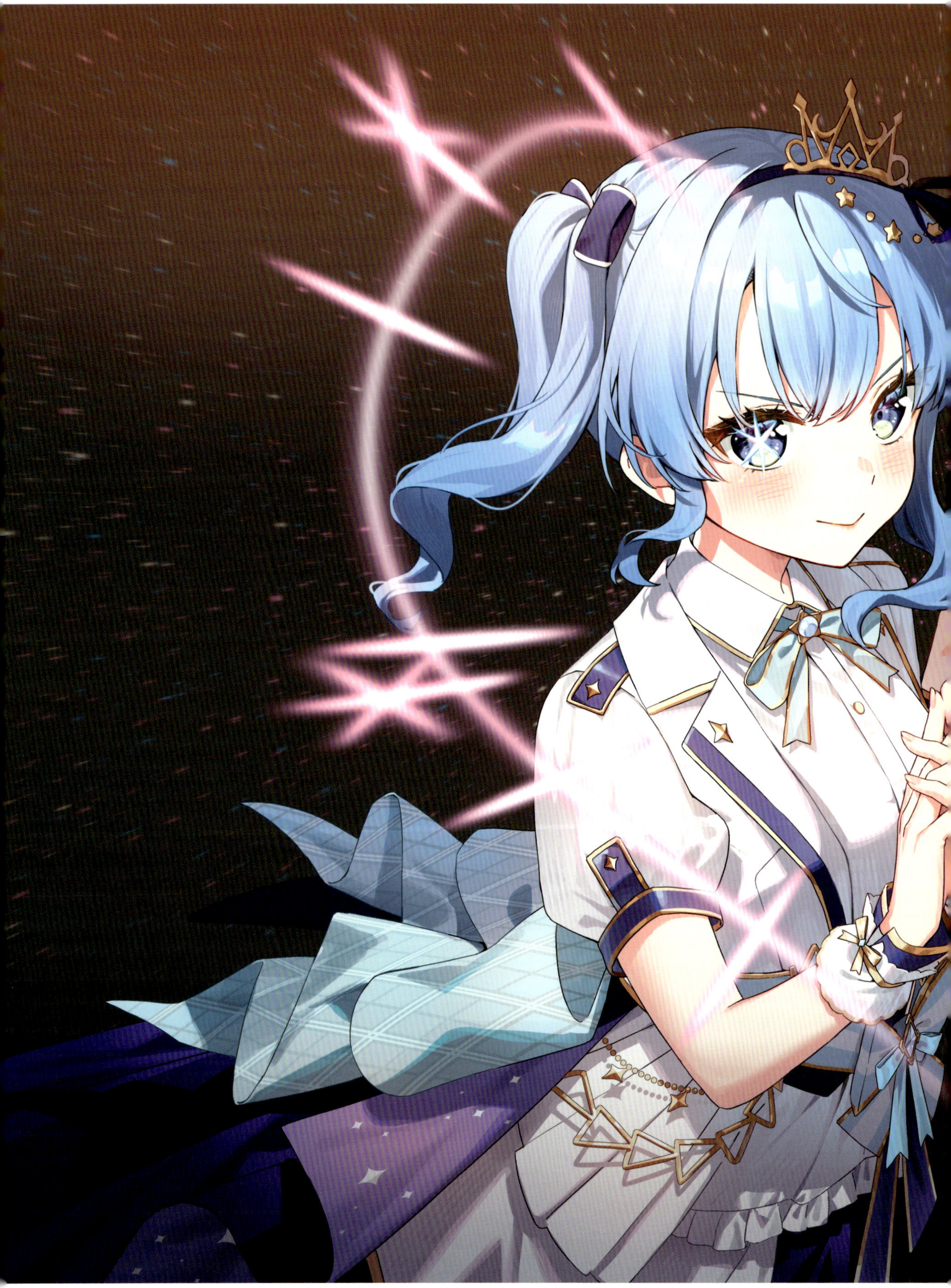

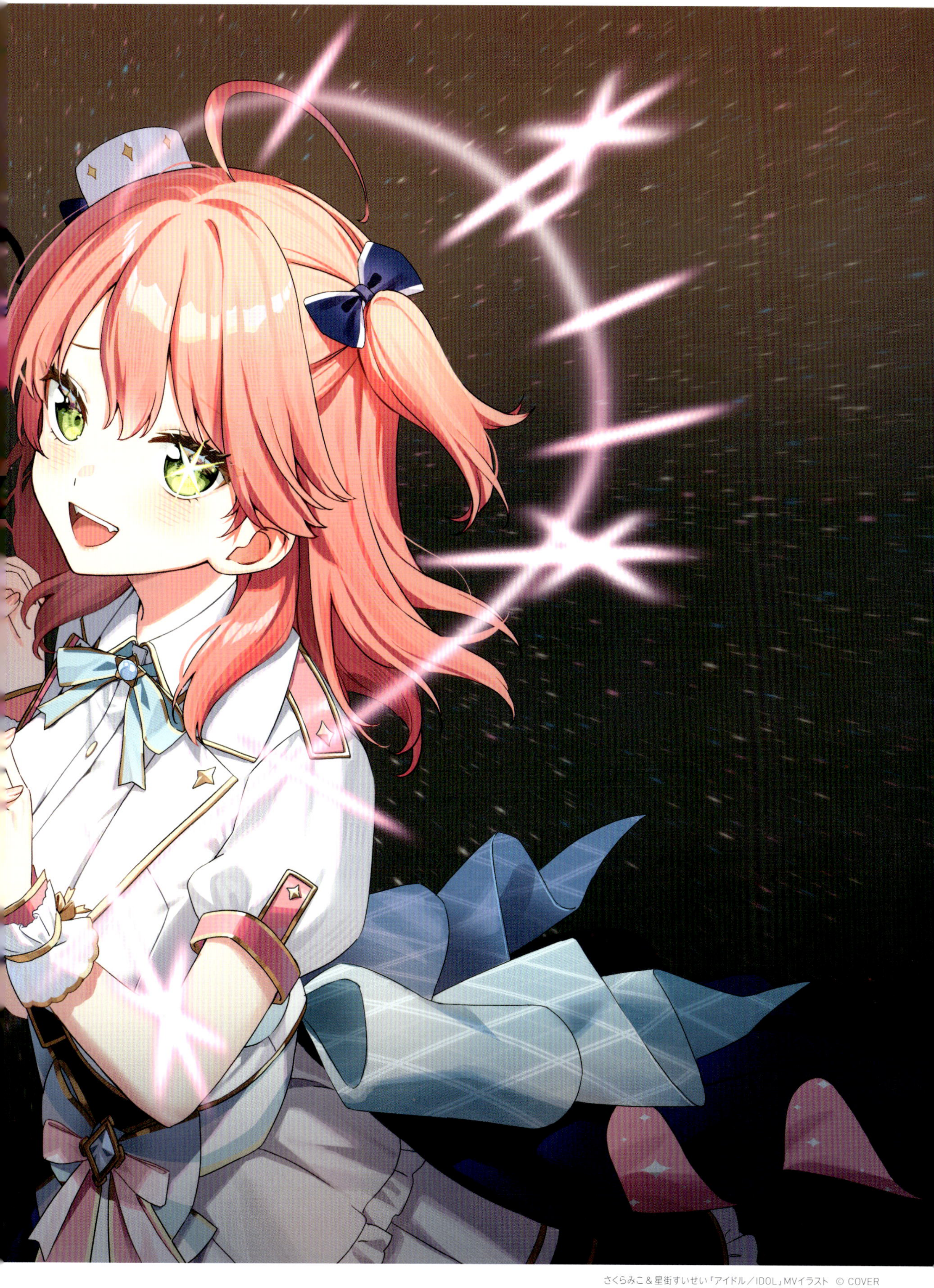

さくらみこ＆星街すいせい「アイドル／IDOL」MVイラスト　© COVER

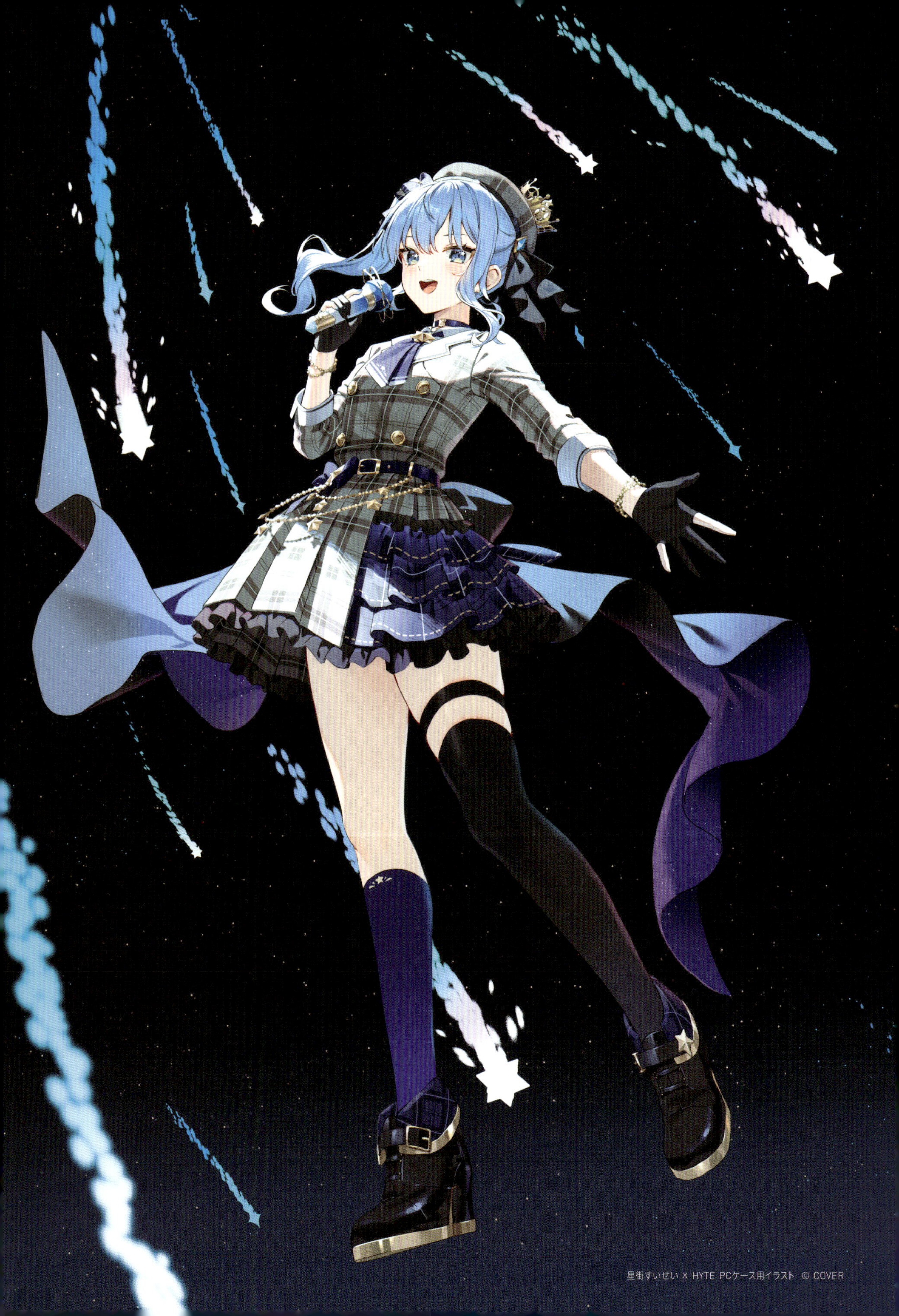

星街すいせい × HYTE PCケース用イラスト © COVER

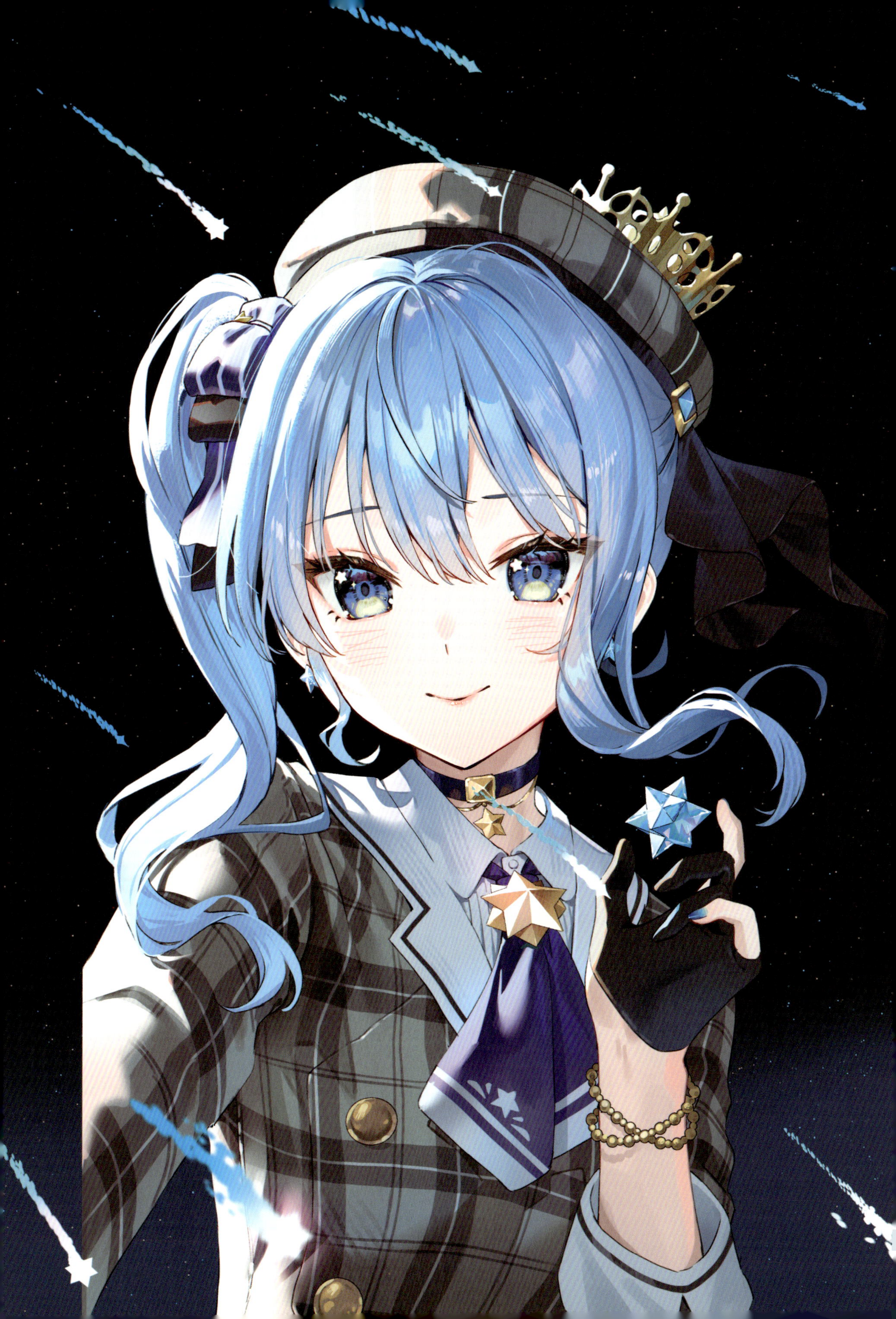

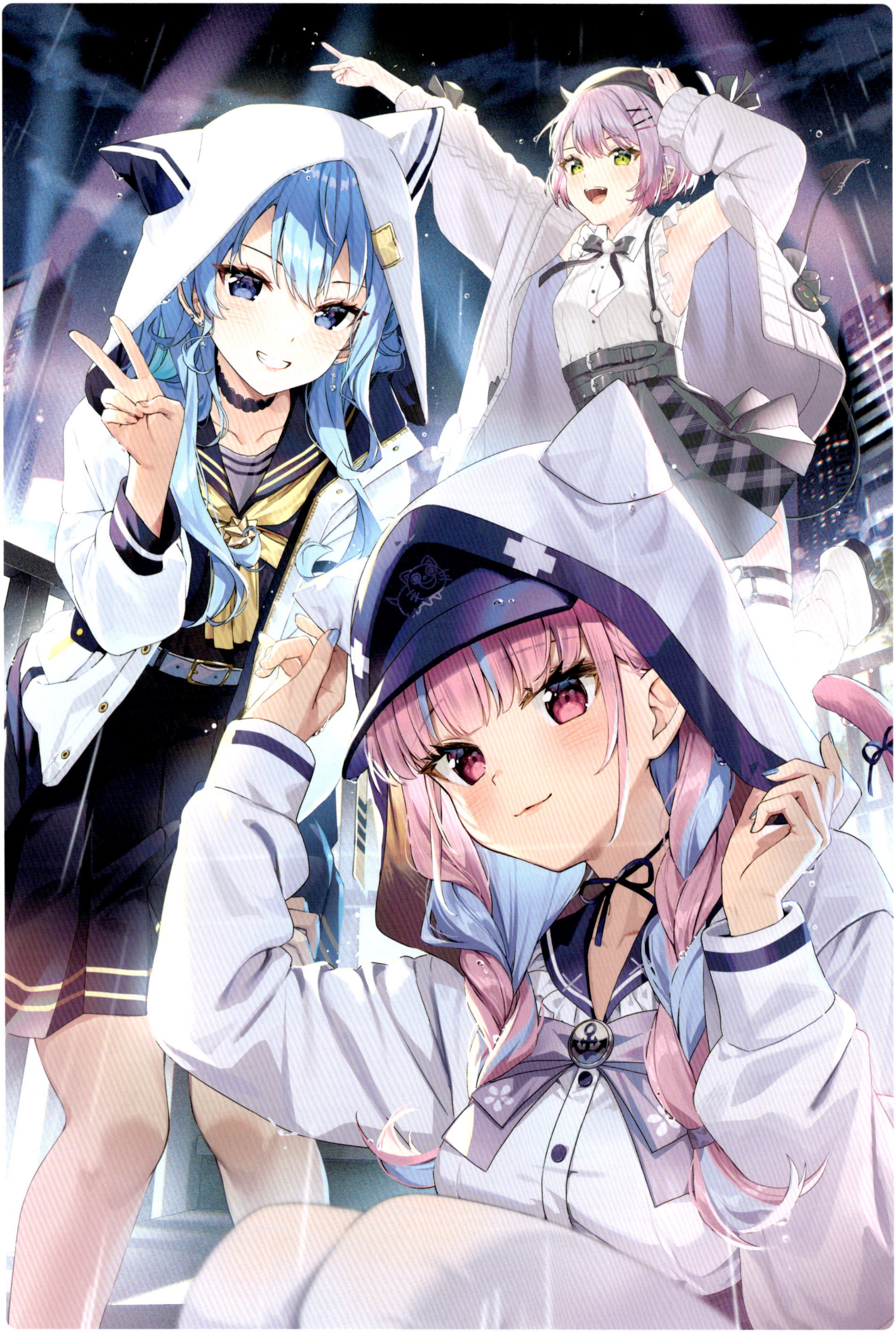

ホロライブクリエイターコンテスト2023 pixiv COLLECTION 描き下ろしイラスト © COVER

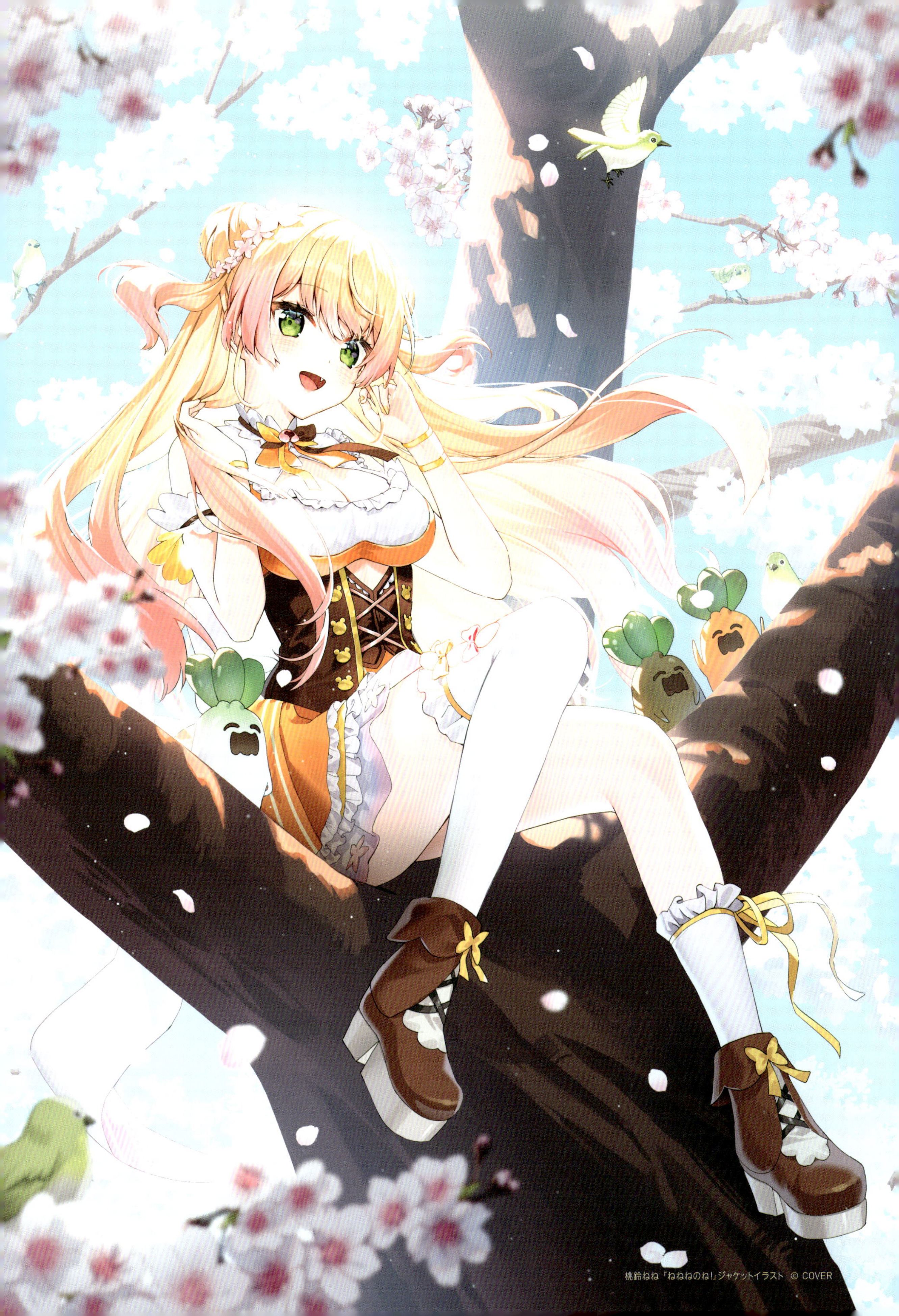

桃鈴ねね『ねねねのね!』ジャケットイラスト © COVER

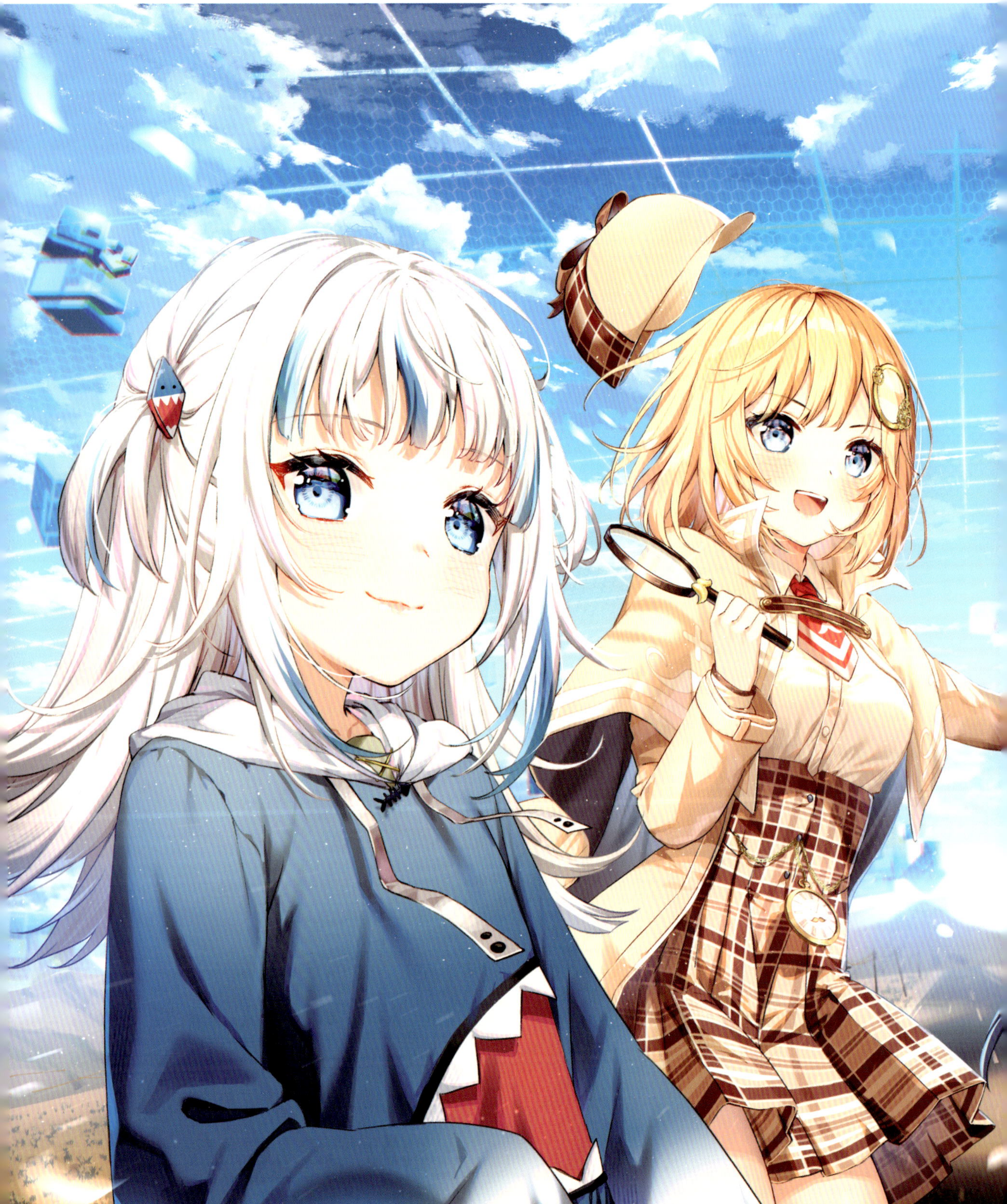

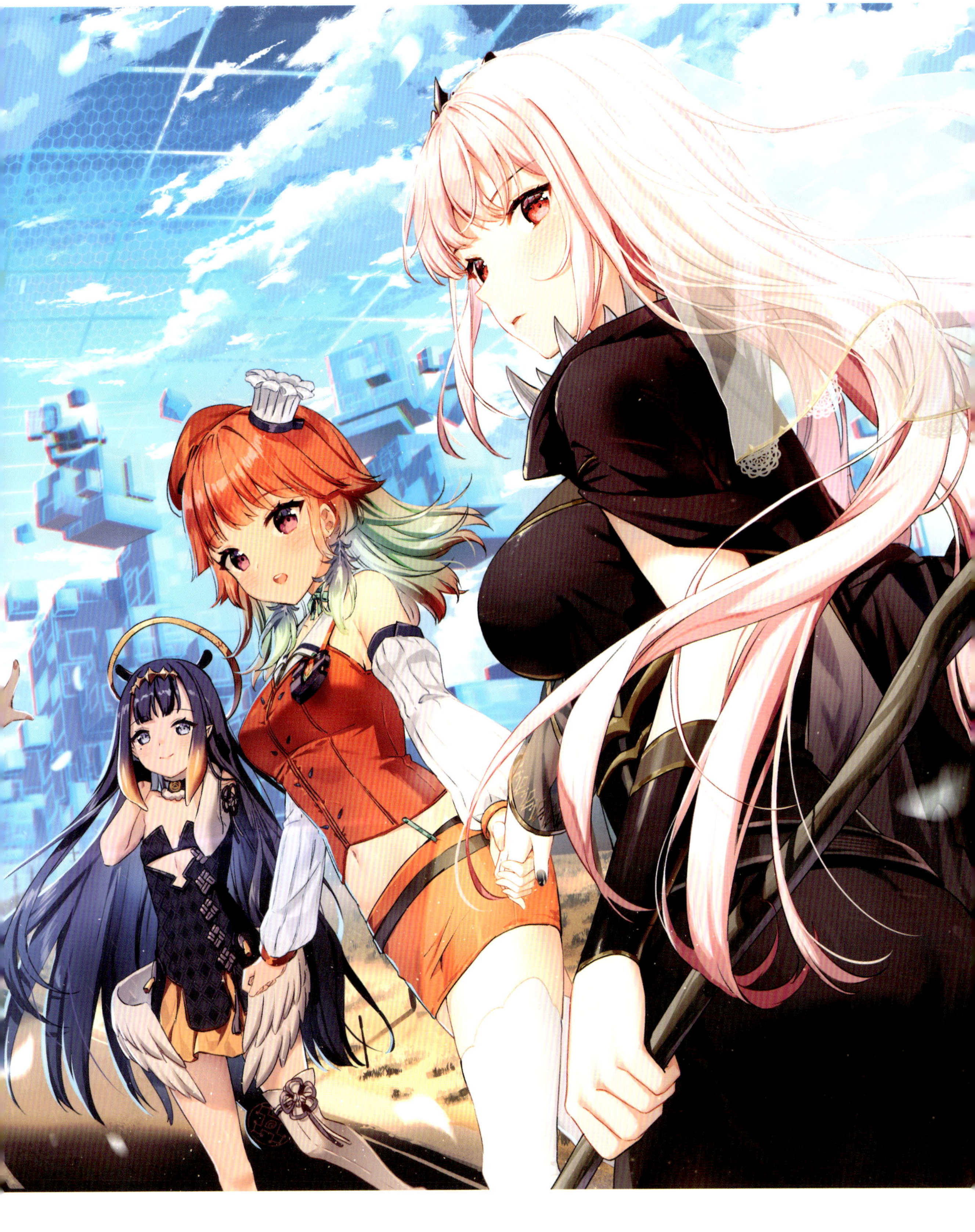

Take Me Home, Country Roads - hololive English -Myth- Cover MVイラスト © COVER

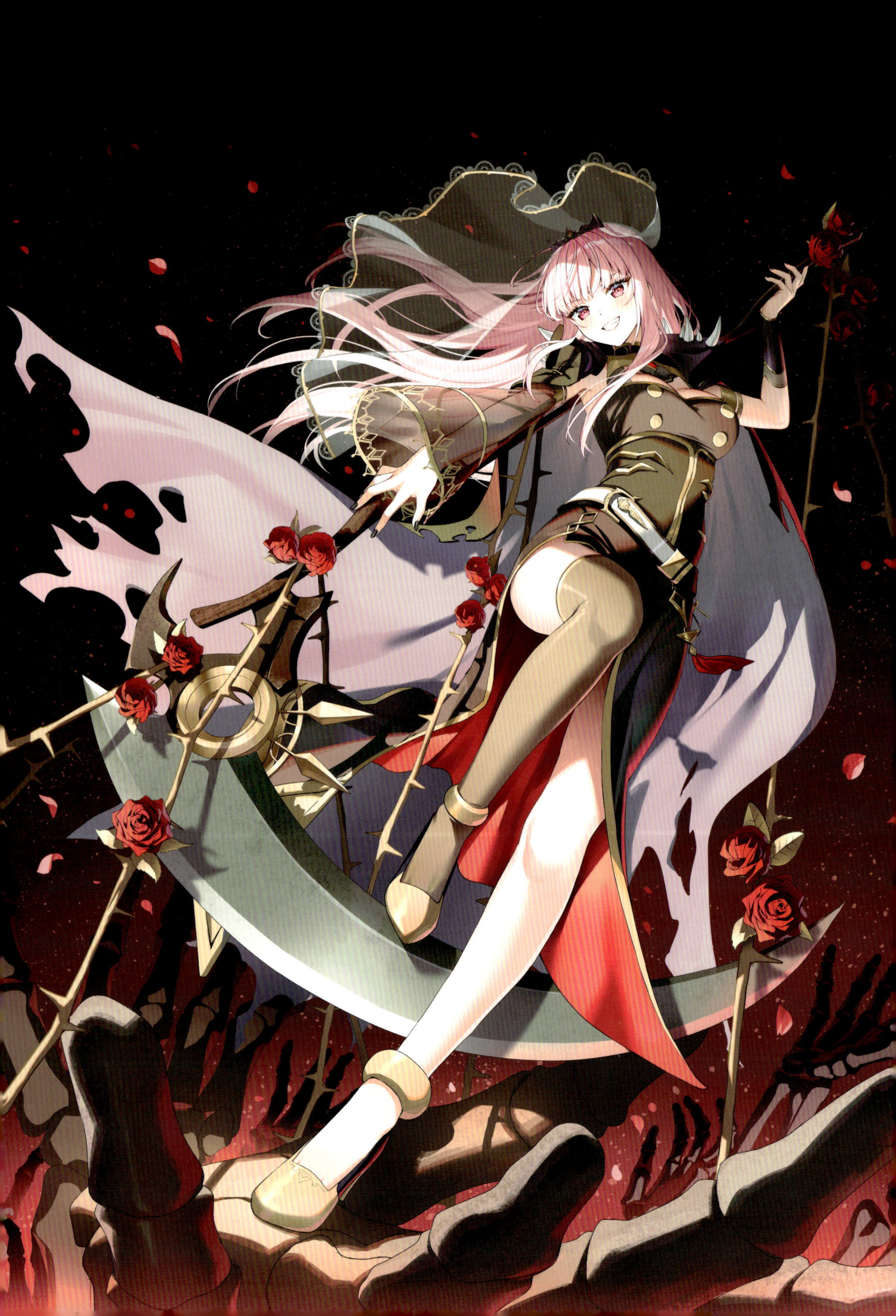

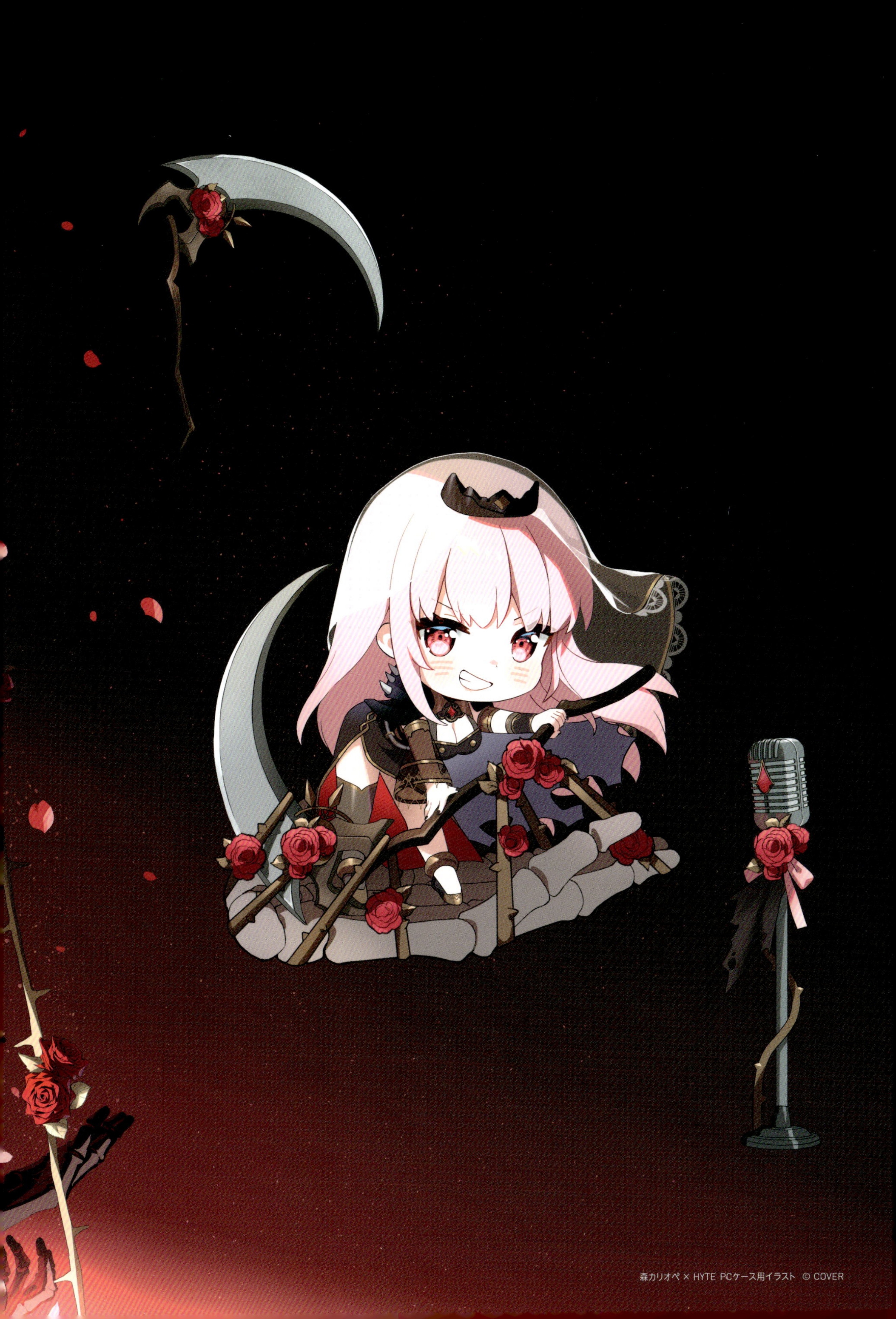

森カリオペ × HYTE PCケース用イラスト © COVER

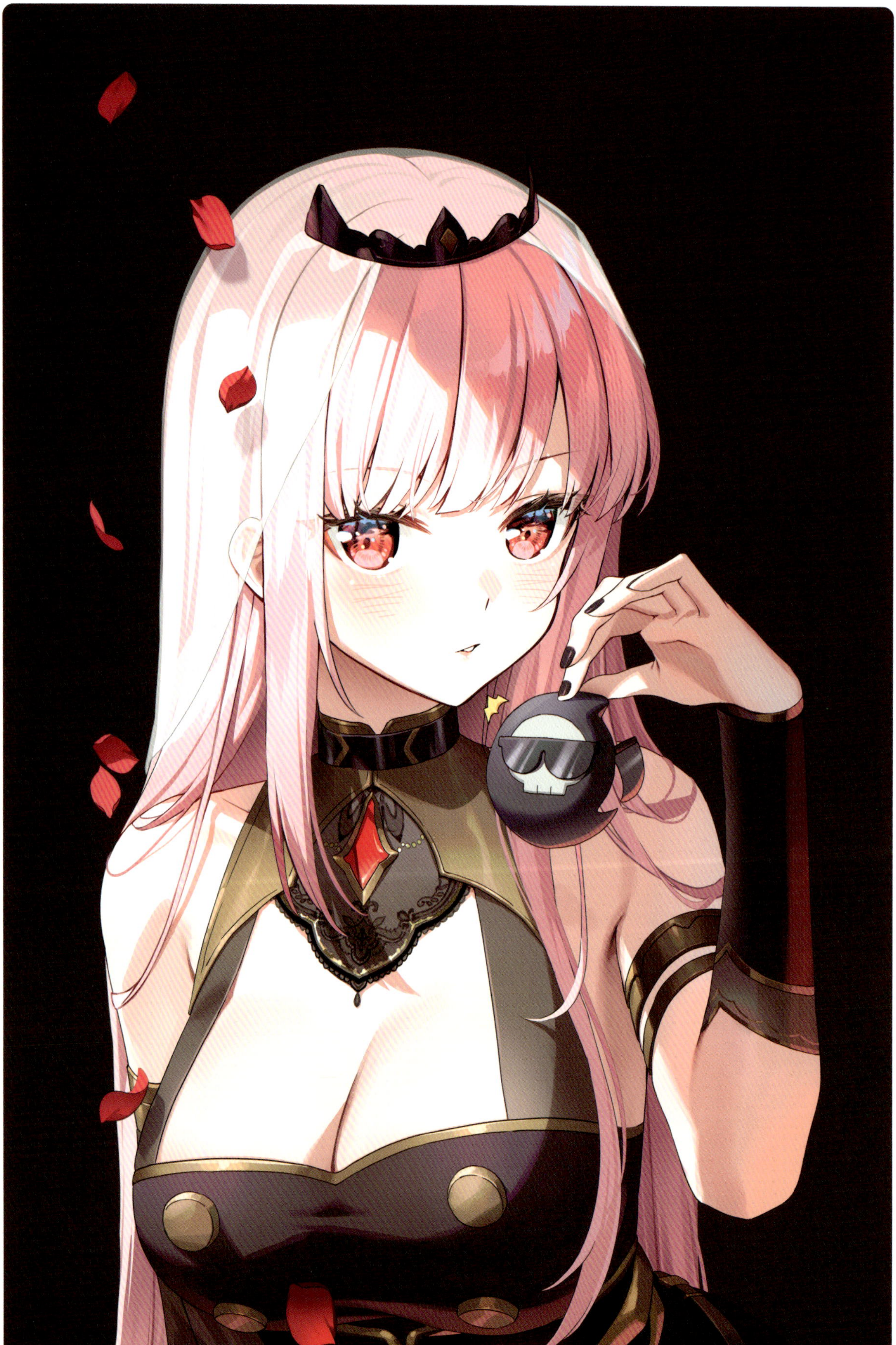

森カリオペ × HYTE PCケース用イラスト © COVER

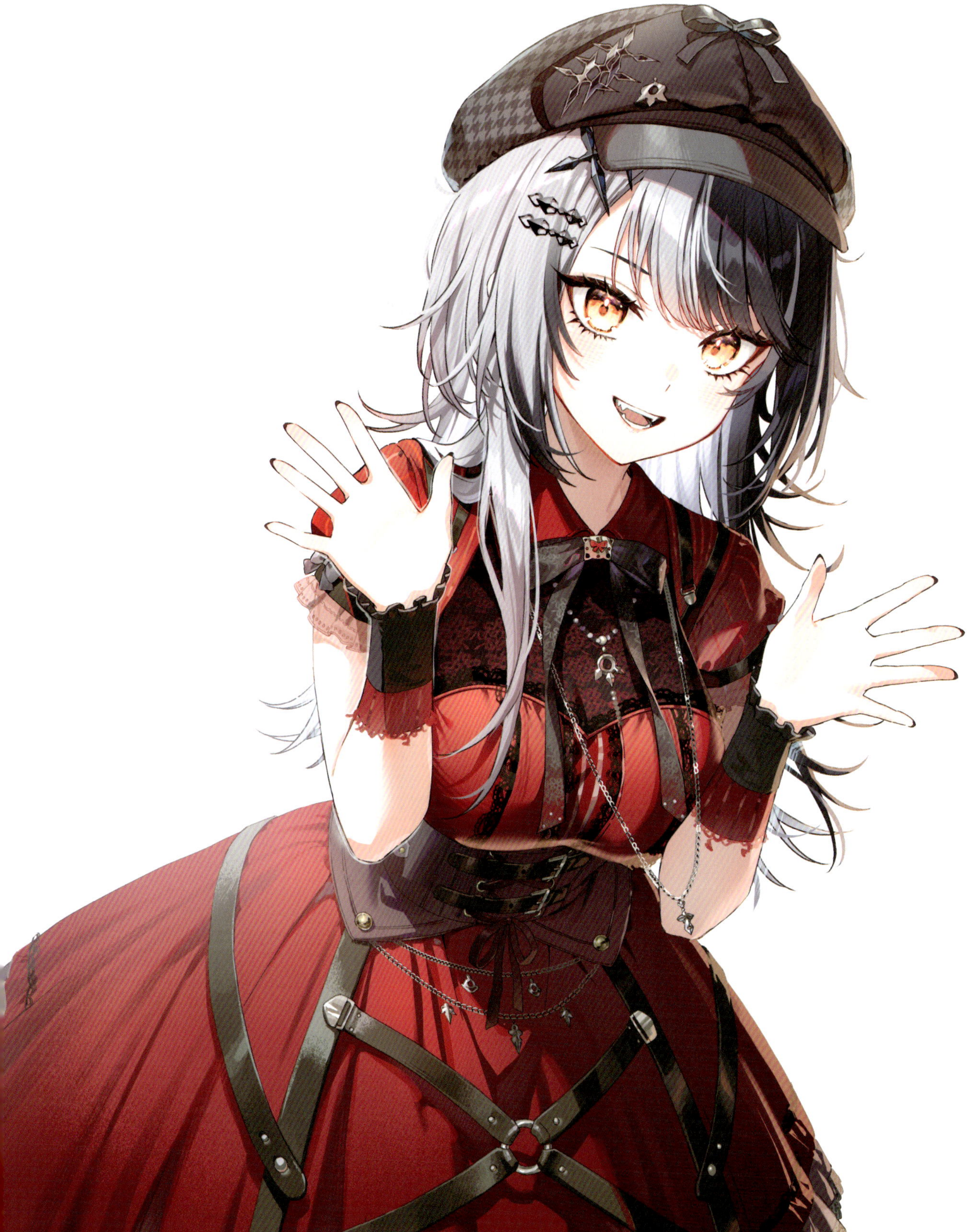

シオリ・ノヴェラ　新衣装グッズイラスト　© COVER

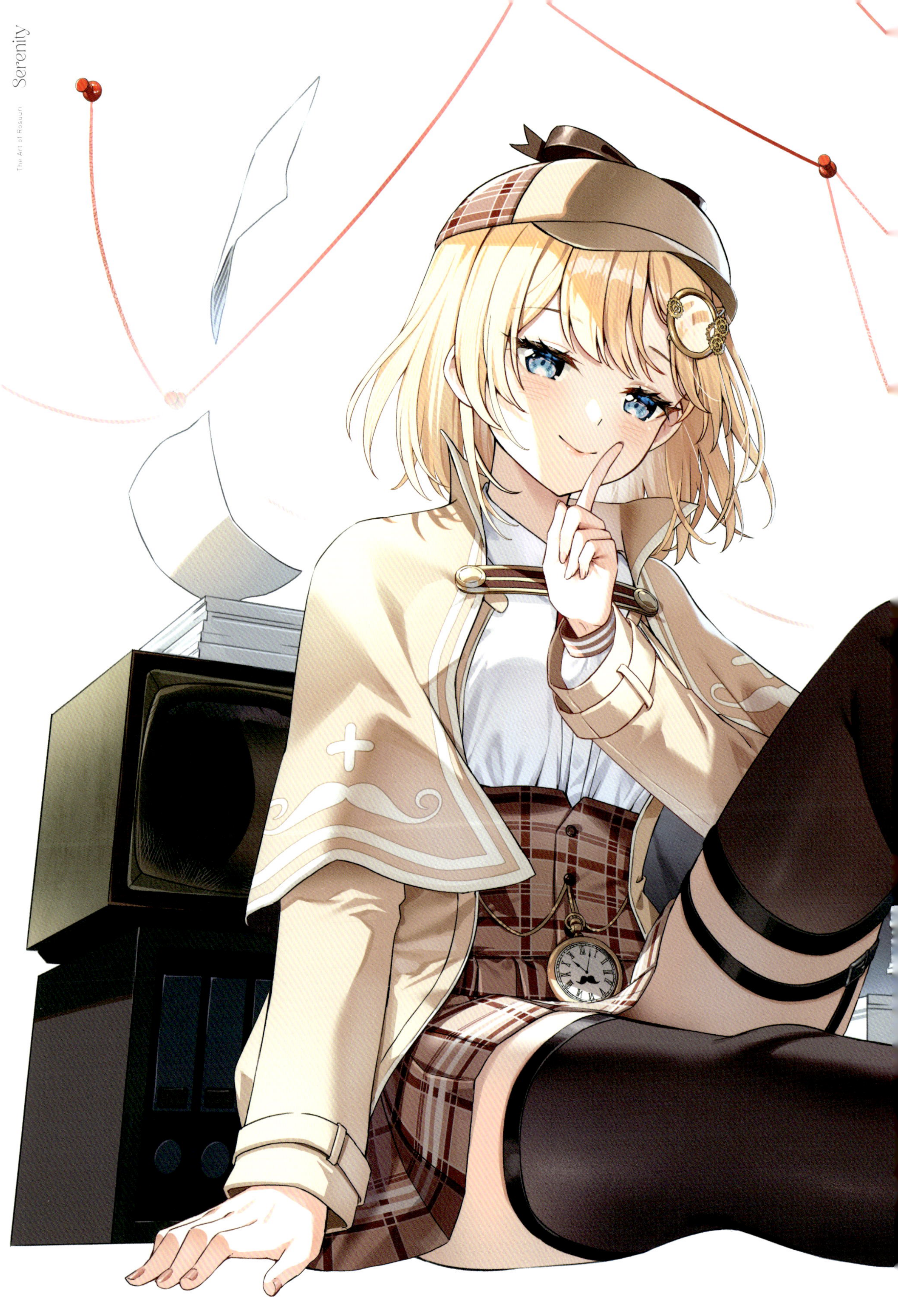

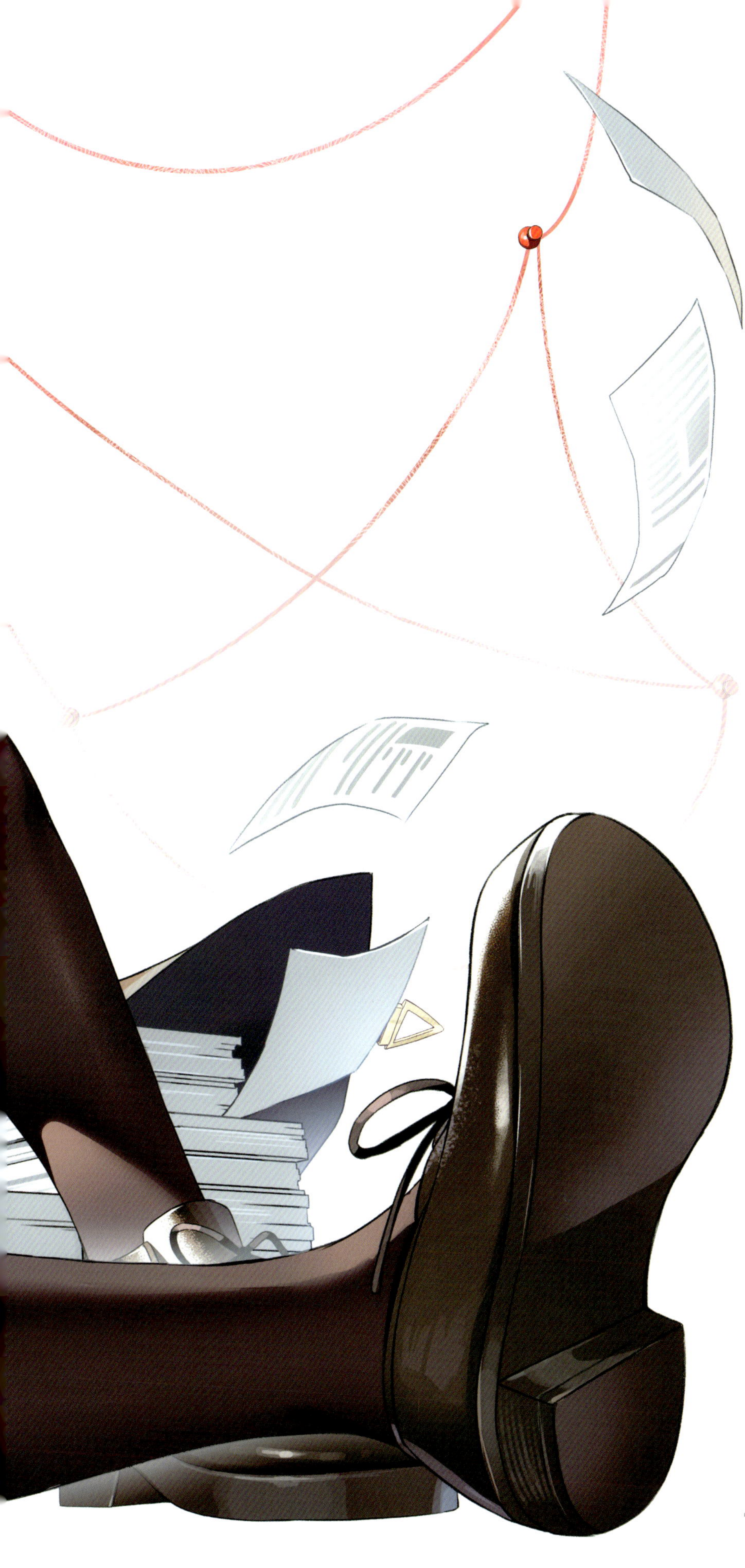

ワトソン・アメリア × HYTE PCケース用イラスト　© COVER

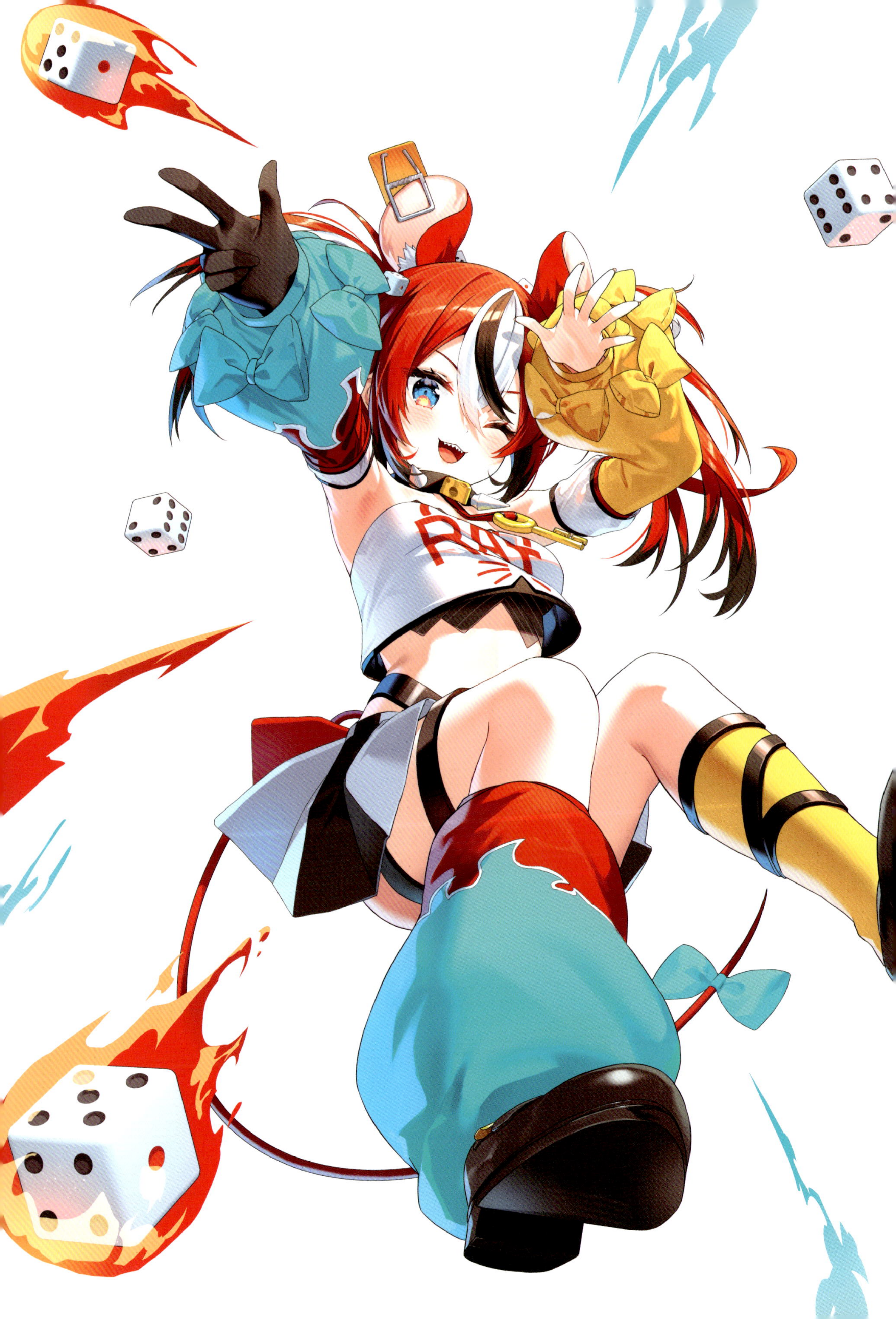

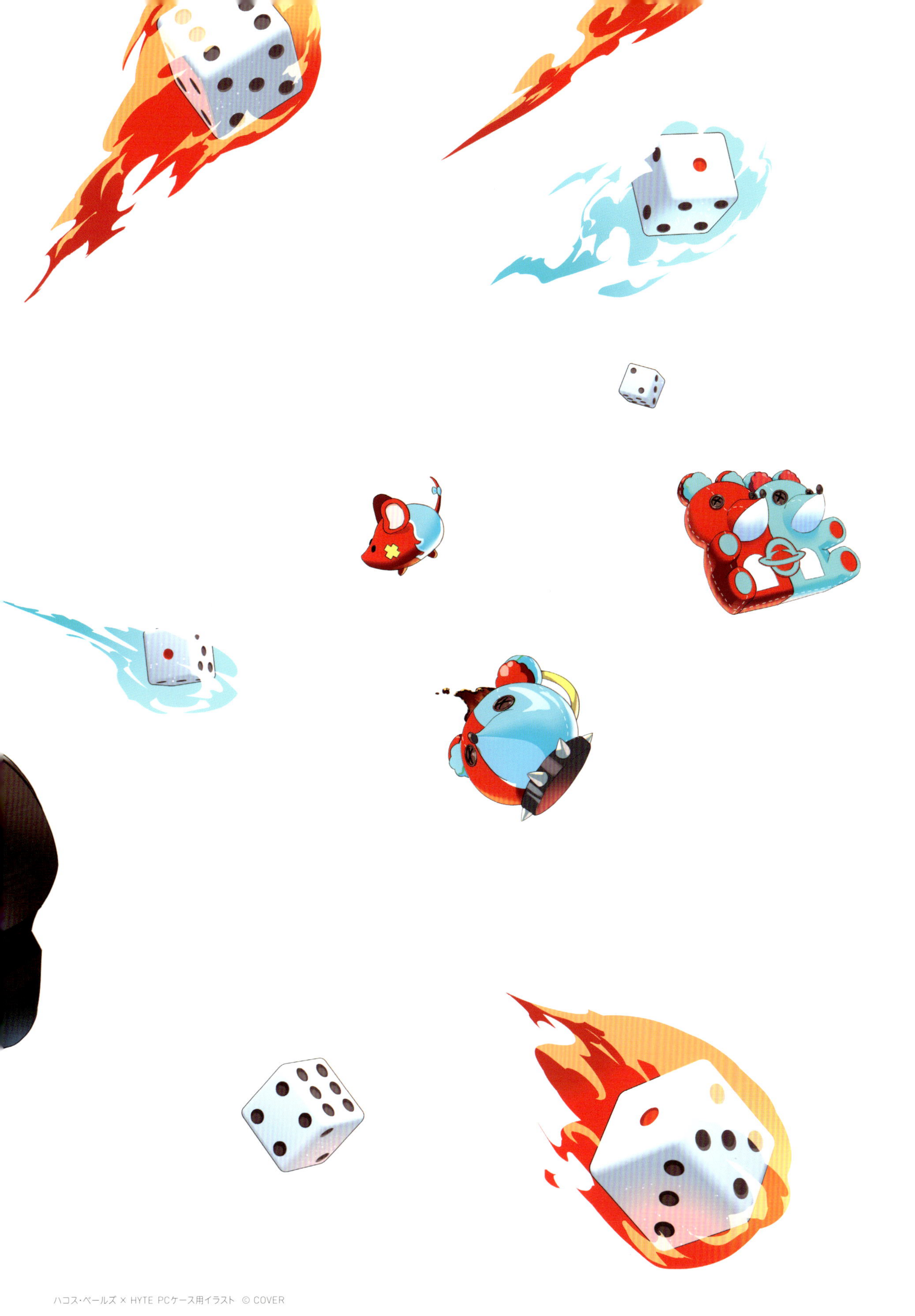

ハコス・ベールズ × HYTE PCケース用イラスト © COVER

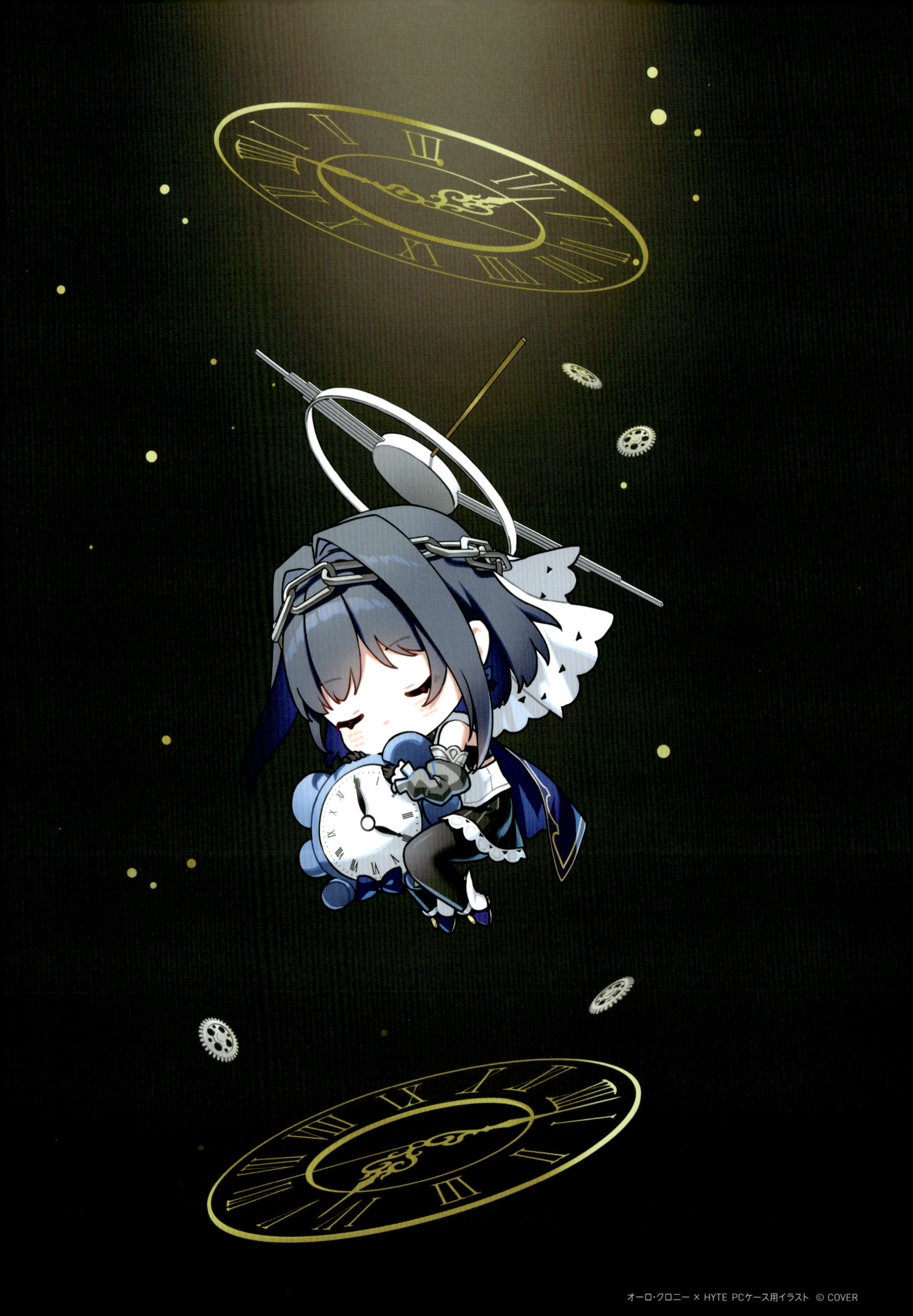

オーロ・クロニー × HYTE PCケース用イラスト

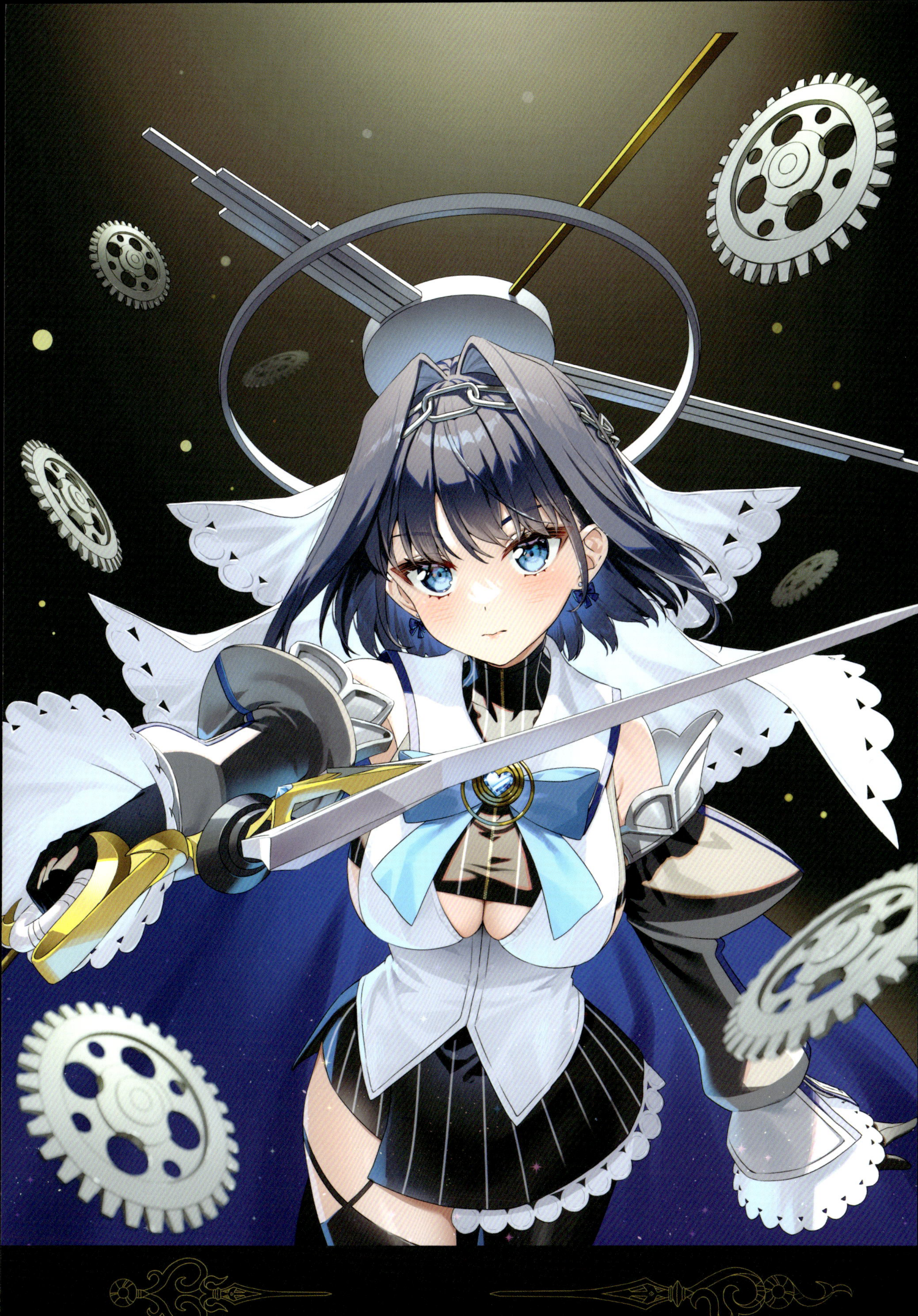

Serenity

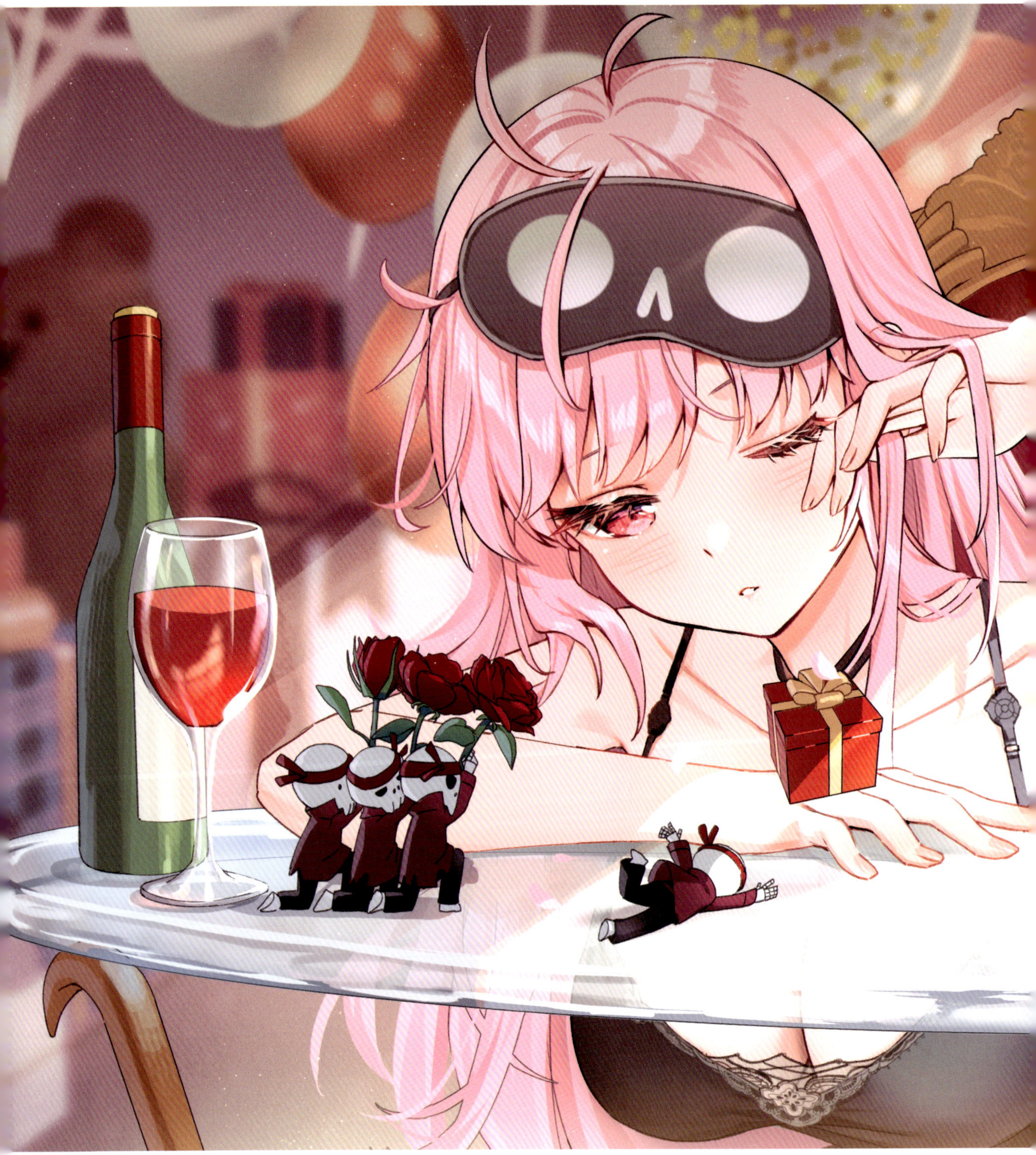

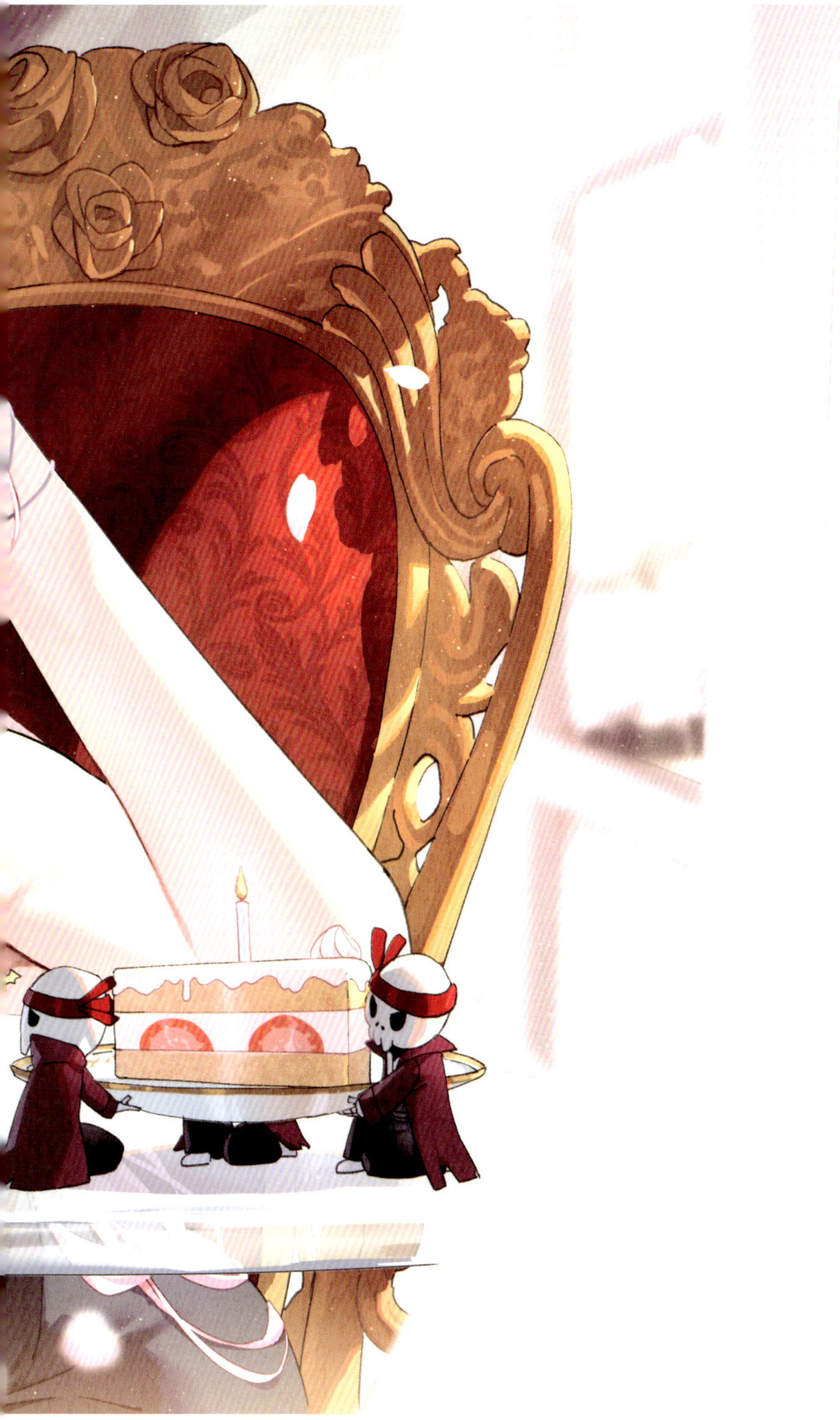

森カリオペ　メンバーシップ壁紙　© COVER

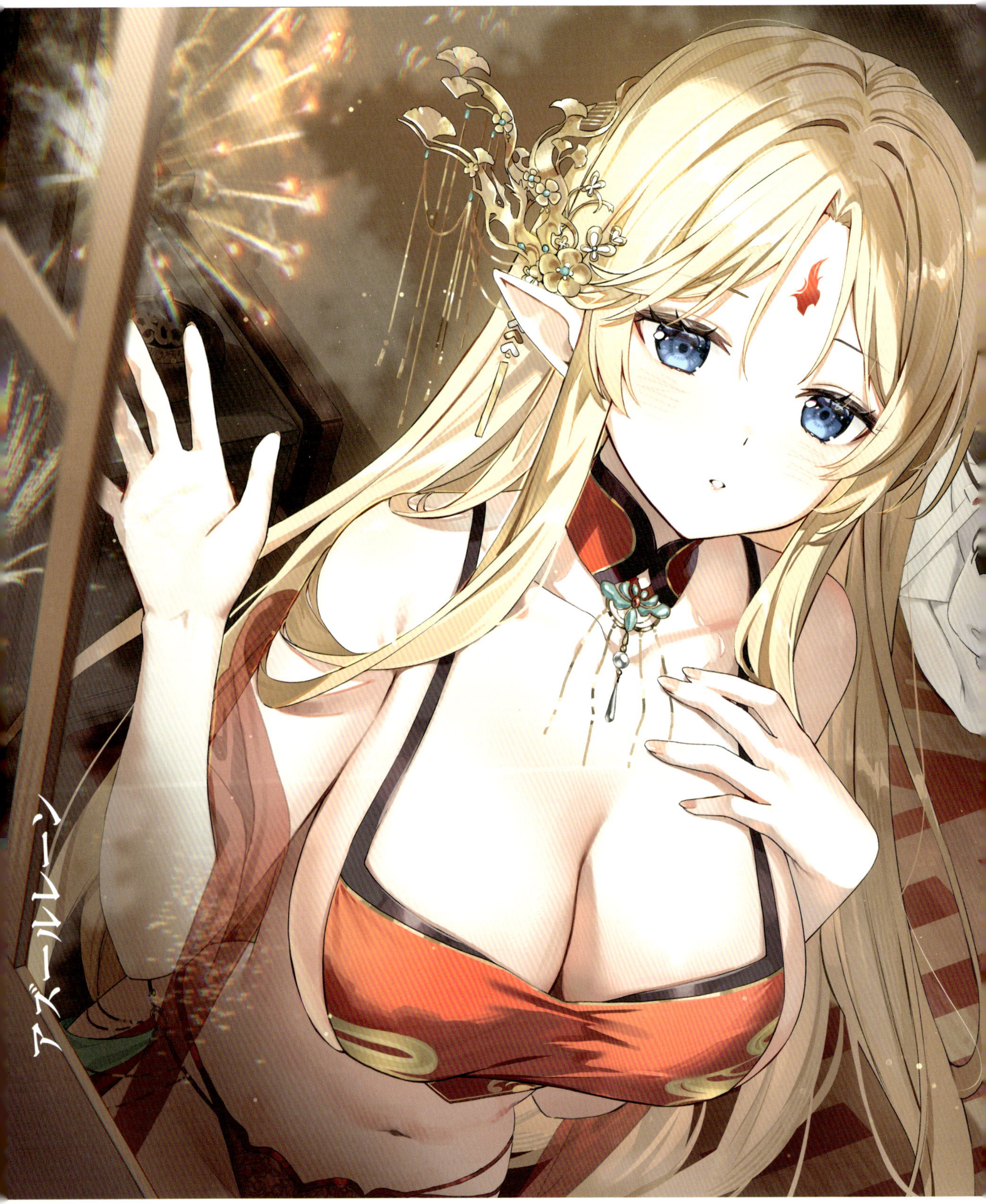
アズールレーン

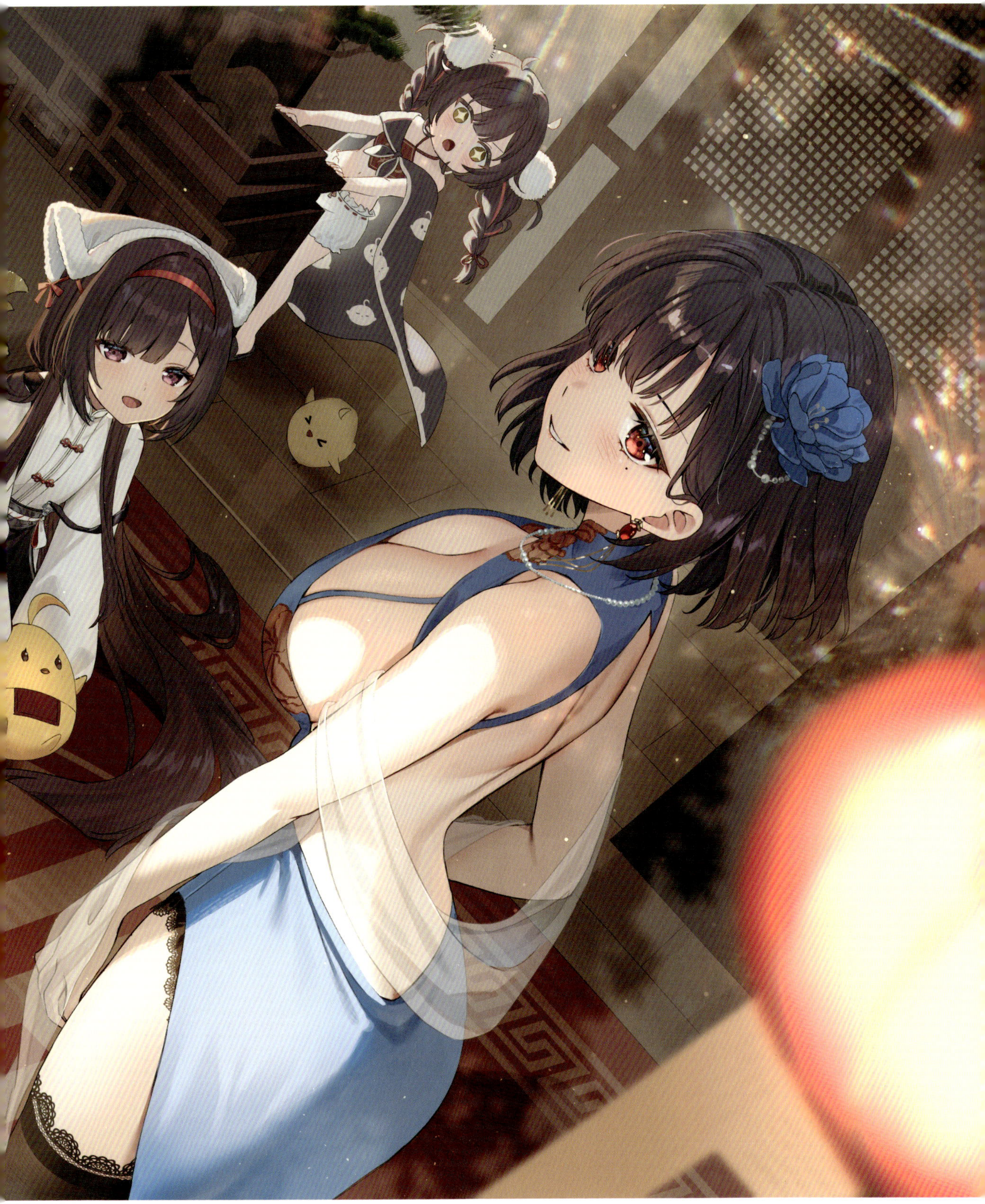

2025 New Year Loading Screen Illustration

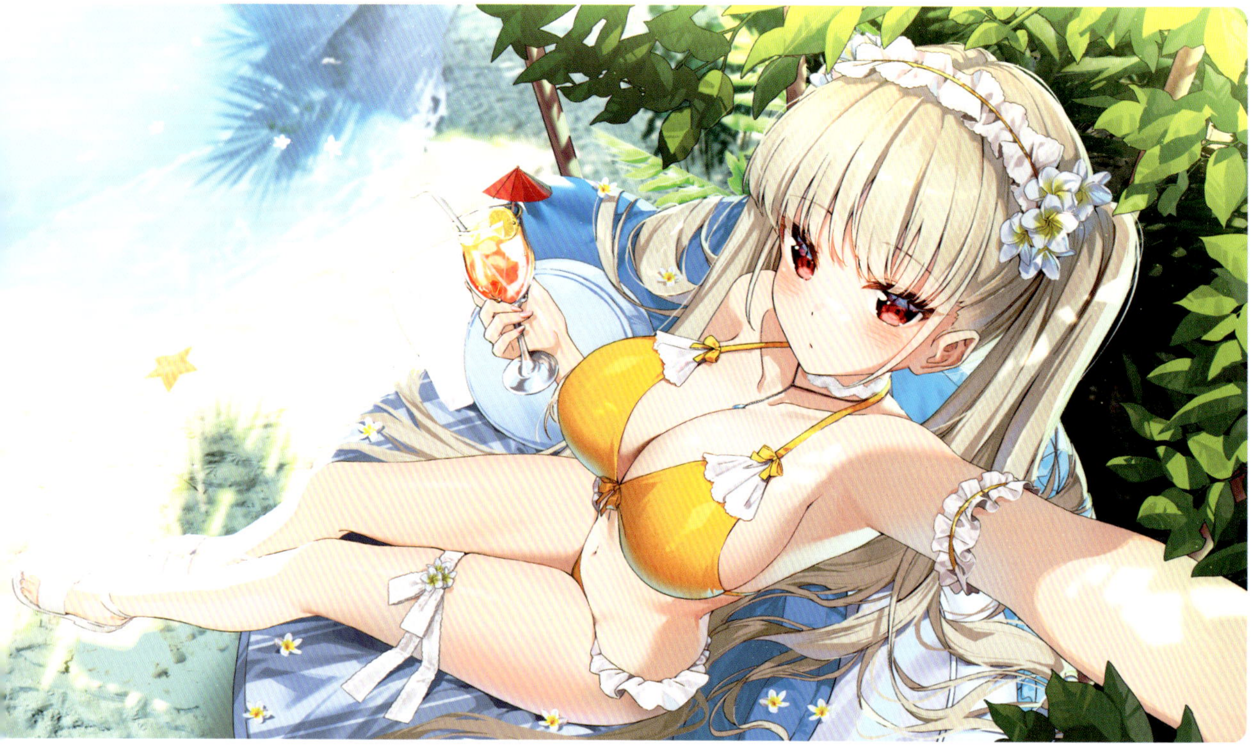

Azur Lane Third Anniversary Art Collection

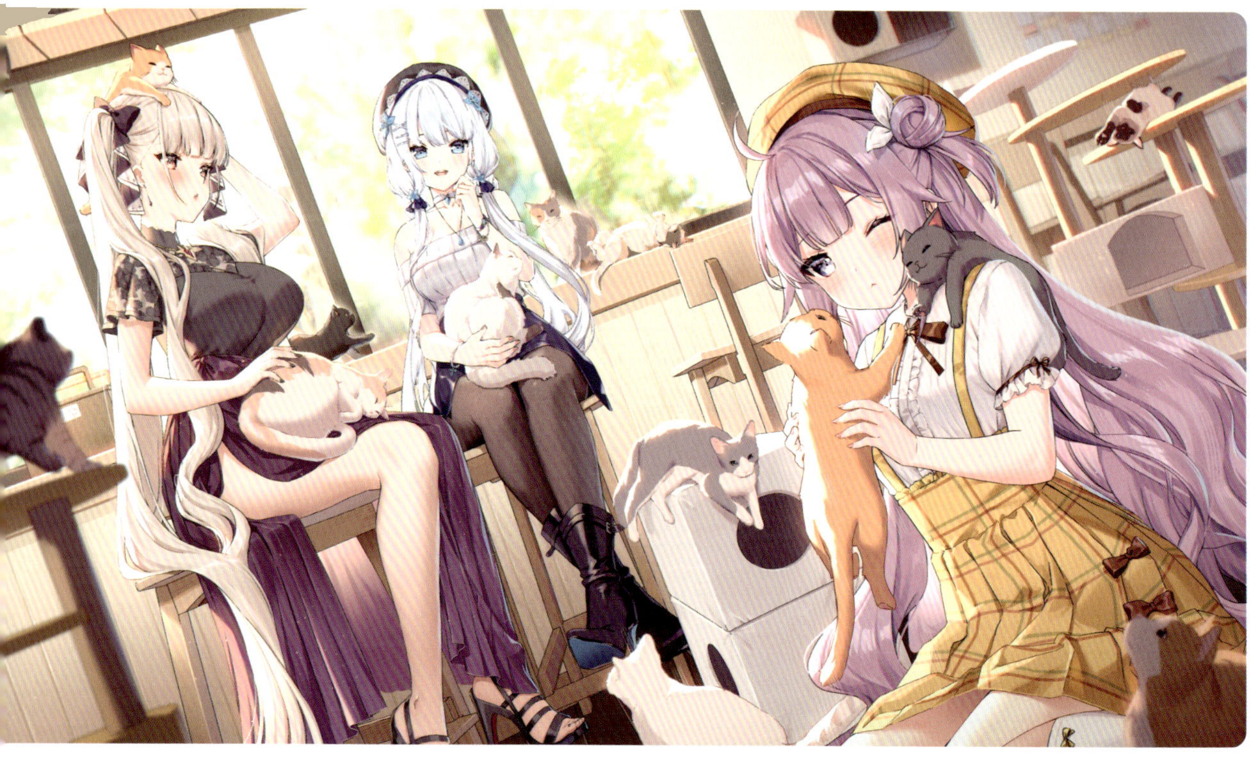

Azur Lane Fourth Anniversary Art Collection

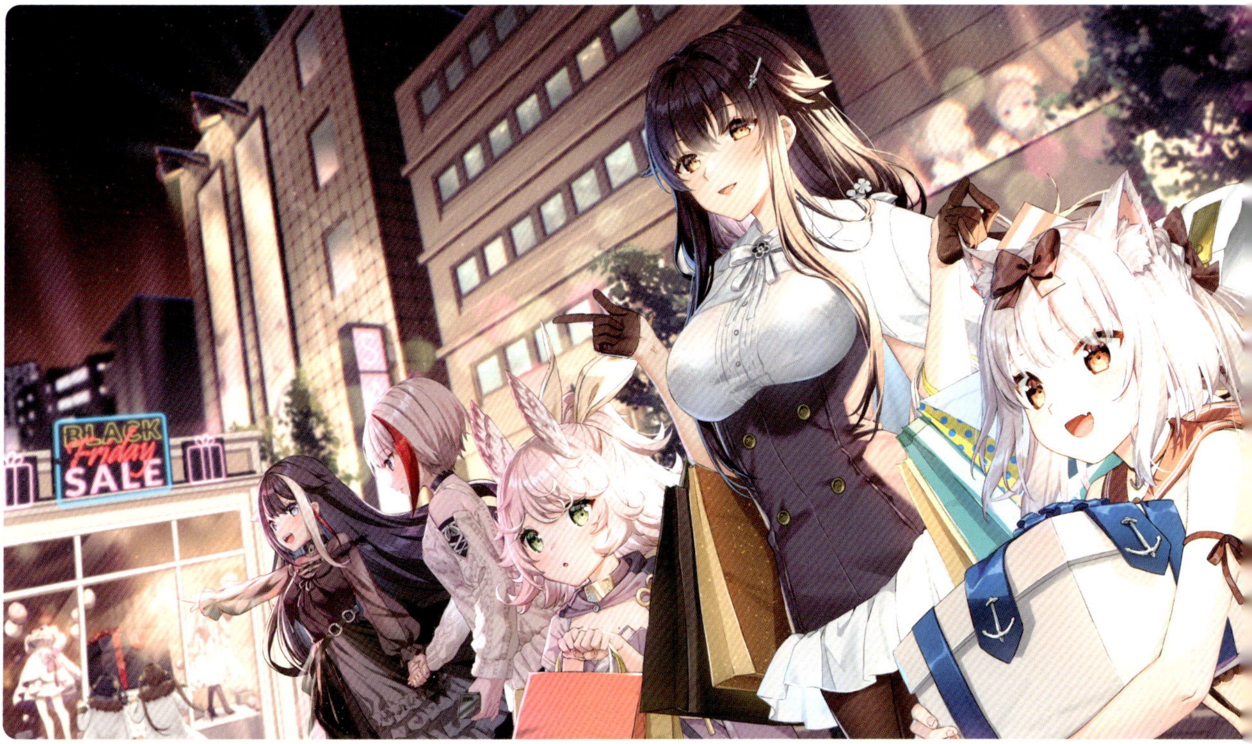

Azur Lane Black Friday Login Screen

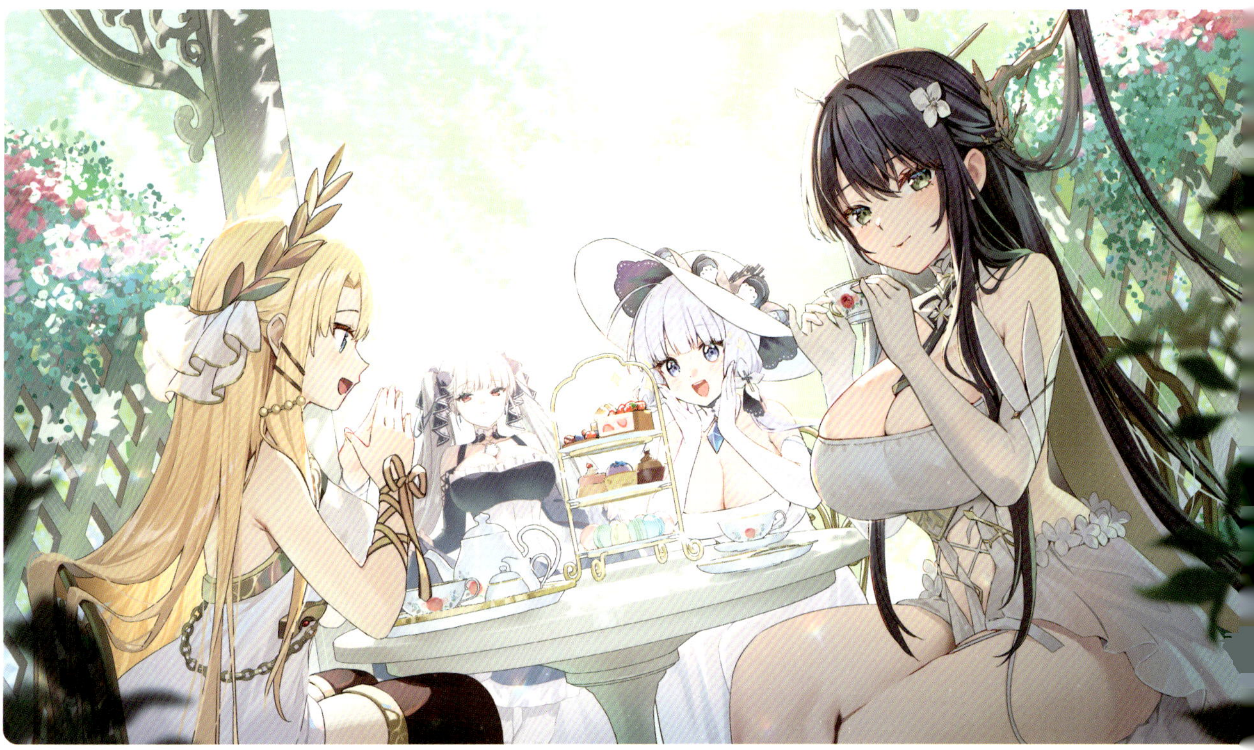

Azur Lane Fifth Anniversary Art Collection

Serenity

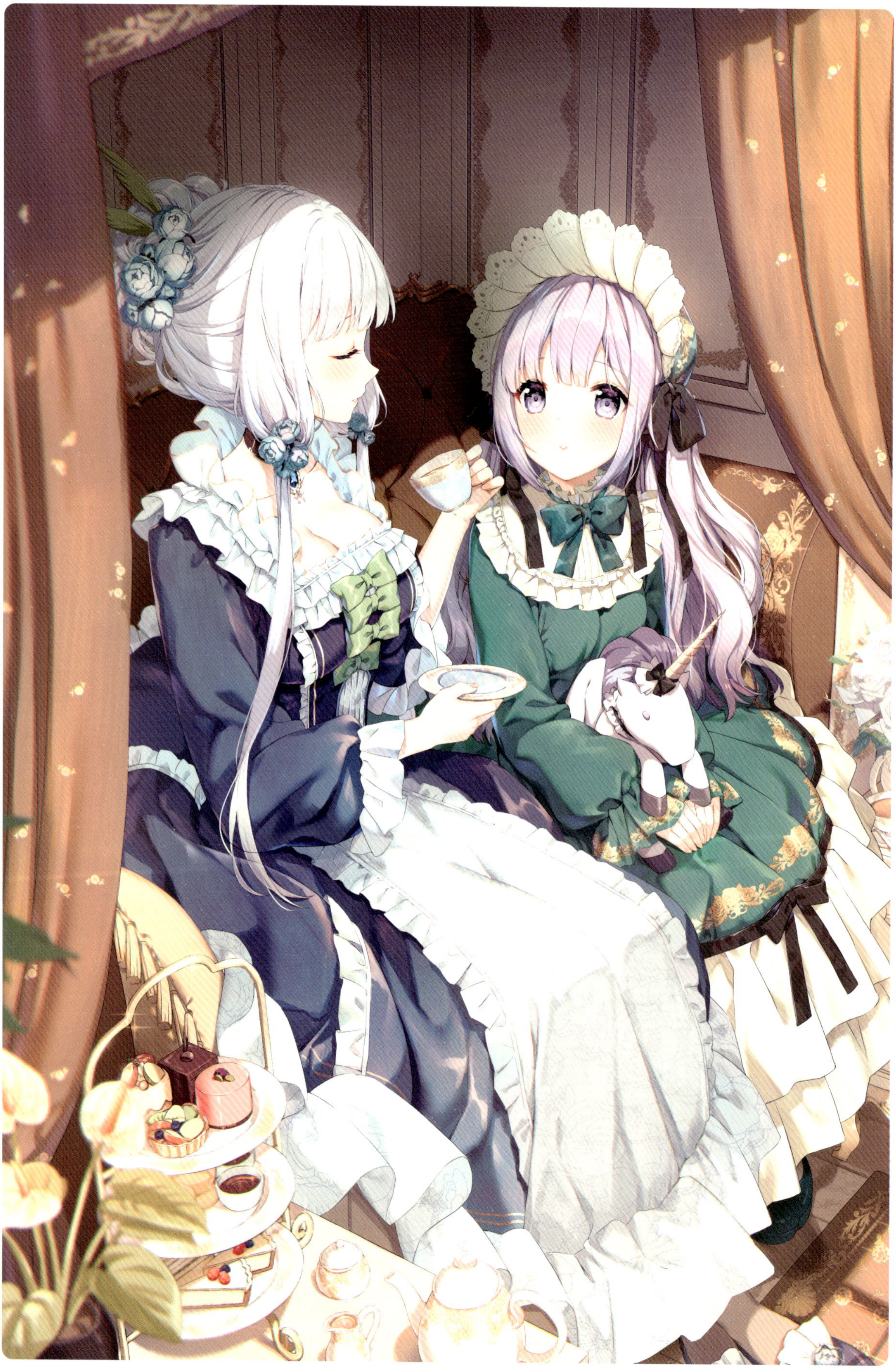

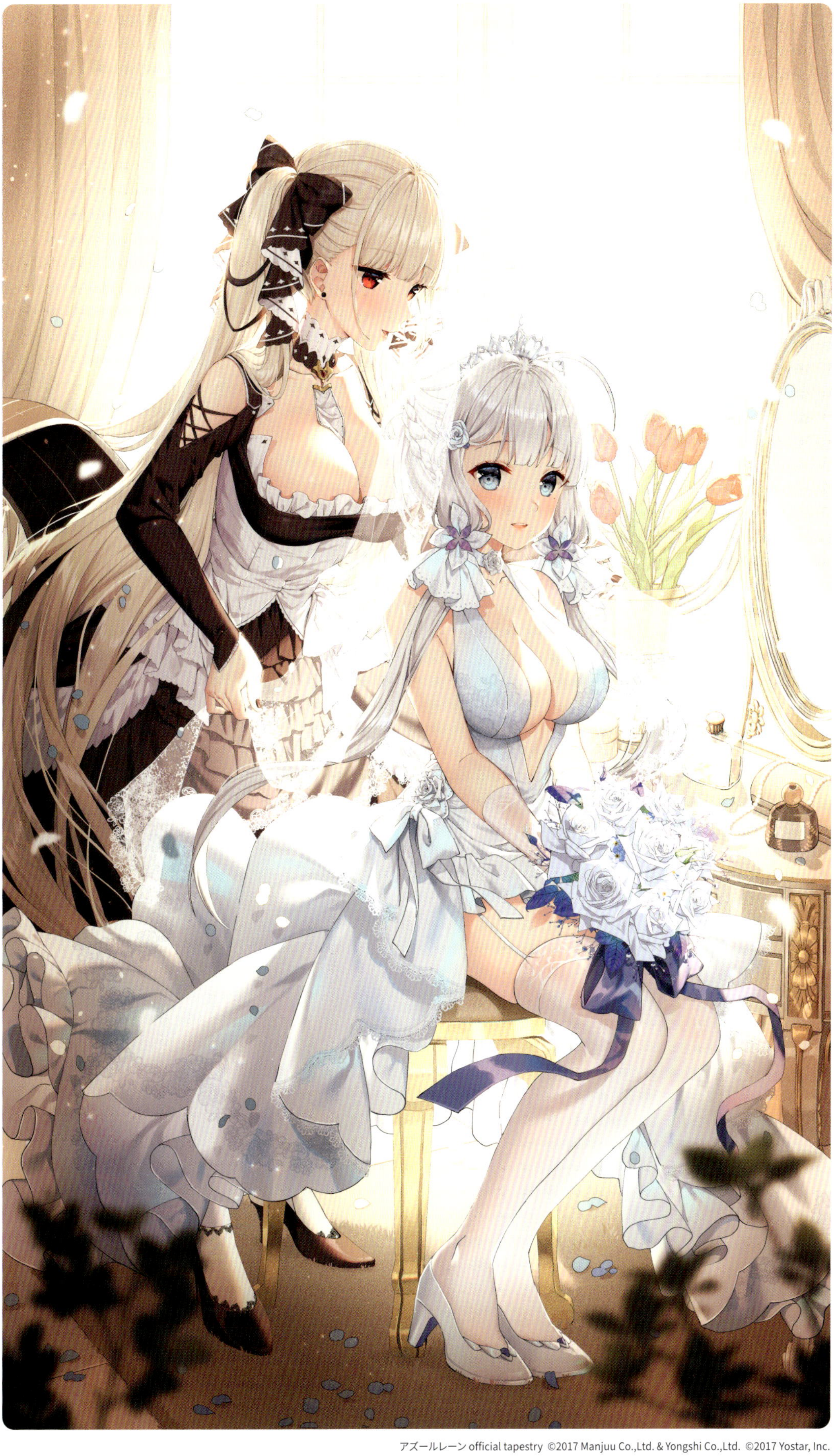

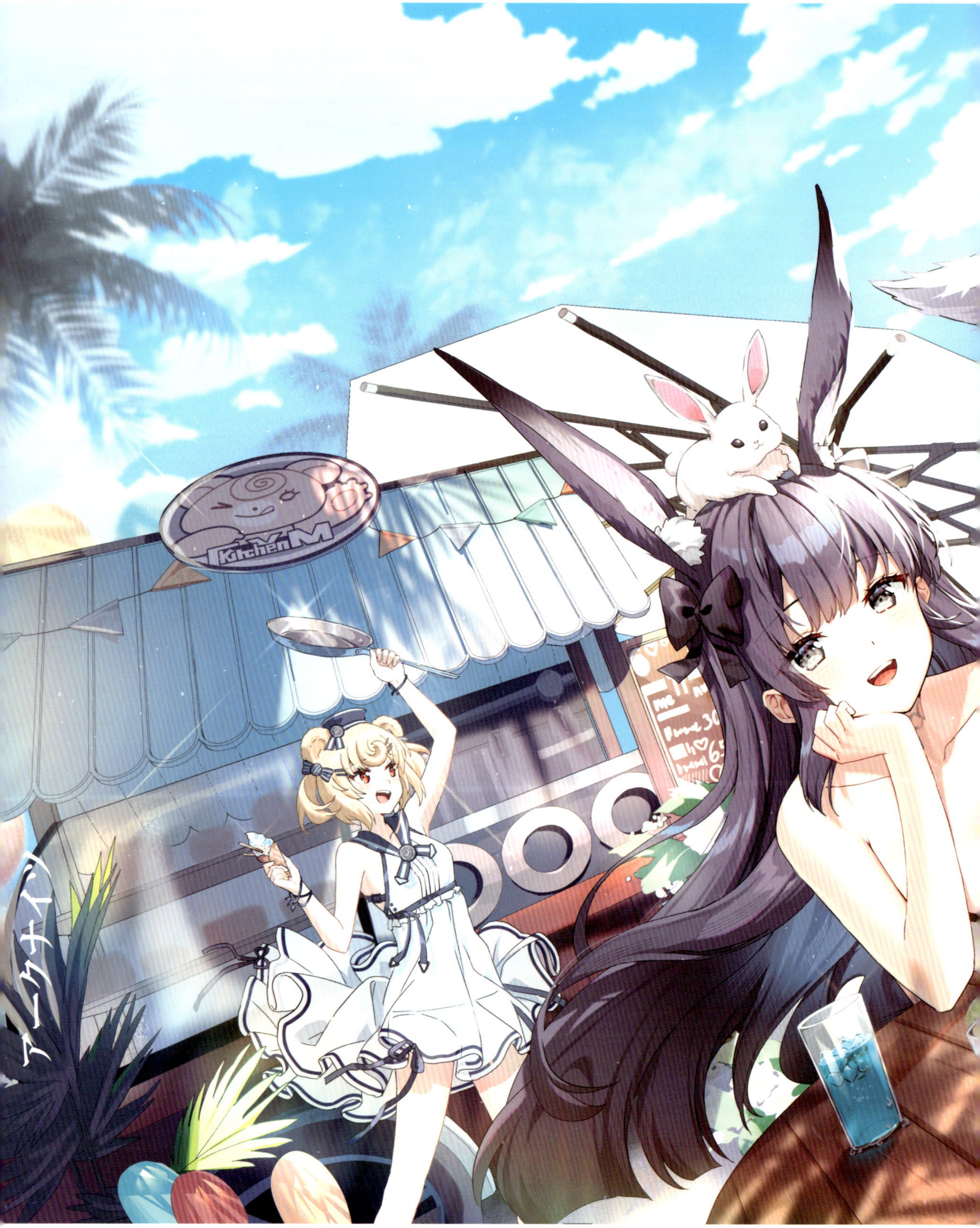

アークナイツ

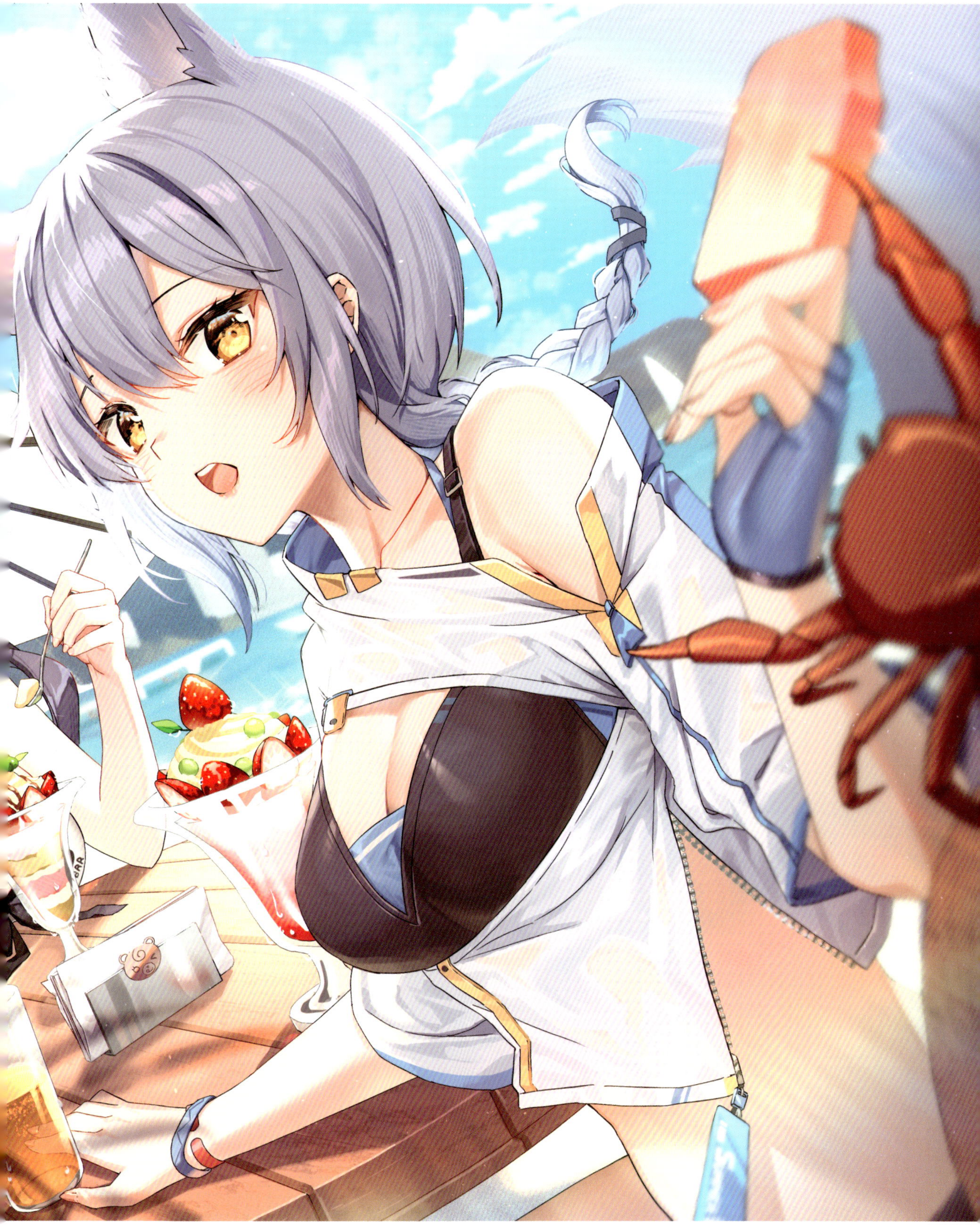

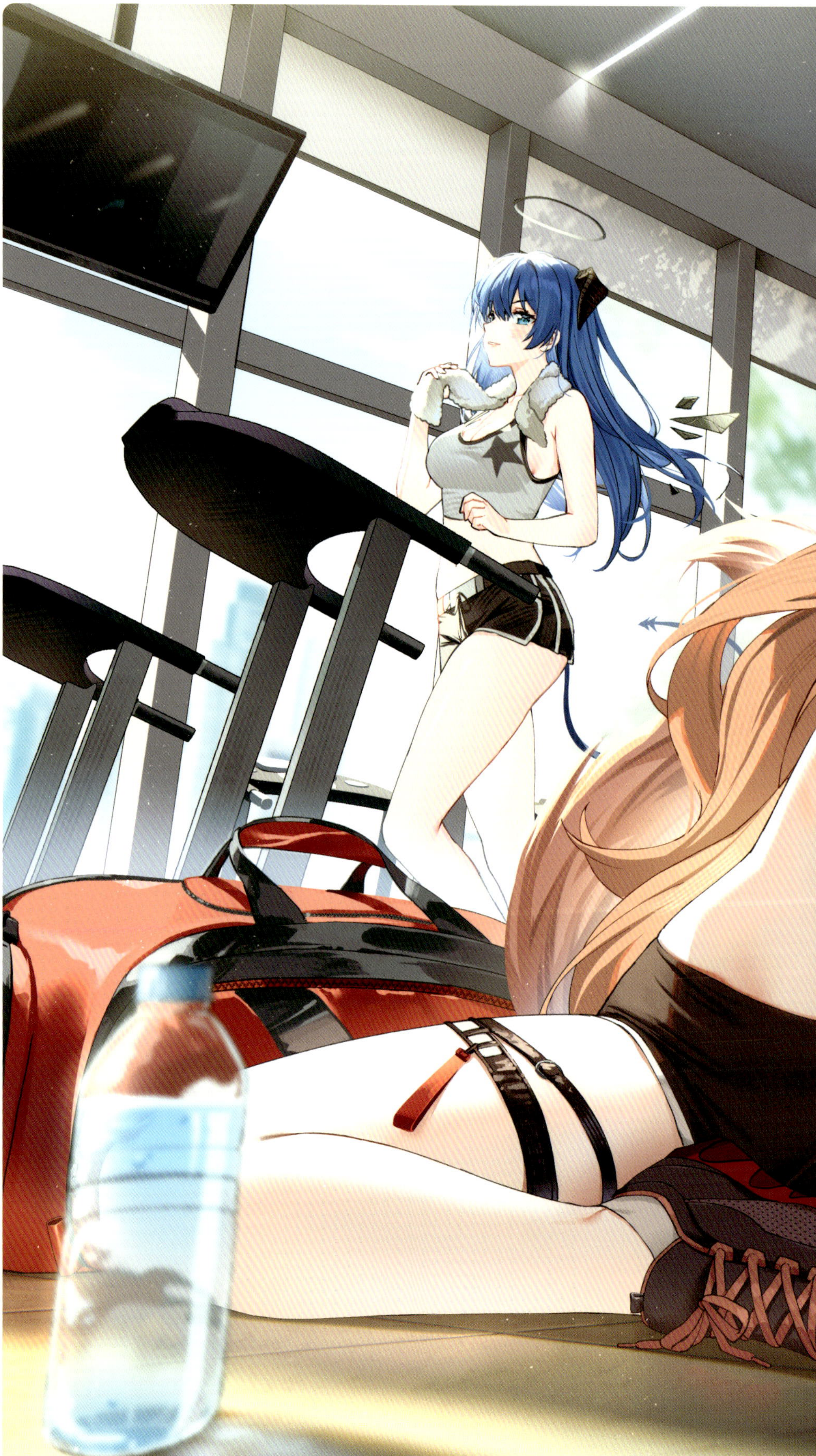

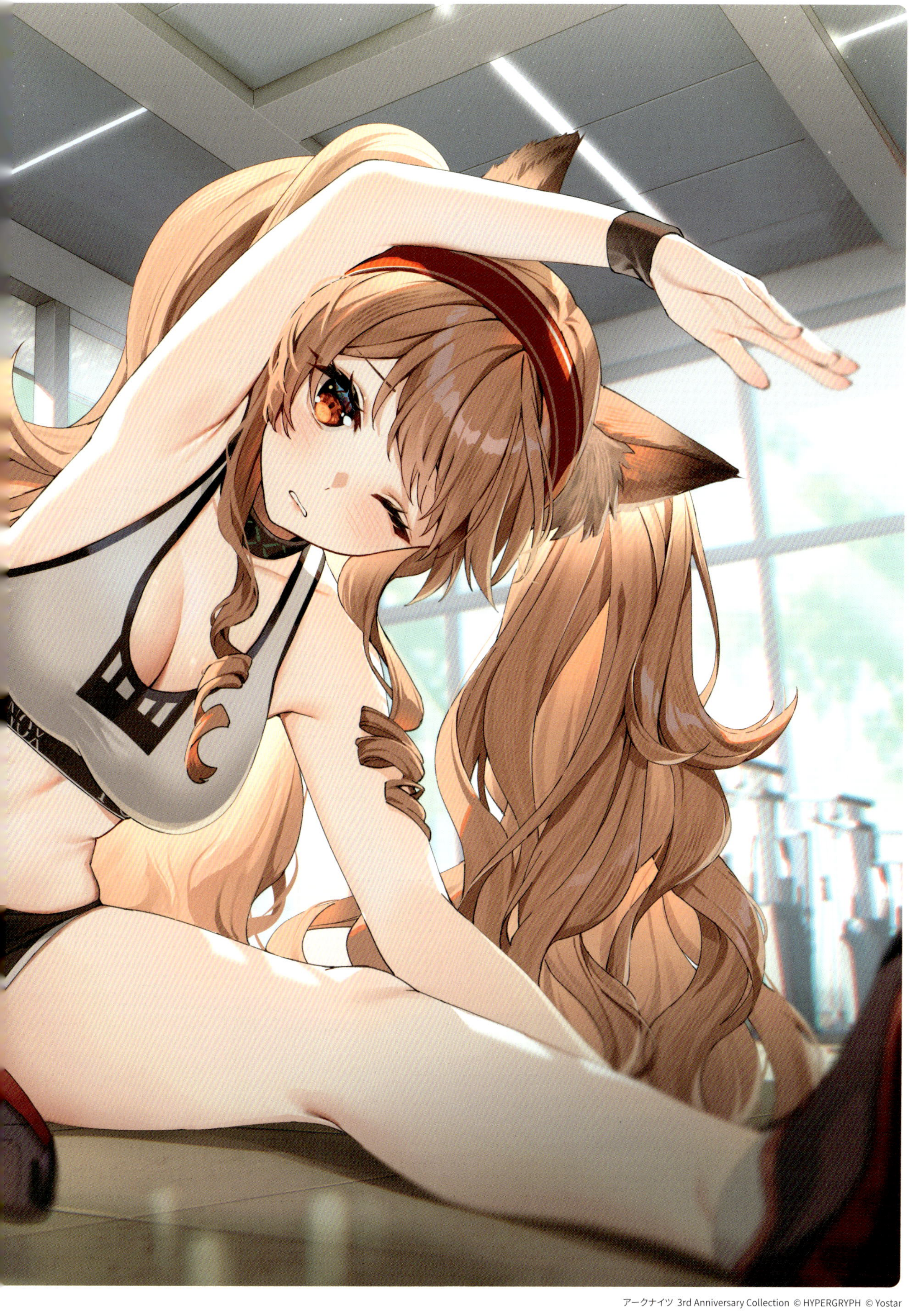

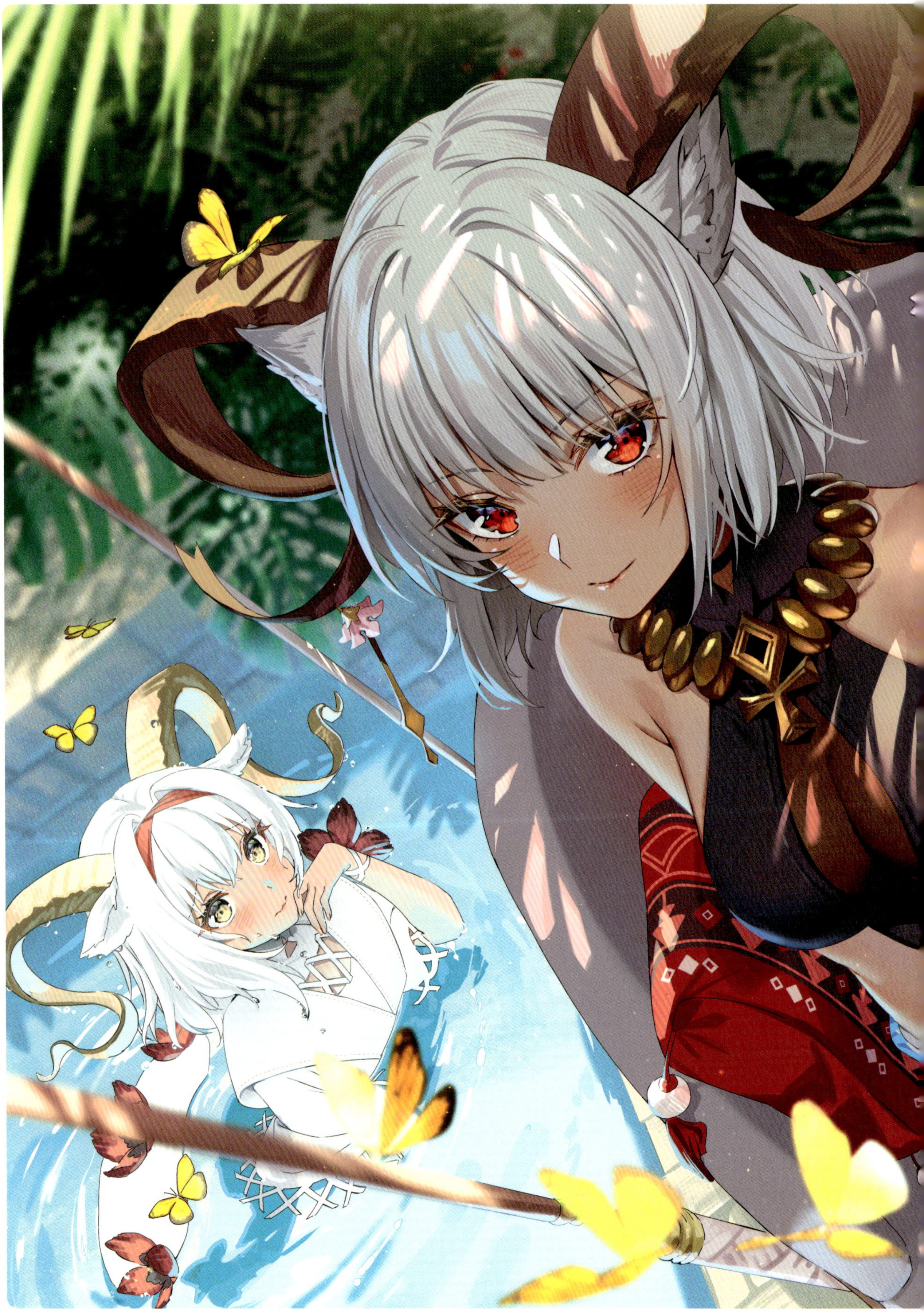

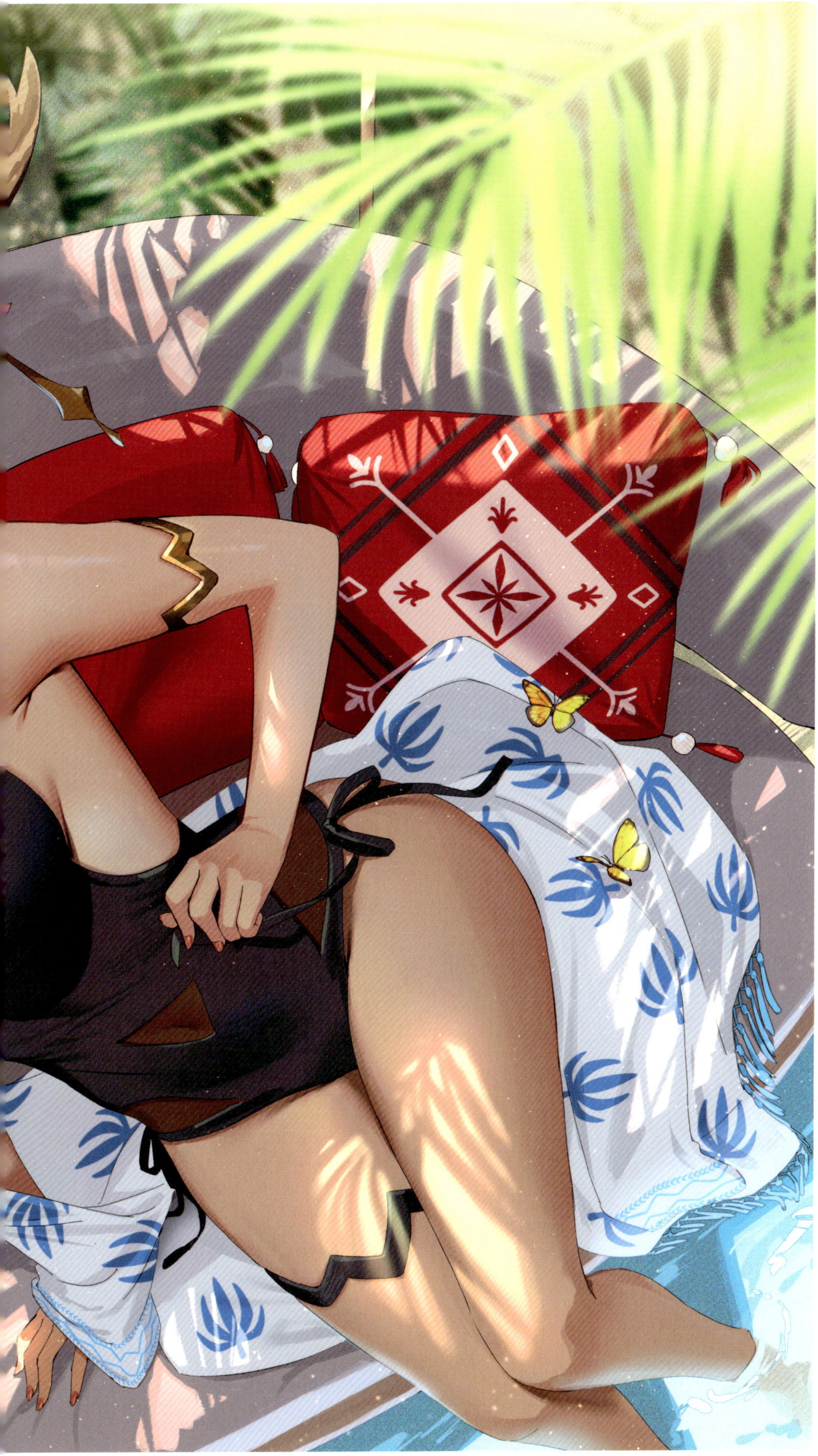

Other Works

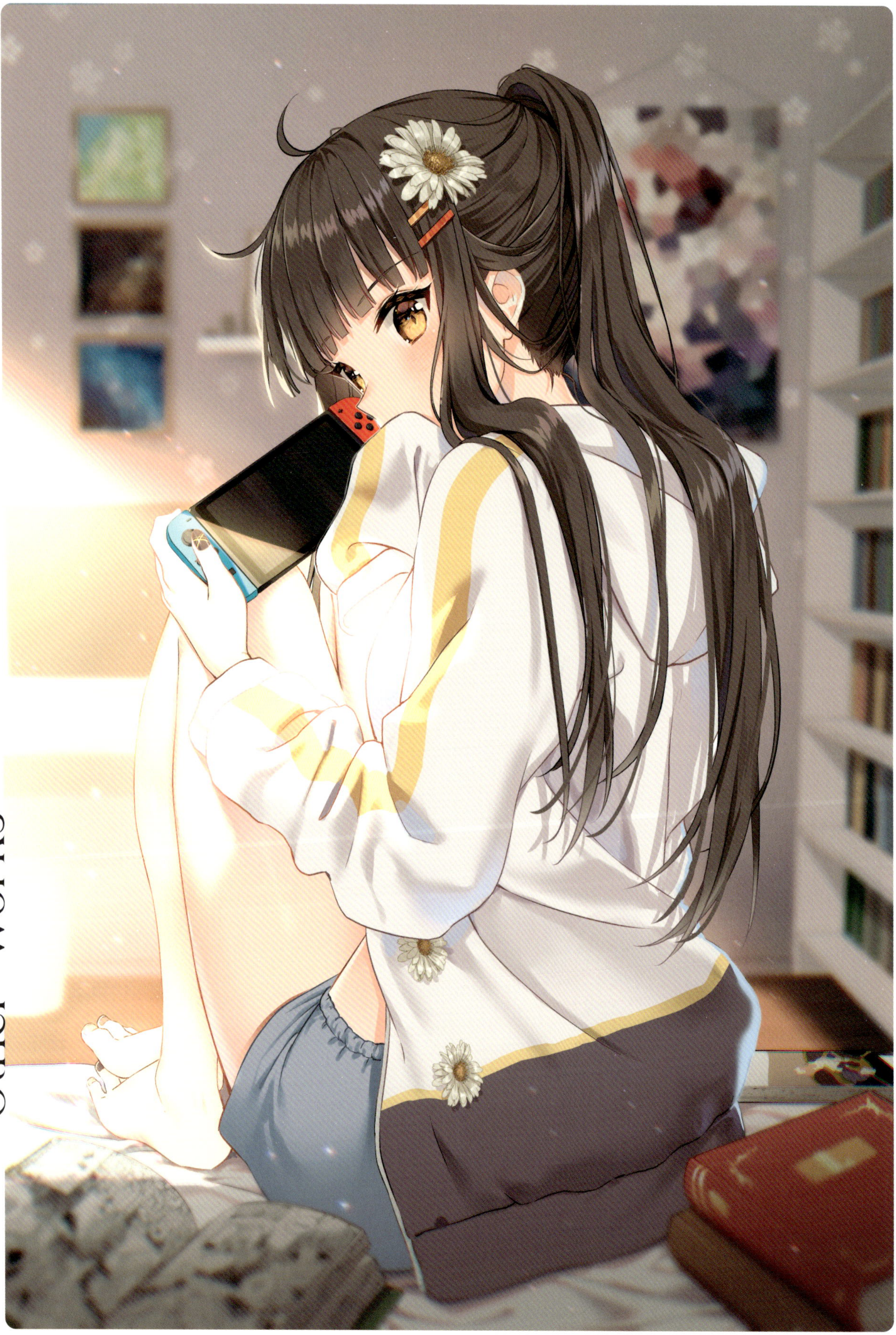

GO MY WAY -有閑×少女- ©ツクルノモリ2019

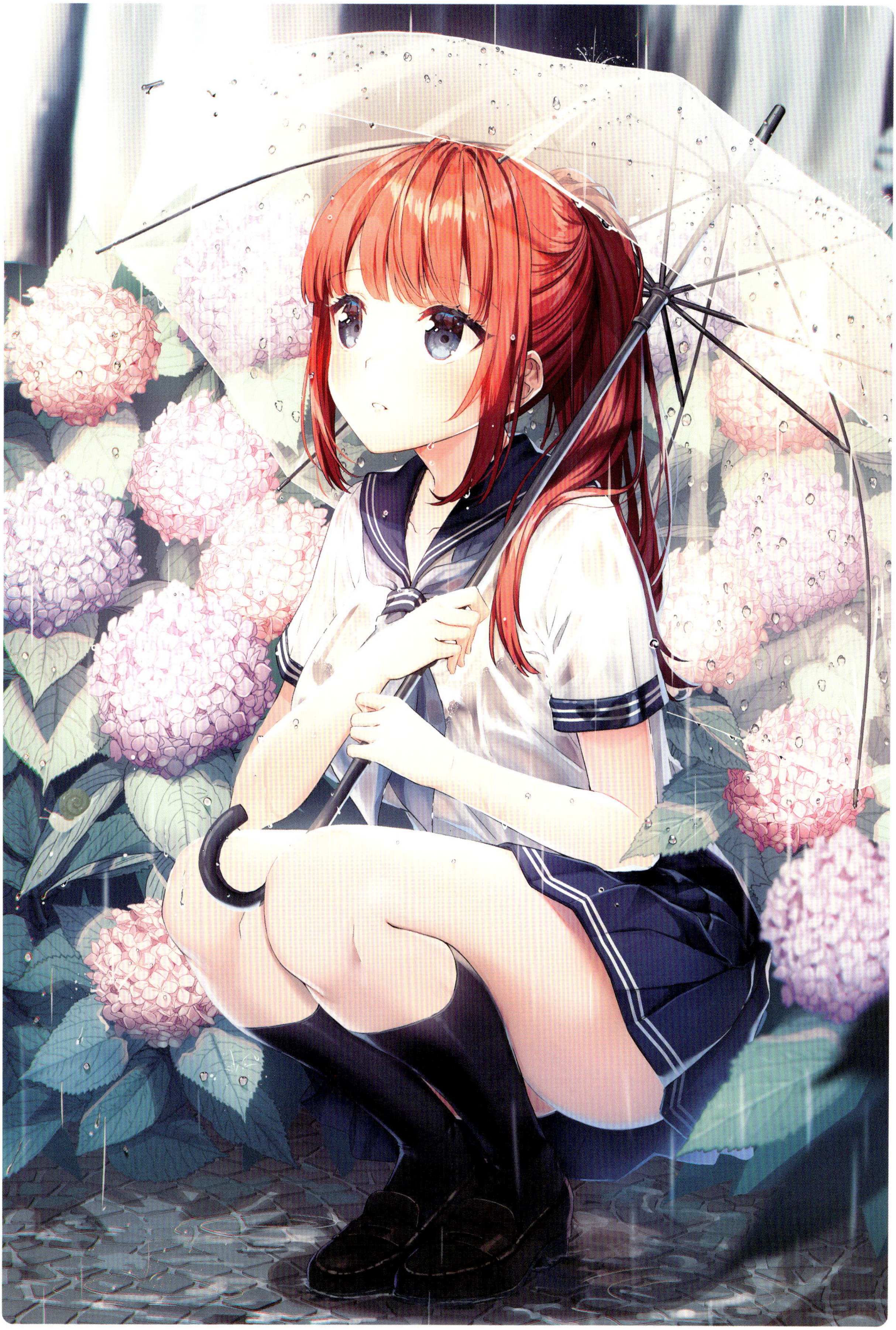

BLUE SKIRT -雨×女子高生- ©ツクルノモリ2019

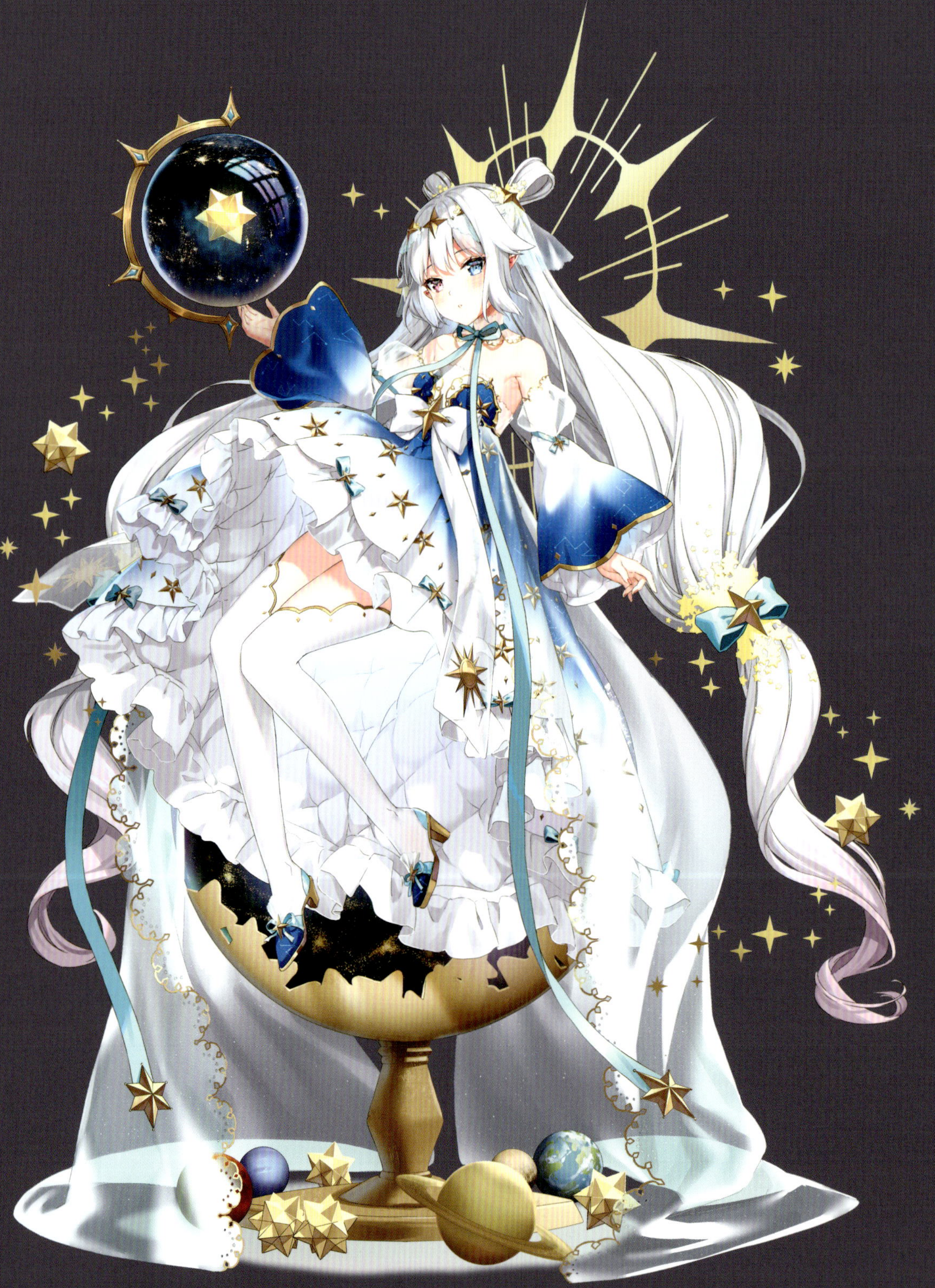

Blue Shift Watcher - Matveiffe Revived Witch ©Yostar ©PixelNeko

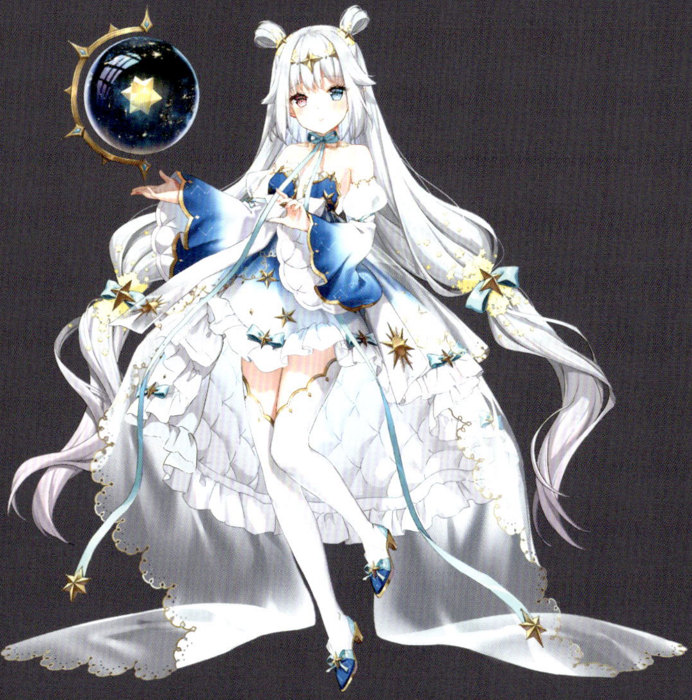

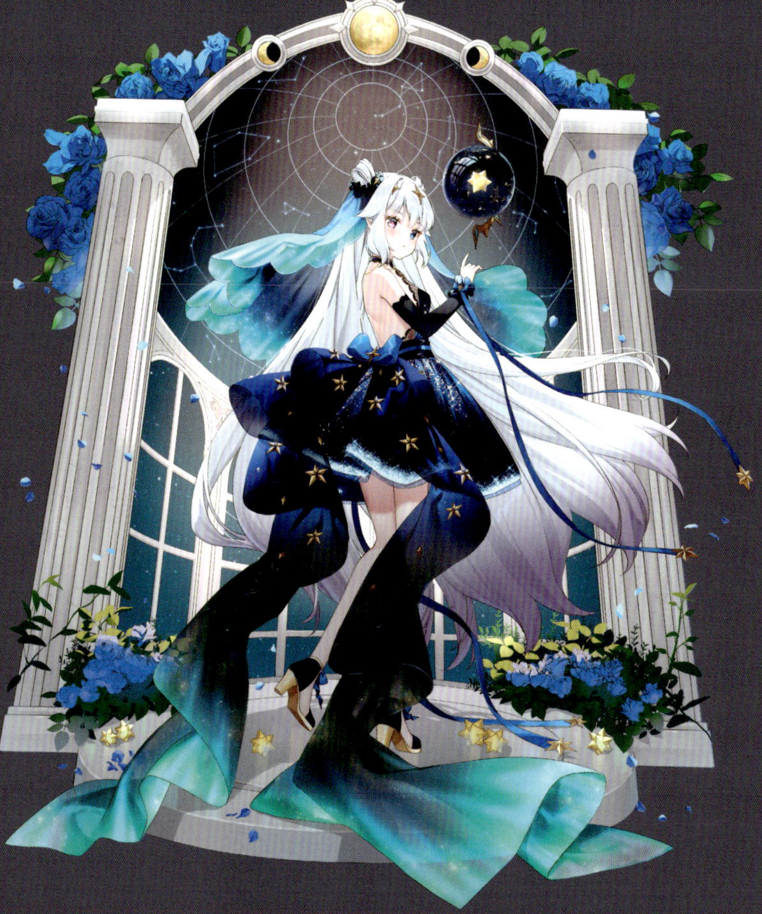

Blue Shift Watcher - Matveiffe New Costume Revived Witch

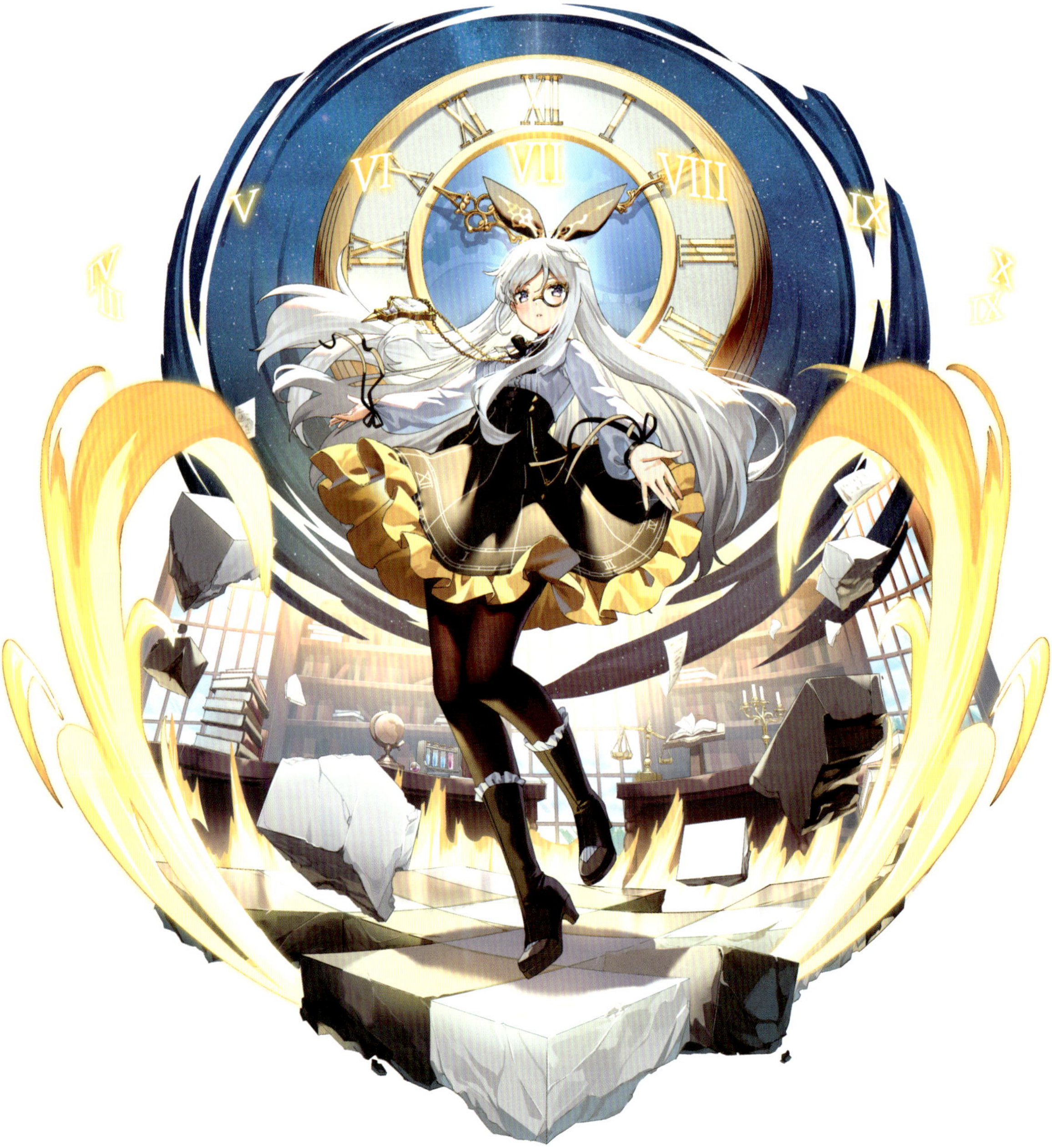

Lost Wail - Phileanosis Revived Witch ©Yostar ©PixelNeko

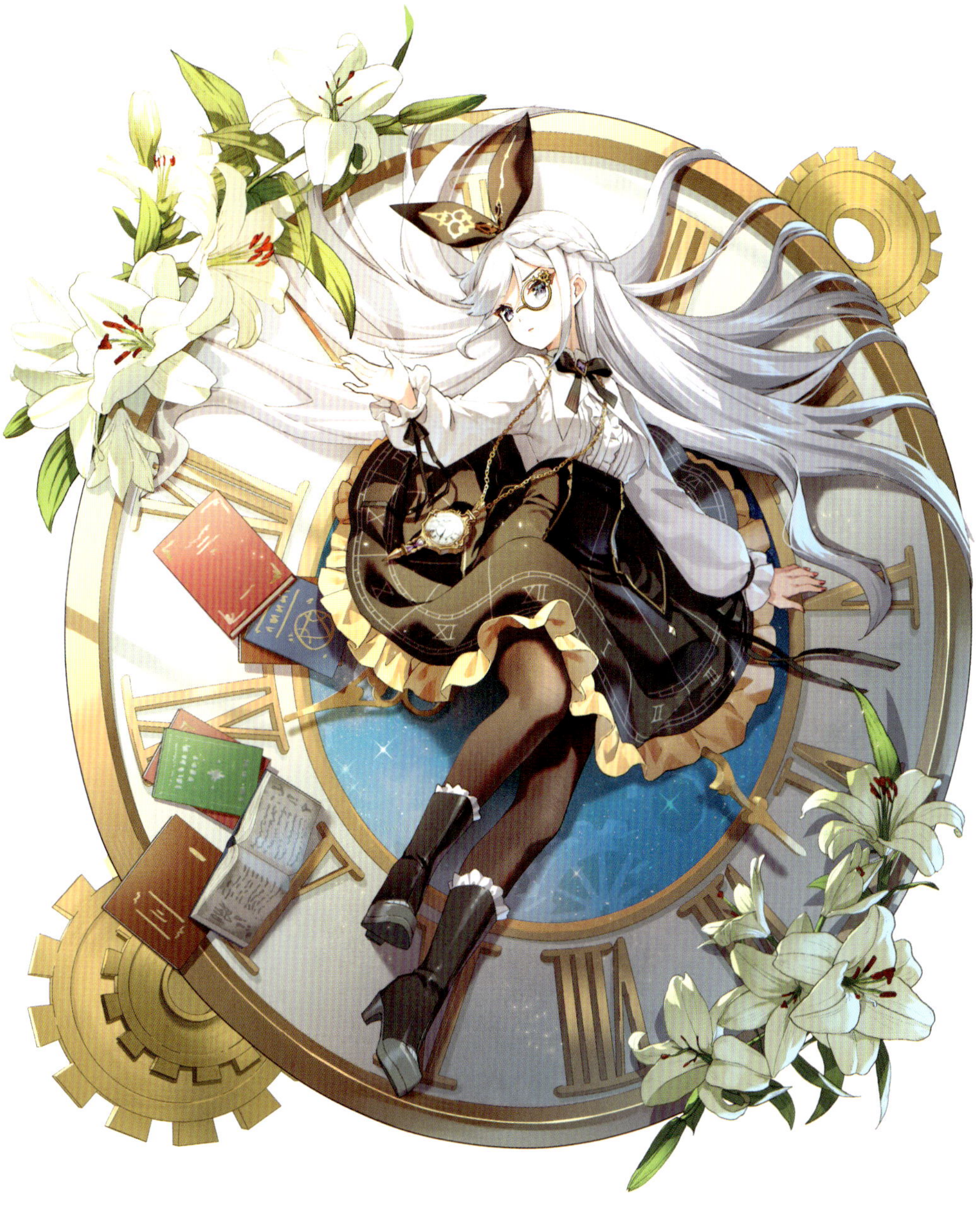

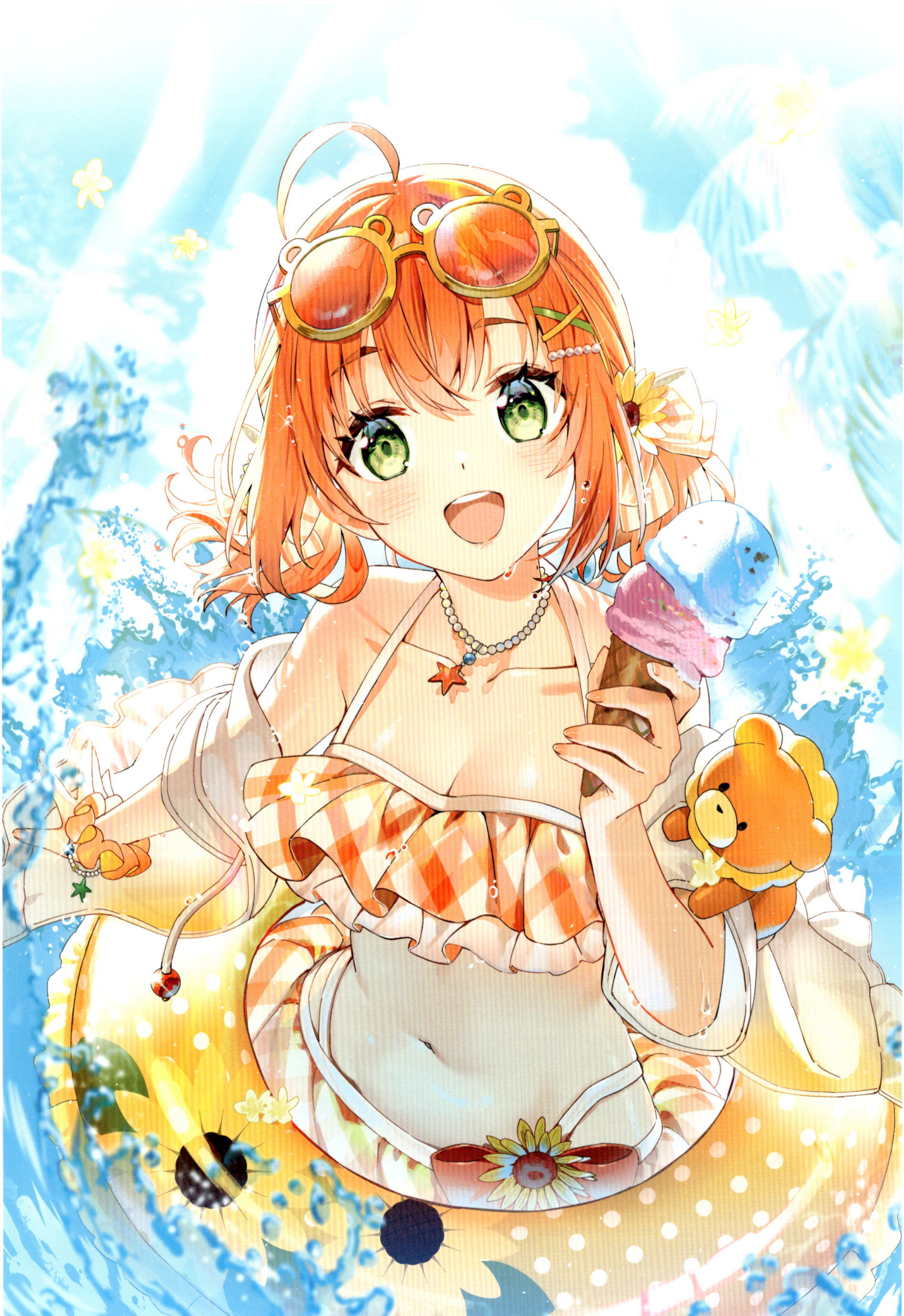

本間ひまわり誕生日グッズイラスト ©ANYCOLOR

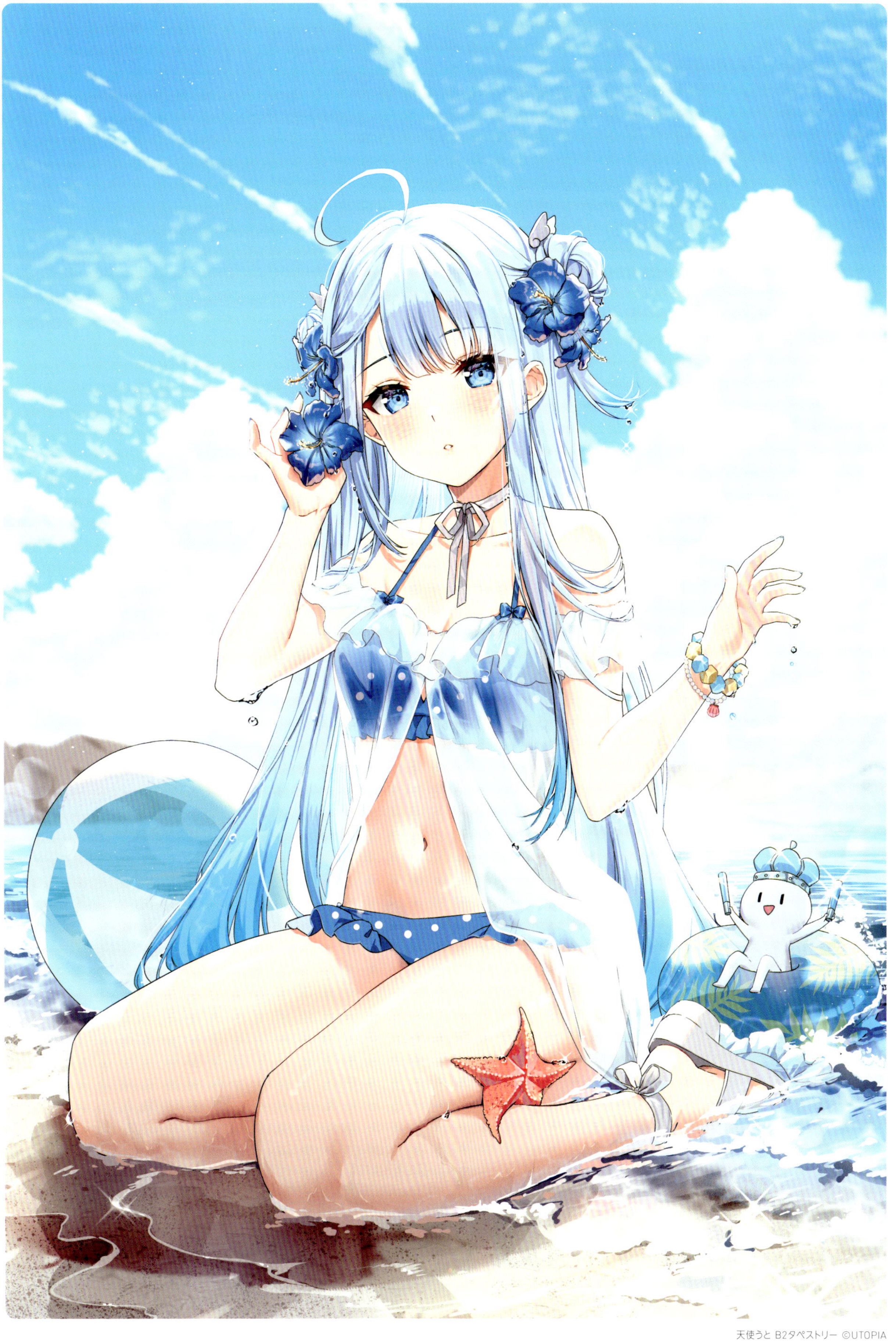

天使うと B2タペストリー ©UTOPIA

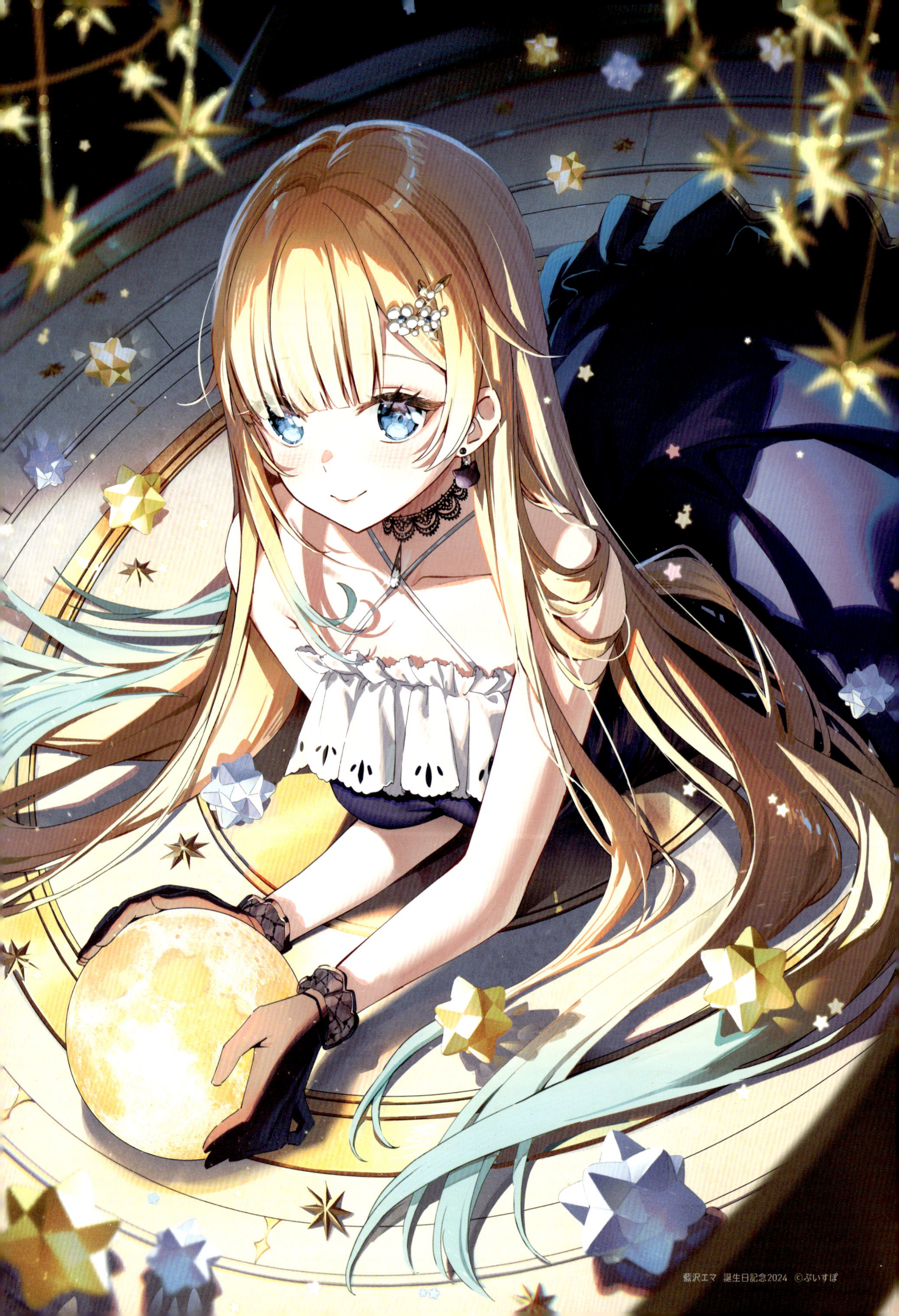

藍沢エマ　誕生日記念2024　©ぶいすぽ

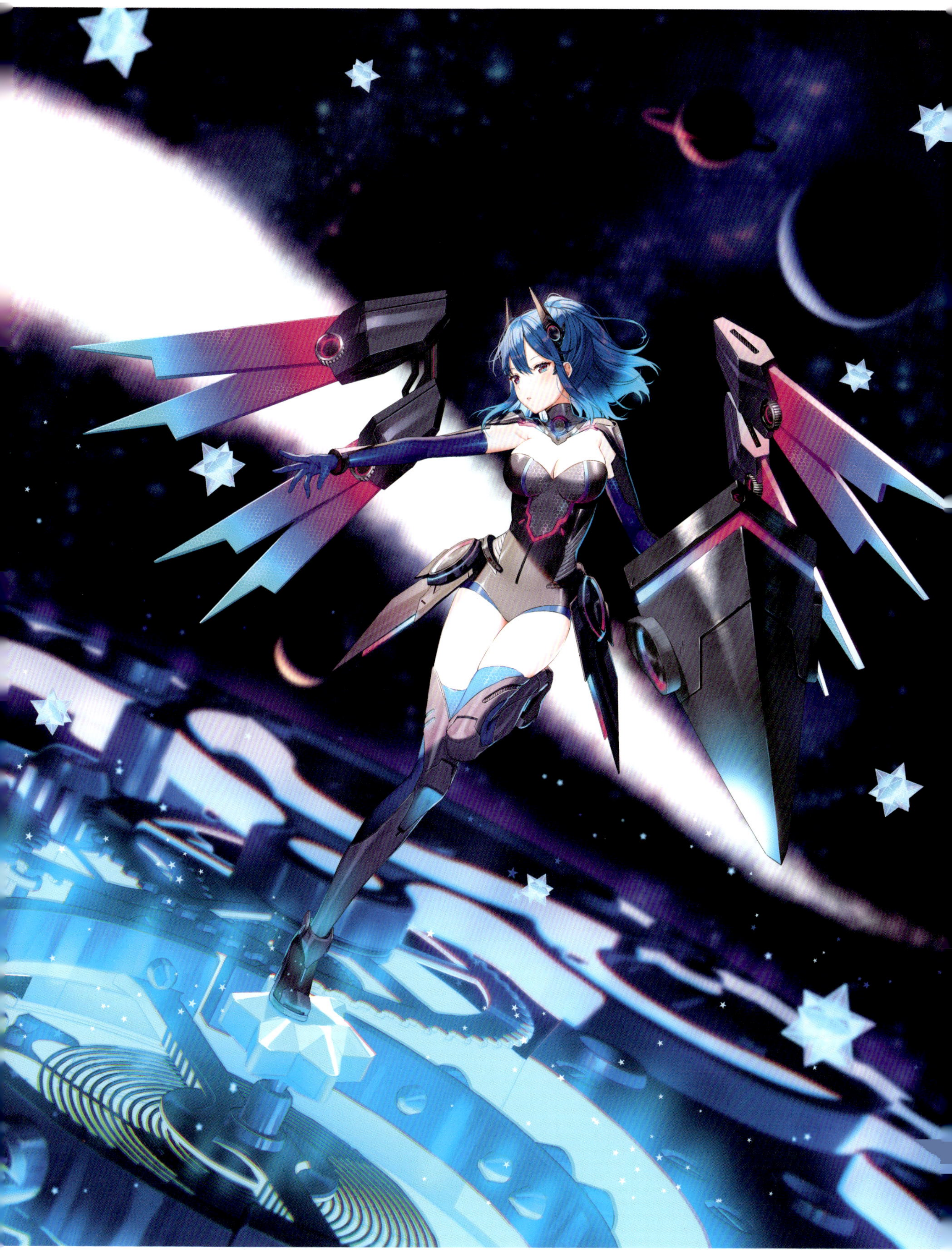

ダイアナは、MSIが展開するゲーミングブランドの世界観を体現するために誕生した公式キャラクターです。
本キャラクターは、国際的に活躍するイラストレーターRosuuri氏とのコラボレーションにより制作され、
革新性と未来感を備えたMSIのゲーミングデスクトップPC「Aegis Ti5」の精神をビジュアルで表現しています。

Aegis-Ti5 キャラクターイラスト

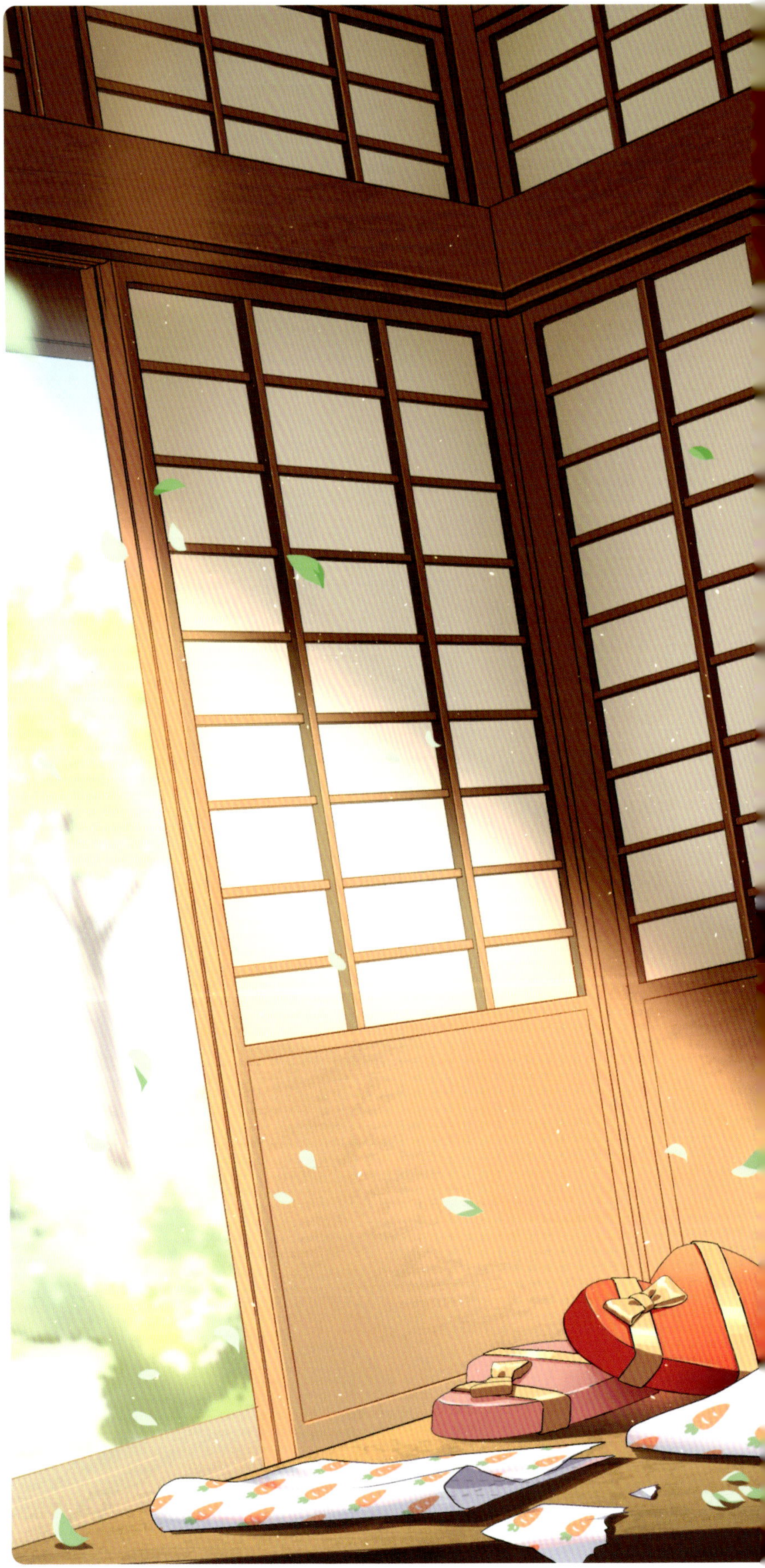

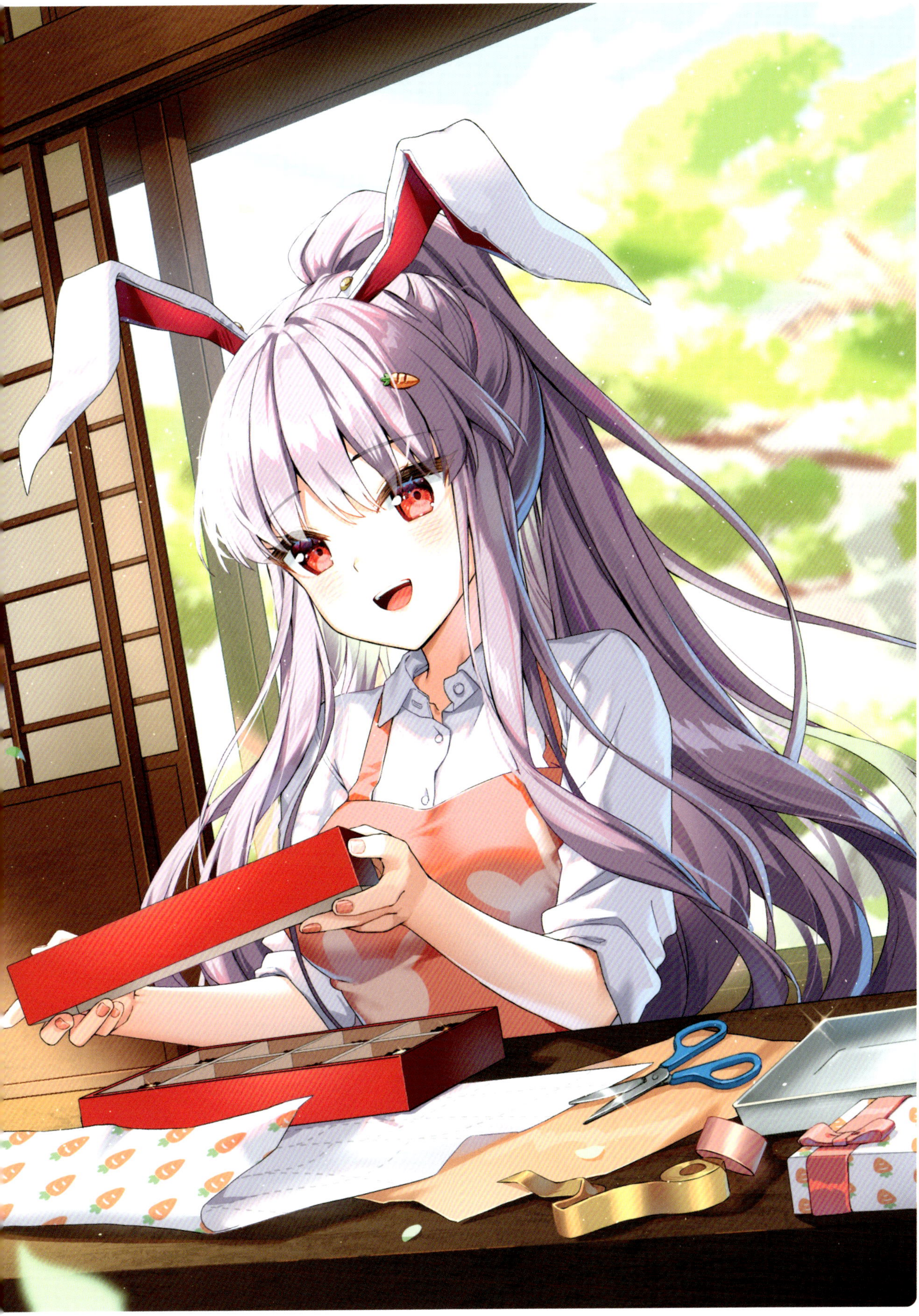

東方ダンマクカグラ ファンタジア・ロストSRミタマカード『【大切な人たちへ想いを込めて】鈴仙・優曇華院・イナバ』

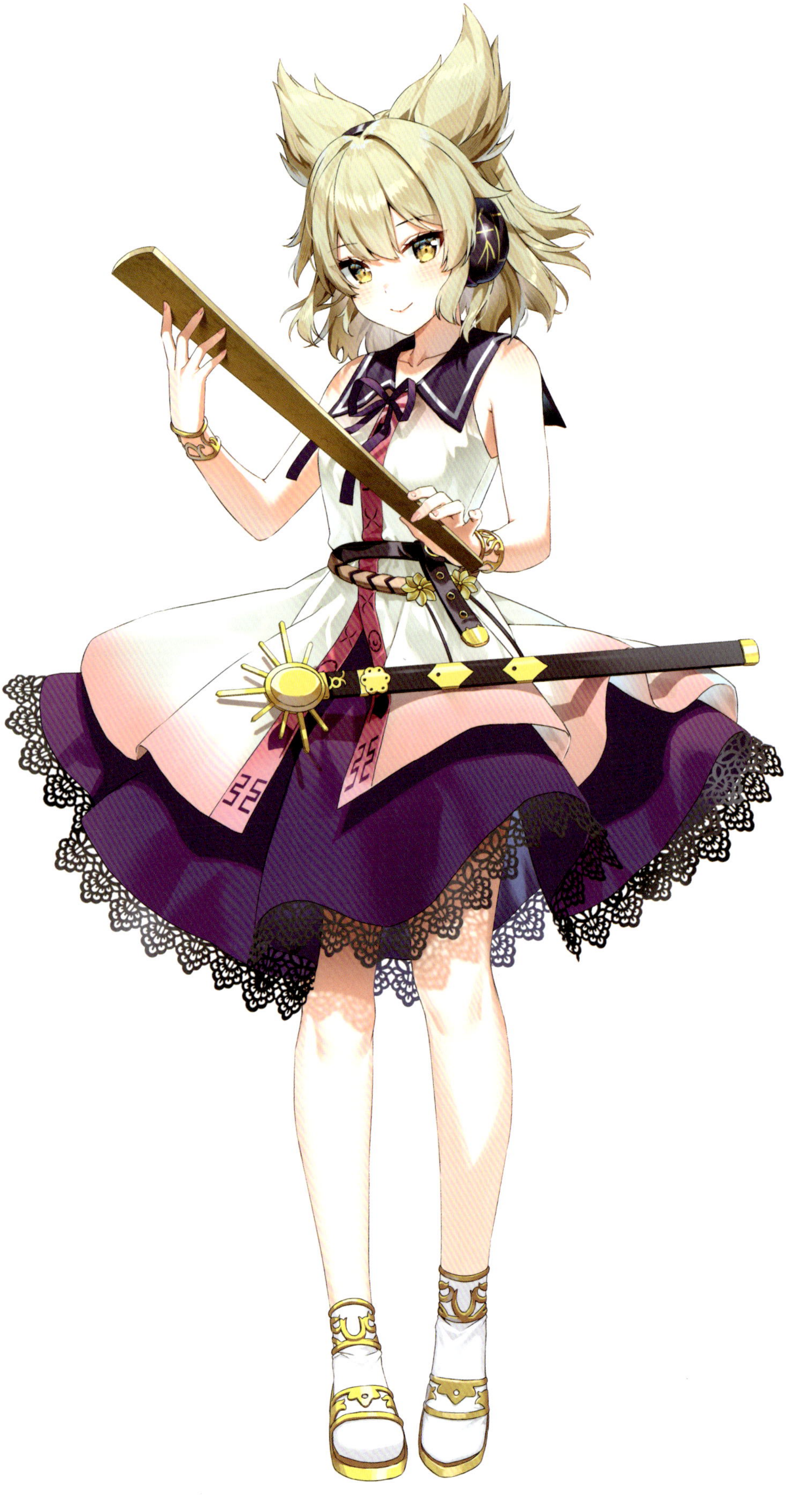

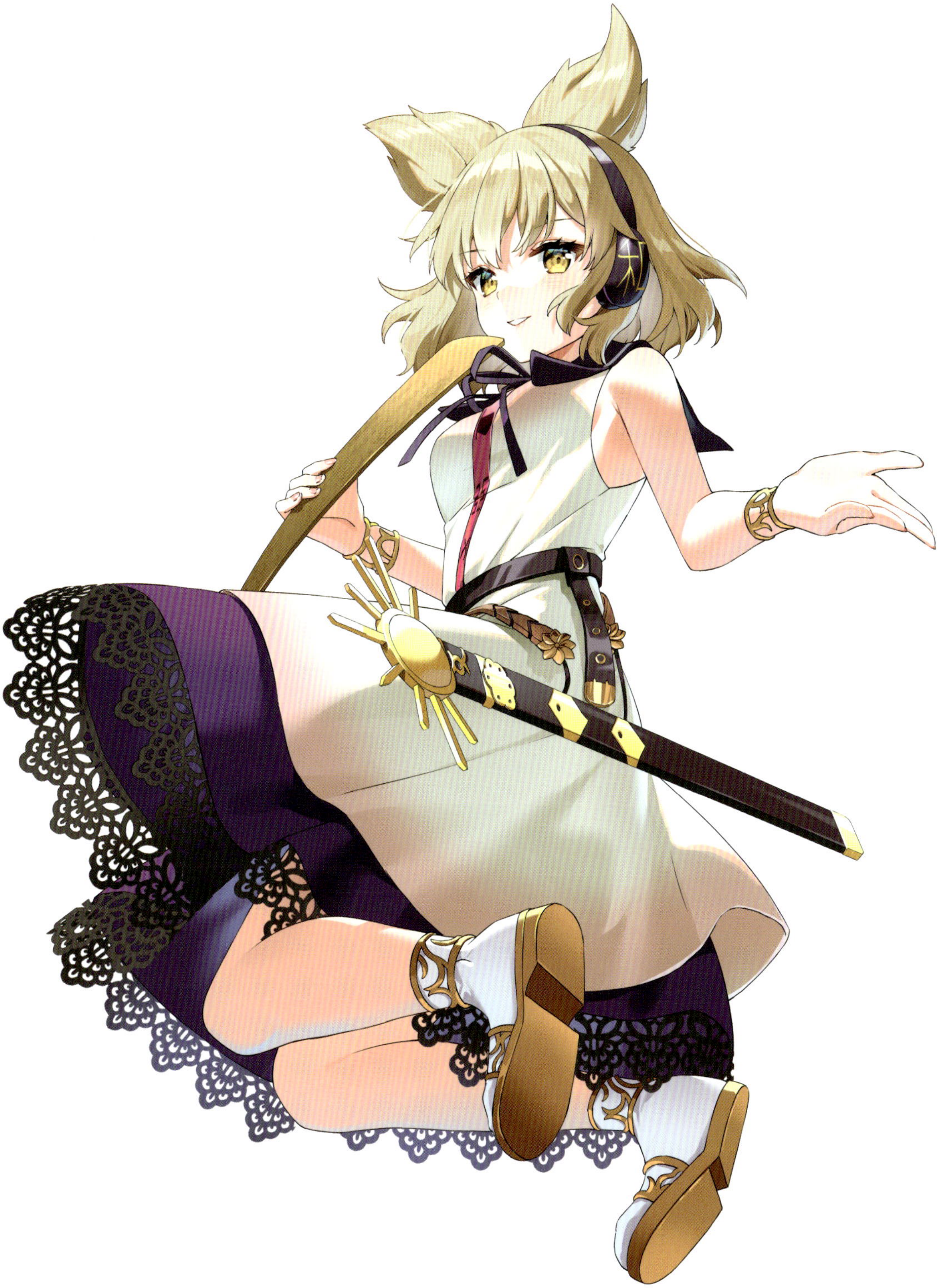

東方スペルバブル 豊聡耳神子 キャラクターアート 東方スペルバブルは東方Projectを原作とした二次創作作品です

Light Novel

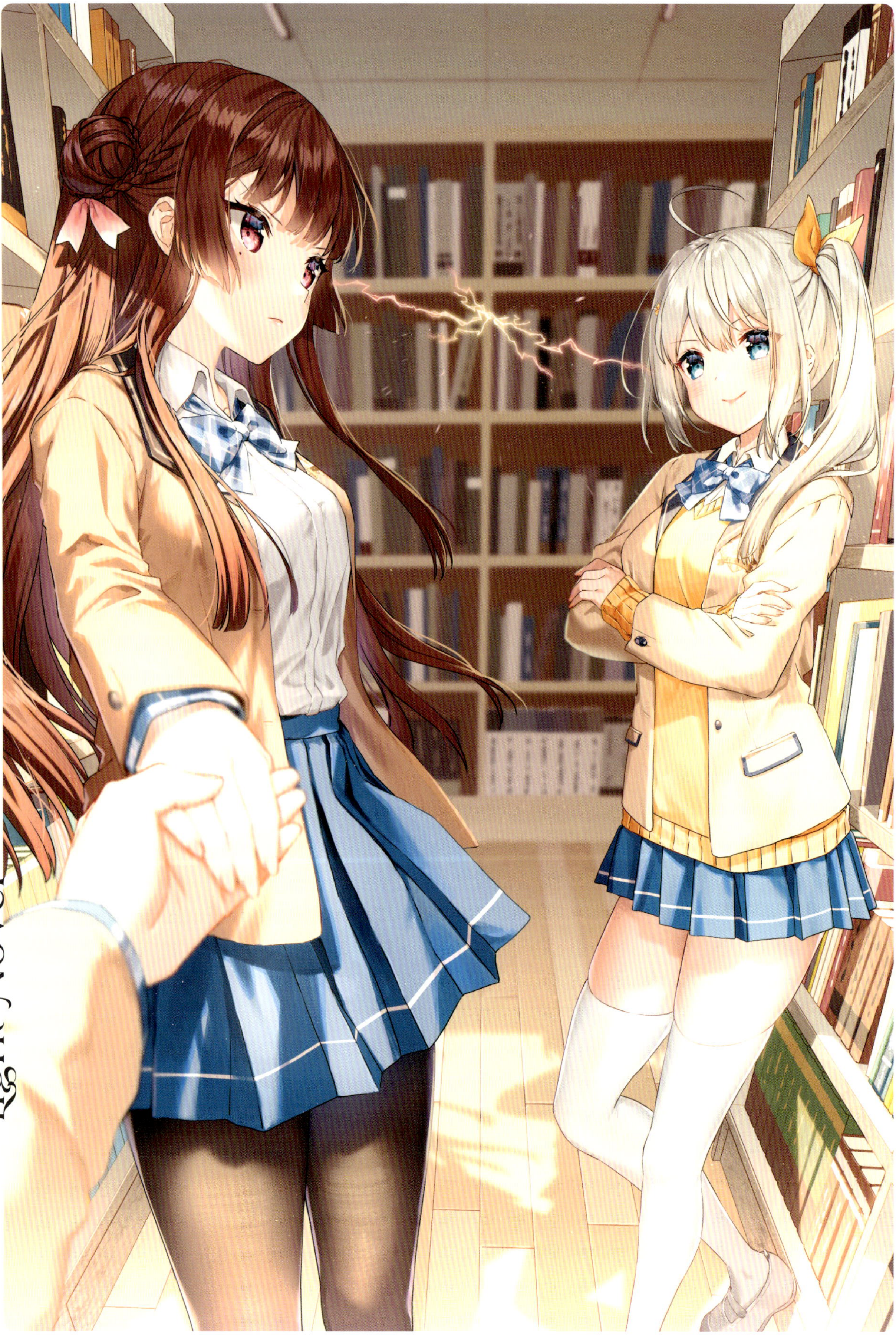

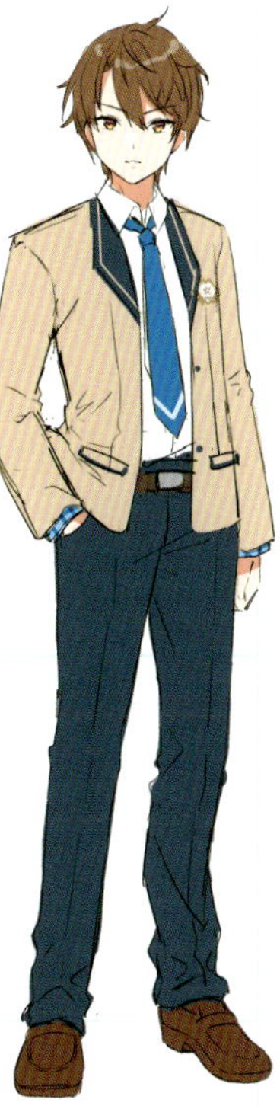

千田薙人

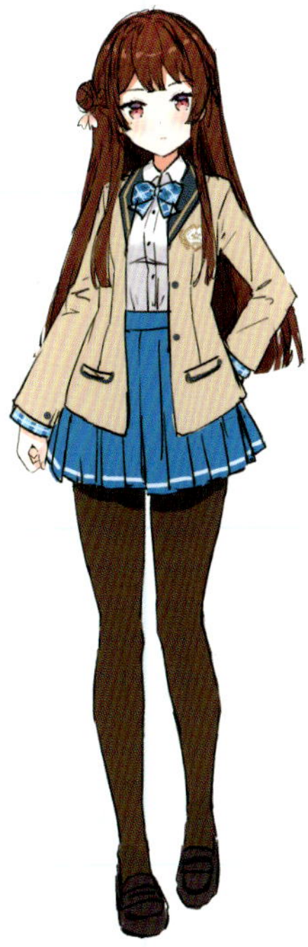

鷹音希

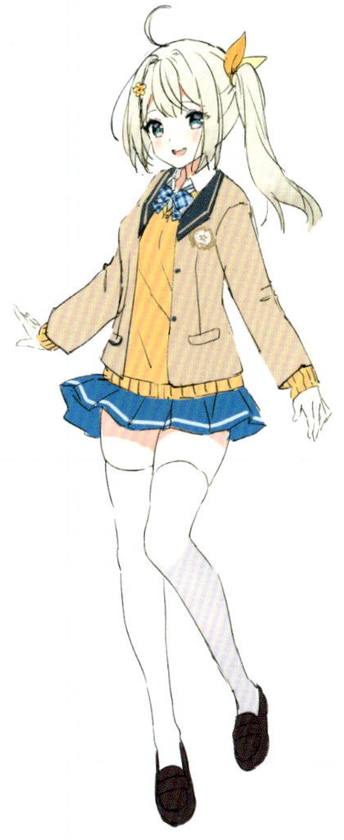

朝谷霧

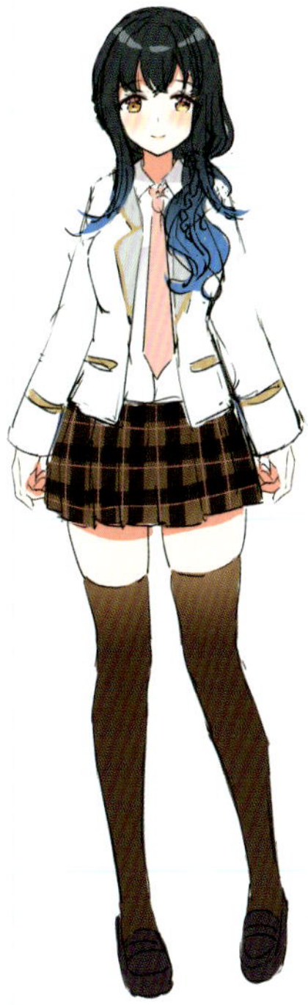

千田流々香

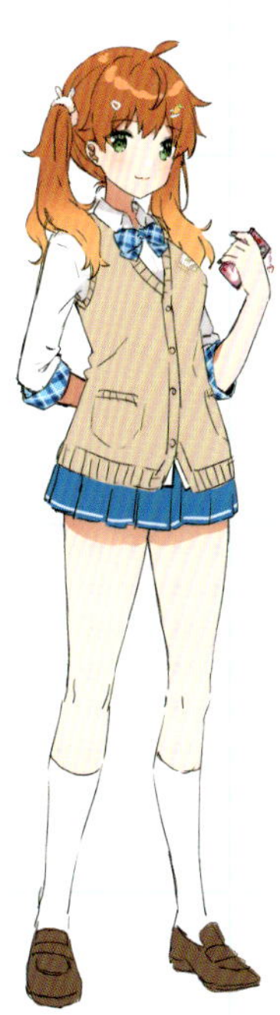

中野唯

角川スニーカー文庫『高嶺の花の今カノは、絶対元カノに負けたくないようです』著:とーわ(KADOKAWA)

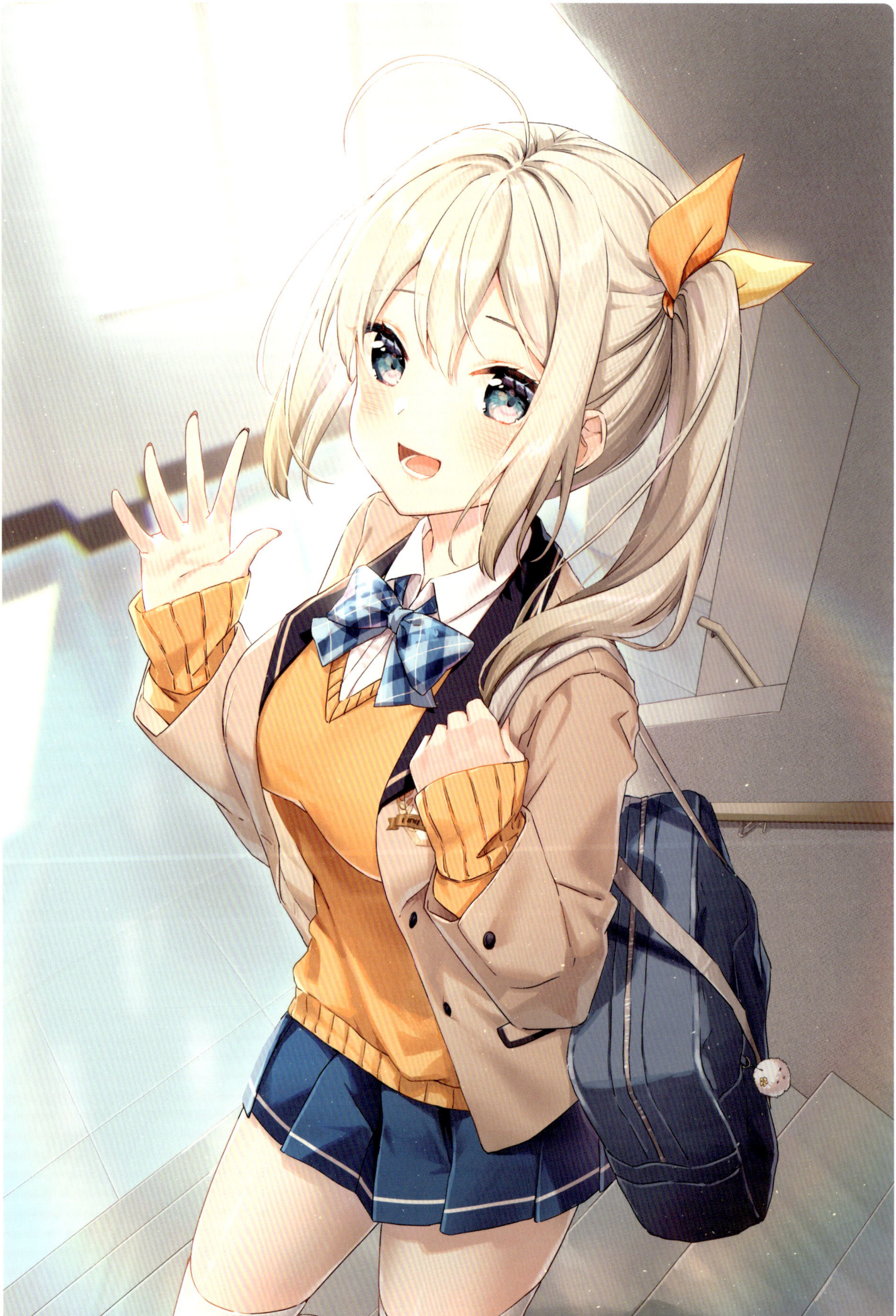

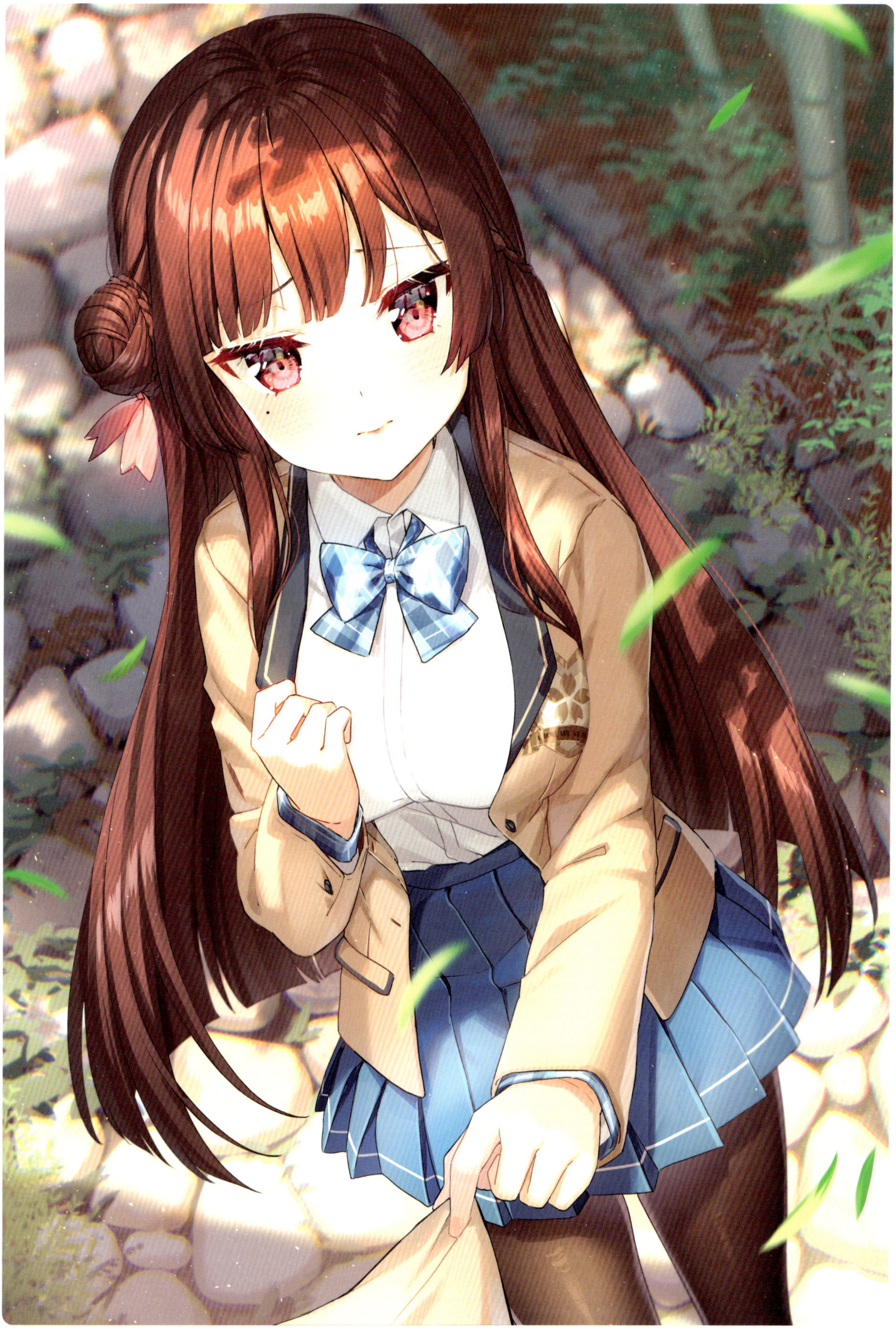

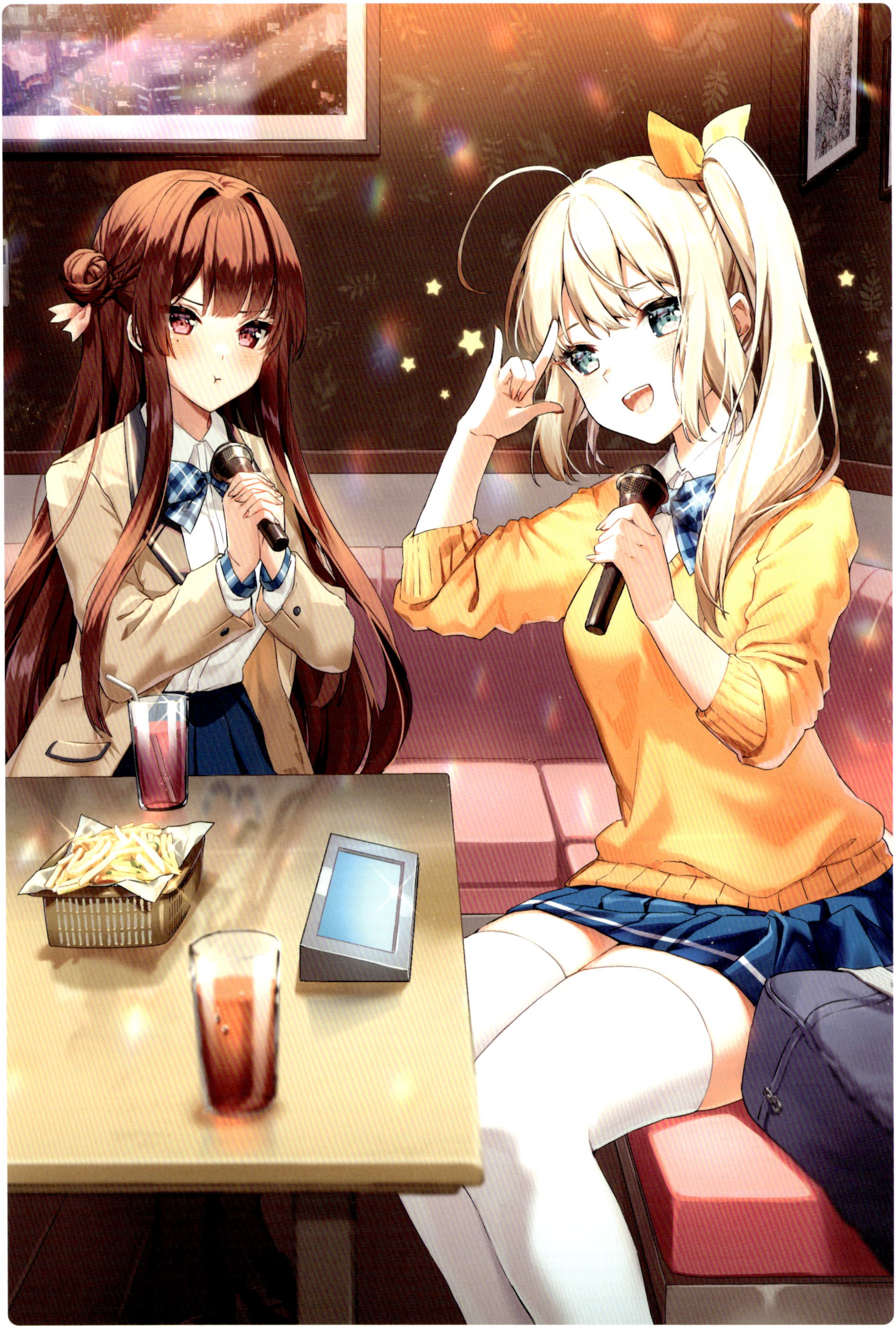

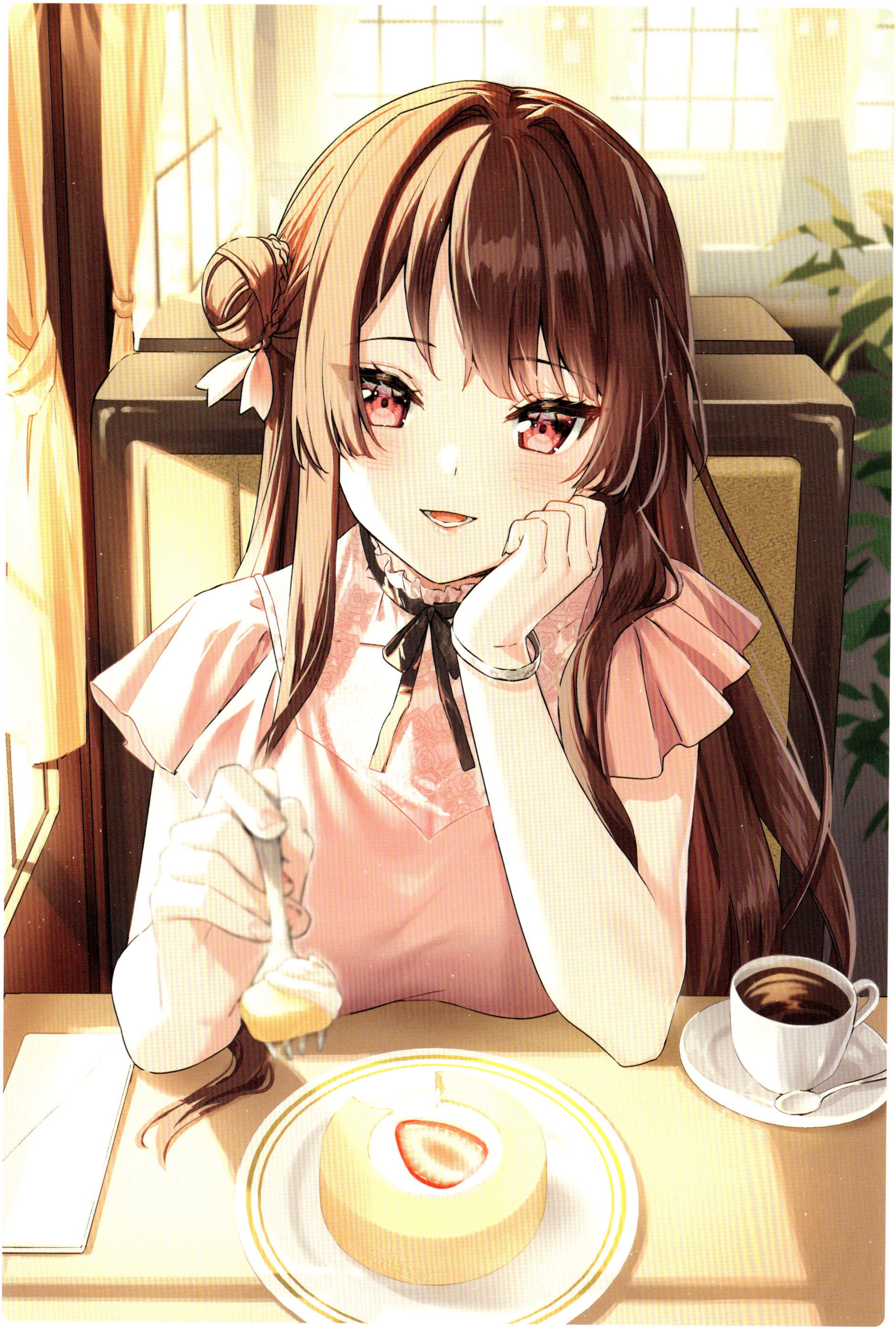

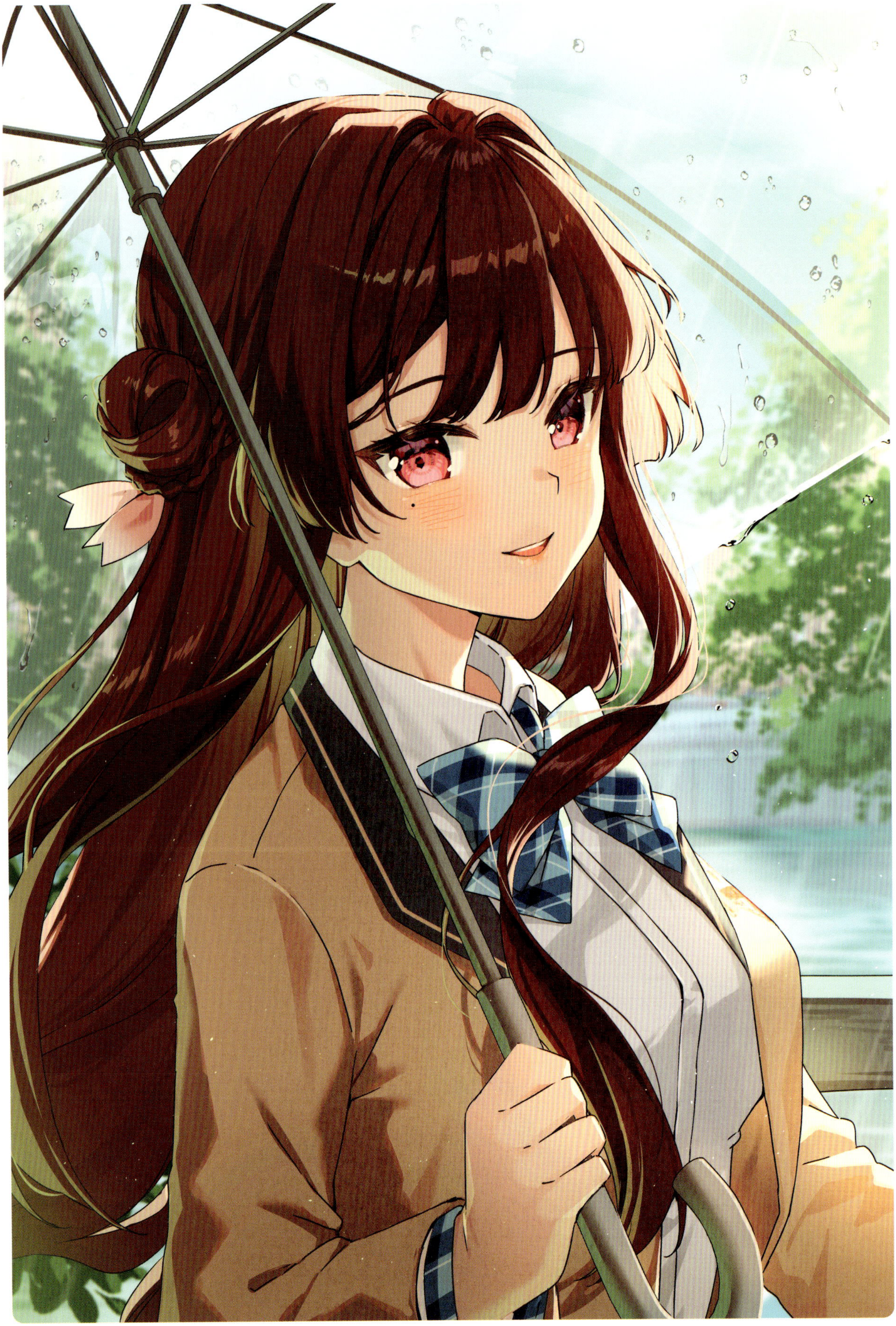

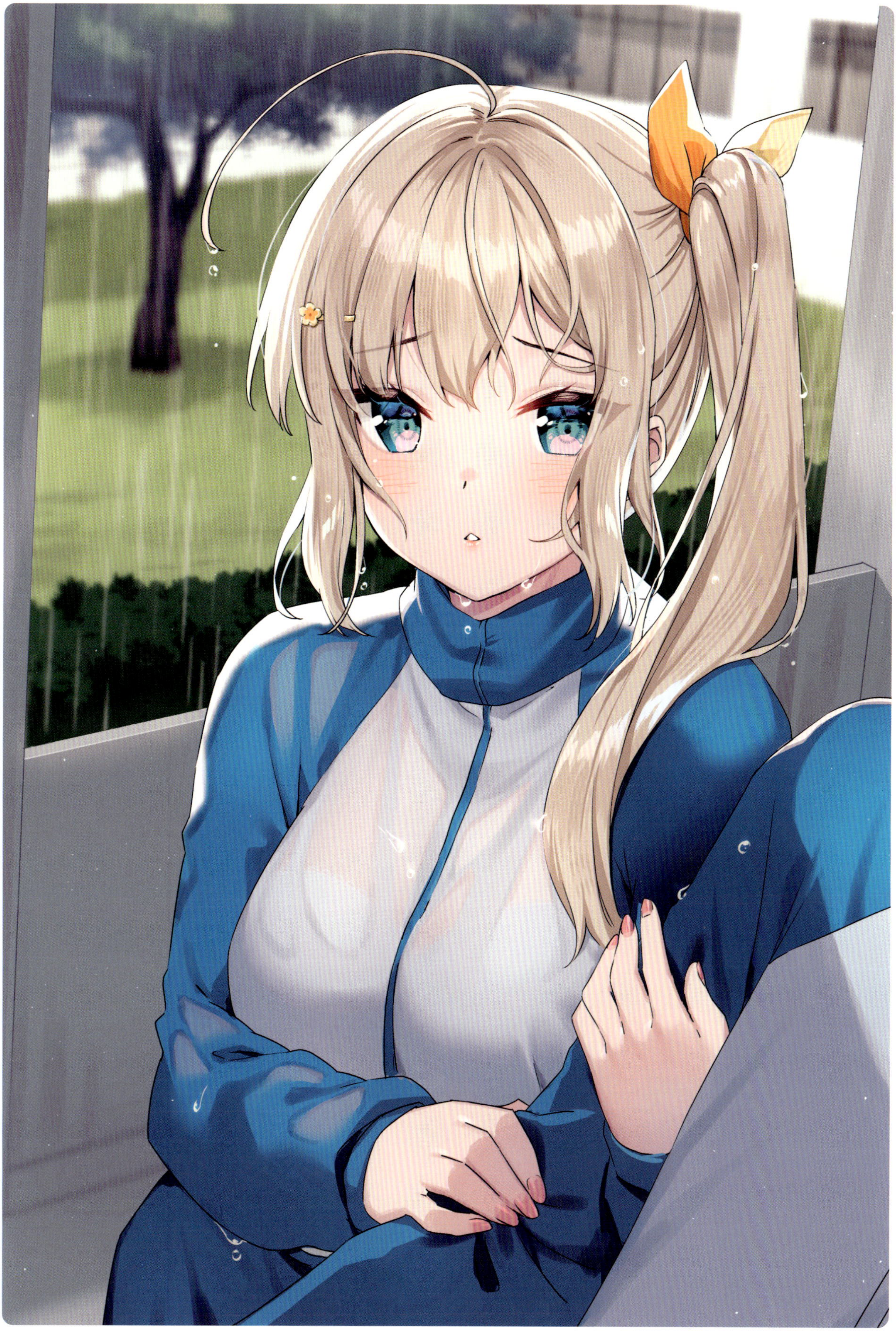

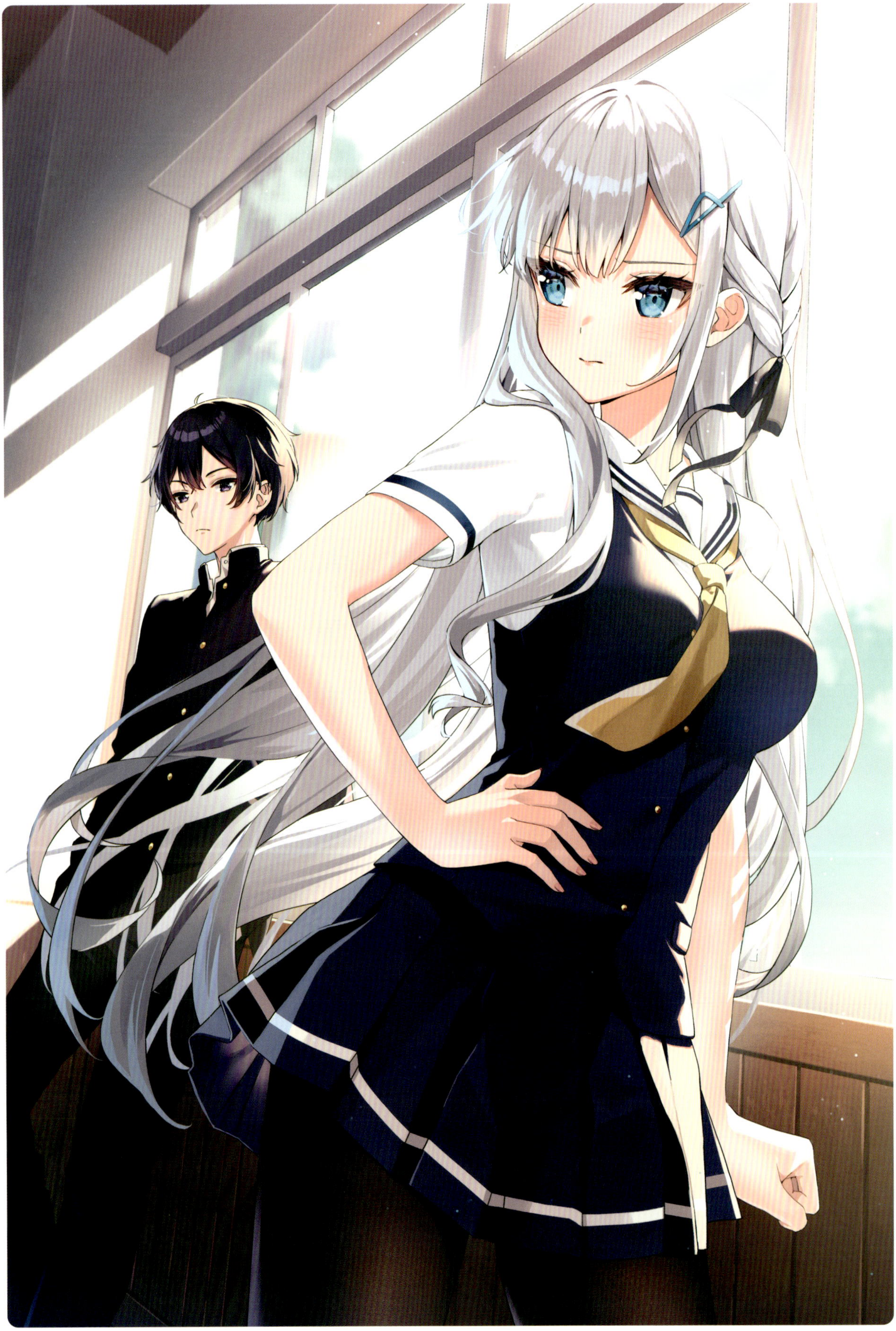

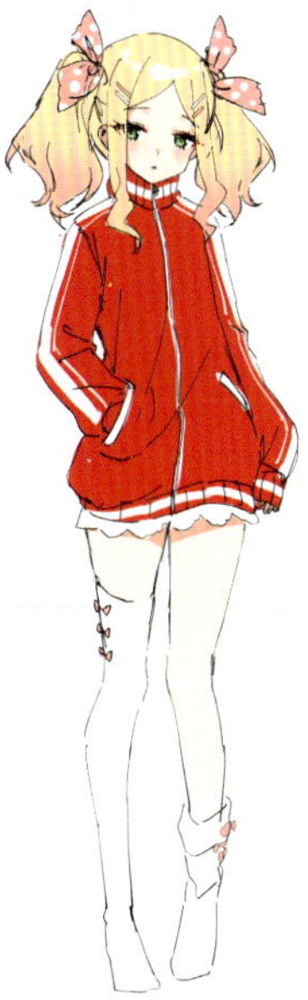

堂本奈乃

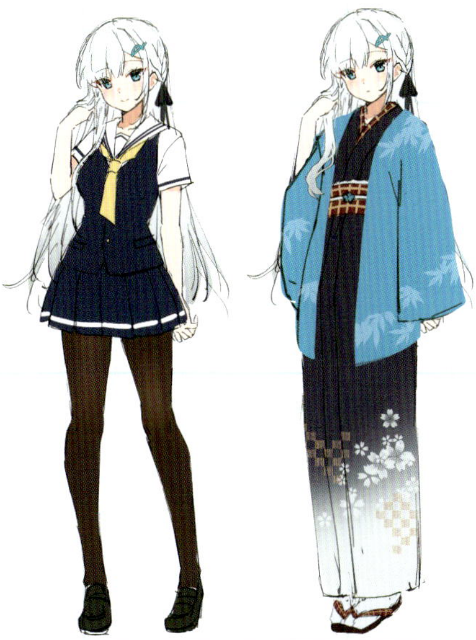

友禅りり

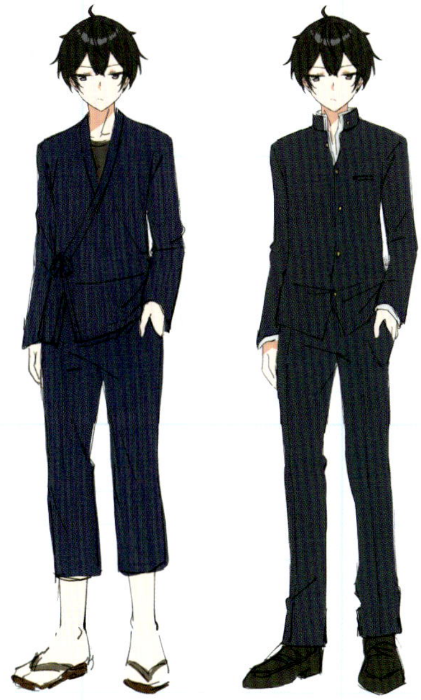

八神錬理

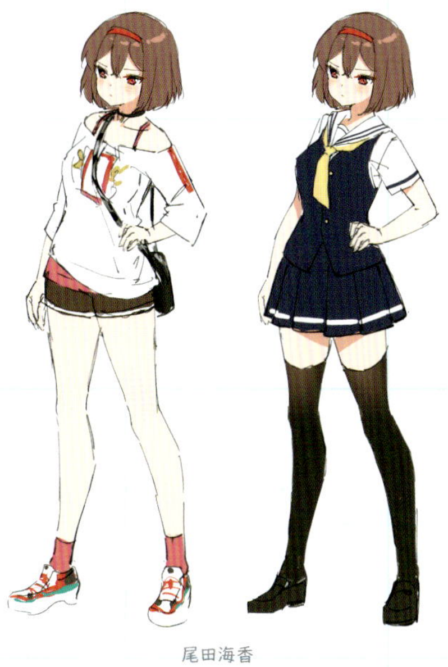

尾田海香

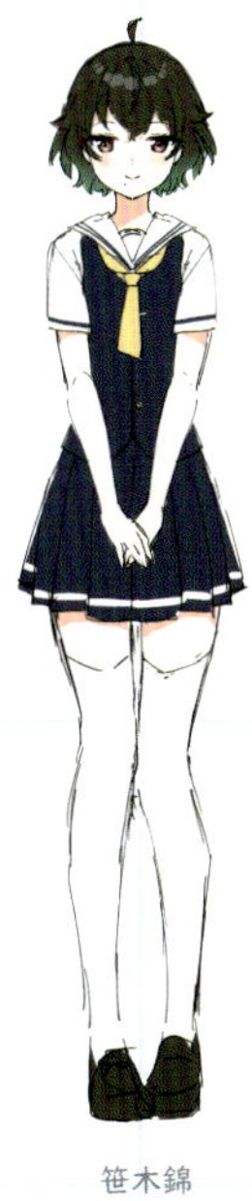

笹木錦

MF文庫J『見た目に反して(僕だけに)甘えたがりの幼なじみを、僕は毎日論破しなければならない。』著：森林 梢(KADOKAWA)

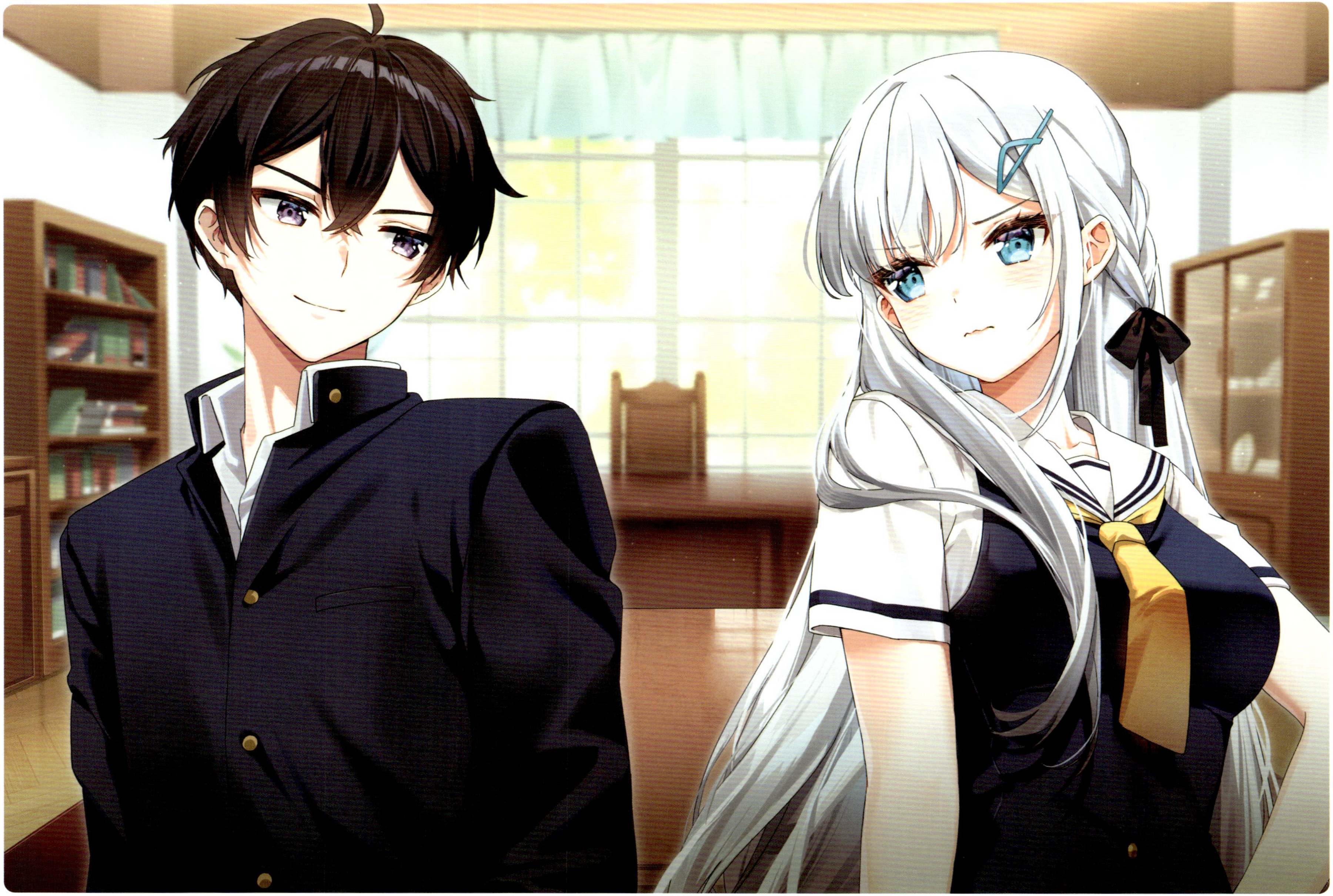

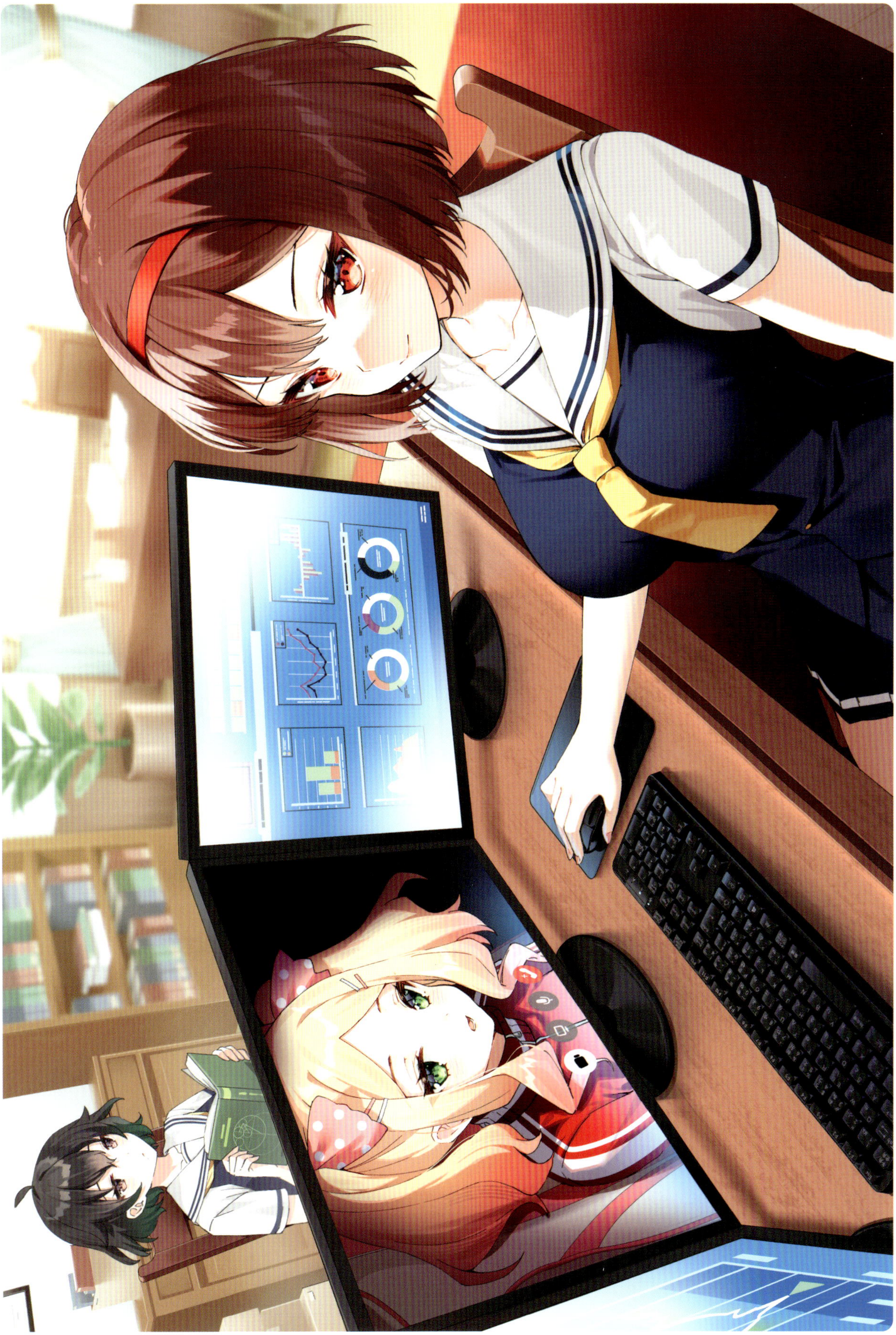

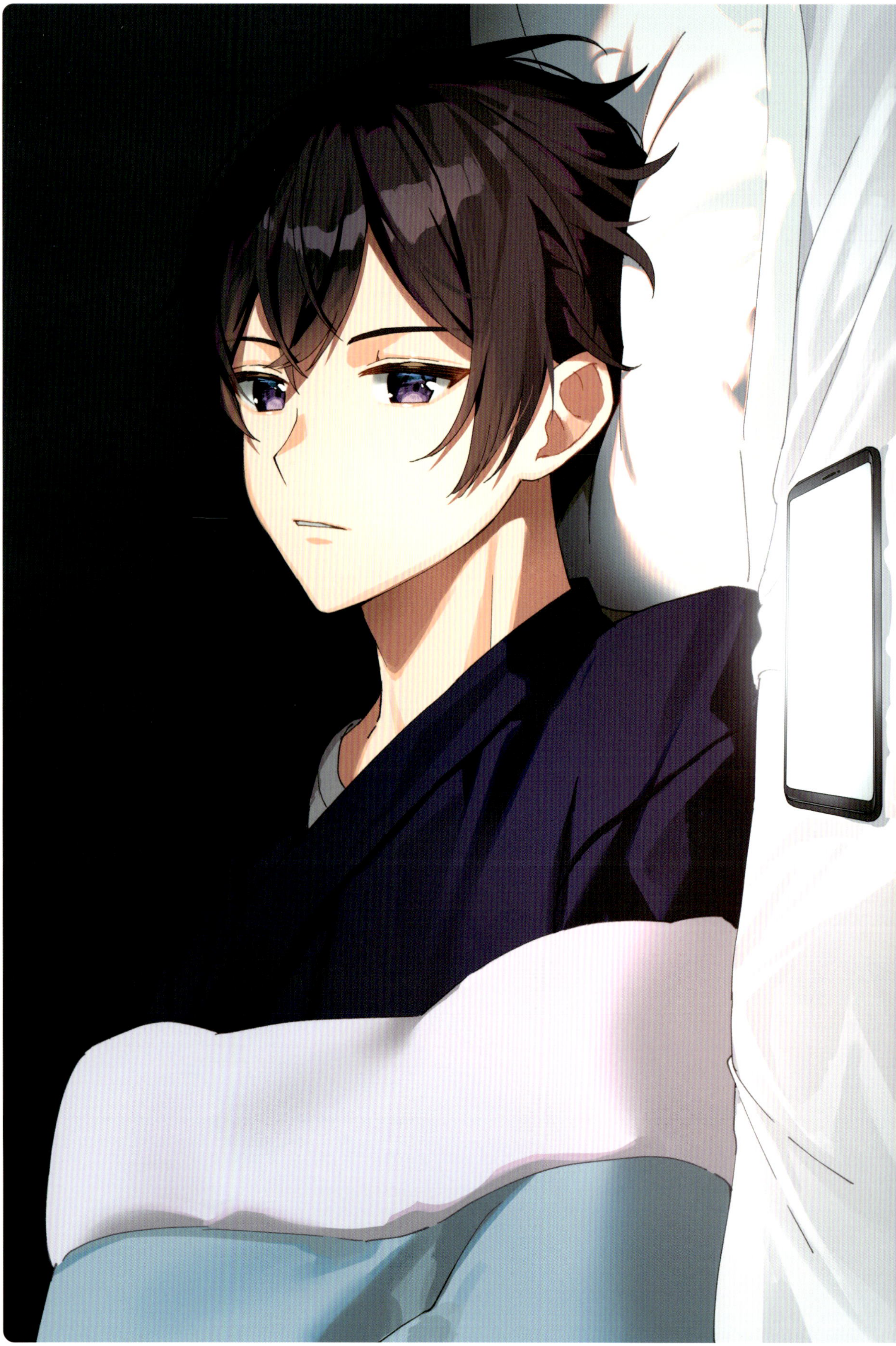

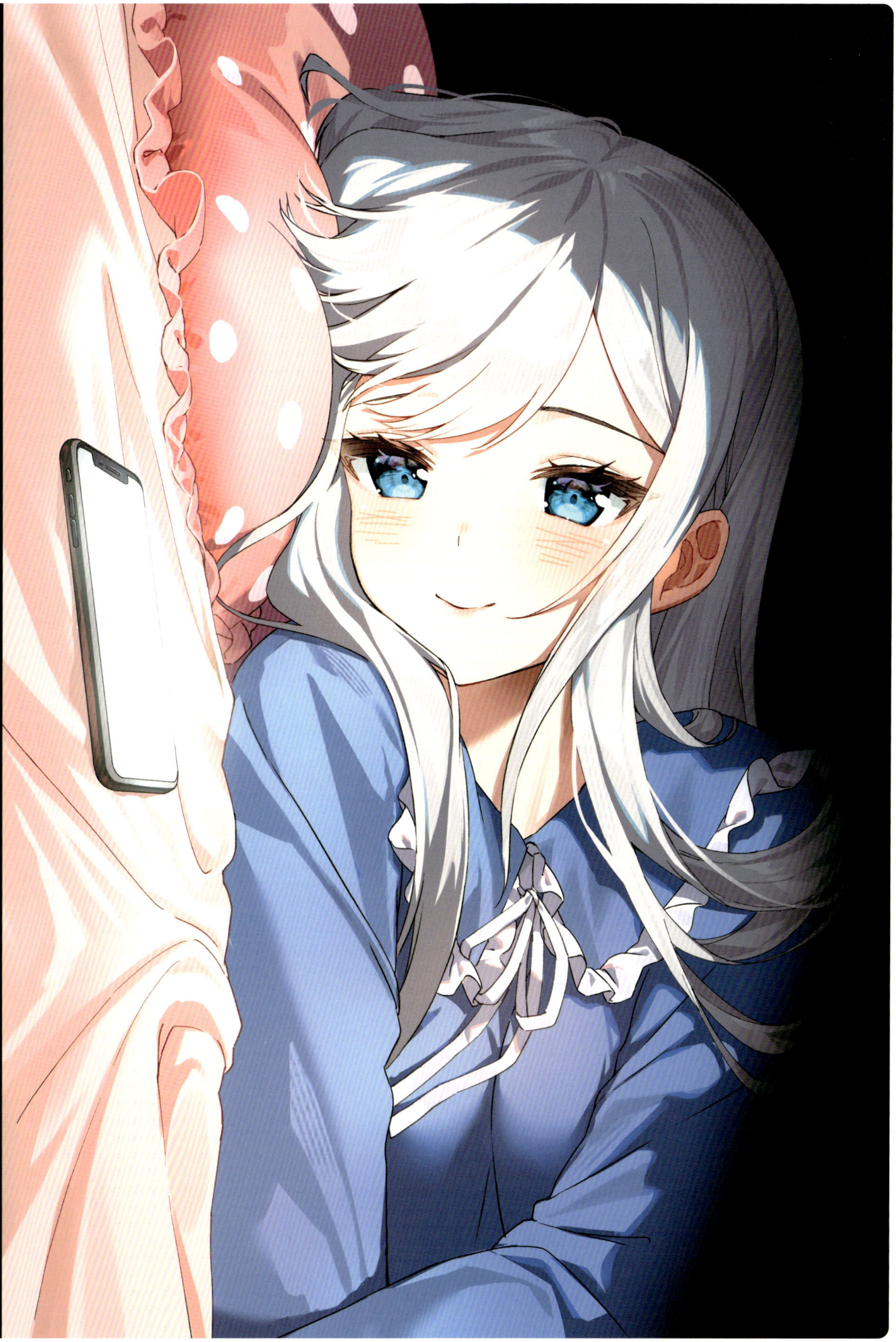

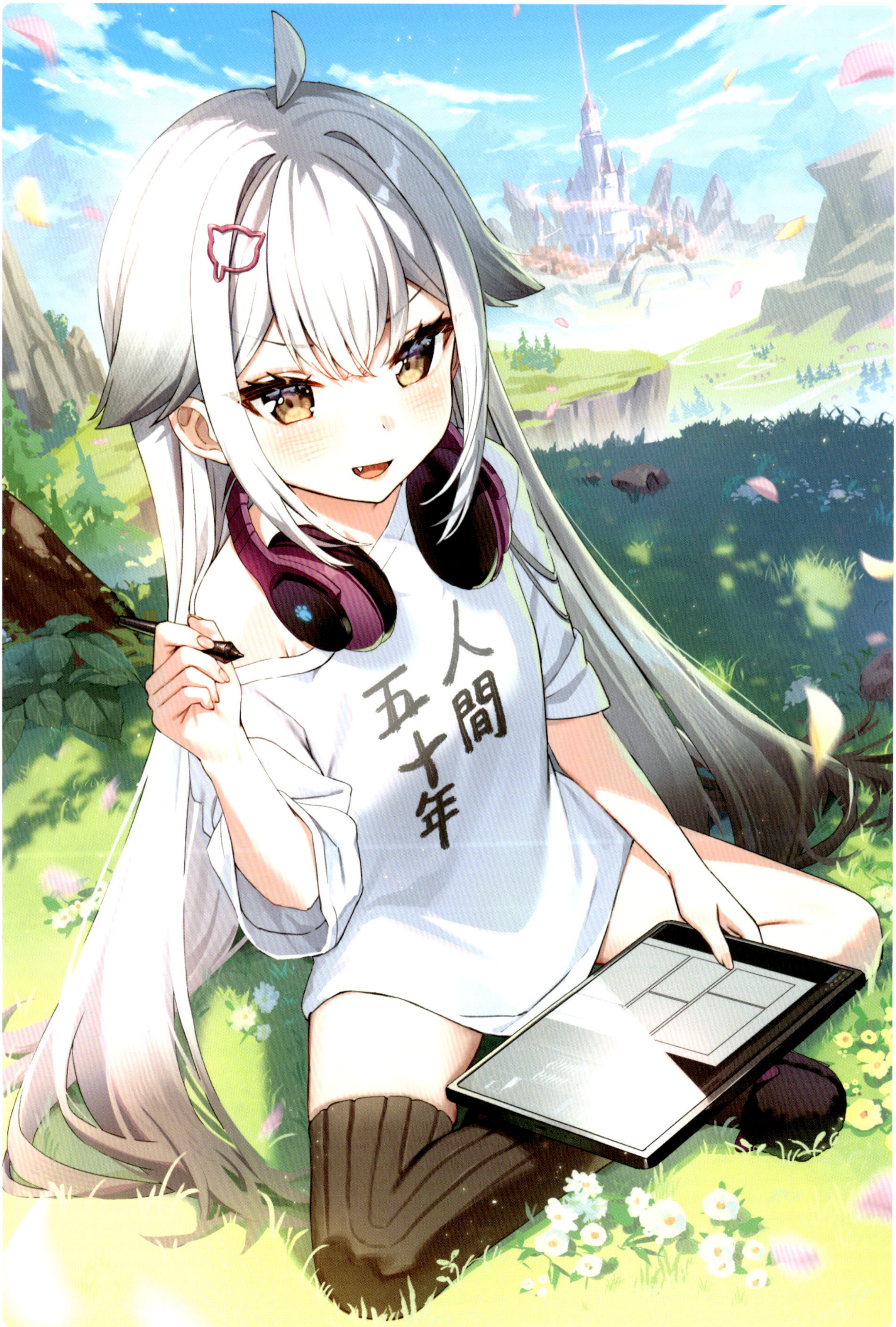
人間
五十年

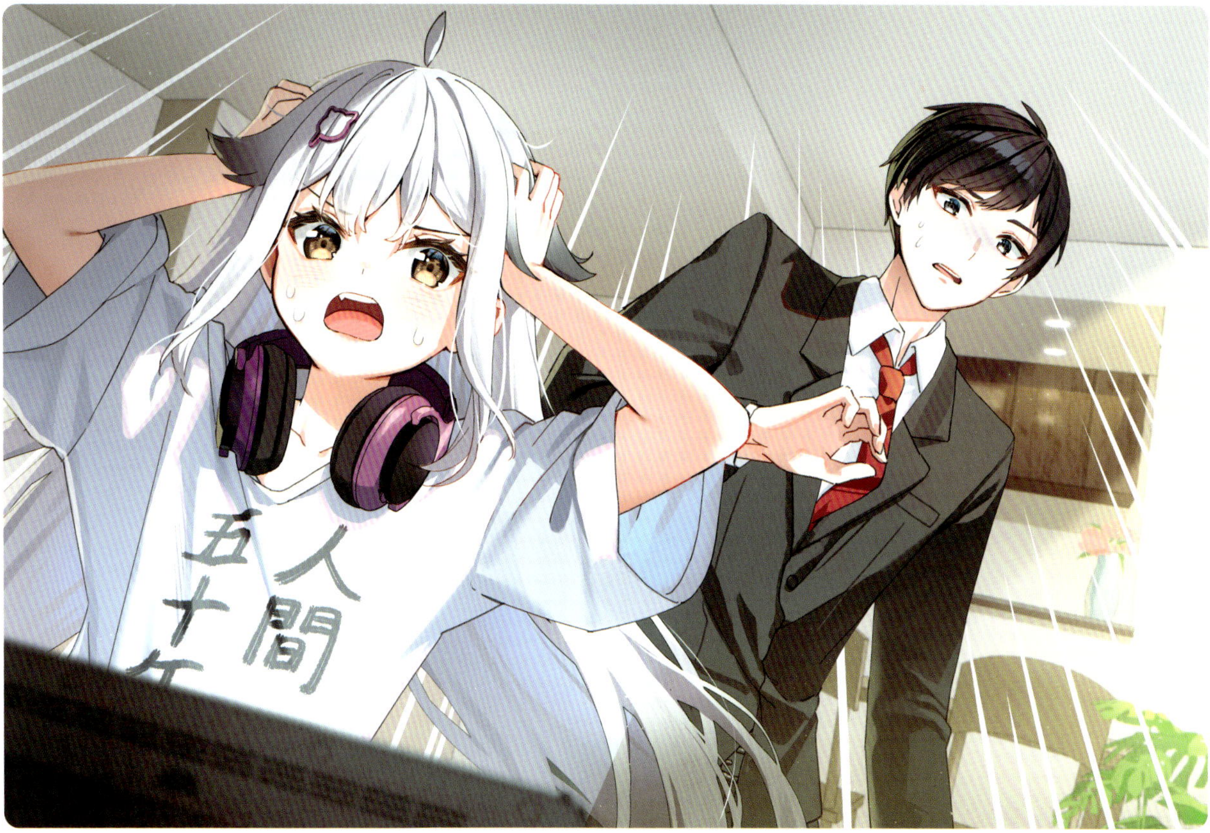

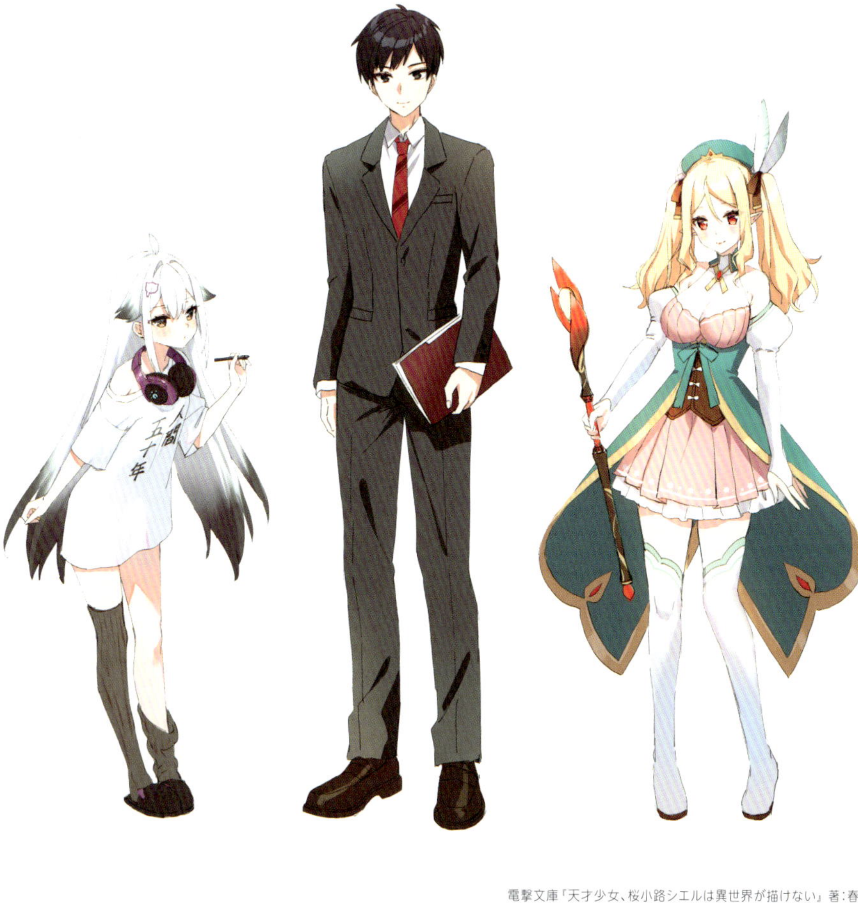

電撃文庫「天才少女、桜小路シエルは異世界が描けない」著：春日みかげ（KADOKAWA）

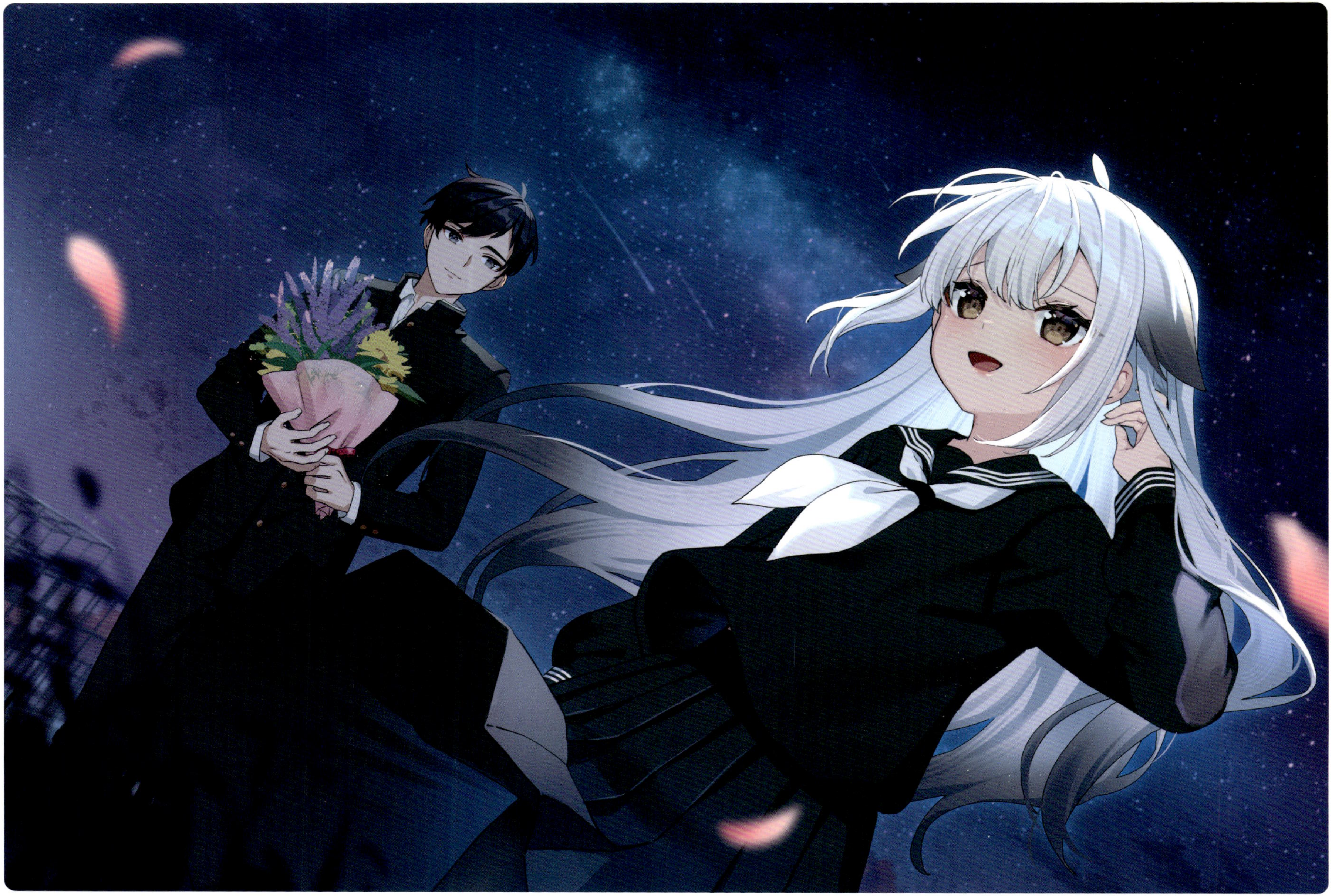

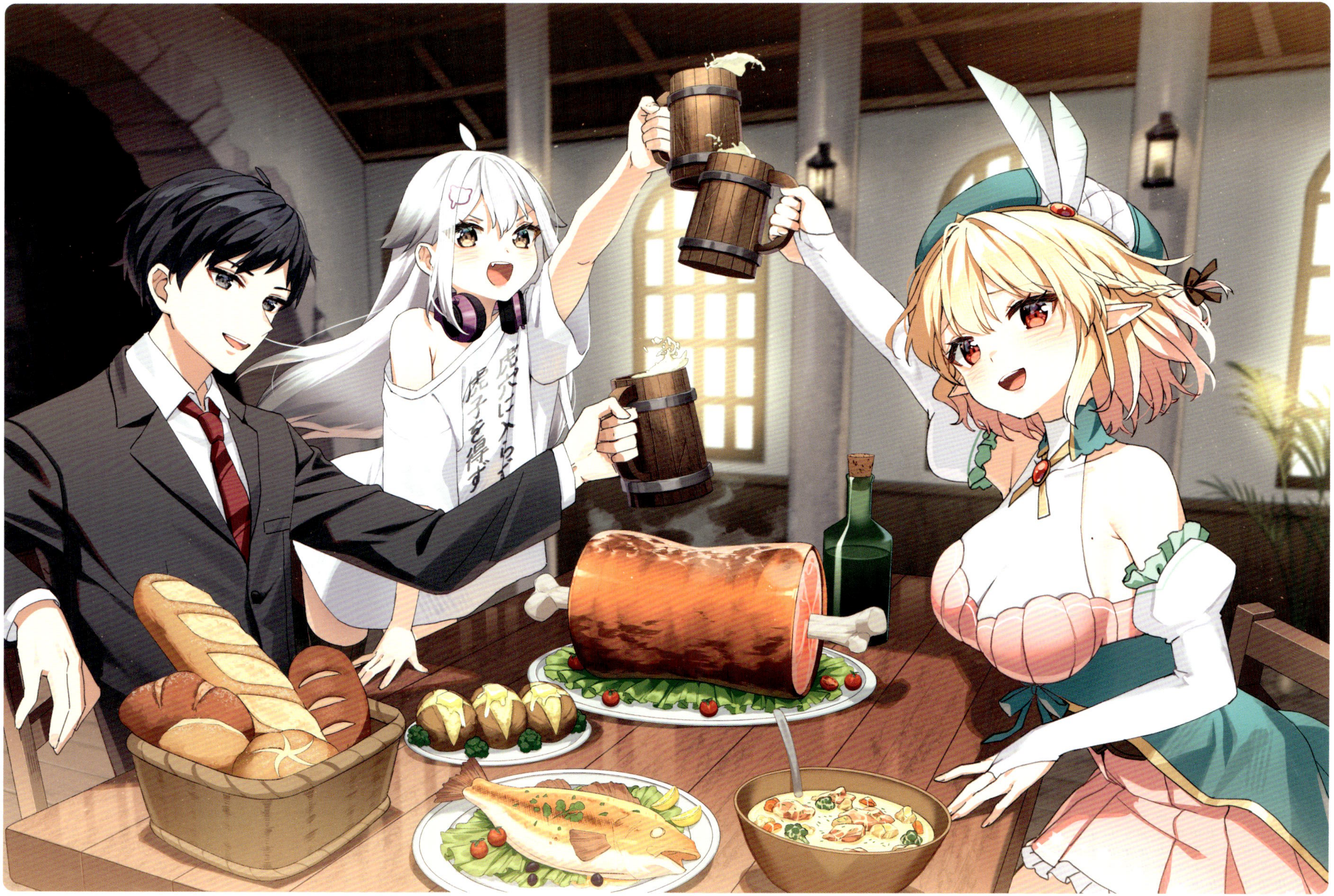
虎子を得ず

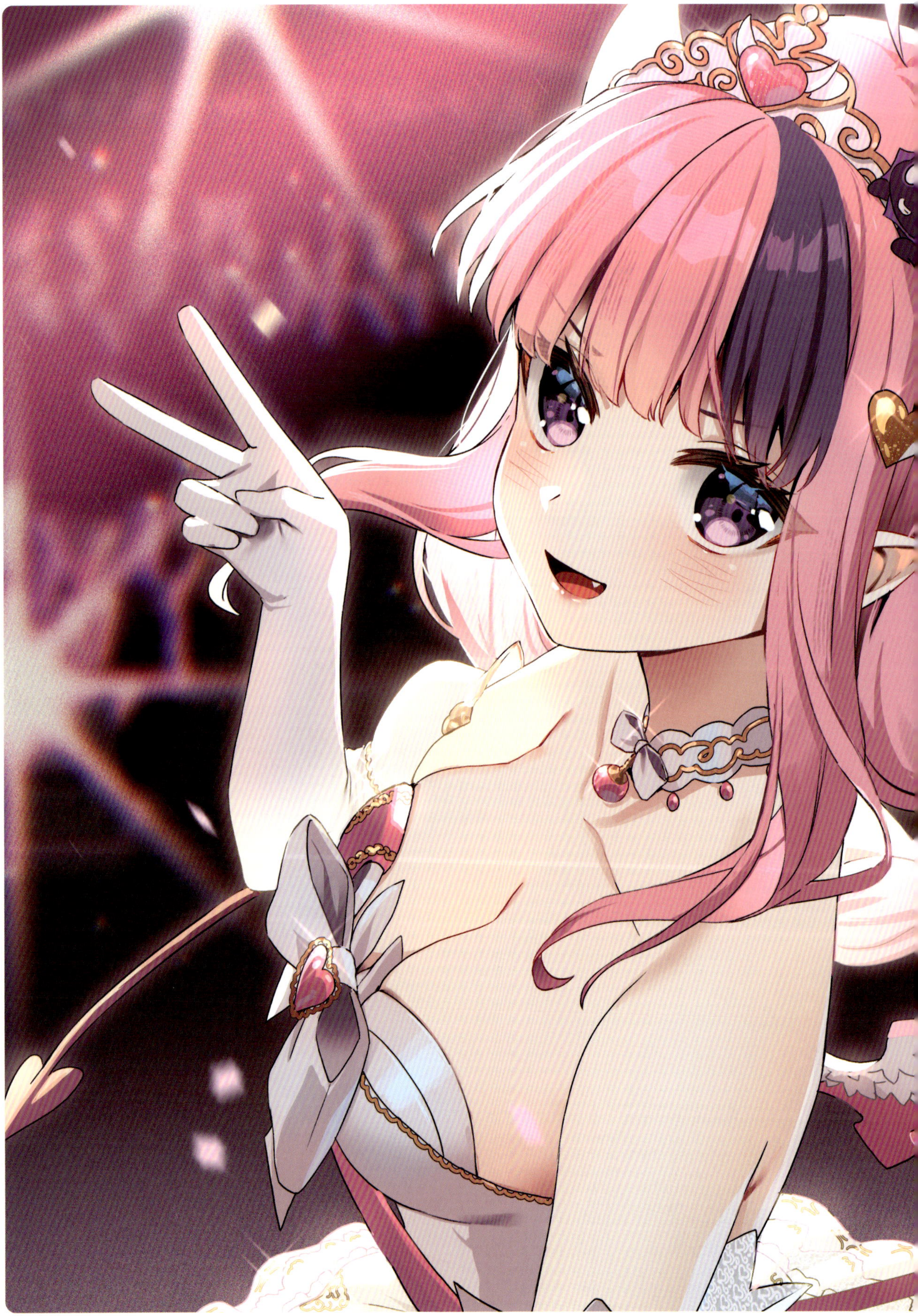

Ironmouse © Ironmouse

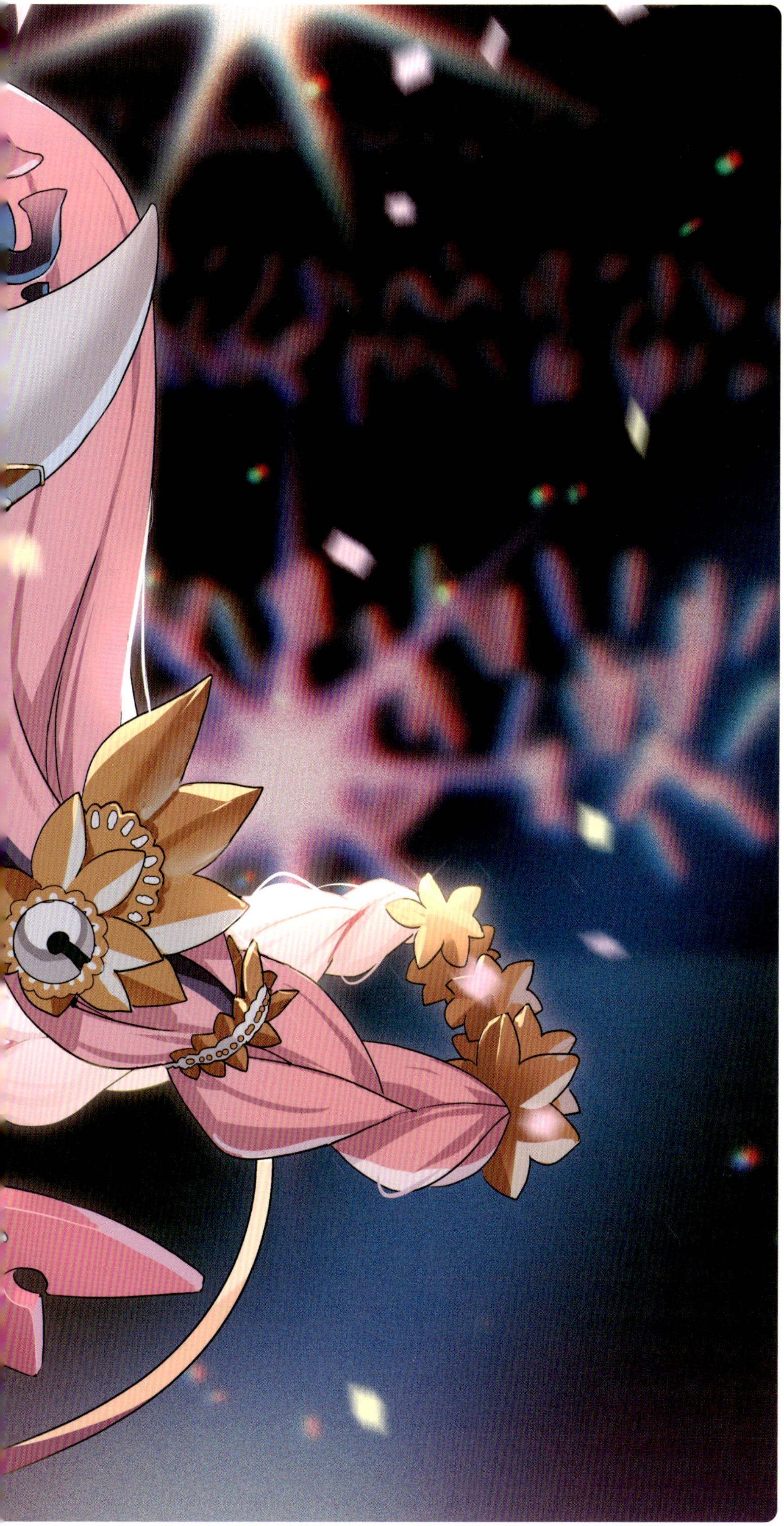

Works as a VTuber Mama

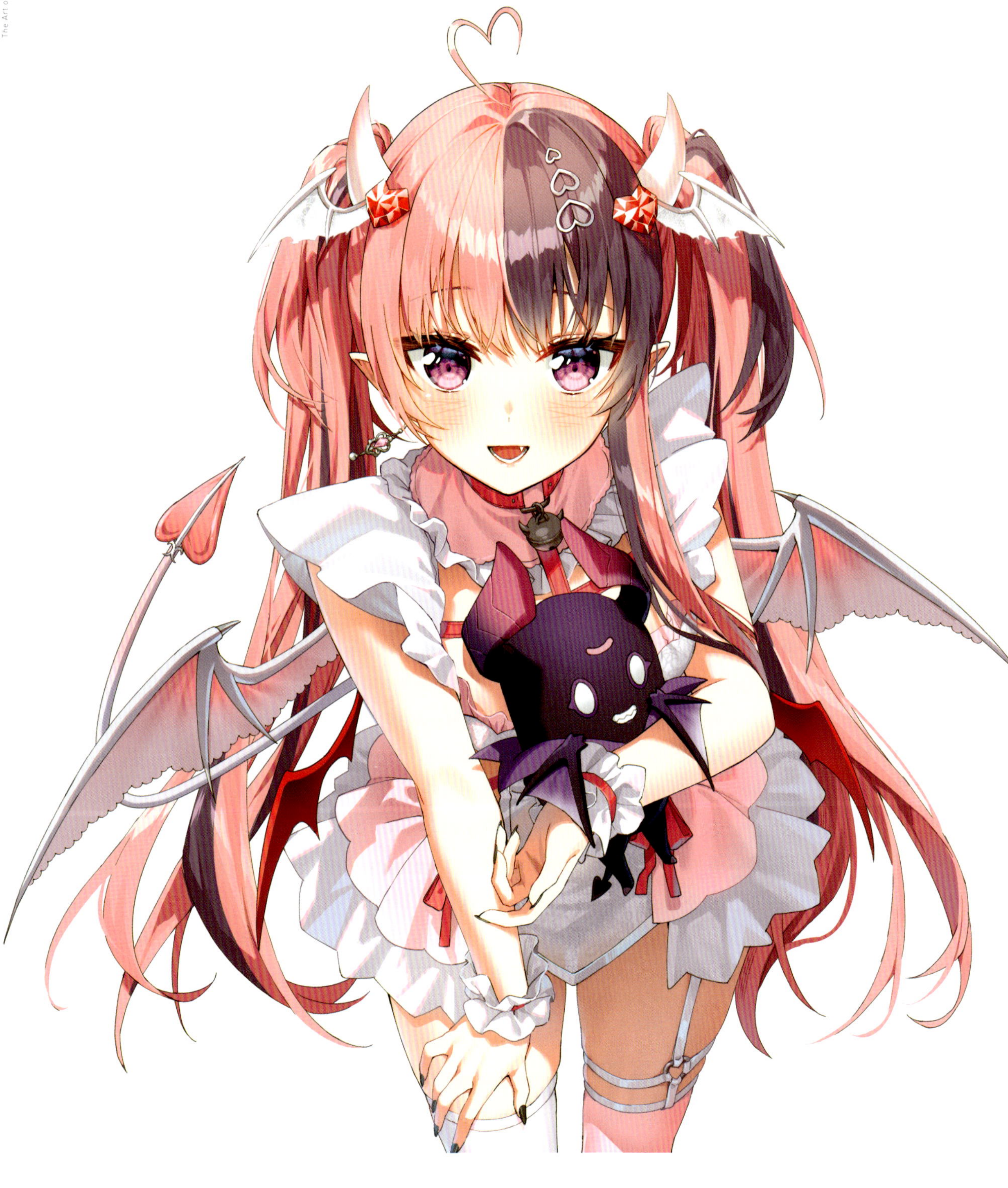

Ironmouse © Ironmouse

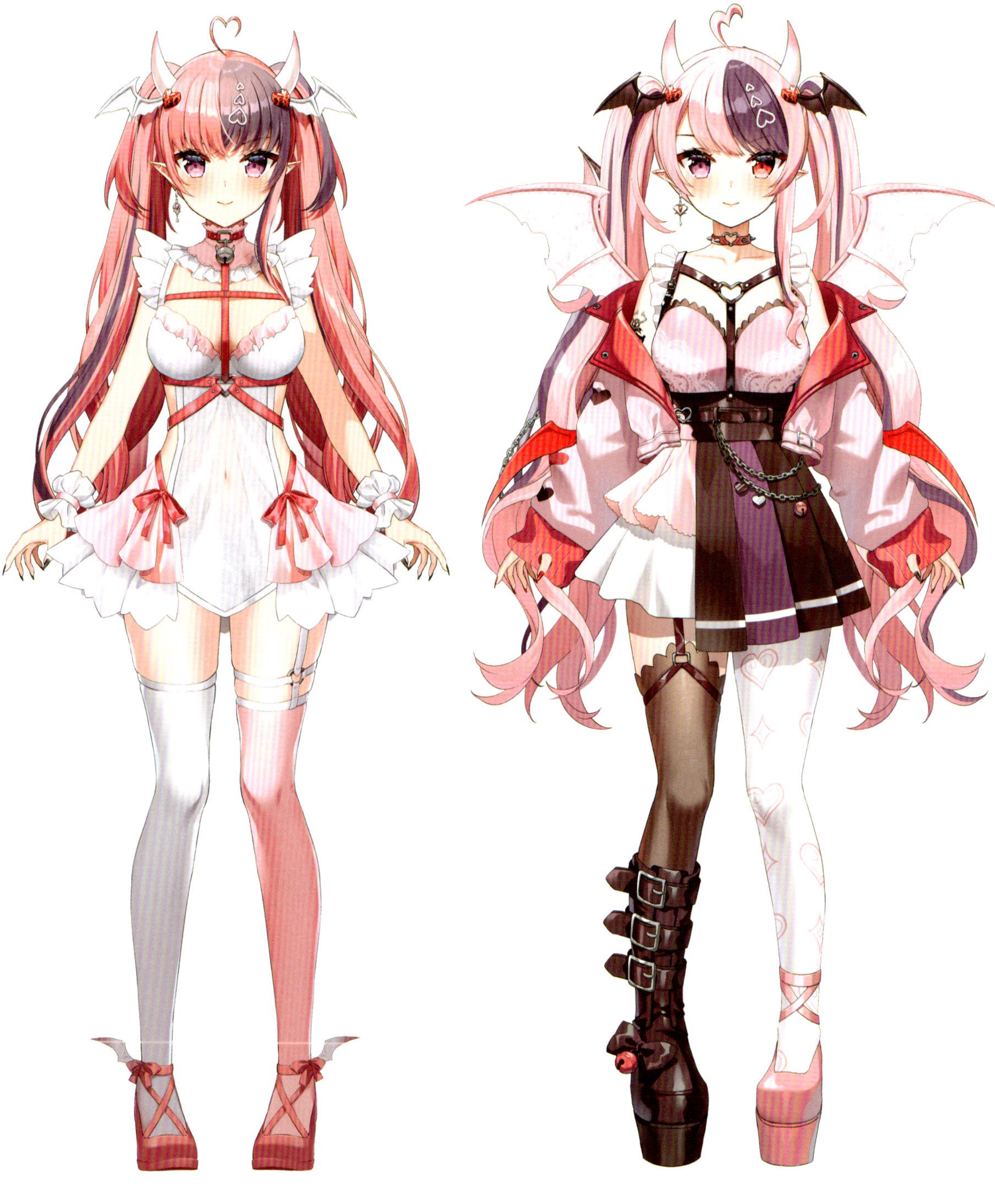

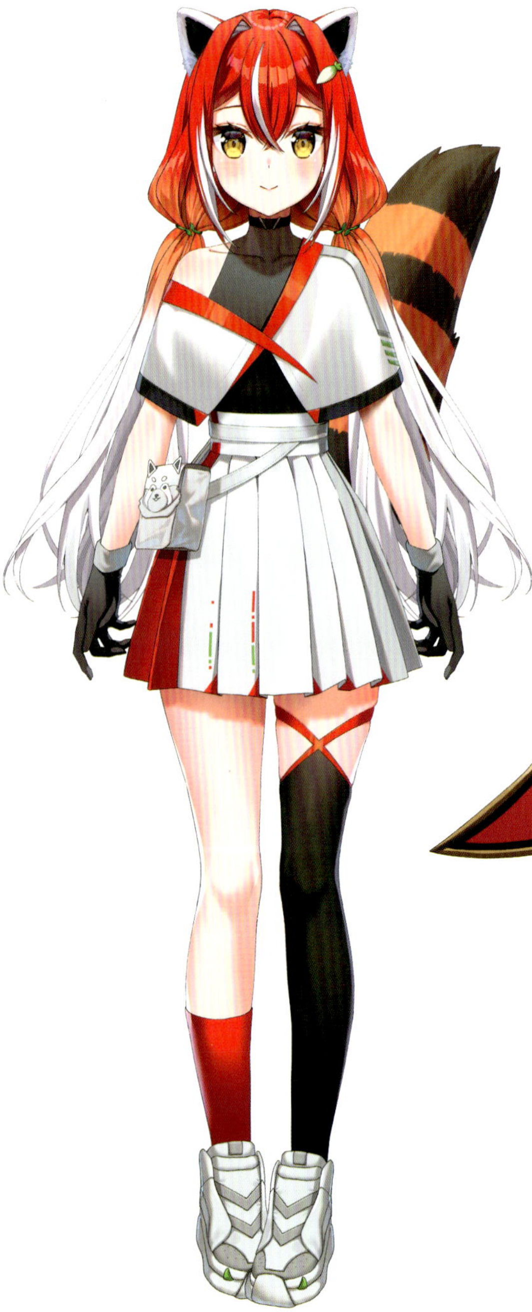

Himura ©HyperX

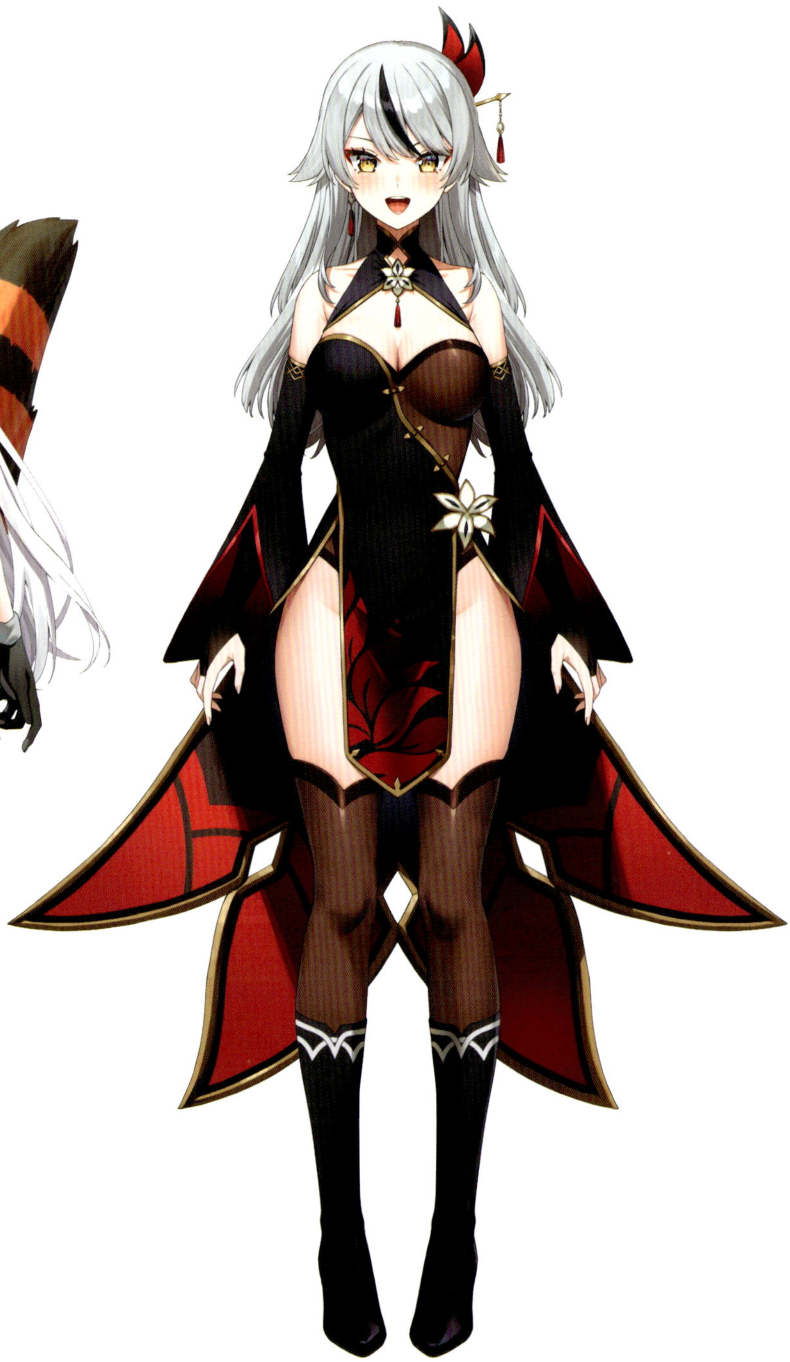

Reya ©LongLiveReya

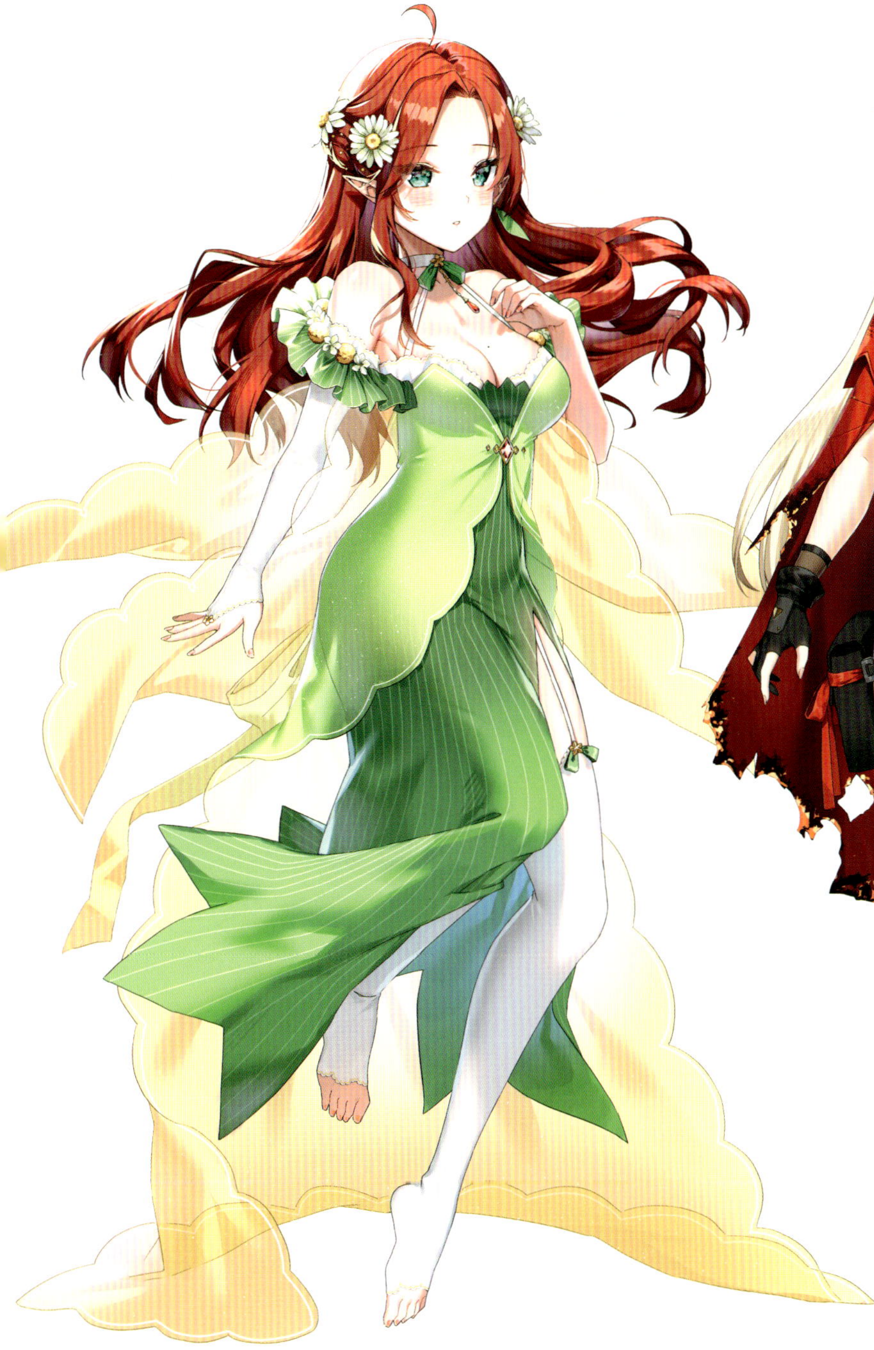

Hal Rayon Vert ©ProPro Inc.

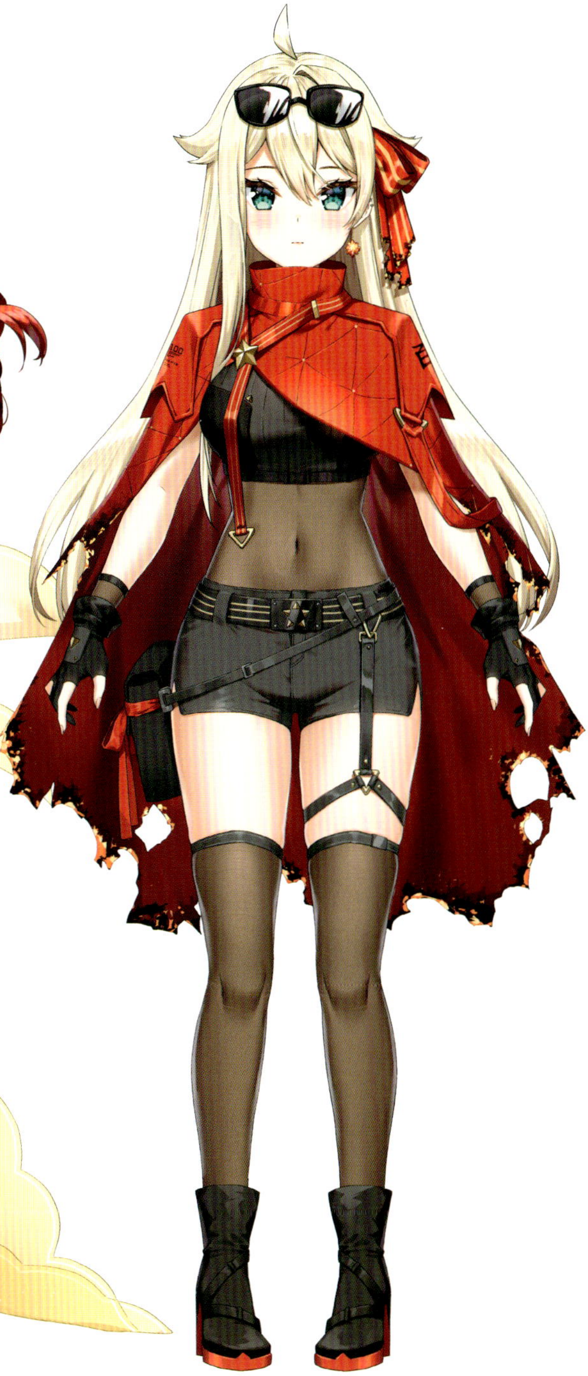

Hoshino Char ©Hoshino Char

Postscript

There's something special about printed artwork; holding the paper in your hands brings it into direct contact with our lives. Each overleaf is a personal adventure that nobody else can experience the same way, in the same space. I imagine you, holding this trove of artwork in your hands, and wish for you a beautiful journey.

In each of my works I aim to capture a feeling, such as wistful longing or joy. I imagine this book as a walk in a calm forest where you can stop and enjoy whatever views resonate with you.
I hope the energy of each piece gives you a chance for reflection, because above all I wish to gift you a moment of serenity.

I'm deeply honored and grateful that this book came to life. Many thanks to my wonderful publisher, who envisioned this project to bring my art into the hands of a wider audience. Likewise, it is thanks to you, dear reader, and our community who support these projects that works of beauty and imagination may continue to flourish. Thank you for being a part of this journey.

紙の上のアート作品には特別な何かが宿ると思います。紙に手を触れることで、それは私たちの生活と直接つながります。それぞれのページは、同じ空間であっても、誰ひとりとして同じ体験にはならない個人的な冒険です。あなたがこのアート作品を手に取り、宝物のような美しい旅を体験されることを願っています。

私は作品のひとつひとつに、懐かしさや喜びといった感情を抱いてもらえることを目指しています。この本は静かな森を散策するようなもので、あなたが立ち止まり、共鳴する景色がきっとあるでしょう。各作品のエネルギーが、あなた自身の内側を深く思索するきっかけになることを願っています。私は何よりもあなたに、心穏やかなひとときを贈りたいと思っています。

この本の完成を光栄に思い、深く感謝しています。素晴らしい出版社の方々が、このプロジェクトを企画し、私の作品をより多くの人々の手に届ける機会を与えてくださいました。心から感謝しています。同様に、親愛なる読者の方々や、これらのプロジェクトを支えてくださるコミュニティの皆様のおかげで、今後も美と想像力にあふれた作品を花開かせることができるのです。この旅路にご参加いただき、誠にありがとうございます。

Rosuuri